Database Solutions

A step-by-step approach to building databases

Database Solutions

A step-by-step approach to building databases

Thomas M. Connolly

Carolyn E. Begg

 Addison-Wesley

HARLOW, ENGLAND ■ READING, MASSACHUSETTS ■ MENLO PARK, CALIFORNIA ■
NEW YORK ■ DON MILLS, ONTARIO ■ AMSTERDAM ■ SYDNEY ■ SINGAPORE ■
TOKYO ■ MADRID ■ SAN JUAN ■ MEXICO CITY ■ SEOUL ■ TAIPEI

PEARSON EDUCATION LIMITED
Head Office:
Edinburgh Gate
Harlow CM20 2JE
England
Tel: +44 (0)1279 623623
Fax: +44 (0)1279 431059

London Office:
128 Long Acre
London WC2E 9AN
Tel: +44 (0)207 477 2000
Fax: +44 (0)207 240 5771

Website: www. awl.com/cseng

First published in Great Britain in 2000

© Pearson Education Limited 2000

The rights of Thomas Connolly and Carolyn Begg to be identified as the authors of this
Work have been asserted by them in accordance with the Copyright, Designs and Patents Act 1988.

ISBN 0-201-67476-9

British Library Cataloguing-in-Publication Data
A CIP catalogue record for this book can be obtained from the British Library.

Library of Congress Cataloging in Publication Data
Applied for.

10 9 8 7 6 5 4 3 2 1

Typeset by Pantek Arts, Maidstone, Kent.
Printed and bound in the United States of America

The Publishers' policy is to use paper manufactured from sustainable forests.

To **Sheena,**

and to my two beautiful children **Kathryn** *and* **Michael,** *to whom I owe so much.*

To **Carolyn,** for her friendship

Thomas M. Connolly

To **Neil,**

and our son, **Calum**

Carolyn E. Begg

Brief contents

Part 5 Second worked example

Appendices

Contents

Part 1   Background

Part 2 Database analysis and design techniques

Part 3 Logical database design

Part 4 Physical database design

Part 5   Second worked example

Appendices

Preface

Background

The database is now the underlying framework of the information system and has fundamentally changed the way many companies and individuals work. The developments in this technology over the past few years have produced database systems that are more powerful and more intuitive to use, and users are creating databases and applications without the necessary knowledge to produce an effective and efficient system. Looking at the literature, we found many excellent books that examine a part of the database development life-cycle. However, we found very few that covered analysis, design, and implementation and described the development process in a simple-to-understand way that could be used by both technical and non-technical readers.

Our original concept therefore was to provide a book primarily for the business community that explained as clearly as possible how to analyze, design, and implement a database. This would cover both simple databases consisting of a few tables and large databases containing tens to hundreds of tables. During the initial reviews that we carried out, it became clear that the book would also be useful for the academic community and provide a very simple and clear presentation of a database design methodology that would complement a more extensive recommended textbook, such as our own book *Database Systems*.

The methodology we present in this book for relational Database Management Systems (DBMSs) – the predominant system for business applications at present – has been tried and tested over the years in both industrial and academic environments. The methodology is divided into two phases:

- a logical database design phase, in which we develop a model of what we're trying to represent while ignoring implementation details;
- a physical database design phase, in which we decide how we're going to realize the implementation in the target DBMS, such as Access, Paradox, Oracle, Informix, or SQL Server.

We present each phase as a series of simple-to-follow steps. For the inexperienced designer, we expect that the steps will be followed in the order described, and guidelines are provided throughout to help with this process. For the experienced designer, the methodology can be less prescriptive, acting more as a framework or checklist.

Helping to understand database design

To help you use the methodology and understand the important issues, we provide a comprehensive worked example that is integrated through the book based on a video rental company called *StayHome*. To reinforce the methodology we work through a second case study in Chapters 18 and 19 based on a veterinary clinic called *Perfect Pets*.

To help you further, we have included additional database solutions in Appendix D (with corresponding SQL scripts included on the accompanying CD-ROM). Each solution has a small introduction, which you may like to read and then try to produce the database design yourself before looking at our sample solution.

Common data models

As well as providing you with additional experience of designing databases, Appendix D also provides you with many common data models that you may find useful. In fact, it has been estimated that one-third of a data model consists of common constructs that are applicable to most companies and the remaining two-thirds are either industry-specific or company-specific. Thus, most database design work consists of re-creating constructs that have already been produced many times before in other companies. The models featured may not represent your company exactly, but they may provide a starting point from which you can develop a more suitable model that matches your company's specific requirements. Some of the models we provide cover the following common business areas:

■ Customer order entry

■ Inventory control

■ Asset management

■ Project management

■ Course management

■ Human resource management

■ Payroll management.

UML (Unified Modeling Language)

Increasingly, companies are standardizing the way in which they model data by selecting a particular approach to data modeling and using it throughout their database development projects. A popular high-level data model used in logical database design, and the one we use in this book, is based on the concepts of the Entity-Relationship (ER) model. Currently there is no standard notation for an ER model. Most books that cover database design for relational DBMSs tend to use one of two conventional notations:

■ Chen's notation, consisting of rectangles representing entities and diamonds representing relationships, with lines linking the rectangles and diamonds;

■ Crow's Feet notation, again consisting of rectangles representing entities and lines between entities representing relationships, with a crow's foot at the end of a line representing a one-to-many relationship.

Both notations are well supported by current CASE tools. However, they can be quite cumbersome to use and a bit difficult to explain. In this book, we instead use the class diagram notation from the latest object-oriented modeling language called UML (Unified Modeling Language). UML is a notation that combines elements from the three major strands of object-oriented design: Rumbaugh's OMT modeling, Booch's Object-Oriented Analysis and Design, and Jacobson's Objectory. It is anticipated that UML will become a standard, and the Object Management Group (OMG) has adopted UML as the standard notation for object methods.

We believe you will find this notation easier to understand and use. To help, we provide access to evaluation copies of the Rational Rose visual modeling tool on the accompanying CD-ROM. This tool supports UML and will allow you to create your ER diagrams.

Showing how to implement a design

We believe it is important to show you how to convert a database design into a physical implementation. In this book, we show how to implement the first case study (the video rental company called *StayHome*) in the Microsoft Access 97 DBMS. In contrast, we show how to implement the database design for the second case study (the veterinary clinic called *Perfect Pets*) in the Oracle 8 DBMS.

Who should read this book?

Who should read this book? We have tried to write this book in a self-contained way. The exception to this is physical database design, where you need to have a good understanding of how the target DBMS operates. Our intended audience is anyone who needs to develop a database, including but not limited to the following:

■ information modelers and database designers;

■ database application designers and implementers;

■ database practitioners;

■ data and database administrators;

■ Information Systems, Business IT, and Computing Science professors specializing in database design;

■ database students, both undergraduate, advanced undergraduate, and graduate;

■ anyone wishing to design and develop a database application.

Structure of this book

We have divided the book into five parts and a set of four appendices:

■ Part 1 – Background. We provide an introduction to DBMSs and the relational model in Chapters 1 and 2. We also provide an overview of the database application lifecycle in Chapter 3.

■ Part 2 – Database analysis and design techniques. We discuss techniques for database analysis in Chapter 4 and show how to use some of these techniques to analyze the requirements for the video rental company *StayHome*. We show how to draw Entity-Relationship (ER) diagrams using UML in Chapter 5 and how to apply the rules of normalization in Chapter 6. ER models and normalization are important techniques that are used in the methodology we describe in Part 3.

■ Part 3 – Logical database design methodology. We describe a step-by-step approach for logical database design. In Step 1, we create a local logical data model for each view of the company. In Step 2, we map each model to a set of database tables, and in Step 3 we merge the local data models together to provide a global model of the company.

■ Part 4 – Physical database design methodology. We describe a step-by-step approach for physical database design. In Step 4, we design a set of base tables for the target DBMS. In Step 5, we choose file organizations and indexes. In Step 6, we consider the introduction of controlled redundancy to achieve improved performance. In Step 7, we design the security measures that will protect the data from unauthorized access. Finally, in Step 8 we monitor and tune the operational system. As we've just mentioned, we show you how to implement the design for the *StayHome* database application in Microsoft Access 97.

■ Part 5 – Second worked example. In Chapters 18 and 19, we work through a second case study for the veterinary clinic *Perfect Pets*. We show you how to implement the design for the *Perfect Pets* database application in Oracle 8.

■ Appendices. Appendix A examines the two main alternative ER notations: Chen's notation and the Crow's Feet notation. Appendix B provides a summary of the methodology as a quick reference guide. Appendix C provides some background information on file organization and storage structures that may help you understand some aspects of the physical database design methodology presented in Part 3. Appendix D provides a set of 15 common data models.

To make the book as readable as possible, we have adopted the following style and structure:

■ A set of objectives for each chapter, clearly highlighted at the start of the chapter.

■ A summary at the end of each chapter covering the main points introduced.

■ Each important concept that is introduced is clearly defined and highlighted by placing the definition in a box.

■ A series of notes and tips – you'll see these throughout the book with an icon adjacent to highlight them.

■ Diagrams are liberally used throughout to support and clarify concepts.

■ A very practical orientation. Each chapter contains many worked examples to illustrate the points covered.

■ A glossary at the end of the book, which you may find useful as a quick reference guide. We also tend to use the margins to give you a reference to the section of the book that defines a concept we're discussing.

Accompanying CD-ROM

The accompanying CD-ROM contains the following aids to help you with this book:

(1) Easy access to up-to-date evaluation versions of the visual modeling tool, Rational Rose.

(2) An implementation of the *StayHome* database application in Microsoft Access 97.

(3) An SQL script to create an implementation of the *Perfect Pets* database application. This script can be used to create a database in many relational DBMSs, such as Oracle, Informix, and SQL Server.

(4) An SQL script for each common data model defined in Appendix D to create the corresponding set of base tables for the database application. Once again, these scripts can be used to create a database in many relational DBMSs.

Corrections and suggestions

As this type of textbook is so vulnerable to errors, disagreements, omissions, and confusion, your input is solicited for future reprints and editions. Comments, corrections, and constructive suggestions should be sent to Addison-Wesley at Pearson Education, or by electronic mail to:

thomas.connolly@paisley.ac.uk

Acknowledgments

This book is the outcome of many years of our work in industry, research, and academia. It is therefore difficult to name all the people who have directly or indirectly helped us in our efforts. For those people we are about to omit, we apologize now. However, special thanks and apologies must first go to our families, who over the years have been neglected while we have been writing our books.

We would like to thank Sally Mortimore, our editor, Alison Birtwell, publishing coordinator, Susan Harrison, production editor, and Annette Abel, copyeditor, for their marvelous help, advice, and encouragement. We would also like to thank the reviewers of this book, who contributed their comments, suggestions, and advice. In particular, we would like to mention Stuart Anderson, Andy Osborn, and Willie Favero.

We would also like to thank our secretaries Lyndonne MacLeod and June Blackburn, for their help and support during the years.

Thomas M. Connolly

Carolyn E. Begg

Glasgow, September 1999

Part One

Background

Chapter 1

Introduction

In this chapter you will learn:

Some common uses of database systems. ◀

The meaning of the term database. ◀

The meaning of the term Database Management System (DBMS). ◀

The major components of the DBMS environment. ◀

The typical functions and services a DBMS should provide. ◀

The advantages and disadvantages of DBMSs. ◀

The database is now such an integral part of our day-to-day life that often we're not aware we are using one. To start our discussion of databases, we briefly examine some applications of database systems. For the purposes of this discussion, we consider a **database** to be a collection of related data and the **Database Management System (DBMS)** to be the software that manages and controls access to the database. We also use the more inclusive term *database system* to be a collection of application programs that interact with the database. We provide more accurate definitions in Section 1.2. Later in the chapter, we'll look at the typical functions of a modern DBMS and briefly review the main advantages and disadvantages of DBMSs.

1.1 Examples of the use of database systems

Purchases from the supermarket

When you purchase goods from your local supermarket, it's likely that a database is accessed. The checkout assistant uses a bar code reader to scan each of your purchases. This is linked to an application program that uses the bar code to find the price of the item from a product database. The program then reduces the number of such items in stock and displays the price on the cash register. If the reorder level falls below a specified threshold, the database system may automatically place an order to obtain more stocks of that item.

Purchases using your credit card

When you purchase goods using your credit card, the assistant normally checks that you have sufficient credit left to make the purchase. This check may be carried out by telephone or it may be done automatically by a card reader linked to a computer system. In either case, there is a database somewhere that contains information about the purchases that you've made using your credit card. To check your credit, there is a database application program that uses your credit card number to check that the price of the goods you wish to buy, together with the sum of the purchases you've already made this month, is within your credit limit. When the purchase is confirmed, the details of your purchase are added to this database. The application program also accesses the database to check that the credit card is not on the list of stolen or lost cards before authorizing the purchase. There are other database application programs to send out monthly statements to each cardholder and to credit accounts when payment is received.

Booking a holiday at the travel agents

When you make inquiries about a holiday, the travel agent may access several databases containing holiday and flight details. When you book your holiday, the database system has to make all the necessary booking arrangements. In this case, the system has to ensure that two different agents don't book the same holiday or overbook the seats on the flight. For example, if there is only one seat left on the flight from London to New York and two agents try to reserve the last seat at the same time, the system has to recognize this situation, allow one booking to proceed, and inform the other agent that there are now no seats available. The travel agent may have another, usually separate, database for invoicing.

Using the local library

Whenever you visit your local library, there is probably a database containing details of the books in the library, details of the readers, reservations, and so on. There will be a computerized index that allows readers to find a book based on its title, or its authors, or its subject area. The database system handles reservations to allow a reader to reserve a book and to be informed by mail when the book is available. The system also sends out reminders to borrowers who have failed to return books on the due date. Typically, the system will have a bar code reader, similar to that used by the supermarket described earlier, which is used to keep track of books coming into and going out of the library.

These are only a few of the applications for database systems, and you'll no doubt be aware of plenty of others. Although we take many of these applications for granted, behind them lies some highly complex technology. At the center of this technology is the database itself. For the system to support the applications that the end-users want, in as efficient a manner as possible, requires a suitably structured database. Producing this structure is known as *database design,* and it's this important activity that we're going to concentrate on in this book. Whether the database you wish to build is small, or large like the ones above, database design isw a fundamental issue, and the methodology presented in this book will help you build your database correctly with relative ease. Having a well-designed database will allow you to produce a system that satisfies the requirements of the users and, at the same time, provides acceptable performance.

1.2 Database approach

In this section, we provide a more formal definition of the terms *database* and *Database Management System (DBMS)* than we used in the last section.

1.2.1 The database

Let's examine the definition of a database in detail to understand this concept fully. The database is a single, large repository of data, which can be used simultaneously by many departments and users. All data that is required by these users is integrated with a minimum amount of duplication. And importantly, the database is normally not owned by any one department or user but is a shared corporate resource.

> **Database**
> A shared collection of logically related data (and a description of this data), designed to meet the information needs of a company.

As well as holding the company's operational data, the database also holds a description of this data. For this reason, a database is also defined as a *self-describing collection of integrated records*. The description of the data, that is the **meta-data** – the 'data about data', is known as the **system catalog** or **data dictionary**. It is the self-describing nature of a database that provides what's known as **data independence**. This means that if new data structures are added to the database or existing structures in the database are modified then the application programs that use the database are unaffected, provided they don't directly depend upon what has been modified. For example, if we add a new column to a record or create a new table, existing applications are unaffected. However, if we remove a column from a table that an application program uses,

> **System catalog**
> Holds data about all objects in the database.

then that application program is affected by this change and must be modified accordingly.

The final term in the definition of a database that we should explain is 'logically related'. When we analyze the company's information needs, we attempt to identify the important objects that need to be represented in the database and the *logical relationships* between these objects. The methodology we'll present for database design will give you guidelines for identifying these important objects and their logical relationships.

Methodology covered in Chapters 7–16

1.2.2 The Database Management System (DBMS)

The **DBMS** is the software that interacts with the users, application programs, and the database. Among other things, the DBMS allows users to insert, update, delete, and retrieve data from the database. Having a central repository for all data and data descriptions allows the DBMS to provide a general inquiry facility to this data, called a *query language*. The provision of a query language (such as SQL) alleviates the problems with earlier systems where the user has to work with a fixed set of queries or where there is a proliferation of programs, giving major software management problems. We'll discuss the typical functions and services of a DBMS in the next section.

DBMS
A software system that enables users to define, create, and maintain the database and also provides controlled access to this database.

SQL covered in Section 2.4 and Chapter 17

> The Structured Query Language (SQL – pronounced 'S-Q-L' or sometimes 'See-Quel'), is the main query language for relational DBMSs.

Figure 1.1 illustrates the database approach. It shows the Sales and Stock Control Departments using their application programs to access the database through the DBMS. Each set of departmental application programs handles data entry, data maintenance, and the generation of reports. The physical structure and storage of the data are managed by the DBMS.

1.2.3 Views

With the functionality described above, the DBMS is an extremely powerful tool. However, as end-users are not too interested in how complex or easy a task is for the system, it could be argued that the DBMS has made things more complex because they may now see more data than they actually need or want to do their job. In recognition of this problem, a DBMS provides another facility known as a *view mechanism,* which allows each user to have his or her own view of the database, where a view is some subset of the database. As well as reducing

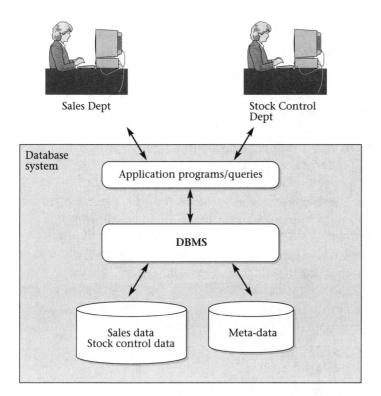

Figure 1.1

Sales and Stock
Control
Departments using a
DBMS.

complexity by letting users see the data in the way they want to see it, views have several other benefits:

- *Views provide a level of security*. Views can be set up to exclude data that some users should not see. For example, we could create a view that allows a branch manager and the Payroll Department to see all staff data, including salary details. However, we could create a second view that excludes salary details, which other staff use.

- *Views provide a mechanism to customize the appearance of the database*. For example, the Stock Control Department may wish to call the Daily Rental Rate column for videos by the simpler name, Daily Rental.

- *A view can present a consistent, unchanging picture of the structure of the database*, even if the underlying database is changed (for example, columns added or removed, relationships changed, data files split, restructured, or renamed). If columns are added or removed from a data file, and these columns are not required by the view, the view is not affected by this change. Thus, a view helps provide additional data independence to that provided by the system catalog, as we described in Section 1.2.1.

1.2.4 Components of the DBMS environment

We can identify five major components in the DBMS environment: hardware, software, data, procedures, and people:

(1) *Hardware* The computer system(s) that the DBMS and the application programs run on. This can range from a single PC, through a single mainframe, to a network of computers.

(2) *Software* The DBMS software and the application programs, together with the operating system, including network software if the DBMS is being used over a network.

(3) *Data* The data acts as a bridge between the hardware and software components and the human components. As we've already said, the database contains both the operational data and the meta-data (the 'data about data').

(4) *Procedures* The instructions and rules that govern the design and use of the database. This may include instructions on how to log on to the DBMS, make backup copies of the database, and how to handle hardware or software failures.

(5) *People* This includes the database designers, database administrators (DBAs), application programmers, and end-users.

1.2.5 DBMS architectures

Before the advent of the Web, generally a DBMS would be divided into two parts:

■ a **client** program that handles the main business and data processing logic and interfaces with the user;

■ a **server** program (sometimes called the **DBMS engine**) that manages and controls access to the database.

This is known as a **two-tier client–server architecture**. Figure 1.2 illustrates a simplified client–server architecture for a video rental company called *StayHome* that has offices throughout America. It shows a centralized database and server located at the company's headquarters in Seattle and a number of clients, located at some of the branches around the US.

StayHome is used throughout this book and discussed more fully in Chapter 4

In the mid-1990s, as applications became more complex and potentially could be deployed to hundreds or thousands of end-users, the client side of this architecture gave rise to two problems:

■ A 'fat' client, requiring considerable resources on the client's computer to run effectively. This includes disk space, RAM, and CPU power.

■ A significant client-side administration overhead.

By 1995, a new variation of the traditional two-tier client–server model appeared to solve these problems called the **three-tier client–server architecture**. This new architecture proposed three layers, each potentially running on a different platform:

Figure 1.2

Simplified two-tier client–server configuration for *StayHome*.

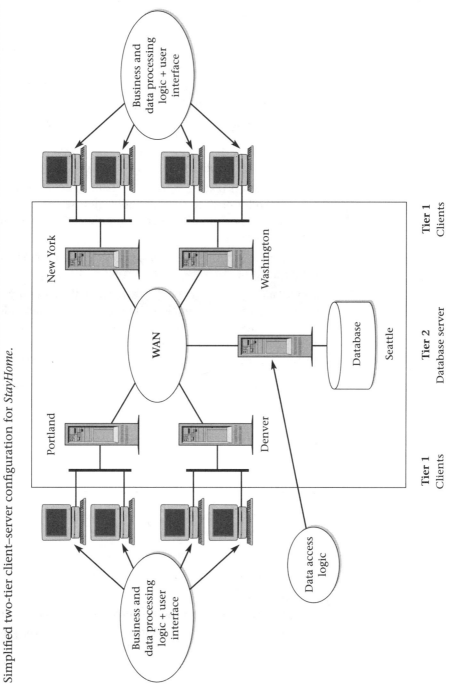

(1) The user interface layer, which runs on the end-user's computer (the *client*).

(2) The business logic and data processing layer. This middle tier runs on a server and is often called the **application server**. One application server is designed to serve multiple clients.

(3) A DBMS, which stores the data required by the middle tier. This tier may run on a separate server called the **database server**.

The three-tier design has many advantages over the traditional two-tier design, such as:

■ A 'thin' client, which requires less expensive hardware.

■ Simplified application maintenance, as a result of centralizing the business logic for many end-users into a single application server. This eliminates the concerns of software distribution that are problematic in the traditional two-tier client–server model.

■ Added modularity, which makes it easier to modify or replace one tier without affecting the other tiers.

■ Easier load balancing, again as a result of separating the core business logic from the database functions. For example, a **Transaction Processing Monitor (TPM)** can be used to reduce the number of connections to the database server. (A TPM is a program that controls data transfer between clients and servers in order to provide a consistent environment for Online Transaction Processing (OLTP).)

An additional advantage is that the three-tier architecture maps quite naturally to the Web environment, with a Web browser acting as the 'thin' client, and a Web server acting as the application server. The three-tier client–server architecture is illustrated in Figure 1.3.

1.3 Functions of a DBMS

In this section, we briefly look at the functions and services we would expect a full-scale DBMS to provide nowadays.

Data storage, retrieval, and update

This is the fundamental function of a DBMS. From our earlier discussion, clearly in providing this functionality the DBMS should hide the internal physical implementation details (such as file organization and storage structures) from the user.

A user-accessible catalog

A key feature of a DBMS is the provision of an integrated *system catalog* to hold data about the structure of the database, users, applications, and so on. The

Figure 1.3

Simplified three-tier client–server configuration for *StayHome*.

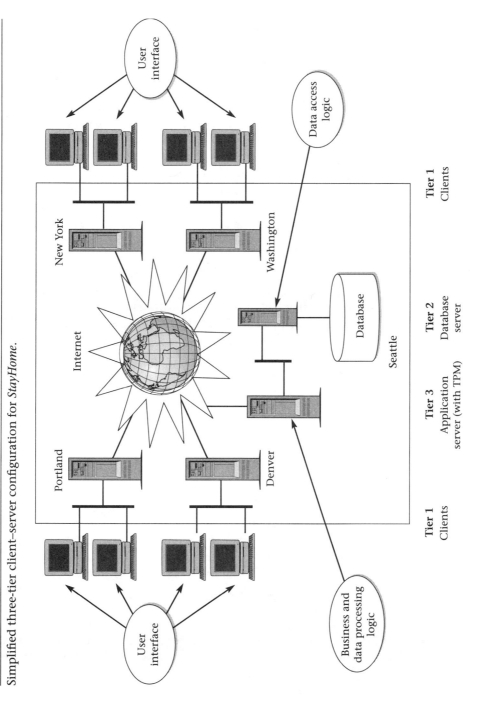

catalog is expected to be accessible to users as well as to the DBMS. The amount of information and the way the information is used vary with the DBMS. Typically, the system catalog stores:

■ names, types, and sizes of data items;

■ integrity constraints on the data;

■ names of authorized users who have access to the data.

Transaction support

Transaction
An action, or series of actions, carried out by a single user or application program, which accesses or changes the contents of the database.

Some simple transactions for the *StayHome* video rental company might be to add a new member of staff to the database, to update the salary of a particular member of staff, or to delete a member from the register. A more complicated example might be to delete a manager from the database *and* to reassign the branch that he or she managed to another member of staff. In this case, there is more than one change to be made to the database. If the transaction fails during execution, perhaps because of a computer crash, the database will be in an *inconsistent* state: some changes will have been made and others not. For example, a branch is not allocated a new manager. Consequently, the changes that have been made will have to be undone to return the database to a consistent state again.

To overcome this, a DBMS should provide a mechanism that will ensure that either all the updates corresponding to a given transaction are made or that none of them are made.

Concurrency control services

One major objective in using a DBMS is to enable many users to access shared data concurrently, this is known as **concurrency control**. Concurrent access is relatively easy if all users are only reading data, as there is no way that they can interfere with one another. However, when two or more users are accessing the database simultaneously and at least one of them is updating data, there may be interference that can result in inconsistencies. For example, consider two transactions T_1 and T_2 that are executing concurrently as illustrated in Figure 1.4.

T_2 is withdrawing \$20 from a *StayHome* member's account (with a balance, bal_x, currently \$50) and T_1 is crediting \$5 to the same account. If these transactions were executed one after the other with no interleaving of operations, the final balance would be \$35 regardless of which was performed first. Transactions T_1 and T_2 start at nearly the same time and both read the balance as \$50. T_2 decreases bal_x by \$20 to \$30 and stores the update in the database. Meanwhile, transaction T_1 increases its copy of bal_x by \$5 to \$55 and stores this value in the database, overwriting the previous update and thereby 'losing' \$20.

Time	T_1	T_2	bal_x
t_1		read(bal_x)	50
t_2	read(bal_x)	$bal_x = bal_x - 20$	50
t_3	$bal_x = bal_x + 5$	write(bal_x)	30
t_4	write(bal_x)		55
t_5			

Figure 1.4

The lost update problem.

When multiple users are accessing the database, the DBMS must ensure that interference like this cannot occur.

Recovery services

When discussing transaction support, we mentioned that if the transaction fails the database has to be returned to a consistent state, this is known as **recovery control**. This may be a result of a system crash, media failure, a hardware or software error causing the DBMS to stop, or it may be the result of the user detecting an error during the transaction and aborting the transaction before it completes. In all these cases, the DBMS must provide a mechanism to recover the database to a consistent state.

Authorization services

It's not difficult to envisage instances where we would want to protect some of the data stored in the database from being seen by all users. For example, we may want only branch managers and the Payroll Department to see salary-related information for staff and prevent all other users from seeing this data. Additionally, we may want to protect the database from unauthorized access. The term **security** refers to the protection of the database against unauthorized access, either intentional or accidental. We expect the DBMS to provide mechanisms to ensure the data is secure.

Security covered in Step 7 in Chapter 15

Support for data communication

Most users access the database from terminals. Sometimes, these terminals are connected directly to the computer hosting the DBMS. In other cases, the terminals are at remote locations and communicate with the computer hosting the DBMS over a network. In either case, the DBMS must be capable of integrating with networking/communication software. Even DBMSs for PCs should be capable of being run on a local area network (LAN) so that one centralized database can be established for users to share, rather than having a series of disparate databases, one for each user.

Integrity services

Database integrity refers to the correctness and consistency of stored data. It can be considered as another type of database protection. While it's related to security, it has wider implications; integrity is concerned with the quality of data itself. Integrity is usually expressed in terms of constraints, which are consistency rules that the database is not permitted to violate. For example, we may want to specify a constraint that no member of *StayHome* can rent more than 10 videos at the one time. Here, we would want the DBMS to check when we assign a video to a member that this limit would not be exceeded and to prevent the rental from occurring if the limit has been reached.

Services to promote data independence

Data independence is normally achieved through a view mechanism, as we discussed in Section 1.2.3. There are usually several types of changes that can be made to the physical characteristics of the database without affecting the views, such as using different file organizations or modifying indexes. This is called *physical data independence*. However, complete *logical data independence* is more difficult to achieve. The addition of a new table or column can usually be accommodated, but not their removal. In some systems, any type of change to an existing table is prohibited.

Utility services

Utility programs help the DBA to administer the database effectively. Some examples of utilities are:

- import facilities, to load the database from flat files, and export facilities, to unload the database to flat files;
- monitoring facilities, to monitor database usage and operation.

> The above discussion is general. The actual level of functionality offered by a DBMS differs from product to product. For example, a DBMS for a PC may not support concurrent shared access, and it may only provide limited security, integrity, and recovery control. However, modern, large multi-user DBMS products offer all the above functions and much more. Modern systems are extremely complex pieces of software consisting of millions of lines of code, with documentation comprising many volumes.

The above discussion is intentionally brief but should be sufficient to provide a general overview of DBMS functionality. For more information, the interested reader is referred to Connolly and Begg (1999).

1.4   Database design

Until now, we've taken it for granted that there is a structure to the data in the database. But how do we get this structure? The answer is quite simple: the structure of the database is determined during **database design**. However, carrying out database design can be extremely complex. To produce a system that will satisfy the company's information needs requires a data-driven approach, which means we think of the data first and the applications second. For the system to be acceptable to the end-users, database design is crucial. A poorly designed database will generate errors that may lead to bad decisions being made, which may have serious repercussions for the company. On the other hand, a well-designed database produces a system that provides the correct information for the decision-making process to succeed, in an efficient way.

We devote several chapters to the presentation of a complete methodology for database design (see Chapters 7–16). We present it as a series of simple-to-follow steps, with guidelines provided throughout. In these chapters, we use a case study based on a video rental company called *StayHome*. To help reinforce the methodology, in Chapters 18 and 19 we go through a second case study, this time a veterinary clinic called *Perfect Pets*. In addition, in Appendix D we provide a number of common business data models that you are likely to encounter in one form or another.

Unfortunately, database design methodologies are not very popular, which may be a major cause of failure in the development of database systems. Owing to the lack of structured approaches to database design, the time and resources required for a database project are typically underestimated, the databases developed are inadequate or inefficient in meeting the demands of applications, documentation is limited, and maintenance is difficult.

We hope the methodology presented in this book will help change this attitude.

1.5   Advantages and disadvantages of DBMSs

The fact that you are reading this book probably means that you already know many of the advantages of DBMSs, such as:

■ *Control of **data redundancy**   The database approach eliminates redundancy where possible. However, it does not eliminate redundancy entirely, but controls the amount of redundancy inherent in the database. For example, it's normally necessary to duplicate key data items to model relationships, and sometimes it's desirable to duplicate some data items to improve performance. The reasons for controlled duplication will become clearer when you read the chapters on database design.

■ *Data consistency* By eliminating or controlling redundancy, we're reducing the risk of inconsistencies occurring. If a data item is stored only once in the database, any update to its value has to be performed only once and the new value is immediately available to all users. If a data item is stored more than once and the system is aware of this, the system can ensure that all copies of the item are kept consistent. Unfortunately, many of today's DBMSs don't automatically ensure this type of consistency.

■ *Sharing of data* In a file-based approach, typically files are owned by the people or departments that use them. On the other hand, the database belongs to the entire company and can be shared by all authorized users. In this way, more users share more of the data. Furthermore, new applications can build on the existing data in the database and add only data that is not currently stored, rather than having to define all data requirements again. The new applications can also rely on the functions provided by the DBMS, such as data definition and manipulation, and concurrency and recovery control, rather than having to provide these functions themselves.

■ *Improved data integrity* As we've already stated, database integrity is usually expressed in terms of **constraints**, which are consistency rules that the database is not permitted to violate. Constraints may apply to data items within a single record or they may apply to relationships between records. Again, integration allows us to define, and the DBMS to enforce, integrity constraints.

■ *Improved maintenance through data independence* Since a DBMS separates the data descriptions from the applications, it helps make applications immune to changes in the data descriptions. This is known as *data independence* and its provision simplifies database application maintenance.

Other advantages include: improved security, improved data accessibility and responsiveness, increased productivity, increased concurrency, and improved backup and recovery services.

There are, however, some disadvantages of the database approach, such as:

■ *Complexity* As we've already mentioned, a DBMS is an extremely complex piece of software, and all users (database designers and developers, DBAs, and end-users) must understand this functionality to take full advantage of it.

■ *Cost of DBMS* The cost of DBMSs varies significantly, depending on the environment and functionality provided. For example, a single-user DBMS for a PC may only cost $100. However, a large mainframe multi-user DBMS servicing hundreds of users can be extremely expensive, perhaps $100,000 to $1,000,000. There is also the recurrent annual maintenance cost, which is typically a percentage of the list price.

■ *Cost of conversion* In some situations, the cost of the DBMS and any extra hardware may be insignificant compared with the cost of converting existing applications to run on the new DBMS and hardware. This cost also includes the cost of training staff to use these new systems, and possibly the employment of specialist staff to help with the conversion and running of the system. This cost is one of the main reasons why some companies feel tied to their current systems and cannot switch to more modern database technology. The term 'legacy system' is sometimes used to refer to an older, and usually inferior, system (such as file-based, hierarchical, or network systems).

■ *Performance* Typically, a file-based system is written for a specific application, such as invoicing. As a result, performance is generally very good. However, the DBMS is written to be more general, to cater for many applications rather than just one. The effect is that some applications may not run as fast any more.

■ *Higher impact of a failure* The centralization of resources increases the vulnerability of the system. Since all users and applications rely on the availability of the DBMS, the failure of any component can bring operations to a complete halt until the failure is repaired.

Chapter summary

✓ A **database** is a shared collection of logically related data (and a description of this data), designed to meet the information needs of a company. A **DBMS** is a software system that enables users to define, create, and maintain the database, and also provides controlled access to this database.

✓ All access to the database is through the DBMS. The DBMS provides facilities that allow users to define the database, and to insert, update, delete, and retrieve data from the database.

✓ The DBMS environment consists of hardware (the computer), software (the DBMS, operating system, and applications programs), data, procedures, and people. The people include database administrators (DBAs), database designers, application programmers, and end-users.

✓ The DBMS provides controlled access to the database. It provides security, integrity, concurrency and recovery control, and a user-accessible catalog. It also provides a view mechanism to simplify the data that users have to deal with.

✓ Some advantages of the database approach include control of data redundancy, data consistency, sharing of data, and improved security and integrity. Some disadvantages include complexity, cost, reduced performance, and higher impact of a failure.

Chapter 2

The relational model

In this chapter you will learn:

➤ What a data model is and what its uses are.

➤ The terminology of the relational model.

➤ How tables are used to represent data.

➤ Properties of database relations.

➤ How to identify candidate, primary, alternate, and foreign keys.

➤ The meaning of entity integrity and referential integrity.

➤ About SQL and QBE, the two most widely used relational languages.

The Relational Database Management System (often called an **RDBMS** for short) has become the dominant data-processing software in use today, with estimated sales of approximately $8–10 billion per year ($25 billion with tools sales included), and growing at a rate of about 25 per cent per year. This software represents the second generation of DBMS and is based on the relational data model proposed by Dr E.F. Codd in his seminal paper 'A Relational Model of Data for Large Shared Data Banks' in 1970. In the relational model, all data is logically structured within *relations* (tables). A great strength of the relational model is this simple logical structure. Yet, behind this simple structure is a sound theoretical foundation that is lacking in the first generation of DBMSs (the network and hierarchical DBMSs).

The design methodology we present in this book is based on the relational data model, as this is the one most of you will be using. In this chapter, we discuss the basic principles of the relational data model. Let's start by first looking at what a data model is.

2.1   What is a data model?

A model is a representation of 'real world' objects and events, and their associations. It concentrates on the essential, inherent aspects of a company and ignores the accidental properties. A **data model** attempts to represent the company, or the part of the company, that you wish to model. It should provide the basic concepts and notations that will allow database designers and end-users to communicate their understanding of the company data unambiguously and accurately. A data model can be thought of as comprising three components:

> **Data model**
> An integrated collection of concepts for describing data, relationships between data, and constraints on the data used by a company.

(1) *a structural part*, consisting of a set of rules that define how the database is to be constructed;

(2) *a manipulative part*, defining the types of operations that are allowed on the data (this includes the operations that are used for updating or retrieving data and for changing the structure of the database);

(3) possibly *a set of integrity rules*, which ensures that the data is accurate.

The purpose of a data model is to represent data and to make the data understandable. If it does this, then it can be easily used to design a database. In the remainder of this chapter, we examine one such data model: the *relational data model*.

2.2   Terminology

The relational model is based on the mathematical concept of a **relation**, which is physically represented as a **table**. Codd, a trained mathematician, used terminology taken from mathematics, principally set theory and predicate logic. In this section, we explain the terminology and structural concepts of the relational model. In Section 2.3, we'll discuss the integrity rules for the model and in Section 2.4 we'll examine the manipulative part of the model.

> **Relation**
> A relation is a table with columns and rows.

2.2.1   Relational data structure

A relational DBMS requires only that the database be perceived by the user as tables.

> Note, however, that this perception applies only to the way we view the database; it does not apply to the physical structure of the database on disk, which we can implement using a variety of storage structures (such as a heap file or hash file).

Storage structures discussed in Appendix C

In the relational model, we use relations to hold information about the objects that we want to represent in the database. We represent a relation as a table in which the rows of the table correspond to individual records and the table columns correspond to **attributes**. Attributes can appear in any order and the relation will still be the same relation, and therefore convey the same meaning.

For example, in the *StayHome* video rental company, the information on branches is represented by the Branch relation, with columns for attributes branchNo (the branch number), street, city, state, zipCode, and mgrStaffNo (the staff number corresponding to the manager of the branch). Similarly, the information on staff is represented by the Staff relation, with columns for attributes staffNo (the staff number), name, position, salary, and branchNo (the number of the branch the staff member works at). Figure 2.1 shows instances of the Branch and Staff relations. As you can see from this example, a column contains values for a single attribute; for example, the branchNo columns contain only numbers of branches.

Domains are an important feature of the relational model. Every attribute in a relational database is associated with a domain. Domains may be distinct for each attribute, or two or more attributes may be associated with the same domain. Figure 2.2 shows the domains for some of the attributes of the Branch and Staff relations.

> Note that, at any given time, typically there will be values in a domain that don't currently appear as values in the corresponding attribute. In other words, a domain describes possible values for an attribute.

The domain concept is important because it allows us to define the meaning and source of values that attributes can hold. As a result, more information is available to the system and it can reject operations that don't make sense. For example, it would not be sensible for us to compare a staff number with a branch number, even though the domain definitions for both these attributes are character strings. Unfortunately, you'll find that many RDBMSs don't currently support domains.

The elements of a relation are the **tuples** or **records** in the table. In the Staff relation, each record contains five values, one for each attribute. As with attributes, tuples can appear in any order and the relation will still be the same relation, and therefore convey the same meaning.

A **relational database** consists of tables that are appropriately structured. We refer to this appropriateness as *normalization*. We'll defer the discussion of normalization until Chapter 6.

Attribute
An attribute is a named column of a relation.

StayHome is used throughout this book and discussed more fully in Chapter 4

Domain
A domain is the set of allowable values for one or more attributes.

Tuple
A tuple is a record of a relation.

Relational database
A collection of normalized tables.

Figure 2.1

An example of the **Branch** and **Staff** relations.

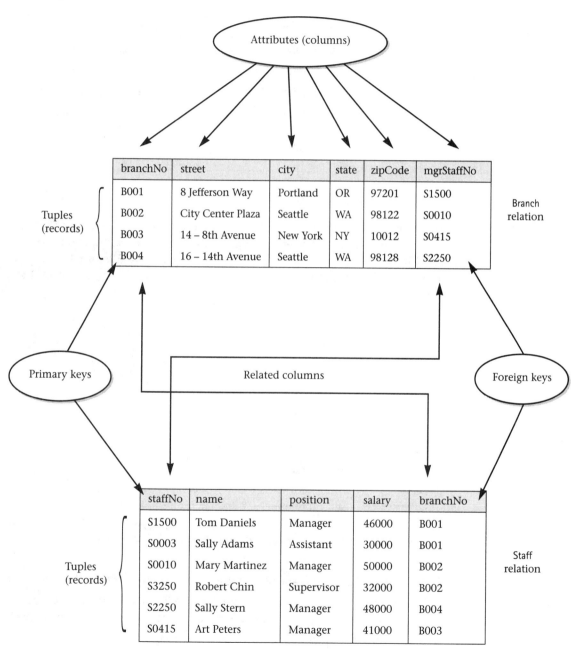

Figure 2.2

Domains for some attributes of the Branch and Staff relations.

Attribute	Domain name	Meaning	Domain definition
branchNo	Branch_Numbers	Set of all possible branch numbers.	Character: size 4, range B001–B999
street	Street_Names	Set of all possible street names.	Character: size 60
staffNo	Staff_Numbers	Set of all possible staff numbers.	Character: size 5, range S0001–S9999
position	Staff_Positions	Set of all possible staff positions.	One of Director, Manager, Supervisor, Assistant, Buyer
salary	Staff_Salaries	Possible values of staff salaries.	Monetary: 8 digits, range $10 000.00–$100 000.00

Alternative terminology

The terminology for the relational model can be quite confusing. In this chapter, we've introduced two sets of terms: (relation, attribute, tuple) and (table, column, record). Other terms that you may encounter are **file** for table, row for record, and **field** for column. You may also find various combinations of these terms, such as table, row, and field.

From now on, we will tend to drop the formal terms of relation, tuple, and attribute, and instead use the more frequently used terms table, record, and column.

2.2.2 Properties of relational tables

A relational table has the following properties:

- The table has a name that is distinct from all other tables in the database.
- Each cell of the table contains exactly one value. (For example, it would be wrong to store several telephone numbers for a single branch in a single cell. In other words, tables don't contain repeating groups. A relational table that satisfies this property is said to be *normalized* or in *first normal form*.)
- Each column has a distinct name.
- The values of a column are all from the same domain.
- The order of columns has no significance. In other words, provided a column name is moved along with the column values, we can interchange columns.
- Each record is distinct; there are no duplicate records.
- The order of records has no significance, theoretically. (However, in practice, the order may affect the efficiency of accessing records, as we'll see in Chapter 13.)

2.2.3 Relational keys

As we've just stated, each record in a table must be unique. This means that we need to be able to identify a column or combination of columns (called *relational keys*) that provides uniqueness. In this section, we explain the terminology used for relational keys.

Since a **superkey** may contain additional columns that are not necessary for unique identification, we're interested in identifying superkeys that contain only the *minimum number* of columns necessary for unique identification.

A **candidate key** for a table has two properties:

■ *Uniqueness* In each record, the values of the candidate key uniquely identify that record.

■ *Irreducibility* No proper subset of the candidate key has the uniqueness property.

There may be several candidate keys for a table. When a key consists of more than one column, we call it a **composite key**. Consider the Branch table shown in Figure 2.1. For a given value of city, we would expect to be able to determine several branches (for example, Seattle has two branches). This column cannot be selected as a candidate key. On the other hand, since *StayHome* allocates each branch a unique branch number, then for a given value of the branch number, branchNo, we can determine at most one record, so that branchNo is a candidate key. Similarly, as no two branches can be located in the same zip code, zipCode is also a candidate key for Branch.

Now consider a table called Role, which represents the characters played by actors in videos. The table comprises an actor number (actorNo), a catalog number (catalogNo), and the name of the character played (character), as shown in Figure 2.3. For a given actor number, actorNo, there may be several different videos the actor has starred in. Similarly, for a given catalog number, catalogNo, there may be several actors who have starred in this video. Therefore, actorNo by itself or catalogNo by itself cannot be selected as a candidate key. However, the combination of actorNo and catalogNo identifies at most one record.

Superkey
A column, or set of columns, that uniquely identifies a record within a table.

Candidate key
A superkey that contains only the minimum number of columns necessary for unique identification.

actorNo	catalogNo	character
A1002	207132	James Bond
A3006	330553	Sean Archer
A3006	902355	Jack Stranton
A2019	330553	Castor Troy
A2019	445624	Stanley Goodspeed
A7525	634817	Captain Steve Hiller
A4343	781132	Cruella De Vil

Figure 2.3

An example of the Role table.

> **TIP** Be careful not to look at sample data and try to deduce the candidate key(s), unless you are certain the sample is representative of the data that will be stored in the table. Generally, an instance of a table cannot be used to prove that a column or combination of columns is a candidate key. The fact that there are no duplicates for the values that appear at a particular moment in time does not guarantee that duplicates are not possible. However, the presence of duplicates in an instance can be used to show that some column combination is not a candidate key. Identifying a candidate key requires that we know the 'real world' meaning of the column(s) involved so that we can decide whether duplicates are possible. Only by using this semantic information can we be certain that a column combination is a candidate key.
>
> For example, from the data presented in Figure 2.1, we may think that a suitable candidate key for the **Staff** table would be **name**, the employee's name. However, although there is only a single value of Tom Daniels in this table at present, if a new member of staff with the same name joins the company, this would invalidate the choice of **name** as a candidate key.

Primary key
The candidate key that is selected to identify records uniquely within the table.

Since a table has no duplicate records, it's always possible to identify each record uniquely. This means that a table always has a **primary key**. In the worst case, the entire set of columns could serve as the primary key, but usually some smaller subset is sufficient to distinguish the records. The candidate keys that are not selected to be the primary key are called **alternate keys**. For the Branch table, if we choose branchNo as the primary key, zipCode would then be an alternate key. For the Role table, there is only one candidate key, comprising actorNo and catalogNo, so these columns would automatically form the primary key.

When a column appears in more than one table, its appearance usually represents a relationship between records of the two tables. For example, in Figure 2.1 the inclusion of branchNo in both the Branch and Staff tables is quite deliberate and links branches to the details of staff working there. In the Branch table, branchNo is the primary key. However, in the Staff table the branchNo column exists to match staff to the branch they work in. In the Staff table, branchNo is a **foreign key**. We say that the column branchNo in the Staff table *targets* the primary key column branchNo in the home table, Branch.

Foreign key
A column, or set of columns, within one table that matches the candidate key of some (possibly the same) table.

> You may recall that we stated in Chapter 1 that one of the advantages of the DBMS approach was control of data redundancy. This is an example of controlled redundancy – these common columns play an important role in modeling relationships, as we'll see in later chapters.

2.2.4 Representing relational databases

A relational database consists of one or more tables. The common convention for representing a description of a relational database is to give the name of each table, followed by the column names in parentheses. Normally, the primary key is underlined. The description of the relational database for the *StayHome* video rental company is:

Branch	(branchNo, street, city, state, zipCode, mgrStaffNo)
Staff	(staffNo, name, position, salary, branchNo)
Video	(catalogNo, title, category, dailyRental, price, directorNo)
Director	(directorNo, directorName)
Actor	(actorNo, actorName)
Role	(actorNo, catalogNo, character)
Member	(memberNo, fName, lName, address)
Registration	(branchNo, memberNo, staffNo, dateJoined)
RentalAgreement	(rentalNo, dateOut, dateReturn, memberNo, videoNo)
VideoForRent	(videoNo, available, catalogNo, branchNo)

Figure 2.4 shows an example of the *StayHome* database.

Branch

branchNo	street	city	state	zipCode	mgrStaffNo
B001	8 Jefferson Way	Portland	OR	97201	S1500
B002	City Center Plaza	Seattle	WA	98122	S0010
B003	14 – 8th Avenue	New York	NY	10012	S0415
B004	16 – 14th Avenue	Seattle	WA	98128	S2250

Staff

staffNo	name	position	salary	branchNo
S1500	Tom Daniels	Manager	46000	B001
S0003	Sally Adams	Assistant	30000	B001
S0010	Mary Martinez	Manager	50000	B002
S3250	Robert Chin	Supervisor	32000	B002
S2250	Sally Stern	Manager	48000	B004
S0415	Art Peters	Manager	41000	B003

Figure 2.4

An example of the *StayHome* video rental database.

Figure 2.4

Continued

Video

catalogNo	title	category	dailyRental	price	directorNo
207132	Tomorrow Never Dies	Action	5.00	21.99	D1001
902355	Primary Colors	Comedy	4.50	14.50	D7834
330553	Face/Off	Thriller	5.00	31.99	D4576
781132	101 Dalmatians	Children	4.00	18.50	D0078
445624	The Rock	Action	4.00	29.99	D5743
634817	Independence Day	Sci-Fi	4.50	32.99	D3765

Director

directorNo	directorName
D1001	Roger Spottiswoode
D7834	Mike Nichols
D4576	John Woo
D0078	Stephen Herek
D5743	Michael Bay
D3765	Roland Emmerick

Actor

actorNo	actorName
A1002	Pierce Brosnan
A3006	John Travolta
A2019	Nicolas Cage
A7525	Will Smith
A4343	Glenn Close

Role

actorNo	catalogNo	character
A1002	207132	James Bond
A3006	330553	Sean Archer
A3006	902355	Jack Stranton
A2019	330553	Castor Troy
A2019	445624	Stanley Goodspeed
A7525	634817	Captain Steve Hiller
A4343	781132	Cruella De Vil

Member

memberNo	fName	lName	address
M250178	Bob	Adams	57 – 11th Avenue, Seattle, WA, 98105
M166884	Art	Peters	89 Redmond Rd, Portland, OR, 97117
M115656	Serena	Parker	22 W. Capital Way, Portland, OR, 97201
M284354	Don	Nelson	123 Suffolk Lane, Seattle, WA, 98117

Registration

branchNo	memberNo	staffNo	dateJoined
B002	M250178	S3250	1-Jul-98
B001	M166884	S0003	4-Sep-99
B001	M115656	S0003	12-May-97
B002	M284354	S3250	9-Oct-98

Figure 2.4

(continued)

RentalAgreement

rentalNo	dateOut	dateReturn	memberNo	videoNo
R753461	4-Feb-00	6-Feb-00	M284354	245456
R753462	4-Feb-00	6-Feb-00	M284354	243431
R668256	5-Feb-00	7-Feb-00	M115656	199004
R668189	2-Feb-00	4-Feb-00	M115656	178643

VideoForRent

videoNo	available	catalogNo	branchNo
199004	N	207132	B001
245456	Y	207132	B002
178643	N	634817	B001
243431	N	634817	B002

2.3 Relational integrity

In the previous section, we discussed the structural part of the relational data model. As we mentioned in Section 2.1, a data model has two other parts: a manipulative part, defining the types of operations that are allowed on the data, and a set of integrity rules, which ensure that the data is accurate. In this section we discuss the relational integrity rules, and in the following section we discuss the main relational manipulation languages.

Since every column has an associated domain, there are constraints (called *domain constraints*) in the form of restrictions on the set of values allowed for the columns of tables. In addition, there are two important relational integrity rules, which are constraints or restrictions that apply to all instances of the database. The two principal rules for the relational model are known as *entity integrity* and *referential integrity*. Before we define these terms, we need first to understand the concept of nulls.

Domains defined in Section 2.2.1

2.3.1 Nulls

A **null** can be taken to mean 'unknown'. It can also mean that a value is not applicable to a particular record, or it could just mean that no value has yet been supplied. Nulls are a way to deal with incomplete or exceptional data. However, a null is not the same as a zero numeric value or a text string filled with spaces; zeros and spaces are values, but a null represents the absence of a value. Therefore, nulls should be treated differently from other values.

For example, suppose it was possible for a branch to be temporarily without a manager, perhaps because the manager has recently left and a new manager has not yet been appointed. In this case, the value for the corresponding mgrStaffNo column would be undefined. Without nulls, it becomes necessary to introduce false data to represent this state or to add additional columns that may not be meaningful to the user. In this example, we may try to represent the absence of a manager with the value 'None at present'. Alternatively, we may add a new column 'currrentManager?' to the Branch table, which contains a value Y (Yes), if there is a manager, and N (No), otherwise. Both these approaches can be confusing to anyone using the database.

We're now in a position to define the two relational integrity rules.

2.3.2 Entity integrity

The first integrity rule applies to the primary keys of base tables.

> A **base table** is a named table whose records are physically stored in the database. This is in contrast to a view, which we mentioned in Section 1.2.3. A view is a 'virtual table' that does not actually exist in the database but is generated by the DBMS from the underlying base tables whenever it's accessed.

From an earlier definition, we know that a primary key is a minimal identifier that is used to identify records uniquely. This means that no subset of the primary key is sufficient to provide unique identification of records. If we allow a null for any part of a primary key, we're implying that not all the columns are needed to distinguish between records, which contradicts the definition of the primary key. For example, as branchNo is the primary key of the Branch table, we should not be able to insert a record into the Branch table with a null for the branchNo column.

2.3.3 Referential integrity

The second integrity rule applies to foreign keys.

In Figure 2.1, branchNo in the Staff table is a foreign key targeting the branchNo column in the home table, Branch. It should not be possible to create a staff record with branch number B300, for example, unless there is already a record for branch number B300 in the Branch table. However, we should be able to create a new staff record with a null branch number to allow for the situation where a new member of staff has joined the company but has not yet been assigned to a particular branch.

2.3.4 Business rules

It's also possible for users to specify additional constraints that the data must satisfy. For example, if *StayHome* has a rule that a member can only rent a maximum of 10 videos at any one time, then the user must be able to specify this rule and expect the DBMS to enforce it. In this case, it should not be possible for a member to rent a video if the number of videos the member currently has rented is 10. Unfortunately, the level of support for relational integrity varies from system to system. We'll discuss the implementation of relational integrity in Chapters 12 and 19.

> **Business rules**
> Additional rules specified by the users or database administrators of a database.

2.4 Relational languages

In Section 2.1, we stated that one part of a data model is the manipulative part, which defines the types of operations that are allowed on the data. This includes the operations that are used for updating or retrieving data from the database, and for changing the structure of the database. The two main languages that have emerged for relational DBMSs are:

- **SQL** (Structured Query Language) and
- **QBE** (Query-by-Example).

SQL has been standardized by the International Standards Organization (ISO), making it both the formal and *de facto* standard language for defining and manipulating relational databases. The main characteristics of SQL are:

- It's relatively easy to learn.
- It's a non-procedural language: you specify *what* information you require, rather than *how* to get it.
- Like most modern languages, SQL is essentially free-format, which means that parts of statements don't have to be typed at particular locations on the screen.
- The command structure consists of standard English words such as CREATE TABLE, INSERT, SELECT. For example, using the tables defined in Figure 2.4, we could list the titles and daily rental rate of all videos in the Action category, sorted according to the video title, using the following SQL statement:

```
SELECT title, dailyrental
FROM video
WHERE category = 'Action'
ORDER BY title ASC;
```

■ SQL can be used by a range of users including Database Administrators (DBAs), management personnel, application programmers, and many other types of end-users.

However, SQL contains only commands to define and manipulate the database; it does not currently contain flow of control commands, such as IF ... THEN ... ELSE, GO TO, DO ... WHILE. Owing to this lack of *computational completeness*, SQL can be used in two ways. The first way is to use SQL *interactively* by entering the statements at a terminal. The second way is to *embed* SQL statements in a procedural language, such as Visual Basic, Delphi, C, C++, Java, COBOL, Fortran, Ada, or Pascal. In the latter case, a popular approach nowadays is to use Microsoft's ODBC (Open Database Connectivity) standard, which provides a DBMS-independent approach to embedding SQL in a programming language, thus making the code more portable between DBMSs.

QBE is an alternative, graphical-based, 'point-and-click' way of querying the database, which is particularly suited for queries that are not too complex, and can be expressed in terms of a few tables. QBE has acquired the reputation of being one of the easiest ways for non-technical users to obtain information from the database. QBE provides a visual means for querying the data through the use of templates. Querying the database is achieved by illustrating the query to be answered. The screen display is used instead of typing in column names and formats; however, we must indicate the columns we want to see and specify data values that we want to use to restrict the query. Languages like QBE can be a highly productive way to query or update the database interactively. Figure 2.5 shows how we would create the SQL query illustrated above using Microsoft Access QBE.

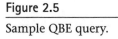

Figure 2.5

Sample QBE query.

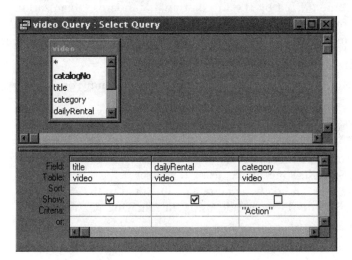

Unfortunately, unlike SQL, there is no official standard for these languages. However, the functionality provided by vendors is generally very similar and the languages are usually more intuitive to use than SQL. We'll return to SQL and QBE in Chapter 17.

Chapter summary

✓ The Relational Database Management System (RDBMS) has become the dominant data-processing software in use today, with estimated sales of approximately \$8–10 billion per year (\$25 billion with tools sales included), and growing at a rate of about 25 per cent per year. This software represents the second generation of DBMS and is based on the relational data model proposed by Dr E.F. Codd.

✓ Relations are physically represented as **tables**, with the records corresponding to individual tuples and the columns to attributes.

✓ Properties of relational tables are: each cell contains exactly one value, column names are distinct, column values come from the same domain, column order is immaterial, record order is immaterial, and there are no duplicate records.

✓ A **superkey** is a column, or set of columns, that identifies records of a table uniquely, while a **candidate key** is a minimal superkey. A **primary key** is the candidate key chosen for use in identification of records. A table must always have a primary key. A **foreign key** is a column, or set of columns, within one table that is the candidate key of another table.

✓ A **null** represents a value for a column that is unknown at the present time or is not defined for this record.

✓ **Entity integrity** is a constraint that states that in a base table no column of a primary key can be null. **Referential integrity** states that foreign key values must match a candidate key value of some record in the home table or be wholly null.

✓ The two main languages for accessing relational databases are SQL (Structured Query Language) and QBE (Query-by-Example).

Chapter 3

The database application lifecycle

In this chapter you will learn:

➤ The main stages of the information systems (IS) lifecycle.

➤ The relationship between the database application and information systems lifecycles.

➤ The main stages of the database application lifecycle.

➤ The activities associated with each stage of the lifecycle.

This chapter begins by first explaining why there is a need for a structured approach to developing software applications. We introduce an example of such an approach called the information systems lifecycle and discuss the relationship between an information system and the database that supports it. We then focus on the database and introduce an example of a structured approach to developing database applications called the database application lifecycle. Finally, we take you through the stages that make up the database application lifecycle.

3.1 The software crisis

You are probably already aware that over the past few decades there has been a dramatic rise in the number of software applications being developed, ranging from small, relatively simple applications consisting of a few lines of code, to large, complex applications consisting of millions of lines of code. Once developed, many of these applications proved to be demanding, requiring constant maintenance. This maintenance involved correcting faults, implementing new user requirements, and modifying the software to run on new or upgraded platforms. With so much software around to support, the effort spent on maintenance began to absorb resources at an alarming rate. As a result, many major software projects were late, over budget, and the software produced was unreliable, difficult to maintain, and performed poorly. This led to what has become known as the 'software crisis'. Although this term was first used in the late 1960s, more than 30 years later, the crisis is still with us. As a result, some people now refer to the software crisis as the 'software depression'. As an indication of the software crisis, a study carried out in the UK by OASIG, a Special Interest Group concerned with the Organizational Aspects of IT, reached the following conclusions (OASIG, 1996):

- 80–90 per cent of systems do not meet their performance goals.
- About 80 per cent are delivered late and over budget.
- Around 40 per cent of developments fail or are abandoned.
- Under 40 per cent fully address training and skills requirements.
- Less than 25 per cent properly integrate business and technology objectives.
- Just 10–20 per cent meet all their success criteria.

There are several major reasons for the failure of software projects, including:

- lack of a complete requirements specification;
- lack of an appropriate development methodology;
- poor decomposition of design into manageable components.

As a solution to these problems, a structured approach to the development of software was proposed and is commonly known as the *Information Systems Lifecycle* or the *Software Development Lifecycle (SDLC)*.

3.2   The information systems lifecycle

An **information system** not only collects, manages, and controls data used and generated by a company but enables the transformation of the data into information. An information system also provides the infrastructure to facilitate the dissemination of information to those who make the decisions critical to the success of a company. The essential component at the *heart* of an information system is the database that supports it.

> **Information system**
> The resources that enable the collection, management, control, and dissemination of data/information throughout a company.

Typically, the stages of the information systems lifecycle include: planning, requirements collection and analysis, design (including database design), prototyping, implementation, testing, conversion, and operational maintenance. Of course, in this book we're interested in the development of the database component of an information system. As a database is a fundamental component of the larger company-wide information system, the database application lifecycle is inherently linked with the information systems lifecycle.

3.3 The database application lifecycle

In this chapter, we describe the database application lifecycle for relational DBMSs. An overview of the stages of the database application lifecycle is shown in Figure 3.1. Below the name of each stage is the section in this chapter that describes that stage. It's important to note that the stages of the database application lifecycle are not strictly sequential, but involve some amount of repetition of previous stages through *feedback loops*. For example, problems encountered during database design may necessitate additional requirements collection and analysis. As there are feedback loops between most stages, we show only some of the more obvious ones in Figure 3.1.

For small database applications with a small number of users, the lifecycle need not be very complex. However, when designing a medium to large database application with tens to thousands of users, using hundreds of queries and application programs, the lifecycle can become extremely complex.

3.4 Database planning

Database planning
The management activities that allow the stages of the database application to be realized as efficiently and effectively as possible.

A starting point for establishing a database project is the creation of a *mission statement* and *mission objectives* for the database application. The mission statement defines the major aims of the database application, while each mission objective identifies a particular task that the database must support. Of course, as with any project, part of the database planning process should also involve some estimation of the work to be done, the resources with which to do it, and the money to pay for it all.

As we've already noted, a database often forms part of a larger company-wide information system and therefore any database project should be integrated with the company's overall IS strategy.

Database planning may also include the development of standards that govern how data will be collected, how the format should be specified, what necessary documentation will be needed, and how design and implementation should proceed. Standards can be very time-consuming to develop and maintain, requiring resources to set them up initially and to continue maintaining them. However, a well-designed set of standards provides a basis for training staff and measuring quality, and ensures that work conforms to a pattern, irrespective of staff skills and experience. Any legal or company requirements concerning the data should be documented, such as the stipulation that some types of data must be treated confidentially or kept for a specific period of time.

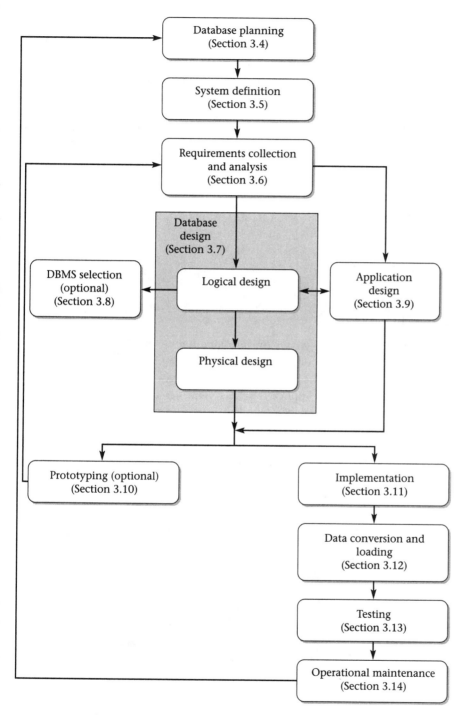

Figure 3.1

Main stages of the
database application
lifecycle.

3.5 System definition

Before attempting to design a database application, it's essential that we first identify the scope and boundary of the system that we're investigating and how it interfaces with other parts of the company's information system. Figure 3.2 shows one example of how to represent the system boundary of a database application for the *StayHome* video rental company. When defining the system boundary for a database application we include not only the current user views but also any known future user views.

Note that this type of diagram can be drawn at any level of detail. A second example of this type of diagram (at a lower level) is shown in Figure 4.9 in the next chapter.

3.5.1 User views

A database application may have one or more user views. Identifying user views is an important aspect of developing a database application because it helps to ensure that no major users of the database are forgotten when developing the requirements for the new application. User views are also particularly helpful in the development of a relatively complex database application by allowing the requirements to be broken down into manageable pieces.

A user view defines what is required of a database application in terms of the data to be held and the transactions to be performed on the data (in other words,

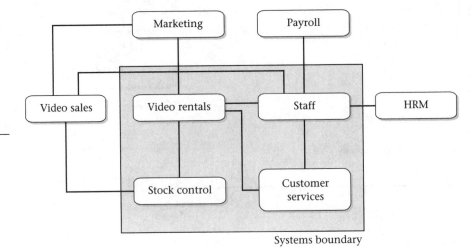

Figure 3.2

Systems boundary of the database application for the *StayHome* video rental company.

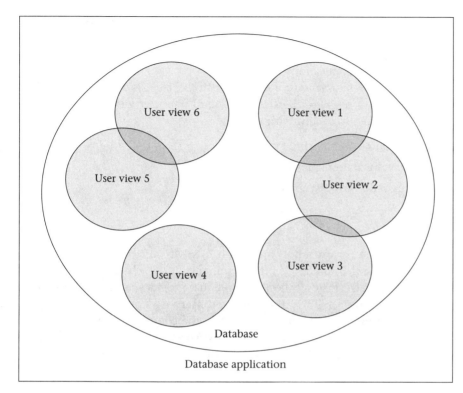

Figure 3.3

A diagram representing a database application with multiple user views: view 4 is distinct; the others have some element of overlap.

what the users will do with the data). The requirements of a user view may be distinct to that view or overlap with other views. Figure 3.3 is a diagrammatic representation of a database application with multiple user views (denoted user view 1 to 6). Note that while user views (1, 2, and 3) and (5 and 6) have overlapping requirements (shown as darker areas), user view 4 has distinct requirements.

3.6 Requirements collection and analysis

In this stage, we collect and analyze information about the company, or the part of the company, to be served by the database. There are many techniques for gathering this information, called fact-finding techniques, which we'll discuss in detail in Chapter 4.

We gather information for each major user view (that is, job role or business application area), including:

■ a description of the data used or generated,

■ the details of how data is to be used or generated,

■ any additional requirements for the new database application.

> **Requirements collection and analysis** The process of collecting and analyzing information about the company to be supported by the database application, and using this information to identify the requirements for the new database application.

We then analyze this information to identify the requirements (or features) to be included in the new database application. These requirements are described in documents collectively referred to as *requirements specifications* for the new database application.

Another important activity associated with this stage is deciding how to deal with the situation where there is more than one user view. There are three major approaches to dealing with multiple user views:

■ the centralized approach,

■ the view integration approach, and

■ a combination of both approaches.

Centralized approach

The **centralized (or one-shot) approach** involves collating the requirements for different views into a single list of requirements, which we refer to simply as a **view**. We give the view a collective name that provides some indication of the functional area covered by all the merged user views. A **global logical data model** representing the entire view (that is, the company, or part of the company being modeled) is created in the next stage (logical database design). A diagram representing the management of user views 1 to 3 using the centralized approach is shown in Figure 3.4.

> **Centralized approach**
> Requirements for each user view are merged into a single set of requirements for the new database application.

Figure 3.4

The centralized approach to managing multiple user views 1 to 3.

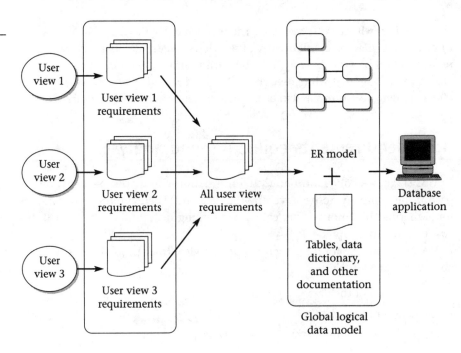

Generally, this approach is preferred when there is a significant overlap in requirements for each user view and the database application is not overly complex.

View integration approach

The **view integration approach** involves leaving the requirements for each view as separate lists of requirements. We create data models representing each user view and then merge the data models at a later stage of database design. A data model that represents a single user view is called a **local logical data model**. A diagram representing the management of user views 1 to 3 using the view integration approach is shown in Figure 3.5.

Generally, this approach is preferred when there are significant differences between user views and the database application is sufficiently complex to justify dividing the work into more manageable parts.

We'll discuss how to manage multiple user views in more detail in Section 4.4.4 using the *StayHome* video rental company and we'll demonstrate how to use the view integration approach in Chapter 10.

> **View integration approach**
> Requirements for each user view are used to build a separate data model to represent that user view. The resulting data models are merged at a later stage in database design.

> **TIP**
>
> Requirements collection and analysis is a preliminary stage to database design. The amount of data gathered depends on the nature of the problem and the policies of the company. Identifying the required functionality for a database application is a critical activity, as systems with inadequate or incomplete functionality will annoy the users, and may lead to rejection or underutilization of the system. However, excessive functionality can also be problematic as it can overcomplicate a system, making it difficult to implement, maintain, use, and learn.

3.7   Database design

> **Database design**
> The process of creating a design for a database that will support the company's operations and objectives.

In Chapter 7, we'll discuss the main aims of the database design stage in more detail and provide an overview of a methodology for database design. **Database design** is made up of two main phases called logical and physical design. During logical database design, we attempt to identify the important objects that need to be represented in the database and the relationships between these objects. During physical database design, we decide how the logical design is to be physically implemented (as tables) in the target DBMS. We'll describe a step-by-step methodology for logical database design in Chapters 8 to 11 and for physical database design in Chapters 12 to 16.

Figure 3.5

The view
integration
approach to
managing multiple
user views 1 to 3.

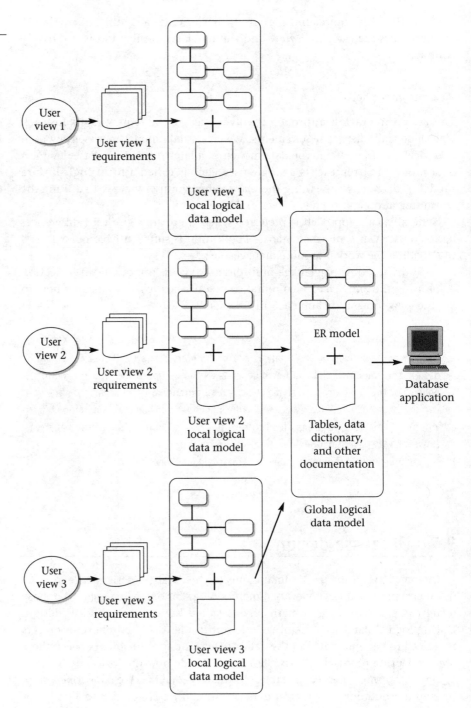

3.8   DBMS selection

If no relational DBMS currently exists in the company, an appropriate part of the lifecycle in which to make a selection is between the logical and physical database design phases. However, selection can be done at any time prior to logical design provided sufficient information is available regarding system requirements such as networking, performance, ease of restructuring, security, and integrity constraints.

Although DBMS selection may be infrequent, as business needs expand or existing systems are replaced, it may become necessary at times to evaluate new DBMS products. In such cases, the aim is to select a system that meets the current and future requirements of the company, balanced against costs that include the purchase of the DBMS product, any additional software/hardware required to support the database system, and the costs associated with changeover and staff training.

A simple approach to selection is to check off DBMS features against requirements. In selecting a new DBMS product, there is an opportunity to ensure that the selection process is well planned, and the system delivers real benefits to the company.

> **TIP**
>
> Nowadays, the World Wide Web is a great source of information and can be used to identify potential candidate DBMSs. Vendors' Web sites can provide valuable information on DBMS products. As a starting point, have a look at *DBMS* magazine's Web site called DBMS ONLINE (available at www.intelligententerprise. com) for a comprehensive index of DBMS products.

DBMS selection
The selection of an appropriate DBMS to support the database application.

Integrity constraints discussed in Section 1.3

3.9   Application design

In Figure 3.1 shown earlier in this chapter, we observed that database and application design are parallel activities of the database application lifecycle. In most cases, we cannot complete the application design until the design of the database itself has taken place. On the other hand, the database exists to support the applications, and so there must be a flow of information between application design and database design.

We must ensure that all the functionality stated in the requirements specifications is present in the application design for the database application. This involves designing the interaction between the user and the data, which we call *transaction design*. In addition to designing how the required functionality is to be achieved, we have to design an appropriate *user interface* to the database application.

Application design
The design of the user interface and the application programs that use and process the database.

3.9.1 Transaction design

Transaction
An action, or series of actions, carried out by a single user or application program, which accesses or changes the contents of the database.

Transactions represent 'real world' events such as the registering of a new member at a video rental company, the creation of a rental agreement for a member to rent a video, or the addition of a new member of staff. These transactions have to be applied to the database to ensure that the database remains current with the 'real world' and to support the information needs of the users (see Section 1.3).

The purpose of transaction design is to define and document the high-level characteristics of the transactions required on the database system, including:

- data to be used by the transaction;
- functional characteristics of the transaction (what the transaction will do);
- output of the transaction;
- importance to the users;
- expected rate of usage.

There are three main types of transactions:

- retrieval transactions;
- update transactions;
- mixed transactions.

Retrieval transactions are used to retrieve data for display on the screen (or as a report) or as input into another transaction. For example, the operation to search for and display the details of a video (given the video number) is a retrieval transaction. *Update transactions* are used to insert new records, delete old records, or modify existing records in the database. For example, the operation to insert the details of a new video into the database is an update transaction. *Mixed transactions* involve both the retrieval and updating of data. For example, the operation to search for and display the details of a video (given the video number) and then update the value of the daily rental rate is a mixed transaction.

3.9.2 User interface design

In addition to designing how the required functionality is to be achieved, we have to design an appropriate user interface for the database application. This interface should present the required information in a *user-friendly* way. The importance of user interface design is sometimes ignored or left until late in the design stages. However, it should be recognized that the interface might be one of the most important components of the system. If it's easy to learn, simple to use, straightforward and forgiving, the users will be inclined to make good use of what information is presented. On the other hand, if the interface has none of these characteristics, the system will undoubtedly cause problems. For example, before implementing a form or report, it's essential that we first design the layout. Useful guidelines to follow when designing forms or reports are listed in Table 3.1 (Shneiderman, 1992).

Table 3.1 Guidelines for form/report design.

Meaningful title

Comprehensible instructions

Logical grouping and sequencing of fields

Visually appealing layout of the form/report

Familiar field labels

Consistent terminology and abbreviations

Consistent use of color

Visible space and boundaries for data-entry fields

Convenient cursor movement

Error correction for individual characters and entire fields

Error messages for unacceptable values

Optional fields marked clearly

Explanatory messages for fields

Completion signal

3.10 Prototyping

> **Prototyping**
> Building a working model of a database application.

At various points throughout the design process, we have the option either to fully implement the database application or to build a prototype.

A prototype is a working model that does not normally have all the required features or provide all the functionality of the final system. The purpose of developing a prototype database application is to allow users to use the prototype to identify the features of the system that work well, or are inadequate, and if possible to suggest improvements or even new features to the database application. In this way, we can greatly clarify the requirements and evaluate the feasibility of a particular system design. Prototypes should have the major advantage of being relatively inexpensive and quick to build.

There are two prototyping strategies in common use today: requirements prototyping and evolutionary prototyping. *Requirements prototyping* uses a prototype to determine the requirements of a proposed database application and once the requirements are complete the prototype is discarded. While *evolutionary prototyping* is used for the same purposes, the important difference is that the prototype is not discarded but with further development becomes the working database application.

3.11 Implementation

Implementation
The physical realization of the database and application designs.

On completion of the design stages (which may or may not have involved prototyping), we're now in a position to implement the database and the application programs. The database implementation is achieved using the *Data Definition Language (DDL)* of the selected DBMS or a graphical user interface (GUI), which provides the same functionality while hiding the low-level DDL statements. The DDL statements are used to create the database structures and empty database files. Any specified user views are also implemented at this stage.

The application programs are implemented using the preferred **third or fourth generation language (3GL or 4GL)**. Parts of these application programs are the database transactions, which we implement using the *Data Manipulation Language (DML)* of the target DBMS, possibly embedded within a host programming language, such as Visual Basic, Delphi, C, C++, Java, COBOL, Fortran, Ada, or Pascal. We also implement the other components of the application design such as menu screens, data entry forms, and reports. Again, the target DBMS may have its own fourth generation tools that allow rapid development of applications through the provision of non-procedural query languages, reports generators, forms generators, and application generators.

Security and integrity controls for the application are also implemented. Some of these controls are implemented using the DDL, but others may need to be defined outside the DDL using, for example, the supplied DBMS utilities or operating system controls.

SQL defined in
Section 2.4

SQL (Structured Query Language) is both a DDL and a DML.

3.12 Data conversion and loading

Data conversion and loading
Transferring any existing data into the new database and converting any existing applications to run on the new database.

This stage is required only when a new database system is replacing an old system. Nowadays, it's common for a DBMS to have a utility that loads existing files into the new database. The utility usually requires the specification of the source file and the target database, and then automatically converts the data to the required format of the new database files. Where applicable, it may be possible for the developer to convert and use application programs from the old system for use by the new system. Whenever conversion and loading are required, the process should be properly planned to ensure a smooth transition to full operation.

3.13 Testing

Before going live, the newly developed database application should be thoroughly tested. This is achieved using carefully planned test strategies and realistic data so that the entire testing process is methodically and rigorously carried out. Note that in our definition of testing we have not used the commonly held view that testing is the process of demonstrating that faults are not present. In fact, testing cannot show the absence of faults; it can show only that software faults are present. If testing is conducted successfully, it will uncover errors in the application programs and possibly the database structure. As a secondary benefit, testing demonstrates that the database and the application programs *appear* to be working according to their specification and that performance requirements appear to be satisfied. In addition, metrics collected from the testing stage provides a measure of software reliability and software quality.

As with database design, the users of the new system should be involved in the testing process. The ideal situation for system testing is to have a test database on a separate hardware system, but often this is not available. If real data is to be used, it is essential to have backups taken in case of error. After testing is complete, the application system is ready to be 'signed off' and handed over to the users.

> **Testing**
> The process of executing the application programs with the intent of finding errors.

3.14 Operational maintenance

In this stage, the database application now moves into a maintenance stage, which involves the following activities:

- Monitoring the performance of the database application. If the performance falls below an acceptable level, the database may need to be tuned or reorganized.

- Maintaining and upgrading the database application (when required). New requirements are incorporated into the database application through the preceding stages of the lifecycle.

We'll examine this stage in more detail in Chapter 16.

> **Operational maintenance**
> The process of monitoring and maintaining the system following installation.

Chapter summary

 An **information system** is the resources that enable the collection, management, control, and dissemination of data/information throughout a company.

✓ The **database** is a fundamental component of an **information system**. The lifecycle of an information system is inherently linked to the life-cycle of the database that supports it.

✓ The main stages of the database application lifecycle include: database planning, system definition, requirements collection and analysis, database design, DBMS selection (optional), application design, prototyping (optional), implementation, data conversion and loading, testing, and operational maintenance.

✓ **Database planning** is the management activities that allow the stages of the database application to be realized as efficiently and effectively as possible.

✓ **System definition** involves identifying the scope and boundaries of the database application, including its major user views. A user view can represent a job role or business application area.

✓ **Requirements collection and analysis** is the process of collecting and analyzing information about the company (or part of the company) that is to be supported by the database application, and using this information to identify the requirements for the new system.

✓ There are three major approaches to dealing with multiple views, namely the centralized approach, the view integration approach, and a combination of both. The **centralized** (or **one-shot**) **approach** involves collating the users' requirements for different user views into a single list of requirements. A data model representing all the user views is created during the database design stage. The **view integration approach** involves leaving the users' requirements for each user view as separate lists of requirements. Data models representing each user view are created and then merged at a later stage of database design.

✓ **Database design** is the process of creating a design for a relational database that will support the company's operations and objectives. This stage includes the logical and physical design of the database.

✓ The aim of **DBMS selection** is to select a system that meets the current and future requirements of the company, balanced against costs that include the purchase of the DBMS product and any additional software/hardware, and the costs associated with changeover and training.

✓ **Application design** involves designing the user interface and the application programs that use and process the database. This stage involves two main activities: transaction design and user interface design.

✓ **Prototyping** involves building a working model of the database application, which allows the designers or users to visualize and evaluate the system.

✓ **Implementation** is the physical realization of the database and application designs.

✓ **Data conversion and loading** involves transferring any existing data into the new database and converting any existing applications to run on the new database.

✓ **Testing** is the process of executing the application programs with the intent of finding errors.

✓ **Operational maintenance** is the process of monitoring and maintaining the system following installation.

Part Two

Database analysis and design techniques

Chapter 4

Fact-finding

In this chapter you will learn:

When fact-finding techniques are used in the database application lifecycle. ◄

The types of facts collected throughout the database application lifecycle. ◄

The types of documentation produced throughout the database application lifecycle. ◄

The most commonly used fact-finding techniques. ◄

How to use each fact-finding technique and the advantages and disadvantages of each. ◄

About a video rental company called *StayHome*. ◄

How to apply fact-finding techniques to the early stages of the database application lifecycle. ◄

In Chapter 3, we learned about the stages of the database application lifecycle. There are many occasions during these stages when it's critical that the database developer captures the necessary facts to build the required database application. The necessary facts cover the business and the users of the database application, including the terminology, problems, opportunities, constraints, requirements, and priorities. These facts are captured using **fact-finding** techniques.

In this chapter, we discuss when a database developer might use fact-finding techniques and what types of facts should be captured. We present an overview of how these facts are used to generate the main types of documentation used throughout the database application lifecycle. We briefly describe the most commonly used fact-finding techniques and identify the advantages and disad-

> **Fact–finding**
> The formal process of using techniques such as interviews and questionnaires to collect facts about systems, requirements, and preferences.

vantages of each. We finally demonstrate how some of these techniques may be used during the earlier stages of the database application lifecycle using a video rental company called *StayHome*. In Chapters 8 to 16, we'll use the *StayHome* case study to demonstrate the methodology for database design.

Throughout this chapter we use the term 'database developer' to refer to a person or group of people responsible for the analysis, design, and implementation of a database application.

4.1 When are fact–finding techniques used?

There are many occasions for fact-finding during the database application lifecycle. However, fact-finding is particularly crucial to the early stages of the lifecycle, including the database planning, system definition, and requirements collection and analysis stages. It's during these early stages that the database developer learns about the terminology, problems, opportunities, constraints, requirements, and priorities of the business and the users of the system. Fact-finding is also used during database design and the later stages of the lifecycle, but to a lesser extent. For example, during physical database design, fact-finding becomes technical as the developer attempts to learn more about the DBMS selected for the database application. Also, during the final stage, operational maintenance, fact-finding is used to determine whether a system requires tuning to improve performance or is further developed to include new requirements.

> Note that it's important to have a rough estimate of how much time and effort is to be spent on fact-finding for a database project. Too much study too soon leads to *paralysis by analysis*. However, too little thought can result in an unnecessary waste of both time and money due to working on the wrong solution to the wrong problem.

4.2 What facts are collected?

Throughout the database application lifecycle, the database developer needs to capture facts about the current or future system. Table 4.1 provides examples of the sorts of data captured and the documentation produced for each stage of the lifecycle. As we mentioned in Chapter 3, the stages of the database application lifecycle are not strictly sequential, but involve some amount of repetition of previous stages through feedback loops. This is also true for the data captured and the documentation produced at each stage. For example, problems encountered during database design may necessitate additional data capture on the requirements for the new system.

Table 4.1 Examples of the data captured and the documentation produced for each stage of the database application lifecycle.

Stage of database application lifecycle	Examples of data captured	Examples of documentation produced
Database planning	Aims and objectives of database project	Mission statement and objectives of database application
System definition	Description of major user views (includes job roles and/ or business application areas)	Definition of scope and boundary of database application; definition of user views to be supported
Requirements collection and analysis	Requirements for user views	Users' and system requirements specifications
Database design	Users' responses to checking the logical database design; functionality provided by target DBMS	Logical database design (includes ER model(s), data dictionary, and tables); physical database design
Application design	Users' responses to checking interface design	Application design (includes description of programs and user interface)
DBMS selection	Functionality provided by target DBMS	DBMS evaluation and recommendations
Prototyping	Users' responses to prototype	Modified users' requirements and systems specification
Implementation	Functionality provided by target DBMS	
Data conversion and loading	Format of current data; data import capabilities of target DBMS	
Testing	Test results	Testing strategies used; analysis of test results
Operational maintenance	Performance testing results; new or changing user and system requirements	User manual; analysis of performance results; modified users' requirements and systems specification

In Section 4.4, we'll return to examine the first three stages of the database application lifecycle, namely database planning, system definition, and requirements collection and analysis. For each stage, we demonstrate the process of collecting data using fact-finding techniques and then producing documentation for the *StayHome* video rental company. However, before this section, we first present a review of the most commonly used fact-finding techniques.

4.3 Fact–finding techniques

A database developer normally uses several fact-finding techniques during a single database project. There are five common fact-finding techniques:

■ Examining documentation
■ Interviewing
■ Observing the business in operation
■ Research
■ Questionnaires.

4.3.1 Examining documentation

Examining documentation can be useful when you're trying to gain some insight as to how the need for a database arose. You may also find that documentation can be helpful to provide information on the business (or part of the business) associated with the problem. If the problem relates to the current system there should be documentation associated with that system. Examining documents, forms, reports, and files associated with the current system is a good way to quickly gain some understanding of the system. Examples of the types of documentation that you should examine are listed in Table 4.2.

4.3.2 Interviewing

Interviewing is the most commonly used, and normally most useful, fact-finding technique. You can interview to collect information from individuals face-to-face. There can be several objectives to using interviewing such as finding out facts, verifying facts, clarifying facts, generating enthusiasm, getting the end-user involved, identifying requirements, and gathering ideas and opinions. However, using the interviewing technique requires good communication skills for dealing effectively with people who have different values, priorities, opinions, motivations, and personalities. As with other fact-finding techniques, interviewing isn't always the best method for all situations. The advantages and disadvantages of using interviewing as a fact-finding technique are listed in Table 4.3.

Table 4.2 Examples of types of documentation that should be examined.

Purpose of documentation	Examples of useful sources
Describes problem and need for database	Internal memos, e-mails, and minutes of meetings Employee/customer complaints, and documents that describe the problem Performance reviews/reports
Describes business (or part of business) affected by problem	Organizational chart, mission statement, and strategic plan of the business Objectives for the part of the business being studied Task/job descriptions Samples of manual forms and reports Samples of computerized forms and reports Completed forms/reports
Describes current system	Various types of flowcharts and diagrams Data dictionary Database application design Program documentation User/training manuals

Table 4.3 Advantages and disadvantages of using interviewing as a fact-finding technique.

Advantages	Disadvantages
Allows interviewee to respond freely and openly to questions	Very time-consuming and costly, and therefore may be impractical
Allows interviewee to feel part of project	Success is dependent on communication skills of interviewer
Allows interviewer to follow up on interesting comments made by interviewee	
Allows interviewer to adapt or reword questions during interview	
Allows interviewer to observe interviewee's body language	

There are two types of interviews, unstructured and structured. *Unstructured interviews* are conducted with only a general objective in mind and with few, if any, specific questions. The interviewer counts on the interviewee to provide a framework and direction to the interview. This type of interview frequently loses focus and, for this reason, you may find that it doesn't usually work well for database analysis and design.

In *structured interviews*, the interviewer has a specific set of questions to ask the interviewee. Depending on the interviewee's responses, the interviewer will direct additional questions to obtain clarification or expansion. *Open-ended questions* allow the interviewee to respond in any way that seems appropriate. An example of an open-ended question is: 'Why are you dissatisfied with the report on member registration?' *Closed-ended questions* restrict answers to either specific choices or short, direct responses. An example of such a question might be: 'Are you receiving the report on member registration on time?' or 'Does the report on member registration contain accurate information?' Both questions require only a 'Yes' or 'No' response.

To ensure a successful interview you should select appropriate individuals to interview, prepare extensively for the interview, and conduct the interview in an efficient and effective manner.

4.3.3 Observing the business in operation

Observation is one of the most effective fact-finding techniques you can use to understand a system. With this technique, you can either participate in, or watch a person performing activities to learn about the system. This technique is particularly useful when the validity of data collected through other methods is in question or when the complexity of certain aspects of the system prevents a clear explanation by the end-users.

As with the other fact-finding techniques, successful observation requires much preparation. To ensure that the observation is successful, you will want to know as much about the individuals and the activity to be observed as possible. For example, when are the low, normal, and peak periods for the activity being observed and will the individuals be upset by having someone watch and record their actions? The advantages and disadvantages of using observation as a fact-finding technique are listed in Table 4.4.

4.3.4 Research

A useful fact-finding technique is to research the application and problem. Computer trade journals, reference books, and the Internet are good sources of information. They can provide you with information on how others have solved similar problems, plus you can learn whether or not software packages exist to solve your problem. The advantages and disadvantages of using research as a fact-finding technique are listed in Table 4.5.

4.3.5 Questionnaires

Another fact-finding technique is to conduct surveys through questionnaires. Questionnaires are special-purpose documents that allow you to gather facts from a large number of people while maintaining some control over their

Table 4.4 Advantages and disadvantages of using observation as a fact-finding technique.

Advantages	Disadvantages
Allows the validity of facts and data to be checked	People may knowingly or unknowingly perform differently when being observed
Observer can see exactly what is being done	May miss observing tasks involving different levels of difficulty or volume normally experienced during that time period
Observer can also obtain data describing the physical environment of the task	Some tasks may not always be performed in the manner in which they are observed
Relatively inexpensive	May be impractical
Observer can do work measurements	

Table 4.5 Advantages and disadvantages of using research as a fact-finding technique.

Advantages	Disadvantages
Can save time if solution already exists	Can be time-consuming
Researcher can see how others have solved similar problems or met similar requirements	Requires access to appropriate sources of information
Keeps researcher up to date with current developments	May ultimately not help in solving problem because problem is not documented elsewhere

Table 4.6 Advantages and disadvantages of using questionnaires as a fact-finding technique.

Advantages	Disadvantages
People can complete and return questionnaires at their convenience	Number of respondents can be low, possibly only 5–10%
Relatively inexpensive way to gather data from a large number of people	Questionnaires may be returned incomplete
People more likely to provide the real facts as responses can be kept confidential	No opportunity to adapt or reword questions that may have been misinterpreted
Responses can be tabulated and analyzed quickly	Can't observe and analyze the respondent's body language
	Can be time-consuming to prepare questionnaire

responses. When dealing with a large audience, no other fact-finding technique can tabulate the same facts as efficiently. The advantages and disadvantages of using questionnaires as a fact-finding technique are listed in Table 4.6.

There are two formats for questionnaires, free-format and fixed-format. *Free-format questionnaires* offer the respondent greater freedom in providing answers. A question is asked and the respondent records the answer in the space provided after the question. Examples of free-format questions are: 'What reports do you currently receive and how are they used?' and 'Are there any problems with these reports? If so, please explain.' The problems with free-format questions are that the respondent's answers may prove difficult to tabulate and, in some cases, may not match the questions asked.

The second type of questionnaire is fixed-format. *Fixed-format questionnaires* contain questions that require specific responses from individuals. Given any question, the respondent must choose from the available answers. This makes the results much easier to tabulate. On the other hand, the respondent cannot provide additional information that might prove valuable. An example of a fixed-format question is: 'The current format of the report on the video rentals is ideal and should not be changed.' The respondent may be given the option to answer Yes or No to this question, or be given the option to answer from a range of responses including Strongly Agree, Agree, No Opinion, Disagree, and Strongly Disagree.

4.4 The *StayHome* case study

In this section, we first describe the *StayHome* case study. We then use the *StayHome* case study to illustrate how you would establish a database project in the early stages of the database application lifecycle by going through the database planning, system definition, and requirements collection and analysis stages.

4.4.1 The *StayHome* case study – an overview

This case study describes a company called *StayHome*, which rents out videos to its members. The first branch of *StayHome* was established in 1982 in Seattle but the company has now grown and has many branches throughout the United States. The company's success is due to the first-class service it provides to its members and the wide and varied stock of videos available for rent.

StayHome currently has about 2000 staff working in 100 branches. When a member of staff joins the company, the *StayHome* staff registration form is used. The staff registration form for Mary Martinez is shown in Figure 4.1.

Each branch has a Manager and several Supervisors. The Manager is responsible for the day-to-day running of a given branch and each Supervisor is responsible for supervising a group of staff. An example of the first page of a report listing the members of staff working at the branch in Seattle is shown in Figure 4.2.

StayHome
Staff Registration Form

Staff Number S0010	**Branch Number** B002
Full Name	**Branch Address**
Mary Martinez	City Center Plaza,
Position	
	Seattle, WA 98122
Manager	
Salary	**Telephone Number(s)**
50000	205-555-6756/206-555-8836

Figure 4.1

The *StayHome* staff registration form for Mary Martinez.

StayHome
Staff Listing

Branch Number B002	**Branch Address**
Telephone Number(s)	City Center Plaza, Seattle,
206-555-6756/206-555-8836	WA 98122

Staff Number	Name	Position
S0010	Mary Martinez	Manager
S3250	Robert Chin	Supervisor
S3190	Anne Hocine	Supervisor
S5889	Annet Longhorn	Assistant
S5980	Chris Lawrence	Assistant
S6112	Sofie Walters	Assistant

Page 1

Figure 4.2

Example of the first page of a report listing the members of staff working at a *StayHome* branch in Seattle.

Figure 4.3

Example of the first page of a report listing the videos available at the *StayHome* branch in Seattle.

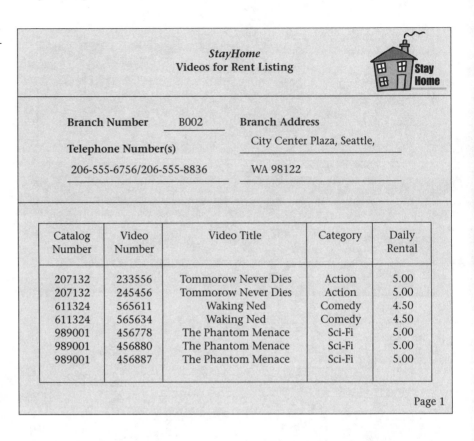

Catalog Number	Video Number	Video Title	Category	Daily Rental
207132	233556	Tommorow Never Dies	Action	5.00
207132	245456	Tommorow Never Dies	Action	5.00
611324	565611	Waking Ned	Comedy	4.50
611324	565634	Waking Ned	Comedy	4.50
989001	456778	The Phantom Menace	Sci-Fi	5.00
989001	456880	The Phantom Menace	Sci-Fi	5.00
989001	456887	The Phantom Menace	Sci-Fi	5.00

Each branch of *StayHome* has a stock of videos for hire. Each video is uniquely identified using a catalog number. However, in most cases, there are several copies of each video at a branch, and the individual copies are identified using the video number. An example of the first page of a report listing the videos available at the branch in Seattle is shown in Figure 4.3.

Before renting a video, a customer must first join as a member of *StayHome*. When a customer joins, he or she is requested to complete the *StayHome* member registration form. The member registration form for Don Nelson is shown in Figure 4.4. *StayHome* currently has about 100 000 members. A customer may choose to register at more than one branch; however, a new member registration form must be filled out on each occasion. An example of the first page of a Manager's report listing the members registered at the branch in Seattle is shown in Figure 4.5.

Once registered, a member is free to rent videos, up to a maximum of 10 at any one time. When a member chooses to rent one or more videos, the *StayHome* video rental form is completed. An example of a completed form for Claire Sinclair renting *Waking Ned* and *The Phantom Menace* is shown in Figure 4.6.

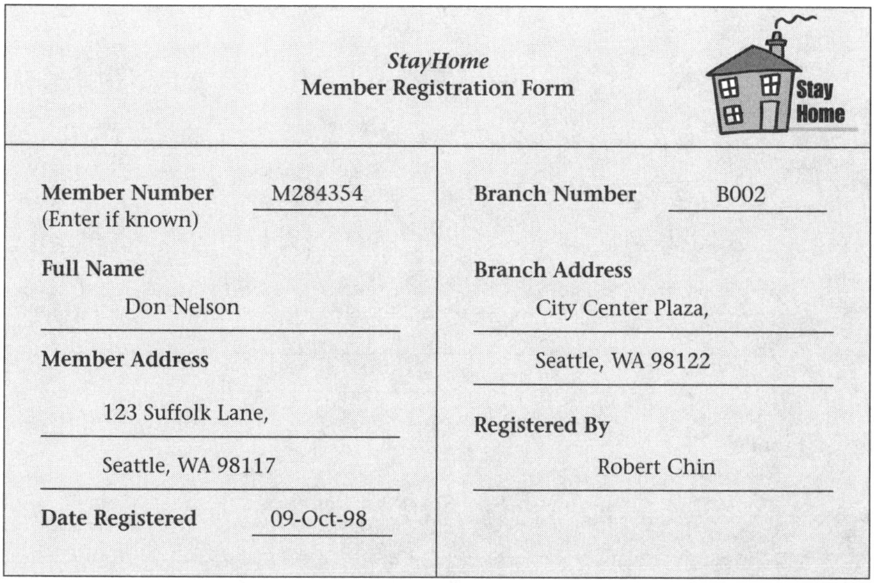

StayHome
Member Registration Form

Stay Home

Member Number (Enter if known) M284354	**Branch Number** B002
Full Name Don Nelson	**Branch Address** City Center Plaza, Seattle, WA 98122
Member Address 123 Suffolk Lane, Seattle, WA 98117	**Registered By** Robert Chin
Date Registered 09-Oct-98	

Figure 4.4

The *StayHome* member registration form for Don Nelson.

As *StayHome* has grown, so have the difficulties in managing the increasing amount of data used and generated by the company. To ensure the continued success of the company, the Director of *StayHome* has urgently requested that a database application be built to help solve the increasing problems of data management.

4.4.2 The *StayHome* case study – database planning

The first step in developing a database application is to clearly define the **mission statement** for the database project. The mission statement defines the major aims of the database application. Those driving the database project within the business (such as the Director and/or owner) normally define the mission statement. A mission statement helps to clarify the purpose of the database project and provides a clearer path towards the efficient and effective creation of the required database application.

Once the mission statement is defined, the next activity involves identifying the **mission objectives**. Each mission objective should identify a particular task that the database must support. The assumption is that if the database supports the mission objectives then the mission statement should be met. The mission statement and objectives may be accompanied by some additional information that specifies, in general terms, the work to be done, the resources with which to do it, and the money to pay for it all.

Figure 4.5

Example of the first page of a report listing the members registered at the *StayHome* branch in Seattle.

	StayHome Members Listing		

Branch Number B002	**Branch Address**	
Telephone Number(s)	City Center Plaza,	
206-555-6756/206-555-8836	Seattle, WA 98122	

Member Number	Name	Address	Date Joined
M129906	Karen Homer	634–12th Avenue, Seattle, WA 98123	10-Jan-94
M189976	John Hood	4/4 Rosie Lane, Seattle	21-May-95
M220045	Jamie Peters	5A–22nd Street, Seattle, WA 98451	20-May-96
M228877	Claire Sinclair	44B–16th Street, Seattle, WA 98123	28-Aug-96
M265432	Janet McDonald	1 Lincoln Way, Seattle, WA 98234	19-Aug-97
M284354	Don Nelson	123 Suffolk Lane, Seattle, WA 98117	09-Oct-98
M284666	William Carring	1 Sparrowhill Way, Seattle, WA 98111	10-Oct-99

Page 1

Creating the mission statement for the StayHome *database application*

You should begin the process of creating a mission statement for the *StayHome* database application by conducting interviews with the Director of the company and any other appropriate staff, as indicated by the Director. Open-ended questions are normally the most useful at this stage of the process. For example, you (the database developer) may start the interview by asking the Director of *StayHome* the following questions:

Database developer 'What is the purpose of your company?'

Director   'We provide a wide range of videos for rent to members registered at our branches throughout the US.'

Video Number	Video Title	Daily Rental	Date Out	Date In	Total Rental
565611	Walking Ned	4.50	12-Dec-99	14-Dec-99	4.50
476667	The Phantom Manace	5.00	13-Dec-99	15-Dec-99	5.00

StayHome Video Rental

Member Number M228877 Branch Number B002

Member Name: Claire Sinclair

Branch Address: City Center Plaza, Seattle, WA 98122

Figure 4.6

Example of a *StayHome* video rental form for Claire Sinclair.

Database developer 'Why do you feel that you need a database?'

Director 'To be honest we can't cope with our own success. Over the past few years, we've opened several new branches, and at each branch we now offer a larger selection of videos to a growing number of members. However, this success has been accompanied by increasing data management problems, which means that the level of service we provide is falling. Also, there's a lack of cooperation and sharing of information between branches, which is a very worrying development.'

Database developer 'How do you know that a database will solve your problems?'

Director 'All I know is that we are drowning in paperwork. We need something that will speed up the way we work, that is, something to automate a lot of the day-to-day tasks that seem to take forever these days. Also, I want the branches to start working together. Databases do this, don't they?'

Responses to these types of questions should help you formulate the mission statement. For example, the mission statement for the *StayHome* database is shown in Figure 4.7. When you feel that you have a clear and unambiguous mission statement that the staff of *StayHome* agree with, you can move on to define the mission objectives.

Figure 4.7

Mission statement
for the *StayHome*
database
application.

'The purpose of the *StayHome* database application is to maintain the data that we generate, to support the video rentals business for our members, and to facilitate the cooperation and sharing of information between branches.'

Creating the mission objectives for the StayHome database application

The process of creating mission objectives involves conducting interviews with appropriate members of staff. Again, open-ended questions are normally the most useful at this stage of the process. To obtain the complete range of mission objectives, you should interview various members of staff with different roles in *StayHome*. Examples of typical questions you might ask are as follows:

'What is your job description?'

'What kinds of tasks do you perform in a typical day?'

'What kinds of data do you work with?'

'What types of reports do you use?'

'What types of things do you need to keep track of?'

'What service does your company provide to your members?'

These questions (or similar) are put to the Director and members of staff in the role of Manager, Supervisor, Assistant, and Buyer of *StayHome*. Of course, it may be necessary to adapt the questions as required depending on whom you are interviewing.

Director

Database developer 'What role do you play for the company?'

Director 'I oversee the running of the company to ensure that we continue to provide the best possible video rental service to our members.'

Database developer 'What kinds of tasks do you perform in a typical day?'

Director 'I monitor the running of each branch by our Managers. I try to ensure that the branches work well together and share important information about videos and members. I oversee the work carried out by the Buyer for our company; that's the person responsible for buying videos for all our branches. I normally try to keep a high profile with our branch Managers by calling into each branch once or twice a month.'

Database developer 'What kinds of data do you work with?'

Director 'I need to be able to get my hands on everything used or generated by our company. That includes data about staff, videos, rentals, members, video suppliers, and video orders. I mean everything!'

Database developer 'What types of reports do you use?'

Director 'I need to know what's going on at all the branches. I get my information from various reports on staff, videos in stock, video rentals, members, video suppliers, and orders.'

Database developer 'What types of things do you need to keep track of?'

Director 'As I said before, I need to track everything, I need to see the whole picture, OK?'

Database developer 'What service does your company provide to your members?'

Director 'We try to provide the best and most competitively priced video rental service in the US.'

Manager

Database developer 'What is your job description?'

Manager 'My job title is Manager. I oversee the day-to-day running of my branch to provide the best service to our members.'

Database developer 'What kinds of tasks do you perform in a typical day?'

Manager 'I ensure that the branch has the appropriate type and number of staff on duty at any time of the day. I monitor the hiring of videos to ensure that we have an appropriate selection of videos for our membership, although I don't actually do the buying of videos myself – that's done by the company Buyer. I monitor the registering of new members and the hiring activity of our current members.'

Database developer 'What kinds of data do you work with?'

Manager 'I need data about staff, videos, rentals, and members.'

Database developer 'What types of reports do you use?'

Manager 'Various reports on staff, videos in stock, video rentals, and members.'

Database developer 'What types of things do you need to keep track of?'

Manager 'Staff, videos in stock, video rentals, and members.'

Database developer 'What service does your company provide to your members?'

Manager 'We try to provide the best video rentals service in the area.'

Supervisor

Database developer 'What is your job description?'

Supervisor 'My job title is Supervisor. I supervise a small group of staff and deal directly with our members in providing a video rental service.'

Database developer   'What kinds of tasks do you perform in a typical day?'

Supervisor   'I allocate staff to particular duties, such as dealing with members, restocking shelves, and the filing of paperwork. I answer queries from members about videos for rent. I process the renting out and return of videos. I keep members' details up to date and register customers when they want to join the company as one of our members.'

Database developer   'What kinds of data do you work with?'

Supervisor   'I work with data about staff, videos, rentals, and members.'

Database developer   'What types of reports do you use?'

Supervisor   'Reports on staff and videos in stock.'

Database developer   'What types of things do you need to keep track of?'

Supervisor   'Whether certain videos are available for hire and whether the details on our membership are up to date.'

Assistant

Database developer   'What is your job description?'

Assistant   'My job title is Assistant. I deal directly with our members in providing a video rental service.'

Database developer   'What kinds of tasks do you perform in a typical day?'

Assistant   'I answer queries from members about videos for rent. You know what I mean: "Do you have such and such a video?" I process the renting out and return of videos. I restock the shelves with returned videos, and when we are not too busy I try to file paperwork.'

Database developer   'What kinds of data do you work with?'

Assistant   'Data about videos, rentals, and members.'

Database developer   'What types of reports do you use?'

Assistant   'None.'

Database developer   'What types of things do you need to keep track of?'

Assistant   'Whether certain videos are available for hire.'

Database developer   'What service does your company provide to your members?'

Assistant   'We try to answer questions about videos in stock such as: "Do you have videos starring Ewan MacGregor?" and "Who starred in or directed *2001 A Space Odyssey*?" You wouldn't believe what our members expect us to know, but luckily most of us work here because we're really into films, so if I don't know the answer, one of the others will.'

Buyer

Database developer 'What is your job description?'

Buyer 'My job title is Buyer. I'm responsible for buying videos for rent for all branches of the company.'

Database developer 'What kinds of tasks do you perform in a typical day?'

Buyer 'I work directly with branch Managers and video suppliers. I respond to requests from Managers to supply them with certain videos. It's my job to ensure that I get the best possible deal for the company when dealing with video suppliers. Of course, I depend on Managers doing their homework – I don't want to order videos that a branch doesn't need or find that a branch doesn't stock sufficient copies of a popular video. When I have time, I do my own checking by monitoring the renting of videos at each branch to check that each branch has an appropriate selection of videos.'

Database developer 'What kinds of data do you work with?'

Buyer 'I need access to data on branches, videos, video rentals, members, video orders, and suppliers.'

Database developer 'What types of reports do you use?'

Buyer 'I need reports on orders I have placed for videos. I need various reports that show me videos in stock, video rentals, and members at each branch and across all branches.'

Database developer 'What types of things do you need to keep track of?'

Buyer 'I need to have up-to-date information about my orders for videos; it's important to deal only with suppliers who won't let us down. I also need to know what's going on at each branch in terms of their stock of videos and video rentals. As I said before, I don't want to order videos that a branch doesn't need.'

Database developer 'What service does your company provide to your members?'

Buyer 'We try to provide the best selection of videos at the cheapest possible rental rate.'

Responses to these types of questions should help you to formulate the mission objectives. For example, the mission objectives for the *StayHome* database are shown in Figure 4.8.

4.4.3 The *StayHome* case study – system definition

The purpose of the system definition stage is to define the scope and boundary of the database application and its major user views. A user view represents the requirements that should be supported by a database application as defined by

Figure 4.8

Mission objectives
for the *StayHome*
database
application.

To maintain (enter, update, and delete) data on branches.
To maintain (enter, update, and delete) data on staff.
To maintain (enter, update, and delete) data on videos.
To maintain (enter, update, and delete) data on members.
To maintain (enter, update, and delete) data on video rentals.
To maintain (enter, update, and delete) data on video suppliers.
To maintain (enter, update, and delete) data on orders to suppliers for videos.
To perform searches on videos.
To perform searches on staff.
To perform searches on video rentals.
To perform searches on members.
To perform searches on video suppliers.
To perform searches on video orders.
To track the status of videos in stock.
To track the status of videos rentals.
To track the status of video orders.
To report on staff at each branch.
To report on videos at each branch.
To report on members at each branch.
To report on video rentals at each branch.
To report on video suppliers.
To report on video orders.

a particular job role (such as Manager or Assistant) or business application area
(such as video rentals or stock control).

Defining the systems boundary for the StayHome *database application*

During this stage of the database application lifecycle, you should use interviews to clarify or expand on data captured in the previous stage. However,
you may also use additional fact-finding techniques, including examining
the sample documentation shown in Section 4.4.1. You should now analyze
the data collected so far to define the boundary of the database application.
The systems boundary for the *StayHome* database application is shown in
Figure 4.9. Contained within the boundary is a representation of the main
types of data mentioned in the interviews and a rough guide as to how this
data is related.

Identifying the major user views for the StayHome *database application*

You should now analyze the data collected so far to define the main user views
of the database application. The majority of data about the user views was col-

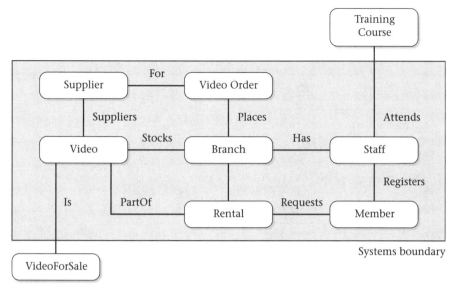

Figure 4.9

Systems boundary
for the *StayHome*
database
application.

lected during interviews with the Director and members of staff in the role of Manager, Supervisor, Assistant, and Buyer. The main user views for the *StayHome* database application are shown in Figure 4.10.

4.4.4 The *StayHome* case study – requirements collection and analysis

During this stage, you should continue to gather more details on the user views identified in the previous stage, to create a *users' requirements specification* that describes in detail the data to be held in the database and how the data is to be used. While gathering more information on the user views, you should also try to collect any general requirements for the system. The purpose of gathering this information is to create a *systems specification*, which describes any features to be included in the new database application such as networking and shared access requirements, performance requirements, and the levels of security required.

While you are collecting the data on the requirements for the user views and the system in general, you will learn about how the current system works. Of course, you are building a new database application and should try to retain the good things about the old system while introducing the benefits that will be part of using the new system.

An important activity associated with this stage is deciding how you want to deal with the situation where you have more than one user view. As we discussed in Section 3.6, there are three major approaches to dealing with multiple user views, namely the *centralized approach*, the *view integration approach*, and a

Figure 4.10

Major user views for the *StayHome* database application.

User view	Requirements
Director	To report on staff at all branches.
	To report on videos at all branches.
	To report on members at all branches.
	To report on video rentals at all branches.
	To report on video suppliers.
	To report on video orders.
Manager	To maintain (enter, update, and delete) data on a given branch.
	To maintain (enter, update, and delete) data on staff at a given branch.
	To perform searches on staff at all branches.
	To report on staff at a given branch.
	To report on videos at a given branch.
	To report on members at a given branch.
	To report on video rentals at a given branch.
Supervisor	To maintain (enter, update, and delete) data on videos at a given branch.
	To maintain (enter, update, and delete) data on members at a given branch.
	To maintain (enter, update, and delete) data on video rentals at a given branch.
	To perform searches on videos at all branches.
	To perform searches on video rentals at a given branch.
	To perform searches on members at a given branch.
	To track the status of videos in stock at a given branch.
	To track the status of video rentals at a given branch.
	To report on staff at a given branch.
Assistant	To maintain (enter, update, and delete) data on video rentals at a given branch.
	To maintain (enter, update, and delete) data on members at a given branch.
	To perform searches on videos at all branches.
	To perform searches on video rentals at a given branch.
	To perform searches on members at a given branch.
	To track the status of videos in stock at a given branch.
	To track the status of video rentals at a given branch.
Buyer	To maintain (enter, update, and delete) data on videos.
	To maintain (enter, update, and delete) data on video suppliers.
	To maintain (enter, update, and delete) data on video orders.
	To perform searches on videos at all branches.
	To perform searches on video suppliers.
	To perform searches on video orders.
	To track the status of video orders.
	To report on videos at all branches.
	To report on video rentals at all branches.
	To report on members at all branches.
	To report on video suppliers.
	To report on video orders.

combination of both approaches. We'll show how you can use these approaches shortly.

Gathering more information on the user views of the StayHome *database application*

To find out more about the requirements for each user view, you may again use a selection of fact-finding techniques, including interviews and observing the business in operation. Examples of the types of questions that you may ask about the data (represented as X) required by a user view includes:

'What type of data do you need to hold on X?'

'What sorts of things do you do with the data on X?'

For example, you may ask a branch Manager the following questions:

Database developer 'What type of data do you need to hold on staff?'

Manager 'The types of data held on a member of staff are his or her name, position, and salary. Each member of staff is given a staff number, which is unique throughout the company.'

Database developer 'What sorts of things do you do with the data on staff?'

Manager 'I need to be able to enter the details of new members of staff and delete their details when they leave. I need to keep the details of staff up to date and print reports that list the name, position, and salary of each member of staff at my branch. I need to be able to allocate Supervisors to look after staff. Sometimes when I need to communicate with other branches, I need to find out the names of Managers at the other branches'.

You need to ask similar questions about all the important data to be stored in the database. Responses to these questions should help you identify the necessary details for the users' requirements specification.

Gathering information on the system requirements of the StayHome
database application

While conducting interviews about user views, you should also collect more general information on the system requirements. Examples of the types of questions that you may ask about the system include:

'What transactions run frequently on the database?'

'What transactions are critical to the operation of the business?'

'When do the critical transactions run?'

'When are the low, normal, and high workload periods for the critical transactions?'

'What type of security do you want for the database application?'

'Is there any highly sensitive data that should only be accessed by certain members of staff?'

'What historical data do you want to hold?'

'What are the networking and shared access requirements for the database system?'

'What type of protection from failures or data loss do you want for your database application?'

For example, you may ask a Manager the following questions:

Database developer 'What transactions run frequently on the database?'

Manager 'We frequently get requests either by phone or by members who call into our branch to search for a particular video and see if it's available for rent. Of course, we also do a lot of renting out and returning of videos.'

Database developer 'What transactions are critical to the operation of the business?'

Manager 'Again, critical operations include being able to search for particular videos and the renting out and returning of videos. Members would go elsewhere if we couldn't provide these basic services.'

Database developer 'When do the critical transactions run?'

Manager 'Every day.'

Database developer 'When are the low, normal, and high workload periods for the critical transactions?'

Manager 'We tend to be quiet in the mornings and get busier as the day progresses. The busiest time each day for dealing with members is between 6 and 9pm. We even have to double the staff on duty during this period on Fridays and Saturdays'.

You may ask the Director the following questions:

Database developer 'What type of security do you want for the database application?'

Director 'I don't suppose a database holding information for a video rental company holds very sensitive data, but I wouldn't want any of our competitors to see our data on members and their video rentals. Staff should only see the data necessary to do their job in a form that suits what they're doing. For example, although it's necessary for Supervisors and Assistants to see member details, member records should only be displayed one at a time and not as a report.'

Database developer 'Is there any highly sensitive data that should only be accessed by certain members of staff?'

Director 'As I said before, staff should only see the data necessary to do their jobs. For example, although Supervisors need to see staff details, I should be the only one to see salary details'.

Database developer 'What historical data do you want to hold?'

Director 'I want to be able to keep members' details for a couple of years after their last video rental, so that we can mailshot them, tell them about our latest promotional offers, and generally try to attract them back. I also want to be able to keep rental information for a couple of years so that we can analyze it to find out which types of videos are the most popular, which age groups hire videos most frequently, and so on.'

Database developer 'What are the networking and shared access requirements for the database system?'

Director 'I want all the branches networked to our Headquarters here in Seattle, so that staff can access the system from wherever and whenever they need to. At most branches, I would expect about two or three staff to be accessing the system at any one time, but remember we have about 100 branches. Most of the time the staff should be just accessing local branch data. However, I don't really want there to be any restrictions about how or when the system can be accessed, unless it's got real financial implications.'

Database developer 'What type of protection from failures or data loss do you want for your database application?'

Director 'The best, of course. All our business is going to be conducted using the database, so if it goes down, we're sunk. To be serious for a minute, I think we probably have to back up our data every evening when the branch closes, what do you think?'

You need to ask similar questions about all the important aspects of the system. Responses to these questions should help you identify the necessary details for the system requirements specification.

Managing the user views of the StayHome database application

How do you decide whether to use the centralized or view integration approach to manage multiple user views? One way to help you make a decision is to examine the overlap in terms of the data used between the user views identified during the system definition stage. Table 4.7 cross-references the Director, Manager, Supervisor, Assistant, and Buyer user views with the main types of data used by the *StayHome* database application (namely Supplier, Video Order, Video, Branch, Staff, Rental, and Member).

Table 4.7 Cross-reference of user views with the main types of data used by the *StayHome* database application.

	Supplier	Video Order	Video	Branch	Staff	Rentals	Member
Director	X	X	X	X	X	X	X
Manager			X	X	X	X	X
Supervisor			X	X	X	X	X
Assistant			X	X		X	X
Buyer	X	X	X	X		X	X

You can see from this table that there is an overlap in the data used by all the user views. However, the Director and Buyer views are distinct in requiring additional data (namely, Supplier and Video Order) to that used by the other user views. Based on this analysis, you could use the centralized approach to first merge the requirements for the Director and Buyer user views (given the collective name of *Business view)* and the requirements for the Manager, Supervisor, and Assistant user views (given the collective name of *Branch view*). You could then develop data models representing the Business and Branch views and then use the view integration approach to merge the two data models.

> Of course, for a simple case study like *StayHome*, you could easily use the centralized approach for all user views but we'll stay with our decision to create two views so that we can demonstrate how the view integration approach works in practice in Chapter 10.

It's difficult to give precise rules as to when it's appropriate to use the centralized or view integration approaches. As the database developer, you should base your decision on an assessment of the complexity of the database application and the degree of overlap between the various user views. However, whether you use the centralized or view integration approach or a mixture of both to build the underlying database, ultimately you need to create the original user views for the working database application. We'll discuss the establishment of the user views for the database in Chapter 15.

In the remainder of this chapter, we present the users' requirements specification for the Branch view and we'll return to discuss the requirements for the Business view in Chapter 10.

Creating the users' requirements specification for the Branch view of the StayHome *database application*

The users' requirements specification for the Branch view is listed in two sections:

- the 'data requirements' section describes the data used by the Branch view;
- the 'transaction requirements' section provides examples of how the data is used by the Branch view (that is, the transactions that staff have to perform on the data).

Data requirements

The data held on a branch of *StayHome* is the branch address made up of street, city, state, and zip code, and the telephone numbers (maximum of three lines). Each branch is given a branch number, which is unique throughout the company.

Each branch of *StayHome* has staff, which includes a Manager, one or more Supervisors, and a number of other staff. The Manager is responsible for the day-to-day running of a given branch. Each branch has several Supervisors and each Supervisor is responsible for supervising a group of staff. The data held on a member of staff is his or her name, position, and salary. Each member of staff is given a staff number, which is unique throughout the company.

Each branch of *StayHome* is allocated a stock of videos. The data held on a video is the catalog number, video number, title, category, daily rental rate, purchase price, status, and the names of the main actors (and the characters played), and the director. The catalog number uniquely identifies each video. In most cases, there are several copies of each video at a branch, and the individual copies are identified using the video number. A video is given a category such as Action, Adult, Children, Thriller, Horror, or Sci-Fi. The status indicates whether a specific copy of a video is available for rent.

Before renting a video from the company, a customer must first register as a member of a local branch of *StayHome*. The data held on a member is the first and last name, address, and the date that the member registered at the branch. Each member is given a member number, which is unique across all branches and is used even when a member chooses to register at more than one branch. The name of the member of staff responsible for processing the registration of a member at a branch is also noted.

Once registered, a member is free to rent videos, up to a maximum of 10 at any one time. The data held on each video rented is the rental number, the member's full name and member number, the video number, title, and daily rental cost, and the dates the video is rented out and returned. The rental number is unique throughout the company.

Transaction requirements

Data entry

(a) Enter the details of a new branch.

(b) Enter the details of a new member of staff at a branch (such as an employee Tom Daniels at branch B001).

(c) Enter the details for a newly released video (such as details of a video called *Independence Day*).

(d) Enter the details of copies of a new video at a given branch (such as three copies of *Independence Day* at branch B001).

(e) Enter the details of a new member registering at a given branch (such as a member Bob Adams registering at branch B002).

(f) Enter the details of a rental agreement for a member renting a video (such as member Don Nelson renting *Tomorrow Never Dies* on 4-Feb-2000).

Data update/deletion

(g) Update/delete the details of a branch.

(h) Update/delete the details of a member of staff at a branch.

(i) Update/delete the details of a given video.

(j) Update/delete the details of a copy of a video.

(k) Update/delete the details of a given member.

(l) Update/delete the details of a given rental agreement for a member renting a video.

Data queries

The database should be capable of supporting the following sample queries:

(m) List the details of branches in a given city.

(n) List the name, position, and salary of staff at a given branch, ordered by staff name.

(o) List the name of each Manager at each branch, ordered by branch number.

(p) List the title, category, and availability of all videos at a specified branch, ordered by category.

(q) List the title, category, and availability of all videos for a given actor's name at a specified branch, ordered by title.

(r) List the title, category, and availability of all videos for a given director's name at a specified branch, ordered by title.

(s) List the details of all videos a specified member currently has on rent.

(t) List the details of copies of a given video at a specified branch.

(u) List the titles of all videos in a specified category, ordered by title.

(v) List the total number of videos in each video category at each branch, ordered by branch number.

(w) List the total cost of the videos at all branches.

(x) List the total number of videos featuring each actor, ordered by actor name.

(y) List the total number of members at each branch who joined in 1999, ordered by branch number.

(z) List the total possible daily rental for videos at each branch, ordered by branch number.

Creating the systems specification for the StayHome database application

The systems specification should list all the important features for the *StayHome* database application. Examples of the types of features that should be described in the systems specification include:

■ Initial database size

■ Database rate of growth

■ The types and average number of record searches

■ Networking and shared access requirements

■ Performance

■ Security

■ Backup and recovery

■ Legal issues.

Initial database size

(a) There are approximately 20 000 video titles and 400 000 videos for rent distributed over 100 branches. There are an average of 4000 and a maximum of 10 000 videos for rent at each branch.

(b) There are approximately 2000 staff working across all branches. There are an average of 15 and a maximum of 25 members of staff working at each branch.

(c) There are approximately 100 000 members registered across all branches. There are an average of 1000 and a maximum of 1500 members registered at each branch.

(d) There are approximately 400 000 video rentals across all branches. There are an average of 4000 and a maximum of 10 000 video rentals at each branch.

(e) There are approximately 1000 directors and 30 000 main actors in 60 000 starring roles.

(f) There are approximately 50 video suppliers and 1000 video orders.

Database rate of growth

(a) Approximately 100 new video titles and 20 copies of each video are added to the database each month.

(b) Once a copy of a video is no longer suitable for renting out (this includes those of poor visual quality, lost, or stolen), the corresponding record is deleted from the database. Approximately 100 records of videos for rent are deleted each month.

(c) Approximately 20 members of staff join and leave the company each month. The records of staff who have left the company are deleted after one year. Approximately 20 staff records are deleted each month.

(d) Approximately 1000 new members register at branches each month. If a member does not rent out a video at any time within a period of two years, his or her record is deleted. Approximately 100 member records are deleted each month.

(e) Approximately 5000 new video rentals are recorded across 100 branches each day. The details of video rentals are deleted two years after the creation of the record.

(f) Approximately 50 new video orders are placed each week. The details of video orders are destroyed two years after the creation of the record.

The types and average number of record searches

(a) Searching for the details of a branch – approximately 10 per day.

(b) Searching for the details of a member of staff at a branch – approximately 20 per day.

(c) Searching for the details of a given video – approximately 5000 per day (Sunday to Thursday), approximately 10 000 per day (Friday and Saturday). Peak workload 6–9pm daily.

(d) Searching for the details of a copy of a video – approximately 10 000 per day (Sunday to Thursday), approximately 20 000 per day (Friday and Saturday). Peak workload 6–9pm daily.

(e) Searching for the details of a specified member – approximately 100 per day.

(f) Searching for the details of a rental agreement for a member renting a video – approximately 10 000 per day (Sunday to Thursday), approximately 20 000 per day (Friday and Saturday). Peak workload 6–9pm daily.

Networking and shared access requirements

(a) All branches should be securely networked to a centralized database located at the company's HQ in Seattle.

(b) The system should allow for at least three people concurrently accessing the system from each branch. Consideration needs to be given to the licensing requirements for this number of concurrent accesses.

Performance

(a) During opening hours but not during peak periods expect less than 1-second response for all single record searches. During peak periods (6–9pm daily) expect less than 5-second response for all searches.

(b) During opening hours but not during peak periods expect less than 5-second response for all multiple record searches. During peak periods (6–9pm daily) expect less than 10-second response for all multiple record searches.

(c) During opening hours but not during peak periods expect less than 1-second response for all updates/saves. During peak periods (6–9pm daily) expect less than 5-second response for all searches.

Security

(a) The database should be password protected.

(b) Each member of staff should be assigned database access privileges appropriate to a particular user view, namely Director, Manager, Supervisor, Assistant, or Buyer.

(c) Staff should see only the data necessary to do their job in a form that suits what they're doing.

Backup and recovery

The database should be backed up each day at 12 midnight.

Legal issues

Each country has laws that govern the way that the computerized storage of personal data is handled. As the *StayHome* database holds data on staff and members, any legal issues that must be complied with should be investigated and implemented.

4.4.5 The *StayHome* case study – database design

In this chapter, we demonstrated the creation of the users' requirements specification for the Branch view and the systems specification for the *StayHome* database application. These documents are the source of information for the next stage of the lifecycle called database design. In Chapters 8 to 16, we'll provide a step-by-step methodology for database design, and we'll use the *StayHome* case study and the documents created for the *StayHome* database application in this chapter to demonstrate the methodology in practice.

Chapter summary

✓ **Fact-finding** is the formal process of using techniques such as interviews and questionnaires to collect facts about systems, requirements, and preferences.

✓ Fact-finding is particularly crucial to the early stages of the database application lifecycle, including the database planning, system definition, and requirements collection and analysis stages.

✓ The five most common fact-finding techniques are examining documentation, interviewing, observing the business in operation, research, and questionnaires.

✓ The first step in developing a database application is to clearly define the **mission statement** and **mission objectives** for the database project. The mission statement defines the major aims of the database application. Each mission objective should identify a particular task that the database must support.

✓ The purpose of the system definition stage is to define the boundaries and user views of the database application.

✓ A user view represents the requirements that should be supported by a database application as defined by a particular job role (such as Manager or Assistant) or business application area (such as video rentals or stock control).

✓ There are two main documents created during the requirements collection and analysis stage, namely the users' requirements specification and the systems specification.

✓ The users' requirements specification describes in detail the data to be held in the database and how the data is to be used.

✓ The systems specification describes any features to be included in the database application such as the required performance and the levels of security.

Chapter 5

Entity-Relationship modeling

In this chapter you will learn:

How to use ER modeling in database design. ◄

The basic concepts of an ER model, called entities, relationships, and attributes. ◄

A diagrammatic technique for displaying an ER model. ◄

How to identify and solve problems called connection traps, which may occur in an ER model. ◄

In Chapter 4, you learned about techniques for gathering and capturing information about what the users require of the database application. Once the requirements collection and analysis stage of the database application lifecycle is complete and you have documented the requirements for the database application, you are ready to begin database design.

Database application lifecycle discussed in Chapter 3.

One of the most difficult aspects of database design is the fact that designers, programmers, and end-users tend to view data and its use in different ways. Unfortunately, unless we can gain a common understanding that reflects how the company operates, the design we produce will fail to meet the users' requirements. To ensure that we get a precise understanding of the nature of the data and how it's used by the company, we need to have a model for communication that is non-technical and free of ambiguities. The Entity-Relationship (ER) model is one such example. Since the introduction of ER modeling in 1976, the model has been extended to include additional advanced modeling concepts. We cover the basic ER concepts in this chapter and introduce some of the more popular advanced concepts in Chapter 11.

Entity-Relationship modeling is a top-down approach to database design. We begin ER modeling by identifying the important data (called entities) and relationships between the data that must be represented in the model. We then add more details such as the information we want to hold about the entities and relationships (called attributes) and any constraints on the entities, relationships, and attributes.

Throughout this chapter, you are introduced to the basic concepts that make up an ER model. Although there is general agreement about what each concept means, there are a number of different ways that you can represent each concept in a diagram. We have chosen a diagrammatic notation that uses an increasingly popular object-oriented modeling language called **UML (Unified Modeling Language)**. However, examples of alternative popular notations for ER models are shown in Appendix A.

> UML is the successor to a number of object-oriented analysis and design methods introduced in the 1980s and 1990s. The Object Management Group (OMG) is currently looking at the standardization of UML, and it's anticipated that UML will be the standard modeling language for object-oriented systems in the near future.

As the ER model forms the basis of the methodology we'll present in Chapters 7 to 16, this chapter may prove to be one of the most important in this book. If you don't understand the concepts immediately, don't worry too much. Try reading the chapter again, and then look at the examples we give in the methodology for additional help. Let's start by introducing the basic concepts of the ER model, namely entities, relationships, and attributes.

5.1 Entities

Entity
A set of objects with the same properties that are identified by a user or company as having an independent existence.

Attributes are discussed in Section 5.3

The basic concept of the ER model is an **entity**, which represents a set of objects in the 'real world' that share the same properties. Each object, which should be uniquely identifiable within the set, is called an **entity occurrence**. An entity has an independent existence and can represent a set of objects with a physical (or 'real') existence or a set of objects with a conceptual (or 'abstract') existence, as shown in Figure 5.1.

We identify each entity by a unique name and a list of properties, called **attributes**. Although an entity has a distinct set of attributes, each entity has its own values for each attribute. A database normally contains many different entities.

Physical existence	Conceptual existence
Member	Role
Video	Rental
Branch	Registration

Figure 5.1

Examples of entities
with physical and
conceptual
existence.

Diagrammatic representation of entities

Each entity is shown as a rectangle labeled with the name of the entity, which is normally a singular noun. In UML, the first letter of each word in the entity name is uppercase (for example, Video, Role, Actor, VideoForRent). Figure 5.2 demonstrates the diagrammatic representation of the Video, Role, and Actor entities.

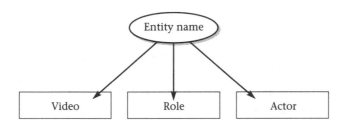

5.2 Relationships

A **relationship** is a set of associations among participating entities. As with entities, each association should be uniquely identifiable within the set. A uniquely identifiable association is called a **relationship occurrence**.

Each relationship is given a name that describes its function. For example, the Actor entity is associated with the Role entity through a relationship called *Plays*, and the Role entity is associated with the Video entity through a relationship called *Features*.

> **Relationship**
> A meaningful
> association among
> entities.

Diagrammatic representation of relationships

Each relationship is shown as a line connecting the associated entities, labeled with the name of the relationship. Normally, a relationship is named using a verb (for example, *Plays* or *Features*) or a short phrase including a verb (for example, *IsPartOf* or *WorksAt*). Again, the first letter of each word in the relationship name is shown in uppercase. Whenever possible, a relationship name should be unique for a given ER model.

A relationship is only labeled in one direction, which usually means that the name of the relationship only makes sense in one direction (for example, Actor

Figure 5.3

Diagrammatic representation of the Video *Features* Role and Actor *Plays* Role relationships.

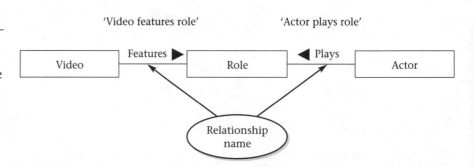

Plays Role makes sense but not Role *Plays* Actor). So once the relationship name is chosen, an arrow symbol is placed beside the name indicating the correct direction for a reader to interpret the relationship name (for example, Actor *Plays* ▶ Role). Figure 5.3 demonstrates the diagrammatic representation of the relationships Video *Features* Role and Actor *Plays* Role.

5.2.1 Degree of a relationship

Degree of a relationship
The number of participating entities in the relationship.

The entities involved in a particular relationship are referred to as participants. The number of participants in a relationship is called the **degree** and indicates the number of entities involved in a relationship. A relationship of degree two is called **binary**. The two relationships shown in Figure 5.3 are **binary relationships**.

A relationship of degree three is called **ternary**. An example of a ternary relationship is *Registers* with three participating entities, namely Branch, Staff, and Member, as shown in Figure 5.4. The purpose of this relationship is to represent the situation where a member of staff registers a member at a particular branch, allowing for members to register at more than one branch, and for members of staff to move between branches.

A relationship of degree four is called quaternary, and a relationship of a higher degree is called *n*-ary. A relationship of a degree higher than binary is called a **complex** relationship. The most popular type of relationship you'll come across is binary, but occasionally you'll come across ternary and less frequently quaternary.

Figure 5.4

Example of a ternary relationship called *Registers*.

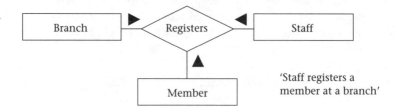

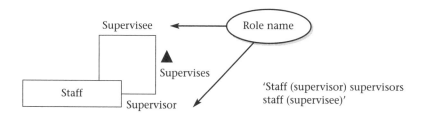

Figure 5.5

Example of a recursive relationship called *Supervises.*

5.2.2 Recursive relationships

Let's consider a recursive relationship called *Supervises*, which represents an association of staff with a supervisor where the supervisor is also a member of staff. In other words, the Staff entity participates twice in the *Supervises* relationship: the first participation as a supervisor, and the second participation as a member of staff who is supervised (supervisee), as shown in Figure 5.5. Recursive relationships are sometimes called *unary* relationships.

Relationships may be given role names to indicate the purpose that each participating entity plays in a relationship. Role names are important for recursive relationships to determine the function of each participating entity. Figure 5.5 shows the use of role names to describe the *Supervises* recursive relationship. The first participation of the Staff entity in the *Supervises* relationship is given the role name Supervisor and the second participation is given the role name Supervisee.

> **Recursive relationship**
> A relationship where the *same* entity participates more than once in *different roles.*

5.3 Attributes

The particular properties of entities are called attributes. Attributes represent what we want to know about entities. For example, a Video entity may be described by the catalogNo, title, category, dailyRental, and price attributes. These attributes hold values that describe each video occurrence, and represent the main source of data stored in the database.

> **Attribute**
> A property of an entity or a relationship.

> A relationship between entities can also have attributes similar to those of an entity, but we'll defer the discussion of relationships that have attributes until Section 5.6.

As we now discuss, we can classify attributes as being: simple or composite; single-valued or multi-valued; or derived.

5.3.1 Simple and composite attributes

Simple attributes cannot be further subdivided. Examples of simple attributes include the category and price attributes for a video. Simple attributes are sometimes called *atomic attributes*.

> **Simple attribute**
> An attribute composed of a single component.

Composite attribute
An attribute composed of multiple single components.

Composite attributes can be further divided to yield smaller components with an independent existence. For example, the name attribute of the Member entity with the value 'Don Nelson' can be subdivided into fName ('Don') and lName ('Nelson').

The decision to model the name attribute as a simple attribute or to subdivide the attribute into fName and lName is dependent on whether the users' transactions access the name attribute as a single unit or as individual components.

5.3.2 Single–valued and multi–valued attributes

Single-valued attribute
An attribute that holds a single value for an entity occurrence.

The majority of attributes are **single-valued** for a particular entity. For example, each occurrence of the Video entity has a single value for the catalogNo attribute (for example, 207132), and therefore the catalogNo attribute is referred to as being single-valued.

Multi-valued attribute
An attribute that holds multiple values for an entity occurrence.

Some attributes have multiple values for a particular entity. For example, each occurrence of the Video entity may have multiple values for the category attribute (for example, 'Children' and 'Comedy'), and therefore the category attribute in this case would be **multi-valued.** A multi-valued attribute may have a set of values with specified lower and upper limits. For example, the category attribute may have between one and three values.

The classification of simple and composite, and the classification of single-valued and multi-valued, are not mutually exclusive. In other words, you can have simple single-valued, composite single-valued, simple multi-valued, and composite multi-valued attributes.

5.3.3 Derived attributes

Derived attribute
An attribute that represents a value that is derivable from the value of a related attribute, or set of attributes, not necessarily in the same entity.

Some attributes may be related for a particular entity. For example, the age of a member of staff (age) is derivable from the date of birth (DOB) attribute, and therefore the age and DOB attributes are related. We refer to the age attribute as a derived attribute, the value of which is derived from the DOB attribute.

In some cases, the value of an attribute is derived from the values in a single entity, like age. But in other cases, the value of an attribute may be derived from the values in more than one entity.

TIP

Age is not normally stored in a database because it would have to be updated regularly. On the other hand, as date of birth never changes and age can be derived from date of birth, date of birth is stored instead, and age is derived from the **DOB** attribute, when needed.

5.3.4 Keys

In Section 2.2.3, we introduced the concept of keys associated with tables. These concepts also apply to entities (see definitions, right).

For example, branchNo (the branch number) and zipCode (the branch's zip code) are candidate keys for the Branch entity, as each has a distinct value for every branch occurrence. If we choose branchNo as the primary key for the Branch entity, then zipCode becomes an alternate key.

Diagrammatic representation of attributes

If an entity is to be displayed with its attributes, we divide the rectangle representing the entity in two. The upper part of the rectangle displays the name of the entity and the lower part lists the names of the attributes. For example, Figure 5.6 shows the ER model for the Video, Role, and Actor entities and their associated attributes.

The first attribute(s) to be listed is the primary key for the entity, if known. The name(s) of the primary key attribute(s) can be labeled with the tag {PK}. In UML, the name of an attribute is displayed with the first letter in lowercase and, if the name has more than one word, with the first letter of each subsequent word in uppercase (for example, character, actorNo, catalogNo). Additional tags that can be used include partial primary key {PPK}, when an attribute only forms part of a composite primary key, and alternate key {AK}.

For simple, single-valued attributes, there is no need to use tags and so we simply display the attribute names in a list below the entity name.

For composite attributes, we list the name of the composite attribute followed below and indented to the right by the names of its simple component parts. For example, in Figure 5.6 the composite attribute name is shown followed below by the names of its component attributes, fName and lName.

For multi-valued attributes, we label the attribute name with an indication of the range of values available for the attribute. For example, if we label the category attribute with the range [1..*], it means that the values for the category attribute is one or more. If we know the precise maximum number of values, we can label the attribute with an exact range. For example, if the category attribute can hold one to a maximum of three values, we would label the attribute with [1..3].

Superkey
An attribute, or set of attributes, that uniquely identifies each entity occurrence.

Candidate key
A superkey that contains only the minimum number of attributes necessary for unique identification.

Primary key
The candidate key that is selected to identify each entity occurrence.

Alternate keys
The candidate keys that are not selected as the primary key of the entity.

Figure 5.6

Diagrammatic
representation of
the attributes for the
Video, Role, and Actor
entities.

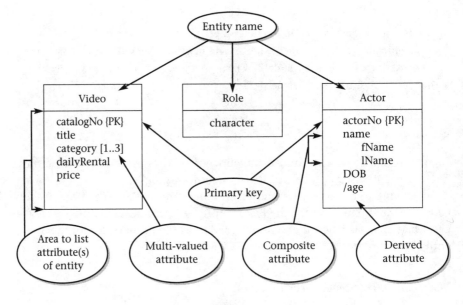

For derived attributes, we prefix the attribute name with a '/'. For example, the derived attribute age is shown in Figure 5.6 as /age.

> Note that no primary key has been identified for the **Role** entity. The presence or absence of a primary key allows us to identify whether an entity is weak or strong. We discuss the concept of strong and weak entities next.

For some simpler database applications, it's possible to show all the attributes for each entity on the data model. However, for more complex database applications, you normally display just the attribute, or attributes, that form the primary key of each entity. When only the primary key attributes are shown in the ER model, you can omit the {PK} tag.

5.4 Strong and weak entities

Strong entity
Entity that is *not*
dependent on the
existence of another
entity for its primary
key.

We can classify entities as being either strong or weak.

For example, as we can distinguish one actor from all other actors and one video from all other videos without the existence of any other entity, the Actor and Video entities are referred to as being **strong**. In other words, the Actor and Video entities are strong because they have their own primary keys, as shown in Figure 5.6.

Figure 5.6 also has an example of a **weak entity** called Role, which represents characters played by actors in videos. If we are unable to uniquely identify one Role entity occurrence from another without the existence of the Actor and Video entities, then Role is referred to as being a weak entity. In other words, the Role entity is weak because it has no primary key of its own.

Strong entities are sometimes referred to as parent, owner, or dominant entities and weak entities as child, dependent, or subordinate entities.

> **Weak entity**
> Entity that is partially or wholly dependent on the existence of another entity, or entities, for its primary key.

5.5 Multiplicity constraints on relationships

We now examine the constraints that may be placed on entities that participate in a relationship. Examples of such constraints include the requirements that a branch must have members and each branch must have staff. The main type of constraint on relationships is called **multiplicity**.

Multiplicity constrains the number of entity occurrences that relate to other entity occurrences through a particular relationship. Multiplicity is a representation of the policies established by the user or company, and is referred to as a **business rule**. Ensuring that all appropriate business rules are identified and represented is an important part of modeling a company.

As we mentioned earlier, the most common degree for relationships is binary. The multiplicity for a binary relationship is generally referred to as one-to-one (1:1), one-to-many (1:*), or many-to-many (*:*). We examine these three types of relationships using the following business rules:

> **Multiplicity**
> The number of occurrences of one entity that may relate to a single occurrence of an associated entity.

- A member of staff manages a branch.
- A branch has members of staff.
- Actors play in videos.

For each business rule, we demonstrate how to work out the multiplicity if, as is sometimes the case, it's not clearly specified in the rule, and show how to represent it in an ER model. In Section 5.5.4, we'll examine multiplicity for relationships of degrees higher than binary.

It's important to note that not all business rules are easily and clearly represented in an ER model. For example, the requirement that a member of staff receives an additional day's holiday for every year of employment with the company may be difficult to represent clearly in an ER model.

5.5.1 One-to-one (1:1) relationships

Let's consider the relationship called *Manages*, which relates the Staff and Branch entities. Figure 5.7(a) displays individual examples of the *Manages* relationship using values for the primary key attributes of the Staff and Branch entities.

Working out the multiplicity

Working out the multiplicity normally requires examining the precise relationships between the data given in a business rule using sample data. The sample data may be obtained by examining filled-in forms or reports or, if possible, from further discussion with the users. However, it's important to stress that to reach the right conclusions about a business rule requires that the sample data examined or discussed is a true representation of all the data.

In Figure 5.7(a), we can see that staffNo S1500 manages branchNo B001 and staffNo S0010 manages branchNo B002, but staffNo S0003 does not manage any

Figure 5.7

Staff *Manages* Branch relationship:
(a) individual examples; (b) the multiplicity.

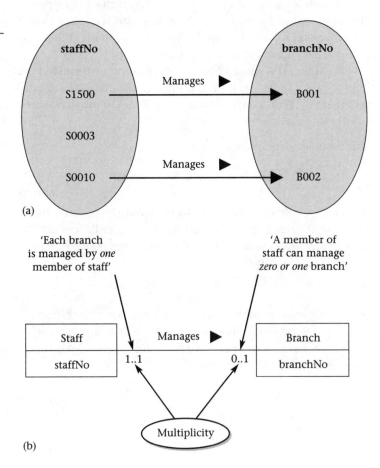

branch. In other words, a member of staff can manage zero or one branch and each branch is managed by a single member of staff. As there is a maximum of one branch for each member of staff and a maximum of one member of staff for each branch involved in the relationship, we refer to this type of relationship as one-to-one, which we usually abbreviate as (1:1).

Diagrammatic representation of 1:1 relationships

An ER model of the Staff *Manages* Branch relationship is shown in Figure 5.7(b). To represent that a member of staff can manage zero or one branch, we place a '0..1' at the opposite end of the relationship from the Staff entity. To represent that a branch always has one manager, we place a '1..1' at the opposite end of the relationship from the Branch entity. (Note that for a 1:1 relationship, we may choose a relationship name that makes sense in either direction.)

5.5.2 One-to-many (1:*) relationships

Let's consider the relationship called *Has*, which again relates the Branch and Staff entities. Figure 5.8(a) displays individual examples of the Branch *Has* Staff

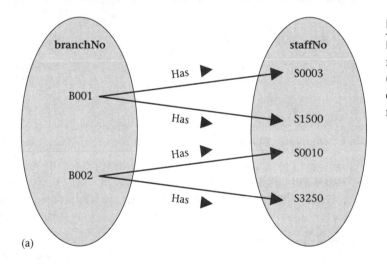

Figure 5.8

Branch *Has* Staff relationship:
(a) individual examples; (b) the multiplicity.

(a)

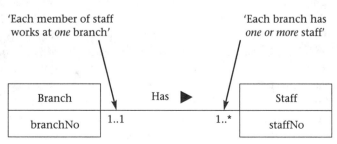

(b)

relationship using values for the primary key attributes of the Branch and Staff entities.

Working out the multiplicity

In Figure 5.8(a), we see that branchNo B001 has staffNos S0003 and S1500, and branchNo B002 has staffNos S0010 and S3250. Therefore, each branch has one or more members of staff and each member of staff works at a single branch. As one branch can have many staff, we refer to this type of relationship as one-to-many, which we usually abbreviate as (1:*).

Diagrammatic representation of 1:* relationships

An ER model of the Branch *Has* Staff relationship is shown in Figure 5.8(b). To represent that each branch can have one or more staff, we place a '1..*' at the opposite end of the relationship from the Branch entity. To represent that each member of staff works at a single branch, we place a '1..1' at the opposite end of the relationship from the Staff entity. (Note that with 1:* relationships, we choose a relationship name that makes sense in the 1:* direction.)

> **TIP**   If you know the actual minimum and maximum values for the multiplicity, you can display these instead. For example, if a branch has between two and ten staff, we can replace the '1..*' by '2..10'.

5.5.3   Many-to-many (*:*) relationships

Let's consider the relationship called *PlaysIn*, which relates the Actor and Video entities. Figure 5.9(a) displays individual examples of the Actor *PlaysIn* Video relationship using values for the primary key attributes of the Actor and Video entities.

Working out the multiplicity

In Figure 5.9(a), we see that actorNo A3006 plays in video catalogNos 902355 and 330553, and actorNo A2019 plays in video catalogNos 330553 and 445624. In other words, a single actor can play in one or more videos. We also see that video catalogNo 330553 has two starring actors but catalogNo 348989 does not have any actors in it, and so we conclude that a single video can star zero or more actors.

In summary, the *PlaysIn* relationship is 1:* from the viewpoint of both the Actor and Video entities. We represent this relationship as two 1:* relationships in both directions, which are collectively referred to as a many-to-many relationship, which we usually abbreviate as (*:*).

Diagrammatic representation of *:* relationships

An ER model of the Actor *PlaysIn* Video relationship is shown in Figure 5.9(b). To represent that each actor can star in one or more videos, we place a '1..*' at the opposite end of the relationship from the Actor entity. To represent that each video can star zero or more actors, we place a '0..*' at the opposite end of the relationship from the Video entity. (Note that for a *:* relationship, we may choose a relationship name that makes sense in either direction.)

5.5.4   Multiplicity for non–binary relationships

Multiplicity for relationships beyond degree two is slightly more complex. For example, the multiplicity for a ternary relationship represents the potential number of entity occurrences in the relationship when the other two values are fixed. Let's consider again the ternary *Registers* relationship between Branch, Staff, and Member shown in Figure 5.4. Figure 5.10(a) displays individual examples of the *Registers* relationship when the values for the Staff and Member entities are fixed.

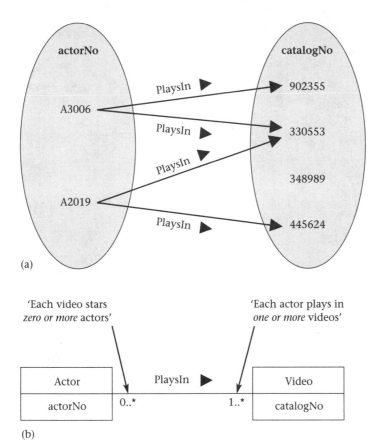

(a)

(b)

Figure 5.9

Actor *PlaysIn* Video relationship:
(a) individual examples;
(b) the muliplicity.

Working out the multiplicity

In Figure 5.10(a), we see that for every combination of staffNo/memberNo values there is always at least one corresponding branchNo value. In particular, staffNo S0003 registers memberNo M166884 at branchNo B001 and B002. This represents the situation where member M166884 has been registered at branch B001 by staff S0003, and has subsequently been registered at B002 by the same member of staff, who has transferred to branch B002 in the intervening period. In other words, from the Branch perspective the multiplicity is 1..*.

If we repeat this test from the Staff perspective, we find that the multiplicity for this relationship is 1..1, and if we examine it from the Member perspective, we find it is 0..*. An ER model of the ternary *Registers* relationship showing multiplicity is illustrated in Figure 5.10(b).

In general, the multiplicity for *n*-ary relationships represents the potential number of entity occurrences in the relationship when the other (*n*-1) values are fixed.

Figure 5.10(a)

The ternary *Registers* relationship from the Branch perspective with the values for Staff and Member fixed: (a) individual examples; (b) multiplicity.

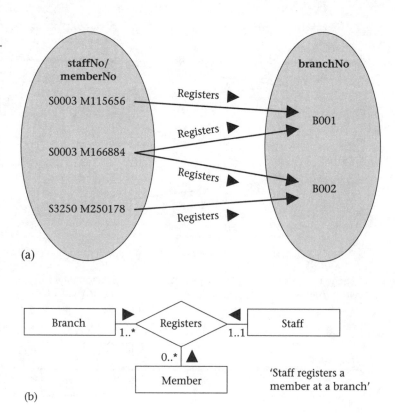

A summary of the possible ways that you may represent multiplicity constraints along with a description of the meaning for each is shown in Table 5.1.

Table 5.1 A summary of ways to represent multiplicity constraints.

Alternative ways to represent multiplicity constraints	Meaning
0..1	Zero or one entity occurrence
1..1 (or just 1)	Exactly one entity occurrence
0..* (or just *)	Zero or many entity occurrences
1..*	One or many entity occurrences
5..10	Minimum of 5 up to a maximum of 10 entity occurrences
0, 3, 6-8	Zero or three or six, seven, or eight entity occurrences

5.5.5 Cardinality and participation constraints

Multiplicity actually consists of two separate constraints known as cardinality and participation.

The **cardinality** of a binary relationship is what we have been referring to as one-to-one, one-to-many, and many-to-many. A **participation constraint** represents whether all entity occurrences are involved in a particular relationship (*mandatory participation*) or only some (*optional participation*). In Figure 5.11, we illustrate the cardinality and participation constraints for the Staff *Manages* Branch relationship shown in Figure 5.7(b). We'll use the participation constraint during the logical database design methodology to determine:

(a) how to create tables for one-to-one relationships (covered in Steps 2.1 and 2.4);

(b) whether a foreign key can have nulls (in Step 2.4).

> **Cardinality**
> Describes the number of possible relationships for each participating entity.

> **Participation**
> Determines whether all or only some entity occurrences participate in a relationship.

Foreign key defined in Section 2.2.3

5.6 Attributes on relationships

As we briefly mentioned in Section 5.3, attributes can also be assigned to relationships. For example, let's consider the relationship *PlaysIn*, which associates the Actor and Video entities. We may wish to record the character played by an actor in a given video. This information is associated with the *PlaysIn* relationship rather than the Actor or Video entities. We create an attribute called character to store this information and assign it to the *PlaysIn* relationship, as illustrated in Figure 5.12. Note, in this figure the character attribute is shown using the symbol for an entity; however, to distinguish between a relationship with an

Figure 5.11

Multiplicity shown as cardinality and participation constraints for the Staff *Manages* Branch 1:1 relationship shown in Figure 5.7(b).

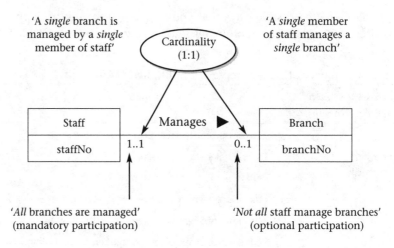

'A *single* branch is managed by a *single* member of staff'

'A *single* member of staff manages a *single* branch'

'*All* branches are managed' (mandatory participation)

'*Not all* staff manage branches' (optional participation)

Figure 5.12

A relationship called *PlaysIn* with an attribute called character.

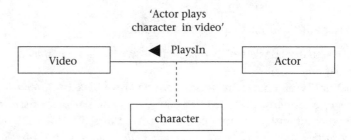

'Actor plays character in video'

attribute and an entity, the rectangle representing the attribute is associated with the relationship using a dashed line.

The presence of one or more attributes assigned to a relationship may indicate that the relationship conceals an unidentified entity. For example, the character attribute associated with an entity called Role was shown earlier in Figure 5.6.

5.7 Design problems with ER models

In this section, we examine two types of problems that may arise when designing an ER model. These problems are collectively referred to as *connection traps,* and normally occur due to a misinterpretation of the meaning of certain relationships. We examine the two main types of connection traps called fan traps and chasm traps, and illustrate how to identify and resolve such problems in ER models.

In general, to identify connection traps we must ensure that the meaning of a relationship (and the business rule that it represents) is fully understood and clearly defined. If we don't understand the relationships we may create a model that is not a true representation of the 'real world'.

5.7.1 Fan traps

A **fan trap** may exist where two or more one-to-many (1:*) relationships fan out from the same entity. A potential fan trap is illustrated in Figure 5.13(a), which shows two 1:* relationships (*Has* and *IsAssigned*) emanating from the same entity called Branch. This model tells us that a single branch has many staff and is assigned many cars. However, a problem arises if we want to know which member of staff uses a particular car. To appreciate the problem, let's examine some examples of the *Has* and *IsAssigned* relationships, using values for the primary key attributes of the Staff, Branch, and Car entities, as shown in Figure 5.13(b).

If we attempt to answer the question: 'Which member of staff uses car SH34?', it's impossible to give a specific answer with the current structure. We can only determine that car SH34 is assigned to branch B001 but we cannot tell whether staff S0003 or S1500 uses this car. The inability to answer this question specifically is the result of a fan trap.

We resolve this fan trap by adding a new relationship called Staff *Uses* Car to the original ER model, as shown in Figure 5.13(c). If we now examine the examples of the *Has*, *IsAssigned*, and *Uses* relationships shown in Figure 5.13(d), we can see that staff S1500 uses car SH34.

5.7.2 Chasm traps

A **chasm trap** may occur where there is a relationship with optional participation that forms part of the pathway between entities that are related. A potential chasm trap is illustrated in Figure 5.14(a), which shows the relationships between the Branch, Car, and Staff entities. This model tells us that a single branch is assigned many cars and a member of staff may use one car. In particular, note that not all staff use a car. A problem arises when we want to know at which branch a member of staff works. To appreciate the problem, let's examine some examples of the *IsAssigned* and *Uses* relationships, using values for the primary key attributes of the Branch, Car, and Staff entities, as shown in Figure 5.14(b).

> **Fan trap**
> Two entities have a 1:* relationship that fan out from a third entity, but the two entities should have a direct relationship between them to provide the necessary information.

> **Chasm trap**
> A model suggests the existence of a relationship between entities, but the pathway does not exist between certain entity occurrences.

Staff	◄ Has	Branch	IsAssigned ►	Car
staffNo	1..* 1..1	branchNo	1..1 1..*	vehLicenseNo

Figure 5.13(a)

Example of a fan trap.

Figure 5.13(b)

Examples of the Branch *Has* **Staff** and the Branch *IsAssigned* Car relationships. Cannot tell which member of staff uses car SH34.

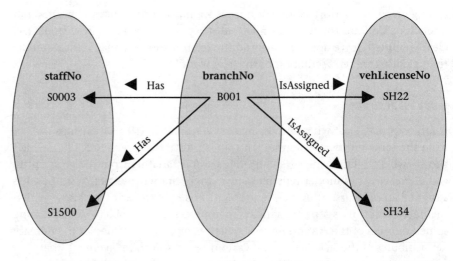

Figure. 5.13(c)

Resolving the fan trap.

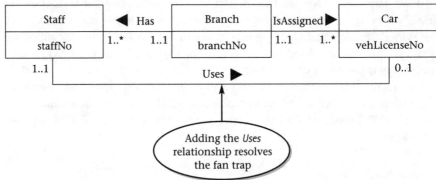

Figure 5.13(d)

Examples of the Branch *Has* Staff, Branch *IsAssigned* Car, and Staff *Uses* Car relationships. Can now tell which car staff use.

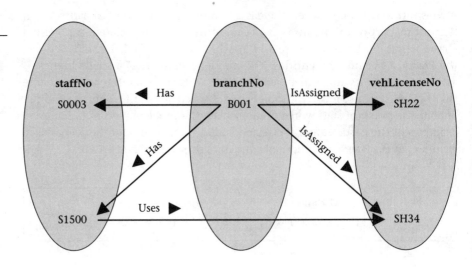

If we attempt to answer the question: 'At which branch does staff S0003 work?', we can't tell with the current structure as not all staff use cars. The inability to answer this question is considered to be a loss of information (as we know a member of staff must work at a branch), and is the result of a **chasm trap**. The optional participation of Staff in the Staff *Uses* Car relationship means that some members of staff are not associated with a branch through the use of cars.

Therefore, to solve this problem and remove the chasm trap, we add a relationship called *Has* between the Branch and Staff entities, as shown in Figure 5.14(c). If we now examine the examples of the *Has*, *IsAssigned*, and *Uses* relationships shown in Figure 5.14(d), we can see that staff S0003 works at branch B001.

The ER concepts described in this chapter sometimes prove inadequate for modeling complex database applications. In Chapter 11, we'll introduce some of the more popular advanced concepts associated with ER models that you may find useful when modeling more complex data.

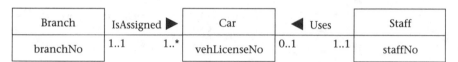

Figure 5.14(a)

Example of a chasm trap.

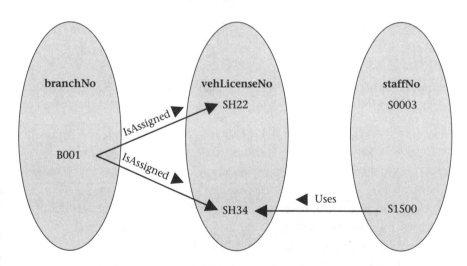

Figure 5.14(b)

Examples of the Branch *IsAssigned* Car and Staff *Uses* Car relationships. Cannot tell which branch staff S0003 works at.

Figure. 5.14(c)

Resolving the chasm trap.

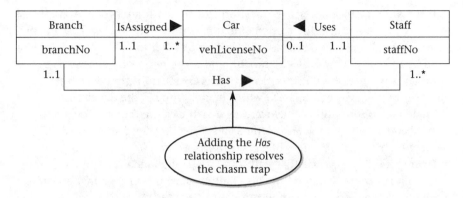

Figure 5.14(d)

Examples of the Branch *Has* Staff, Branch *IsAssigned* Car, and Staff *Uses* Car relationships. Can now tell which branch each member of staff works at.

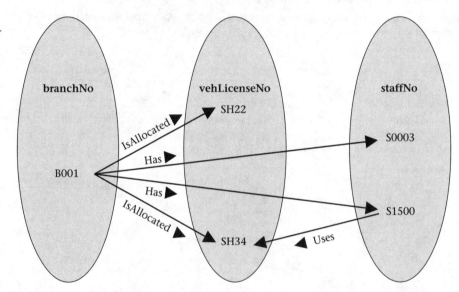

Chapter summary

✓ An **entity** is a set of objects with the same properties that are identified by a user or company as having an independent existence. A uniquely identifiable object is called an **entity occurrence**.

✓ A **relationship** is a meaningful association among entities. A uniquely identifiable association is called a **relationship occurrence**.

✓ The **degree of a relationship** is the number of participating entities in a relationship.

✓ A **recursive relationship** is a relationship where the same entity participates more than once in *different* roles.

✓ An **attribute** is a property of an entity or a relationship.

✓ A **simple attribute** is composed of a single component.

✓ A **composite attribute** is composed of multiple single components.

✓ A **single-valued attribute** holds a single value for an entity occurrence.

✓ A **multi-valued attribute** holds multiple values for an entity occurrence.

✓ A **derived attribute** represents a value that is derivable from the value of a related attribute, or a set of attributes, not necessarily in the same entity.

✓ A **strong entity** is *not* dependent on the existence of another entity for its primary key. A **weak entity** is partially or wholly dependent on the existence of some other entity (or entities) for its primary key.

✓ **Multiplicity** defines the number of occurrences of one entity that may relate to a single occurrence of an associated entity.

✓ The **cardinality** describes the number of possible relationships for each participating entity.

✓ The **participation constraint** determines whether all or only some entity occurrences participate in a relationship.

✓ A **fan trap** occurs when two entities have 1:* relationships that fan out from a third entity, but the two entities should have a direct relationship between them to provide the necessary information.

✓ A **chasm trap** suggests the existence of a relationship between entities, but the pathway does not exist between certain entity occurrences.

Chapter 6

Normalization

In this chapter you will learn:

➤ How the technique of normalization is used in database design.

➤ How tables that contain redundant data can suffer from update anomalies, which can introduce inconsistencies into a database.

➤ The rules associated with the most commonly used normal forms, namely first (1NF), second (2NF), and third (3NF) normal forms.

➤ How tables that break the rules of 1NF, 2NF, or 3NF are likely to contain redundant data and suffer from update anomalies.

➤ How to restructure tables that break the rules of 1NF, 2NF, or 3NF.

In the previous chapter, we learned about Entity-Relationship (ER) modeling, a commonly used top-down approach to database design. In this chapter, we consider another commonly used approach to database design called normalization. Normalization can be used in database design in two ways: the first is to use normalization as a bottom-up approach to database design; the second is to use normalization in conjunction with ER modeling.

Using normalization as a **bottom-up approach** involves analyzing the associations between attributes and, based on this analysis, grouping the attributes together to form tables that represent entities and relationships. However, this approach becomes difficult with a large number of attributes, where it's difficult to establish all the important associations between the attributes.

For this reason, in this book we present a methodology that recommends that you should first attempt to understand the data using a **top-down approach** to database design. In this approach, we use ER modeling to create a data model that represents the main entities and relationships. We then translate the ER model into a set of tables that represents this data. It's at this point that we use normalization to check whether the tables are well designed.

Normalization check performed in Steps 2.2 and 3.2

The purpose of this chapter is to examine why normalization is a useful technique in database design and, in particular, how normalization can be used to check the structure of tables created from an ER model.

6.1 Introduction

In 1972, Dr E.F. Codd developed the technique of **normalization** to support the design of databases based on the *relational model*. Normalization is often performed as a series of tests on a table to determine whether it satisfies or violates the rules for a given **normal form**. There are several normal forms, although the most commonly used ones are called first normal form (1NF), second normal form (2NF), and third normal form (3NF). All these normal forms are based on rules about relationships among the columns of a table.

In the following sections, we first demonstrate how badly structured tables that suffer data redundancy can cause problems called *update anomalies*. Badly structured tables may occur due to errors in the original ER model or in the process of translating the ER model into tables. We then present a definition for first normal form (1NF), second normal form (2NF), and third normal form (3NF), and demonstrate how each normal form can be used to identify and correct different types of problems in our tables.

> **Normalization**
> A technique for producing a set of tables with desirable properties that supports the requirements of a user or company.

6.2 Data redundancy and update anomalies

A major aim of relational database design is to group columns into tables to minimize data redundancy and reduce the file storage space required by the implemented base tables. To illustrate the problems associated with data redundancy, let's compare the Staff and Branch tables shown in Figure 6.1 with the StaffBranch table shown in Figure 6.2.

Base tables defined in Section 2.3.2

The StaffBranch table is an alternative form of the Staff and Branch tables. The tables have the following structure, with the primary key for each table underlined:

Primary key defined in Section 2.2.3

Staff (<u>staffNo</u>, name, position, salary, branchNo)

Branch (<u>branchNo</u>, branchAddress, telNo)

StaffBranch (<u>staffNo</u>, name, position, salary, branchNo, branchAddress, telNo)

In the StaffBranch table there is **redundant data**; the details of a branch are repeated for every member of staff located at that branch. In contrast, the details of each branch appear only once in the Branch table and only the branch number (branchNo) is repeated in the Staff table, to represent where each member of staff is located. Tables that have redundant data may have problems called **update anomalies**, which are classified as insertion, deletion, or modification anomalies.

Figure 6.1

The Staff and Branch tables.

Staff

staffNo	name	position	salary	branchNo
S1500	Tom Daniels	Manager	46000	B001
S0003	Sally Adams	Assistant	30000	B001
S0010	Mary Martinez	Manager	50000	B002
S3250	Robert Chin	Supervisor	32000	B002
S2250	Sally Stern	Manager	48000	B004
S0415	Art Peters	Manager	41000	B003

Branch

branchNo	branchAddress	telNo
B001	8 Jefferson Way, Portland, OR 97201	503-555-3618
B002	City Center Plaza, Seattle, WA 98122	206-555-6756
B003	14 – 8th Avenue, New York, NY 10012	212-371-3000
B004	16 – 14th Avenue, Seattle, WA 98128	206-555-3131

Figure 6.2

The StaffBranch table.

staffNo	name	position	salary	branchNo	branchAddress	telNo
S1500	Tom Daniels	Manager	46000	B001	8 Jefferson Way, Portland, OR 97201	503-555-3618
S0003	Sally Adams	Assistant	30000	B001	8 Jefferson Way, Portland, OR 97201	503-555-3618
S0010	Mary Martinez	Manager	50000	B002	City Center Plaza, Seattle, WA 98122	206-555-6756
S3250	Robert Chin	Supervisor	32000	B002	City Center Plaza, Seattle, WA 98122	206-555-6756
S2250	Sally Stern	Manager	48000	B004	16 – 14th Avenue, Seattle, WA 98128	206-555-3131
S0415	Art Peters	Manager	41000	B003	14 – 8th Avenue, New York, NY 10012	212-371-3000

6.2.1 Insertion anomalies

There are two main types of insertion anomalies, which we illustrate using the StaffBranch table shown in Figure 6.2.

(1) To insert the details of new members of staff into the StaffBranch table, we must include the details of the branch at which the staff are to be located. For example, to insert the details of new staff located at branch B003, we must enter the correct details of branch B003 so that the branch details are

consistent with values for branch B003 in other records of the StaffBranch table. The tables shown in Figure 6.1 do not suffer from this potential inconsistency, because for each staff member we only enter the appropriate branch number into the Staff table. In addition, the details of branch B003 are recorded only once in the database as a single record in the Branch table.

(2) To insert details of a new branch that currently has no members of staff into the StaffBranch table, it's necessary to enter nulls into the staff-related columns, such as staffNo. However, as staffNo is the primary key for the StaffBranch table, attempting to enter nulls for staffNo violates entity integrity, and is not allowed. The design of the tables shown in Figure 6.1 avoids this problem because branch details are entered into the Branch table separately from the staff details. The details of staff ultimately located at that branch can be entered into the Staff table at a later date.

Entity integrity defined in Section 2.3.2

6.2.2 Deletion anomalies

If we delete a record from the StaffBranch table that represents the last member of staff located at a branch, the details about that branch are also lost from the database. For example, if we delete the record for staff S0415 ('Art Peters') from the StaffBranch table, the details relating to branch B003 are lost from the database. The design of the tables in Figure 6.1 avoids this problem because branch records are stored separately from staff records and only the column branchNo relates the two tables. If we delete the record for staff S0415 from the Staff table, the details on branch B003 in the Branch table remain unaffected.

6.2.3 Modification anomalies

If we want to change the value of one of the columns of a particular branch in the StaffBranch table, for example the telephone number for branch B001, we must update the records of all staff located at that branch. If this modification is not carried out on all the appropriate records of the StaffBranch table, the database will become inconsistent. In this example, branch B001 would have different telephone numbers in different staff records.

The above examples illustrate that the Staff and Branch tables of Figure 6.1 have more desirable properties than the StaffBranch table of Figure 6.2. In the following sections, we examine how normal forms can be used to formalize the identification of tables that have desirable properties from those that may potentially suffer from update anomalies.

First normal form (1NF)
A table in which the intersection of every column and record contains one, and only one, value.

6.3 First normal form (1NF)

Only first normal form (1NF) is critical in creating appropriate tables for relational databases. All the subsequent normal forms are optional. However, to avoid the update anomalies discussed in Section 6.2, it's normally recommended that you proceed to third normal form (3NF).

Let's examine the Branch table shown in Figure 6.3, with primary key branchNo. We can see that all the columns of this version of the Branch table comply with our definition of 1NF with the exception of the column telNos. There are multiple values at the intersection of the telNos column with every record. For example, branchNo B001 has three telephone numbers, 503-555-3618, 503-555-2727, and 503-555-6534. As a result, the Branch table is not in 1NF.

Note that although the **branchAddress** column may appear to hold multiple values, this representation of address does not break 1NF. In this example, we have simply chosen the option to hold all the details of an address as a single value.

Figure 6.3

This version of the Branch table is not in 1NF.

branchNo	branchAddress	telNos
B001	8 Jefferson Way, Portland, OR 97201	503-555-3618, 503-555-2727, 503-555-6534
B002	City Center Plaza, Seattle, WA 98122	206-555-6756, 206-555-8836
B003	14 – 8th Avenue, New York, NY 10012	212-371-3000
B004	16 – 14th Avenue, Seattle, WA 98128	206-555-3131, 206-555-4112

Primary key

More than one value, so *not* in 1NF

Converting to 1NF

To convert this version of the Branch table to 1NF, we create a separate table called BranchTelephone to hold the telephone numbers of branches, by removing the telNos column from the Branch table along with a copy of the primary key of the Branch table (branchNo). The primary key for the new BranchTelephone table is the telNo column. The structures for the altered Branch table and the new BranchTelephone table are shown in Figure 6.4. The Branch and BranchTelephone tables are in 1NF as there is a single value at the intersection of every column with every record for each table.

6.4 Second normal form (2NF)

Second normal form applies only to tables with composite primary keys, that is, tables with a primary key composed of two or more columns. A table with a single column primary key is automatically in at least 2NF. A table that is not in 2NF may suffer from the update anomalies discussed in Section 6.2.

Let's examine the TempStaffAllocation table shown in Figure 6.5. This table represents the hours worked per week for temporary staff at each branch. The primary key for the TempStaffAllocation table is made up of both the staffNo and branchNo columns. Note that we use the term 'non-primary-key' columns to refer to those columns that are not part of the primary key. For example, the non-primary-key columns for the TempStaffAllocation table are branchAddress, name, position, and hoursPerWeek. The arrows shown below the TempStaffAllocation table indicate particular relationships between the primary key columns and the non-primary-key columns.

> **Second normal form (2NF)**
> A table that is already in 1NF and in which the values in each non-primary-key column can only be worked out from the values in *all* the columns that make up the primary key.

The particular relationships that we show between the columns of the **TempStaffAllocation** table in Figure 6.5 are more formally referred to as **functional dependencies**. Functional dependency is a property of the meaning of the columns in a table and indicates how columns relate to one another.

For example, consider a table with columns **A** and **B**, where column **B** is functionally dependent on column **A** (denoted **A** → **B**). If we know the value of **A**, we find *only one value* of **B** in all the records that has this value for **A**, at any moment in time. So, when two records have the same value of **A**, they also have the same value of **B**. However, for a given value of **B** there may be several different values of **A**.

Figure 6.4

Altered Branch table is in 1NF owing to the removal of the telNos column and the creation of a new table called BranchTelephone.

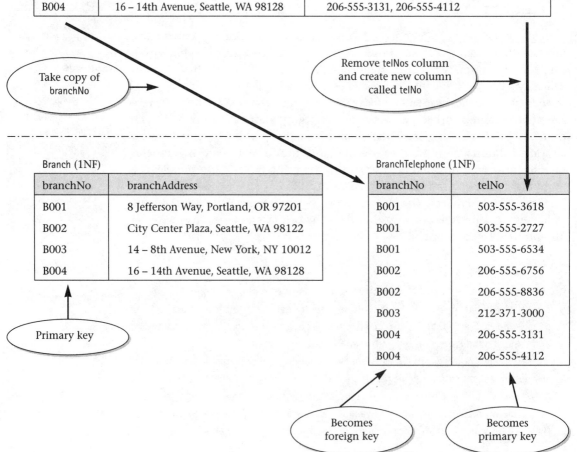

Converting to 1NF

Branch (Not 1NF)

branchNo	branchAddress	telNos
B001	8 Jefferson Way, Portland, OR 97201	503-555-3618, 503-555-2727, 503-555-6534
B002	City Center Plaza, Seattle, WA 98122	206-555-6756, 206-555-8836
B003	14 – 8th Avenue, New York, NY 10012	212-371-3000
B004	16 – 14th Avenue, Seattle, WA 98128	206-555-3131, 206-555-4112

Take copy of branchNo

Remove telNos column and create new column called telNo

Branch (1NF)

branchNo	branchAddress
B001	8 Jefferson Way, Portland, OR 97201
B002	City Center Plaza, Seattle, WA 98122
B003	14 – 8th Avenue, New York, NY 10012
B004	16 – 14th Avenue, Seattle, WA 98128

Primary key

BranchTelephone (1NF)

branchNo	telNo
B001	503-555-3618
B001	503-555-2727
B001	503-555-6534
B002	206-555-6756
B002	206-555-8836
B003	212-371-3000
B004	206-555-3131
B004	206-555-4112

Becomes foreign key

Becomes primary key

Figure 6.5

TempStaffAllocation table is not in 2NF.

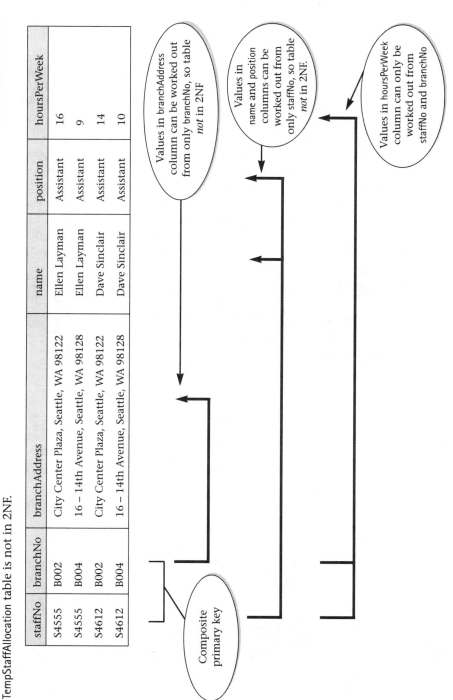

staffNo	branchNo	branchAddress	name	position	hoursPerWeek
S4555	B002	City Center Plaza, Seattle, WA 98122	Ellen Layman	Assistant	16
S4555	B004	16 – 14th Avenue, Seattle, WA 98128	Ellen Layman	Assistant	9
S4612	B002	City Center Plaza, Seattle, WA 98122	Dave Sinclair	Assistant	14
S4612	B004	16 – 14th Avenue, Seattle, WA 98128	Dave Sinclair	Assistant	10

Values in branchAddress column can be worked out from only branchNo, so table *not* in 2NF

Values in name and position columns can be worked out from only staffNo, so table *not* in 2NF.

Values in hoursPerWeek column can only be worked out from staffNo and branchNo

Composite primary key

We can see that the TempStaffAllocation table contains redundant data and may suffer from the update anomalies described in Section 6.2. For example, to change the name of 'Ellen Layman', we have to update two records in the TempStaffAllocation table. If only one record is updated, the database will be inconsistent. The reason that the TempStaffAllocation table contains redundant data is that this table does not comply with our definition for 2NF.

Consider the non-primary-key column branchAddress of the TempStaffAllocation table. The values in the branchAddress column can be worked out from the values in the branchNo column (part of the primary key). In other words, every unique value in the branchNo column has the same value in the branchAddress column. For example, every time the value B002 appears in the branchNo column, the same address 'City Center Plaza, Seattle, WA 98122' appears in the branchAddress column.

Now consider the non-primary-key columns name and position. The values in the name and position columns can be worked out from the values in the staffNo column (part of the primary key). For example, every time S4555 appears in the staffNo column, the name 'Ellen Layman' and position 'Assistant' appear in the name and position columns.

Finally, consider the non-primary-key column hoursPerWeek. The values in the hoursPerWeek column can only be worked out from the values in both the staffNo and branchNo columns (the whole primary key). For example, every time S4555 appears in the staffNo column at the same time B002 appears in the branchNo column, then the value '16' appears in the hoursPerWeek column.

> The formal definition of **second normal form (2NF)** is a table that is in first normal form and every non-primary-key column is **fully functionally dependent** on the primary key. Full functional dependency indicates that if **A** and **B** are columns of a table, **B** is fully functionally dependent on **A**, if **B** is not dependent on any subset of **A**. If **B** is dependent on a subset of **A**, this is referred to as a **partial dependency**. If a partial dependency exists on the primary key, the table is not in 2NF. The partial dependency must be removed for a table to achieve 2NF.

Converting to 2NF

To convert the TempStaffAllocation table shown in Figure 6.5 to 2NF, we need to remove the non-primary-key columns that can be worked out using only part of the primary key. In other words, we need to remove the columns that can be worked out from either the staffNo or the branchNo column but do not require both. For the TempStaffAllocation table, this means that we must remove the branchAddress, name, and position columns and place them in new tables.

To do this we create two new tables called Branch and TempStaff. The Branch table will hold the columns describing the details of branches and the TempStaff table will hold the columns describing the details of temporary staff.

(1) The Branch table is created by removing the branchAddress column from the TempStaffAllocation table along with a copy of the part of the primary key that the column is related to, which in this case is the branchNo column.

(2) In a similar way, the TempStaff table is created by removing the name and position columns from the TempStaffAllocation table along with a copy of the part of the primary key that the columns are related to, which in this case is the staffNo column.

It's not necessary to remove the hoursPerWeek column as the presence of this column in the TempStaffAllocation table does not break the rules of 2NF. The structures for the altered TempStaffAllocation table and the new Branch and TempStaff tables are shown in Figure 6.6. The primary key for the new Branch table is branchNo and the primary key for the new TempStaff table is staffNo.

The TempStaff and Branch tables must be in 2NF because the primary key for each table is a single column. The altered TempStaffAllocation table is also in 2NF because the non-primary-key column hoursPerWeek is related to both the staffNo and branchNo columns.

6.5 Third normal form (3NF)

Although 2NF tables have less redundancy than tables in 1NF, they may still suffer from update anomalies.

Let's examine the BranchManager table shown in Figure 6.7, with primary key branchNo. This table is not in 3NF because of the presence of the name column. Although we can work out the name of the manager at a given branch from the primary key, branchNo, we can also work out the name from another non-primary-key column, mgrStaffNo. For example, when B001 appears in the branchNo column, 'Tom Daniels' appears in the name column. However, when S1500 appears in mgrStaffNo, 'Tom Daniels' also appears in the name column. In other words, the name of a member of staff can be worked out from knowing the value in mgrStaffNo. This is not allowed in 3NF as the values in all non-primary-key columns must be worked out from only the values in the primary key column(s).

> **Third normal form (3NF)**
> A table that is already in 1NF and 2NF, and in which the values in all non-primary-key columns can be worked out from *only* the primary key column(s) and no other columns.

The formal definition for **third normal form (3NF)** is a table that is in first and second normal forms and in which no non-primary-key column is **transitively dependent** on the primary key. Transitive dependency is a type of functional dependency that occurs when a particular type of relationship holds between columns of a table.

For example, consider a table with columns A, B, and C. If B is functionally dependent on A (A → B) and C is functionally dependent on B (B → C), then C is transitively dependent on A via B (provided that A is not functionally dependent on B or C). If a transitive dependency exists on the primary key, the table is not in 3NF. The transitive dependency must be removed for a table to achieve 3NF.

Figure 6.6

Altered TempStaffAllocation table is in 2NF owing to the removal of the branchAddress, name, and position columns and the creation of the new Branch and TempStaff tables.

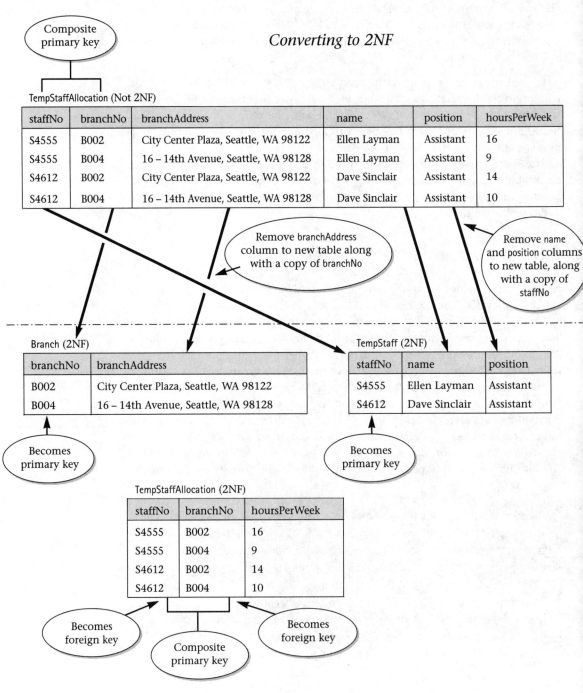

Interestingly, the BranchManager table shown in Figure 6.7 doesn't appear to contain redundant data. This is because the relationship between branches and managers is one-to-one (1:1). In other words, a single branch has a single Manager and a single Manager manages a single branch. For example, the Manager of branchNo B001 is mgrStaffNo S1500 and S1500 is the Manager of branchNo B001 and no other branch. However, the current structure of the BranchManager table is likely to result in a type of redundancy that involves more than one table. For example, the relationship between the mgrStaffNo and name columns in the BranchManager table is likely to exist already in a table in the database that holds all staff details including Managers. For example, see the staffNo and name columns in the Staff table of Figure 6.1.

1:1 relationship defined in Section 5.5.1

Converting to 3NF

To convert the BranchManager table shown in Figure 6.7 into 3NF, we need to remove the name column. We create a new table called ManagerStaff to represent the relationship between the mgrStaffNo and name columns. (Of course, creating a new table would not be necessary if the relationship between mgrStaffNo

Figure 6.7

The BranchManager table is not in 3NF.

branchNo	branchAddress	telNo	mgrStaffNo	name
B001	8 Jefferson Way, Portland, OR 97201	503-555-3618	S1500	Tom Daniels
B002	City Center Plaza, Seattle, WA 98122	206-555-6756	S0010	Mary Martinez
B003	14 – 8th Avenue, New York, NY 10012	212-371-3000	S0145	Art Peters
B004	16 – 14th Avenue, Seattle, WA 98128	206-555-3131	S2250	Sally Stern

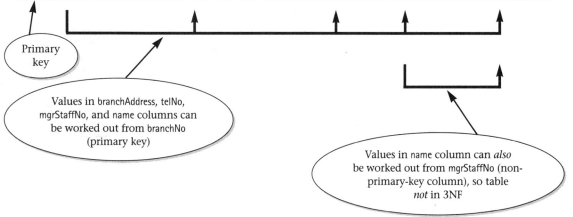

Primary key

Values in branchAddress, telNo, mgrStaffNo, and name columns can be worked out from branchNo (primary key)

Values in name column can *also* be worked out from mgrStaffNo (non-primary-key column), so table *not* in 3NF (staffNo) and name columns already existed in a table in the database.) Following the restructuring of the tables, we rename BranchManager to Branch. The structures for the new Branch and ManagerStaff tables are shown in Figure 6.8.

There are normal forms that go beyond 3NF such as fourth normal form (4NF) and fifth normal form (5NF). However, these later normal forms are not commonly used as they attempt to identify and solve problems in tables that occur

Figure 6.8

The Branch table is in 3NF owing to the removal of the name column.

BranchManager (Not 3NF)

branchNo	branchAddress	telNo	mgrStaffNo	name
B001	8 Jefferson Way, Portland, OR 97201	503-555-3618	S1500	Tom Daniels
B002	City Center Plaza, Seattle, WA 98122	206-555-6756	S0010	Mary Martinez
B003	14 – 8th Avenue, New York, NY 10012	212-371-3000	S0145	Art Peters
B004	16 – 14th Avenue, Seattle, WA 98128	206-555-3131	S2250	Sally Stern

Primary key

Take copy of mgrStaffNo

Remove name column to new table

BranchManager table is renamed Branch

Branch (3NF)

branchNo	branchAddress	telNo	mgrStaffNo
B001	8 Jefferson Way, Portland, OR 97201	503-555-3618	S1500
B002	City Center Plaza, Seattle, WA 98122	206-555-6756	S0010
B003	14 – 8th Avenue, New York, NY 10012	212-371-3000	S0415
B004	16 – 14th Avenue, Seattle, WA 98128	206-555-3131	S2250

ManagerStaff (3NF)

mgrStaffNo	name
S1500	Tom Daniels
S0010	Mary Martinez
S0415	Art Peters
S2250	Sally Stern

Primary key

Becomes foreign key

Primary key

relatively infrequently. If you would like to find out more about 4NF and 5NF you should consult the *Database Systems* book by Connolly and Begg (1999).

Chapter summary

✓ **Normalization** is a technique for producing a set of tables with desirable properties that supports the requirements of a user or company.

✓ Tables that have redundant data may have problems called update anomalies, which are classified as insertion, deletion, or modification anomalies.

✓ The definition for **first normal form (1NF)** is a table in which the intersection of every column and record contains one, and only one, value.

✓ The definition for **second normal form (2NF)** is a table that is already in 1NF and in which the values in each non-primary-key column can only be worked out from the values in *all* the columns that make up the primary key.

✓ The definition for **third normal form (3NF)** is a table that is already in 1NF and 2NF, and in which the values in all non-primary-key columns can be worked out from *only* the primary key column(s) and no other columns.

Part Three

Logical database design

Chapter 7

Overview of the methodology

In this chapter you will learn:

What a design methodology is. ◄

The aims of a database design methodology. ◄

The purpose of data modeling. ◄

Database design has two main phases: logical and physical design. ◄

The steps in the methodology for logical and physical database design. ◄

In Chapter 3, we described the main stages of the database application lifecycle, one of which is database design. This stage starts only after a complete analysis of the company's requirements has been undertaken, as we discussed in Chapter 4. In Chapters 8–16, we'll present a methodology for logical and physical database design. In this chapter, we discuss the aims of a database design methodology and give a brief overview of the methodology presented in this book.

7.1 Introduction to the database design methodology

The aim of this book is to help you design and build a database. However, once the database you require starts to become reasonably complex, you need to have a systematic approach to producing the design of the database that will satisfy the users' requirements and achieve the stated performance requirements for the system (such as response times). This systematic approach is called a database design methodology. As we discussed briefly in Section 3.7, the methodology we present in this book is divided into two main phases, *logical* and *physical database design,* where we build data models to represent the company. Before providing an overview of the methodology, answering the following questions may help clarify some points that you may be wondering about:

(1) What is a database design methodology?

(2) What are the aims of a database design methodology?

(3) Why build data models?

7.1.1 What is a database design methodology?

Design methodology
A structured approach that uses procedures, techniques, tools, and documentation aids to support and facilitate the process of design.

A database **design methodology** consists of phases made up of steps, which guide the designer in the techniques appropriate at each stage of the project. The phases also help the designer to plan, manage, control, and evaluate database development projects. In addition, it is a structured approach for analyzing and modeling a set of requirements for a database in a standardized and organized manner.

7.1.2 What are the aims of a database design methodology?

The major aims of a database design methodology are to:

■ represent the data and the relationships between data required by all major areas and user groups in the company (for example, production, marketing, stock control);

■ provide a data model that supports all the transactions required on the data by the users;

■ specify a minimal design that is appropriately structured to achieve the stated performance requirements for the system (such as response times).

Unfortunately, you'll find that these aims are not always easy to achieve, and that sometimes compromises are required, particularly to achieve acceptable system performance.

The approach we use for database design is referred to as a top-down approach. This approach starts with the development of data models that contain a few entities and relationships and then applies successive top-down refinements to identify attributes and possibly additional entities and relationships. For example, you may:

(1) identify the entities Branch and Staff;

(2) then identify a relationship between these entities, Branch *Has* Staff;

(3) finally, identify the associated attributes, such as Branch (branchNo, street, city, state, zipCode) and Staff (staffNo, name, salary, position).

The top-down approach is considered an appropriate strategy for the design of both simple and complex databases, and is the basis for the approach we'll use in our methodology.

7.1.3 Why build data models?

The two main purposes of building data models are:

(1) to assist in the understanding of the meaning of the data;
(2) to facilitate communication about the information requirements.

Building a data model requires answering questions about entities, relationships, and attributes. In doing so, you discover the meaning of the company's data, which exist whether or not they happen to be recorded in a formal data model. Entities, relationships, and attributes are fundamental to all companies. However, their meaning may remain poorly understood until they have been correctly documented. A data model makes it easier for you to understand the meaning of the data. Therefore, you model data to ensure that you understand:

■ each user's perspective of the data;

■ the nature of the data itself, independent of its physical representations;

■ the use of data within and across applications.

Data models can be used to convey your understanding of the company's data requirements. Provided both parties are familiar with the notation used in the model, it will support communication with the users. We separate database design into two main phases:

■ **Logical database design** – to build the logical representation of the database, which includes identification of the important entities and relationships, and to translate this representation to a set of tables.

Logical design covered in Chapters 8–11

■ **Physical database design** – to decide how the logical design is to be physically implemented (as tables) in the target relational DBMS.

Physical design covered in Chapters 12–16

Logical database design

The process of constructing a model of the data used in a company based on a specific data model, but independent of a particular DBMS and other physical considerations.

Strictly speaking, there is a phase before logical database design known as *conceptual database design*. Conceptual database design is used to produce a global view of the data as seen by high-level managers. The conceptual model is the basis for the identification and description of the main data objects, avoiding unnecessary details. Conceptual database design is independent of all physical considerations, including the underlying data model. However, as we're designing databases specifically for relational DBMSs, we've combined the two phases together and used the more general term 'logical database design'.

Logical database design

The first phase of database design is called logical database design and results in the creation of a logical data model of the company. A logical model is derived knowing the underlying data model of the target DBMS, which as we've just said, is the relational model in this book. However, you ignore any other aspects of the chosen DBMS and, in particular, any physical details, such as file organizations or indexes.

Increasingly, companies are standardizing the way in which they model data by selecting a particular approach to data modeling and using it throughout their database development projects. A popular high-level data model used in logical database design, and the one we use in this book, is based on the concepts of the Entity-Relationship (ER) model.

Throughout the process of developing a logical data model, you continually test and validate the model against the users' requirements:

(1) Using normalization. Normalization ensures that the tables derived from the data model do not display data redundancy, which can cause update anomalies when implemented.

(2) To ensure that the logical data model supports the transactions specified by the users.

The logical data model is a source of information for the physical design process, providing you with a vehicle for making trade-offs that are very important to efficient database design. For example, in the logical data model you may identify that the value of one attribute may be derived from the value of another attribute. During physical design, you may decide to store the second attribute and calculate the value of the other attribute every time you need it. On the other hand, you may decide to store both attributes, thereby increasing the size of the database but making access to the derived attribute more efficient.

The logical model also serves an important role during the operational maintenance stage of the database application lifecycle. Properly maintained and kept up to date, you will find the data model allows future changes to data or transaction requirements to be accurately and efficiently represented in the database.

Logical database design is an iterative process that has a starting point and an almost endless procession of refinements. As you come to understand the workings of the company and the meanings of its data, and express that understanding in the selected data models, the information gained may well necessitate changes to other parts of the design. For example, having identified the entities Branch and Staff and the relationship Branch *Has* Staff, you may identify the entity Member and the relationship Branch *Registers* Member. However, after some further investigation, you may find that there is information that you need to hold about registrations, such as the date of registration and which member of staff registered the new member, and you may change the relationship *Registers* into an entity Registration.

> Logical database design is critical to the overall success of the system. If the design is not a true representation of the company, it will be difficult, if not impossible, to define all the required **user views** or to maintain database integrity. It may even prove difficult to define the physical implementation or to maintain acceptable system performance. If the design is a true representation of the company, it will be possible to implement the system and at the same time achieve acceptable performance. Another hallmark of good database design is the ability to adjust to change. Therefore, it's worthwhile spending the time and effort necessary to produce the best possible design.

User views discussed in Section 3.5.1 and Section 4.4

Physical database design

Physical database design
The process of producing a description of the implementation of the database on secondary storage; it describes the base tables, file organizations, and indexes used to achieve efficient access to the data, and any associated integrity constraints and security restrictions.

Physical database design is the second phase of the database design process, during which you decide how the database is to be implemented. The previous phase of database design involved the development of a logical structure for the database (that is, identifying the entities, relationships, and attributes that are required). Although this structure is DBMS-independent, in this book it's developed for the relational model, and so certain structures that we know cannot be represented in a relational database are removed. However, before developing the physical database design, you must first identify the target DBMS. Therefore, physical design is tailored to a specific DBMS system, such as Microsoft Access 97, Oracle 8, or SQL Server 7. There is feedback between physical and logical design, because decisions are taken during physical design for improving performance that may affect the structure of the logical data model.

In general, the main aim of physical database design is to describe how you intend to physically implement the logical database design. For the relational model, this involves:

See Chapter 12
■ creating tables in the target relational DBMS and implementing the constraints on these tables from the data presented in the global logical data model;

See Chapter 13
■ identifying the specific file organizations and indexes for the data to achieve an optimum performance for the database system;

See Chapter 14
■ considering the structure of the base tables to identify whether relaxing the normalization rules may achieve improved performance;

See Chapter 15
■ designing security protection for the system.

7.1.4 Critical success factors in database design

The following guidelines are important to the success of database design:

■ Work interactively with the users as much as possible.

■ Follow a structured methodology throughout the data modeling process.

■ Employ a data-driven approach.

■ Incorporate structural and integrity considerations into the data models.

■ Combine normalization and transaction validation techniques into the data modeling methodology.

■ Use diagrams to represent as much of the data models as possible.

■ Use a Database Design Language (DBDL) to represent additional information that is known about data but not represented by the model.

■ Build a data dictionary to supplement the data model diagrams.

■ Be willing to repeat steps.

All these guidelines are built into the methodology we're about to introduce in the next section and present in the following chapters. Once you've read these chapters, you may wish to look back at these factors to see how they benefit a database design methodology.

7.2 Overview of the database design methodology

In this section, we present an overview of the database design methodology. The steps in the methodology are shown in Figure 7.1, and the chapter in which the step will be discussed is noted in the adjacent column.

Logical database design is divided into three main steps:

Step 1 covered in Chapter 8
■ *Step 1* decomposes the design into more manageable tasks, by examining different user perspectives on the company. The output of this step is the creation of **local logical data models**, which are a complete and accurate representation of the company as seen by different user groups.

Logical database design	Chapter
Step 1 Build local logical data model for each view	8
Step 1.1 Identify entities	
Step 1.2 Identify relationships	
Step 1.3 Identify and associate attributes with entities or relationships	
Step 1.4 Determine attribute domains	
Step 1.5 Determine candidate and primary key attributes	
Step 1.6 Specialize/Generalize entities (optional step)	
Step 1.7 Remove features not compatible with the relational model	
Step 1.8 Check model supports user transactions	
Step 2 Create and check tables for each local logical data model	9
Step 2.1 Create tables for local logical data model	
Step 2.2 Check table structures using normalization	
Step 2.3 Check tables support user transactions	
Step 2.4 Define integrity constraints	
Step 2.5 Review local logical data model with users	
Step 3 Build and check global logical data model (optional step)	10
Step 3.1 Merge local logical data models into global model	
Step 3.2 Check logical data model	
Step 3.3 Check for future growth	
Step 3.4 Review global logical data model with users	
Physical database design	
Step 4 Translate global logical data model for target DBMS	12
Step 4.1 Design base tables for target DBMS	
Step 4.2 Design business rules for target DBMS	
Step 5 Design physical representation	13
Step 5.1 Analyze transactions	
Step 5.2 Choose file organizations	
Step 5.3 Choose indexes	
Step 6 Consider the introduction of controlled redundancy	14
Step 6.1 Consider derived data	
Step 6.2 Consider duplicating columns or joining tables together	
Step 7 Design security mechanisms	15
Step 7.1 Design user views	
Step 7.2 Design access rules	
Step 8 Monitor and tune the operational system	16

Figure 7.1

Steps in the methodology for logical and physical database design.

■ *Step 2* maps the local logical models to a set of tables. In addition, the logical models are validated using the technique of normalization. Normalization is an effective means of ensuring that the models are structurally consistent, logical, and have minimal redundancy. The data models are also validated against the transactions that they are required to support. Validation is the process of ensuring that you're creating the 'correct' model.

Step 2 covered in Chapter 9

From this point, the data models could be used to generate prototype database implementations for the user views, if necessary.

Step 3 covered in Chapter 10

■ *Step 3* involves the integration of the local logical data models (which represent different user views) to provide a single **global logical data model** of the company (which represents all user views). This global model is validated as before to ensure that it is structurally correct and that it supports the required transactions.

Physical database design is divided into four main steps:

Step 4 covered in Chapter 12

■ *Step 4* involves the design of the base tables and integrity constraints using the available functionality of the target DBMS.

Step 5 covered in Chapter 13

■ *Step 5* involves choosing the file organizations and indexes for the base tables. Typically, DBMSs provide a number of alternative file organizations for data, with the exception of PC DBMSs, which tend to have a fixed storage structure.

Step 6 covered in Chapter 14

■ *Step 6* considers relaxing the normalization constraints imposed on the tables to improve the overall performance of the system. This is a step that you should undertake only if necessary, because of the inherent problems involved in introducing redundancy while still maintaining consistency.

Step 7 covered in Chapter 15

■ *Step 7* involves designing the security measures to protect data from unauthorized access. This means that you decide how each user view should be implemented, and what access controls are required on the base tables.

Step 8 covered in Chapter 16

■ *Step 8* is an ongoing process of monitoring the operational system to identify and resolve any performance problems resulting from the design and to implement new or changing requirements.

Appendix B presents a summary of the methodology for those of you who are already familiar with database design and simply require an overview of the main steps.

Throughout this methodology, users play a critical role in continually reviewing and validating the data model and the supporting documentation.

TIP Database design is an iterative process that has a starting point and an almost endless procession of refinements. Although we present it here as a procedural process, it must be emphasized that this does not imply that it should be performed in this manner. It is likely that the knowledge you gain in one step may alter decisions you made in a previous step. Similarly, you may find it useful to look briefly at a later step to help with an earlier step. The methodology should act as a framework to help guide you through the database design activity effectively.

Some steps may not be necessary depending on the complexity of the company you're analyzing and your need for performance and security. Figure 7.2 shows which steps may be omitted depending on your particular requirements.

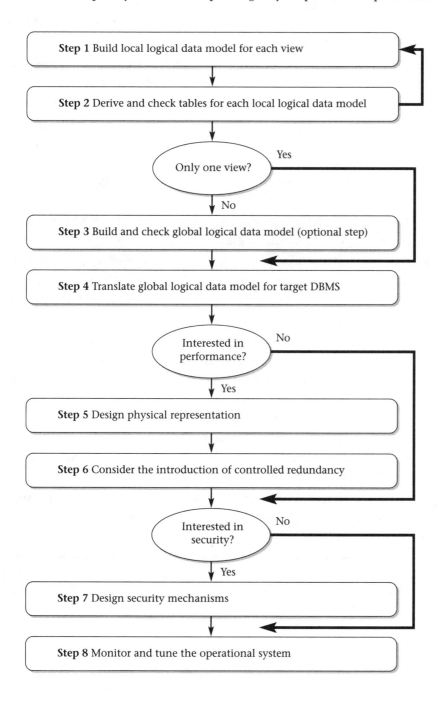

Figure 7.2

Progression through the methodology.

Chapter summary

✓ A **design methodology** is a structured approach that uses procedures, techniques, tools, and documentation aids to support and facilitate the process of design.

✓ The major aims of a database design methodology are to represent all the required data and relationships between data; to provide a data model that supports all required transactions; and to specify a minimal design that is appropriately structured to achieve the stated performance requirements.

✓ The two main purposes of data modeling are to assist in the understanding of the meaning of the data and to facilitate communication about the information requirements.

✓ The database design methodology used in this book has two main phases: logical and physical database design.

✓ **Logical database design** is the process of constructing a model of the information used in a company based on a specific data model, but independent of a particular DBMS and other physical considerations. In our case, logical design is tailored to the relational model.

✓ **Physical database design** is the process of producing a description of the implementation of the database on secondary storage; it describes the file organizations and indexes used to achieve efficient access to the data, and any associated integrity constraints and security restrictions. Physical design is tailored to a specific DBMS system.

✓ There is feedback between physical and logical design, because decisions taken during physical design to improve performance may affect the structure of the logical data model.

✓ There are critical factors for the success of the database design stage including, for example, working interactively with users and being willing to repeat steps.

Chapter 8

Logical database design
– Step 1

In this chapter you will learn:

How to decompose the scope of the design into specific views of ◀
the company.

How to use Entity-Relationship (ER) modeling to build a logical ◀
data model for each view.

How to document the process of logical database design. ◀

Users play an integral role throughout the process of logical ◀
database design.

This chapter covers the first step of our logical database design methodology. In this step, you build a local logical data model for each **view** identified during the earlier analysis stage.

Methodology summarized
in Appendix B

During analysis, you will have identified a number of user views, and depending on the amount of overlap between these views, you may have combined some views together. In the Requirements Collection and Analysis stage discussed in Section 4.4.4, we identified two merged views for *StayHome*:

■ **Branch**, consisting of the Manager, Supervisor, and Assistant user views;
■ **Business**, consisting of the Director and Buyer user views.

In this chapter, you're going to build a local logical data model for the *Branch view* of *StayHome*, and in Chapter 10 we'll show you how to combine the local logical data models for the Branch and Business views together to produce a global logical data model for the entire company.

Step 1 Build local logical data model for each view

Objective
To build a local logical data model of the company for each view.

We refer to the logical data model for each view as the **local logical data model** for that view. Each local logical data model comprises:

■ entities,

■ relationships,

■ attributes and attribute domains,

■ candidate keys, primary keys, and alternate keys,

■ integrity constraints.

The logical data model is supported by documentation, including a data dictionary, which you'll produce throughout the development of the model. We'll detail the types of supporting documentation that you may want to produce as we go through the various steps. The tasks involved in Step 1 are:

■ Step 1.1 Identify entities

■ Step 1.2 Identify relationships

■ Step 1.3 Identify and associate attributes with entities or relationships

■ Step 1.4 Determine attribute domains

■ Step 1.5 Determine candidate and primary key attributes

■ Step 1.6 Specialize/Generalize entities (optional step)

■ Step 1.7 Remove features not compatible with the relational model

■ Step 1.8 Check model supports user transactions.

So, let's start to build the model for the Branch view.

Step 1.1 Identify entities

Objective
To identify the main entities that are required by the view.

The first step in building a local logical data model is to define the main objects that the users are interested in. These objects are the entities for the model. One method of identifying entities is to examine the users' requirements specification. From this specification, you can identify nouns or noun phrases that are mentioned (for example, staff number, staff name, catalog number, title, daily rental rate, purchase price). You should also look for major objects such as people, places, or concepts of interest, excluding those nouns that are merely qualities of other objects.

Entities defined in Section 5.1; users' requirements for Branch view given in Section 4.4.4

For example, you could group staff number and staff name with an entity called Staff, and group catalog number, title, daily rental rate, and purchase price with an entity called Video.

An alternative way of identifying entities is to look for objects that have an existence in their own right. For example, Staff is an entity because staff exist whether or not you know their names, addresses, and salaries. If possible, you should get the user to assist with this activity.

It's sometimes difficult to identify entities because of the way they are presented in the users' requirements specification. Users often talk in terms of examples or analogies. Instead of talking about staff in general, users may mention people's names. In some cases, users talk in terms of job roles, particularly where people or companies are involved. These roles may be job titles or responsibilities, such as Manager, Deputy Manager, Supervisor, or Assistant. To further confuse matters, users frequently use synonyms and homonyms.

> Two words are *synonyms* when they have the same meaning, for example 'branch' and 'outlet'. *Homonyms* occur when the same word can have different meanings depending on the context. For example, the word 'program' has several alternative meanings such as a series of events, a plan of work, a piece of software, and a course of study.

It's not always obvious whether a particular object is an entity, a relationship, or an attribute. For example, how would you model marriage? In fact, depending on the actual requirements you could model marriage as any or all of these. You'll find that analysis is subjective, and different designers may produce different, but equally valid, interpretations. The activity therefore relies, to a certain extent, on judgment and experience. Database designers must take a very selective view of the world and categorize the things that they observe within the context of the company. Thus, there may be no unique set of entities deducible from a given user's requirements specification. However, successive iterations of the analysis process should lead you to the choice of entities that are at least adequate for the system required.

> **TIP** The fact that database design is subjective can initially be quite off-putting. However, by following the methodology we present in this book, you'll find that the task is achievable and that it gets easier with some practice and experience. To help, in Chapters 18 and 19 we'll go through a second case study, and in Appendix D we provide a lot of common business data models you are likely to encounter in one form or another.

StayHome *entities*

For the *StayHome* case study, you may identify the following entities:

Branch	Staff
Video	VideoForRent
Member	RentalAgreement
Actor	Director

Document entities

As you identify entities, assign them names that are meaningful and obvious to the user. Record the names and descriptions of entities in a data dictionary. If possible, document the expected number of occurrences of each entity. If an entity is known by different names, the names are referred to as synonyms or **aliases**, which you should also record in the data dictionary. Figure 8.1 shows an extract from the data dictionary that documents the entities for *StayHome*.

Figure 8.1

Extract from the data dictionary for *StayHome* showing description of entities.

Entity name	Description	Aliases	Occurrence
Branch	Place of work	Outlet and Branch Outlet	One or more *StayHome* branches are located in main cities throughout the US.
Staff	General term describing all staff employed by *StayHome*	Employee	Each member of staff works at a particular branch

Step 1.2 Identify relationships

Objective
To identify the important relationships that exist between the entities that you have identified.

Relationships defined in Section 5.2

Having identified the entities, the next step is to identify all the relationships that exist between these entities. When you identify entities, one method is to look for nouns in the users' requirements specification. Again, you can use the grammar of the requirements specification to identify relationships. Typically, relationships are indicated by verbs or verbal expressions. For example:

- Branch *Has* Staff

- Branch *IsAllocated* VideoForRent

- VideoForRent *IsPartOf* RentalAgreement

The fact that the users' requirements specification records these relationships suggests that they are important to the users, and should be included in the model.

> **TIP**
>
> We're interested only in required relationships between entities. In the previous example, you identified the **Branch** *IsAllocated* **VideoForRent** and **VideoForRent** *IsPartOf* **RentalAgreement** relationships. You may also be inclined to include a relationship between **Branch** and **RentalAgreement** (for example, **Branch** *Handles* **RentalAgreement**). However, although this is a possible relationship, from the requirements it's not a relationship that we're interested in modeling. We discuss this further in Step 1.6.

Take great care to ensure that all the relationships that are either explicit or implicit in the users' requirements specification are noted. In principle, it should be possible to check each pair of entities for a potential relationship between them, but this would be a daunting task for a large system comprising hundreds of entities. On the other hand, it's unwise not to perform some such check. However, missing relationships should become apparent when you check that the model supports the transactions that the users require.

Transaction check covered in Steps 1.8 and 2.3

In most instances, the relationships you find will be binary; in other words, the relationships exist between exactly two entities. However, you should be careful to look out for complex relationships that may involve more than two entities and recursive relationships that involve only one entity. For *StayHome*, you should identify the following non-binary relationships:

Complex and recursive relationships defined in Sections 5.2.1 and 5.2.2

Figure 8.2

First draft of the
relationships for
StayHome.

Entity	Relationship	Entity
Branch	Has	Staff
	IsAllocated	VideoForRent
Branch, Staff[†]	Registers	Member
Staff	Manages	Branch
	Supervises	Staff
Video	Is	VideoForRent
VideoForRent	IsPartOf	RentalAgreement
Member	Requests	RentalAgreement
Actor	PlaysIn	Video
Director	Directs	Video

[†] represents a ternary relationship

Registers	a ternary relationship between Branch, Member, and Staff
Supervises	a recursive relationship between Staff.

StayHome *relationships*

For the *StayHome* case study, you may identify the relationships shown in
Figure 8.2.

Use entity relationship (ER) modeling

It's often easier to visualize a complex system rather than decipher long textual
descriptions of such a system. The use of Entity-Relationship (ER) diagrams
helps you more easily to represent entities and how they relate to one another.
You can represent the above entities and relationships in the first draft ER
model shown in Figure 8.3.

Some other notations
shown in Appendix A Throughout the database design phase, we recommend that ER modeling is
used whenever necessary, to help build up a picture of what you're attempting
to model. Different people use different notations for ER modeling. In this
book, we've used the latest object-oriented notation called **UML** (**Unified
Modeling Language**), but other notations perform a similar function.

Determine the multiplicity constraints of relationships

Multiplicity defined in
Section 5.5 Having identified the relationships you wish to model, you now want to determine the multiplicity of each relationship. If specific values for the multiplicity
are known, or even upper or lower limits, document these values as well.

Figure 8.3

First draft of the ER model for *StayHome* showing entities and relationships.

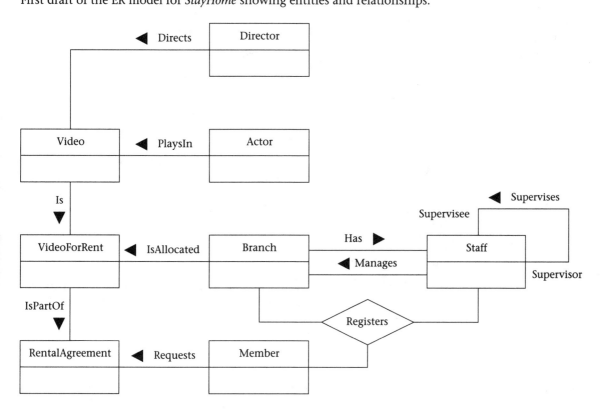

A model that includes multiplicity constraints more explicitly represents the semantics of the relationship and consequently results in a better representation of what you're trying to model. Multiplicity constraints are used to check and maintain the quality of the data. These constraints can be applied when the database is updated to determine whether or not the updates violate the stated rules.

TIP If you have identified any recursive relationships with a minimum multiplicity of one for either role, check the multiplicity constraints again, as this tends to be an unusual situation.

Figure 8.4

Multiplicity constraints for the relationships identified for *StayHome*.

Entity	Multiplicity	Relationship	Entity	Multiplicity
Branch	1..*	Has	Staff	1..1
	1..*	IsAllocated	VideoForRent	1..1
Branch, Staff[†]	1..*, 1..1	Registers	Member	0..*
Staff	0..1	Manages	Branch	1..1
	0..*	Supervises	Staff	0..1
Video	1..*	Is	VideoForRent	1..1
VideoForRent	0..*	IsPartOf	RentalAgreement	1..1
Member	0..*	Requests	RentalAgreement	1..1
Actor	1..*	PlaysIn	Video	0..*
Director	1..*	Directs	Video	1..1

[†] represents a ternary relationship

StayHome multiplicity constraints

For the *StayHome* case study, you should identify the multiplicity constraints shown in Figure 8.4. Figure 8.5 shows the updated ER model with this information added.

Check for fan and chasm traps

Fan and chasm traps discussed in Section 5.7

Having identified the relationships, you should check that each one correctly represents what you want it to represent, and that you've not inadvertently created any fan traps or chasm traps.

Check that each entity participates in at least one relationship

Step 2.1 covered in Chapter 9

Generally, an entity cannot be modeled unrelated to any other entity, otherwise when you map the entity to a table in Step 2.1, there would be no way to navigate to that table. The common exception to this rule is a database with a single table. If you find that you have such an entity, check whether the entity appears elsewhere in the model, perhaps under a different name. Failing this, look at the requirements again to determine whether you've missed any relationships. If this does not identify missing relationships, go back to the users to discuss the use of this particular entity in more detail.

Figure 8.5

Adding multiplicity constraints to the ER model for *StayHome*.

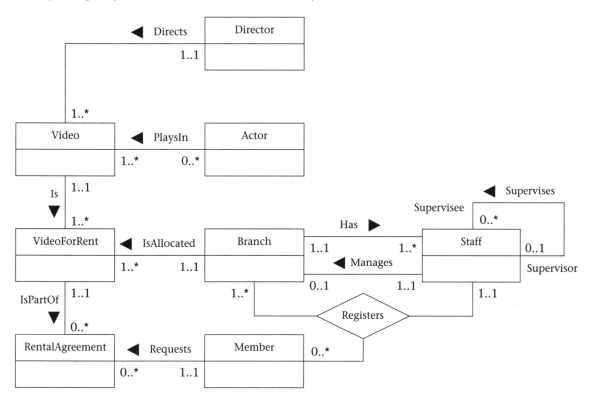

Document relationships

As you identify relationships, assign them names that are meaningful and obvious to the user. Also record relationship descriptions, and the multiplicity constraints in the data dictionary. Figure 8.6 shows an extract from the data dictionary that documents the relationships for *StayHome*.

Step 1.3 Identify and associate attributes with entities or relationships

Objective
To associate attributes with the appropriate entities or relationships.

Attributes defined in
Section 5.3

The next step in the methodology is to identify the types of facts about the entities and relationships that you've chosen to be represented in the database.

Figure 8.6

Extract from the
data dictionary for
StayHome showing
description of
relationships.

Entity	Multiplicity	Relationship	Entity	Multiplicity
Branch	1..*	Has	Staff	1..1
Branch	1..*	IsAllocated	VideoForRent	1..1
Staff	0..1	Manages	Branch	1..1
Staff	0..*	Supervises	Staff	0..1

In a similar way to identifying entities, look for nouns or noun phrases in the users' requirements specification. The attributes can be identified where the noun or noun phrase is a property, quality, identifier, or characteristic of one of the entities or relationships that you've previously found.

> **TIP** By far the easiest thing to do when you've identified an entity or a relationship in the users' requirements specification is to consider '*What information are we required to hold on . . . ?* The answer to this question should be described in the specification. However, in some cases, you may need to ask the users to clarify the requirements. Unfortunately, they may give you answers that also contain other concepts, so users' responses must be carefully considered.

Simple/Composite attributes

Simple/composite
attributes defined in
Section 5.3.1

It's important to note whether an attribute is simple or composite. Composite attributes are made up of simple attributes. For example, an address attribute can be simple and hold all the details of an address as a single value, such as '8 Jefferson Way, Portland, OR, 97201'. However, the address attribute may also represent a composite attribute, made up of simple attributes that hold the address details as separate values in the attributes street ('8 Jefferson Way'), city ('Portland'), state ('OR'), and zipCode ('97201').

The option to represent address details as a simple or composite attribute is deter-mined by the users' requirements. If users do not need to access the separate components of an address, you should represent the address attribute as a simple attribute. On the other hand, if users do need to access the individual components of an **address**, you should represent the **address** attribute as being composite, made up of the required simple attributes.

Single/Multi-valued attributes

In addition to being simple or composite, an attribute can also be single-valued or multi-valued. Most attributes you encounter will be single-valued, but occasion-ally you may encounter a multi-valued attribute: that is, an attribute that holds multiple values for a single entity occurrence. For example, you may identify the Branch attribute telNo (the telephone number) as a multi-valued attribute.

Multi-valued attributes defined in Section 5.3.2

You may have identified branch telephone numbers as a separate entity. This is an alternative, and equally valid, way to model this. As you'll see shortly in Step 1.7, multi-valued attributes are mapped to entities anyway, so both approaches produce the same end result.

Derived attributes

Attributes whose values can be found by examining the values of other attrib-utes are known as derived attributes. Often, these attributes are not shown in the logical data model. However, sometimes the value of the attribute or attrib-utes on which the derived attribute is based may be deleted or modified. In this case, the derived attribute must be shown in the data model to avoid this potential loss of information. If a derived attribute is shown in the model, you must indicate that it's derived by prefixing its name with a '/'.

Derived attributes defined in Section 5.3.3

We'll consider the representation of derived attributes during physical data-base design. Depending on how the attribute is used, new values for a derived attribute may be calculated each time it's accessed or when the value(s) it's derived from change. However, this issue is not the concern of logical database design, and we'll discuss how best to physically represent derived attributes in Step 6.1 in Chapter 14.

Potential problems

When identifying attributes, it's not uncommon for it to become apparent that one or more entities have been omitted from the original selection. In this case, return to the previous steps, document the new entities and re-examine the associated relationships.

> **TIP** It may be useful to produce a list of all attributes given in the users' requirements specification. As you associate an attribute with a particular entity or relationship, you can remove the item from the list. In this way, you can ensure that an attribute is associated with only one entity or relationship and, when the list is empty, that all attributes are associated with some entity or relationship.

You must also be aware of cases where attributes appear to be associated with more than one entity as this can indicate the following:

(1) You've identified several entities that can be represented as a single entity. For example, you may have identified entities Manager and Supervisor both with the attributes staffNo (the staff number), name, and salary, which can be represented as a single entity called Staff with the attributes staffNo, name, salary, and position.

> On the other hand, it may be that these entities share many attributes but there are also attributes that are unique to each entity. In Chapter 11, we'll look at some advanced ER modeling concepts known as specialization and generalization, and provide guidelines for their use. These advanced concepts allow you to represent this type of situation more accurately. We omit these advanced concepts here and consider them as a separate optional step (Step 1.6) to keep the basic methodology as simple as possible.

(2) You've identified a relationship between entities. In this case, you must associate the attribute with only *one* entity, namely the parent entity, and ensure that the relationship was previously identified in Step 1.2. If this is not the case, the documentation should be updated with details of the newly identified relationship. For example, you may have identified the entities Branch and Staff with the following attributes:

Branch   branchNo, street, city, state, zipCode, managerName

Staff   staffNo, name, position, salary

The presence of the managerName attribute in Branch is intended to represent the relationship Staff *Manages* Branch. In this case, however, the managerName attribute should be omitted from Branch and the relationship *Manages* should be added to the model.

StayHome **attributes for entities**

For the *StayHome* case study, you should identify and associate attributes with entities as follows:

Branch	branchNo, address (composite: street, city, state, zipCode), telNo (multi-valued)
Staff	staffNo, name, position, salary
Video	catalogNo, title, category, dailyRental, price
Director	directorName
Actor	actorName
Member	memberNo, name (composite: fName, lName), address
RentalAgreement	rentalNo, dateOut, dateReturn
VideoForRent	videoNo, available

Note that the **address** attribute in **Branch** and the **name** attribute in **Member** have been identified as composite, whereas the **address** attribute in **Member** and the **name** attributes in **Staff**, **Director**, and **Actor** have been identified as simple. This reflects the users' access requirements for these attributes.

StayHome **attributes for relationships**

You may have difficulty associating the attribute representing the date a member registered at a branch, dateJoined, with a particular entity. It cannot be associated with Member because a member can register at more than one branch. In fact, this attribute should not be associated with any of the above entities but should instead be associated with the *Registers* ternary relationship between Member, Branch, and Staff. Similarly, the attribute representing the name of the character an actor plays in a video, character, has to be associated with the many-to-many *PlaysIn* relationship between Actor and Video.

Document attributes

As you identify attributes, assign them names that are meaningful and obvious to the user. Record the following information for each attribute:

- attribute name and description;
- data type and length;
- any aliases or synonyms that the attribute is known by;
- whether the attribute must always be specified (in other words, whether the attribute allows or disallows nulls);
- whether the attribute is multi-valued.
- whether the attribute is composite and if so, what are the simple attributes that make up the composite attribute;
- whether the attribute is derived and if so, how it should be computed;
- default values for the attribute (if specified).

Nulls defined in Section 2.3.1

Figure 8.7 shows an extract from the data dictionary that documents the attributes for *StayHome*.

Step 1.4 Determine attribute domains

Objective
To determine domains for the attributes in the local logical data model.

The objective of this step is to determine domains for the attributes in the logical data model. A **domain** is a pool of values from which one or more attributes draw their values. Examples of the attribute domains for *StayHome* include:

- The attribute domain of valid branch numbers as being a four-character fixed-length string, with the first character as a letter and the next three characters as digits in the range 000–999.
- The attribute domain for valid telephone numbers as being a 10-digit string.
- The possible values for the available attribute of the VideoForRent entity as being either 'Y' or 'N'. The domain of this attribute is a single character string consisting of the values 'Y' or 'N'.

A fully developed data model specifies the domains for each of the model's attributes and includes:

Entity	Attributes	Description	Data type and length	Nulls	Multi-valued	...
Branch	branchNo	Uniquely identifies a branch	4 fixed characters	No	No	
	address:					
	street	Street of branch address	30 variable characters	No	No	
	city	City of branch address	20 variable characters	No	No	
	state	State of branch address	2 fixed characters	No	No	
	zipCode	Zip code of branch address	5 variable characters	No	No	
	telNo	Telephone numbers of branch	10 variable characters	No	Yes	
Staff	staffNo	Uniquely identifies a member of staff	5 fixed characters	No	No	
	name	Name of staff member	30 variable characters	No	No	

Figure 8.7

Extract from the data dictionary for *StayHome* showing description of attributes.

■ the allowable set of values for the attribute;

■ the size and format of the attribute.

Document attribute domains

As you identify attribute domains, record their names and characteristics in the data dictionary. Update the data dictionary entries for attributes to record their domain in place of the data type and length information.

Step 1.5 Determine candidate and primary key attributes

Objective
To identify the candidate key(s) for each entity and, if there is more than one candidate key, to choose one to be the primary key.

Keys defined in Sections 2.2.3 and 5.3.4

This step is concerned with identifying the candidate key(s) for an entity and then selecting one to be the primary key. Be careful to ensure that you choose a candidate key that can never be null (if the candidate key consists of more than one attribute, then this applies to each attribute). If you identify more than one candidate key, you must choose one to be the primary key; the remaining candidate keys are called alternate keys.

TIP Peoples' names generally do not make good candidate keys, as we pointed out in Section 2.2.3. For example, you may think that a suitable candidate key for the **Staff** entity would be **name**, the member of staff's name. However, it's possible for two people with the same name to join *StayHome*, which would clearly invalidate the choice of **name** as a candidate key. We could make a similar argument for the names of *StayHome's* members. In such cases, rather than coming up with combinations of attributes that may provide uniqueness, it may be better to define a new attribute that would always ensure uniqueness, such as a **staffNo** attribute for the **Staff** entity and a **memberNo** attribute for the **Member** entity.

When choosing a primary key from among the candidate keys, you should use the following guidelines to help make the selection:

■ the candidate key with the minimal set of attributes;
■ the candidate key that is less likely to have its values changed;
■ the candidate key that is less likely to lose uniqueness in the future;
■ the candidate key with fewest characters (for those with textual attribute(s));
■ the candidate key with the smallest maximum value (for numerical attributes);
■ the candidate key that is easiest to use from the users' point of view.

Weak entities defined in Section 5.4

In the process of identifying primary keys, note whether an entity is strong or weak. If you can assign a primary key to an entity, the entity is referred to as being **strong**. On the other hand, if you can't identify a primary key to an entity, the entity is referred to as being **weak**.

The primary key of a weak entity can only be identified when you map the weak entity to a table, which we'll describe in Step 2.1 in Chapter 9.

StayHome **primary keys**

For the *StayHome* case study, you should identify the primary keys shown in Figure 8.8.

> From the given users' requirements for *StayHome* there are no obvious keys for the **Director** and **Actor** entities. In fact, the only attributes that have been identified for the entities are the director's name for the **Director** entity and the actor's name for the **Actor** entity. And as we've just said, these are not suitable as primary keys, so we've made up a primary key for each of these entities, which we've called **directorNo** and **actorNo**, respectively.

Figure 8.8

ER model for *StayHome* showing primary keys.

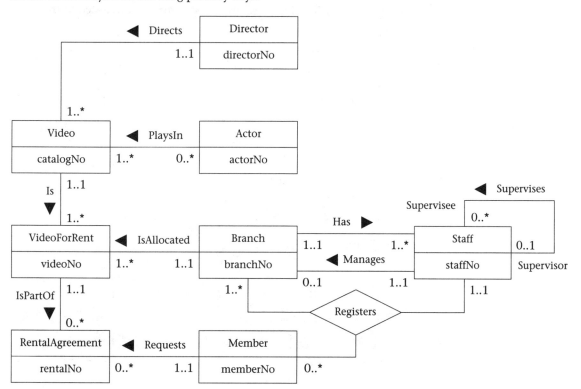

Document candidate, primary, and alternate keys

Record the identification of candidate, primary, and alternate keys (when available) in the data dictionary. Figure 8.9 shows an extract from the data dictionary that documents the attributes for *StayHome* with the keys identified.

Step 1.6 Specialize/Generalize entities (optional step)

Objective
To identify superclass and subclass entities, where appropriate.

In this step, you have the option to continue the development of the logical data model using the process of specialization or generalization. The modeling of superclasses and subclasses adds more information to the data model, but also adds more complexity as well. Consequently, as this is an optional step, we'll omit the details of specialization and generalization for now and consider it separately in Chapter 11 for those readers who may be interested in this.

Figure 8.9

Extract from the data dictionary for *StayHome* showing attributes with primary and alternate keys identified.

Entity	Attributes	Description	Key	Nulls	...
Branch	branchNo	Uniquely identifies a branch	Primary key	No	
	address:				
	street	Street of branch address		No	
	city	City of branch address		No	
	state	State of branch address		No	
	zipCode	Zip code of branch address	Alternate key	No	
	telNo	Telephone numbers of branch		No	
Staff	staffNo	Uniquely identifies a member of staff	Primary key	No	
	name	Name of staff member		No	

Step 1.7 Remove features not compatible with the relational model

Objective
To refine the local logical data model to remove features that are not compatible with the relational model.

At this point, you have a local data model for the Branch view of the company. However, the data model may contain some structures that are not easily modeled by conventional relational DBMSs. In this step, you transform such data structures into a form that is more easily handled by such systems. More specifically then, the objectives of this step are to:

(1) Remove many-to-many (*:*) binary relationships.

(2) Remove many-to-many (*:*) recursive relationships.

(3) Remove complex relationships.

(4) Remove multi-valued attributes.

(5) Re-examine one-to-one (1:1) relationships.

(6) Remove redundant relationships.

Remove many-to-many (*:*) binary relationships

If a many-to-many (*:*) relationship is represented in the logical data model, you should decompose this relationship to identify an intermediate entity. You replace the *:* relationship with two one-to-many (1:*) relationships to the newly identified entity.

: relationships defined in Section 5.5.3

For example, consider the *:* relationship Actor *PlaysIn* Video shown in Figure 8.10(a). If we decompose the *PlaysIn* relationship, we identify the Role entity and two new 1:* relationships (*Plays* and *Features*). The *:* *PlaysIn* relationship is now represented as Actor *Plays* Role and Video *Features* Role, as shown in Figure 8.10(b).

This example also illustrates that any attributes associated with *:* relationships should become attributes of the newly created intermediate entity. However, this applies only to attributes associated with *:* relationships; attributes associated with 1:1 or 1:* relationships can be handled without creating any new entities, as you'll see in Step 2.1 in the next chapter.

Figure 8.10

(a) The Actor *PlaysIn* Video many-to-many (*:*) relationship; (b) decomposing the *PlaysIn* *:* relationship into two one-to-many (1:*) relationships (*Plays* and *Features*) by introducing the weak entity Role.

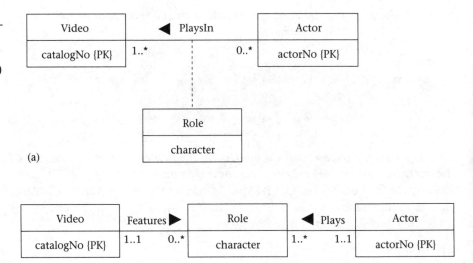

Note that the **Role** entity is shown as a weak entity (no primary key identified) because of its existence dependency on the owner entities **Actor** and **Video**.

Remove many–to–many (*:*) recursive relationships

Recursive relationships defined in Section 5.2.2

A recursive relationship is a particular type of relationship in which an entity has a relationship with itself. There are three types of recursive relationships:

■ one-to-one (1:1) recursive;

■ one-to-many (1:*) recursive;

■ many-to-many (*:*) recursive.

Participation defined in Section 5.5.5

The first two relationships can be represented as a single table in the relational model without any restructuring, although if a 1:* recursive relationship has optional participation on the many side, it may be more efficient to create a second table to reduce the number of nulls that may be stored. We'll consider how to represent 1:1 and 1:* recursive relationships in Step 2.1 in the next chapter. However, if you've identified a *:* recursive relationship, you should decompose this relationship to identify an intermediate entity.

We have no *:* recursive relationships in the *StayHome* case study, although we do have a 1:* recursive relationship Staff *Supervises* Staff. However, to demonstrate how we can restructure such relationships to be compatible with the relational model, let's assume that this is a *:* recursive relationship representing the situation where staff can be supervised by many supervisors, as shown in Figure 8.11(a).

You simplify a *:* recursive relationship in much the same way as a *:* relationship between different entities. An intuitive way of resolving this problem is first to represent Staff as two entities, giving us a familiar binary *:* relationship, as shown in Figure 8.11(b). As before, you resolve this *:* relationship by introducing an intermediate (weak) entity SupervisedStaff, as shown in Figure 8.11(c). You can then recombine the two parts of the split Staff entity, taking care not to lose any relationships, giving the final model shown in Figure 8.11(d).

Remove complex relationships

A complex relationship is a relationship between three or more entities. If a complex relationship is represented in the logical data model, you should decompose this relationship to identify an intermediate entity. The complex relationship is replaced with the required number of 1:* (binary) relationships to the newly identified entity.

Complex relationships defined in Section 5.2.1

For example, the ternary *Registers* relationship represents the association of the member of staff who registers a new member at a branch (a member can register at different branches), as shown in Figure 8.12(a). You can simplify this relationship by introducing a new entity and defining (binary) relationships between each of the original entities and the new entity. In this example, you decompose the *Registers* relationship to identify a new weak entity called Registration. The new entity is associated with the original entities through three new binary relationships: Branch *Registers* Registration, Staff *Processes* Registration, and Member *Agrees* Registration, as shown in Figure 8.12(b).

Multiplicity for Registers relationship covered in Section 5.5.4

Remove multi-valued attributes

A multi-valued attribute holds multiple values for a single entity. If a multi-valued attribute is represented in the logical data model, you should decompose this attribute to identify an entity.

Multi-valued attributes defined in Section 5.3.2

For example, to represent the situation where a single branch has up to three telephone numbers, we've defined the telNo attribute of the Branch entity as being a multi-valued attribute, as shown in Figure 8.13(a). You remove this multi-valued attribute and identify a new entity called Telephone, with the multi-valued attribute telNo now represented as a simple (primary key) attribute, and a new relationship called *Provides*, as shown in Figure 8.13(b).

Figure 8.11

(a) The *Supervises* many-to-many (*:*) recursive relationship. (b) Showing the *Supervises* *:* recursive relationship as a familiar binary relationship. (c) Resolving the *:* relationship *Supervises* to create a new (weak) entity called SupervisedStaff and an additional relationship called *SupervisedBy*. (d) Recombining the two Staff entities to resolve the *:* recursive relationship.

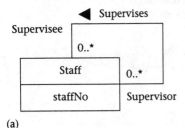

(a)

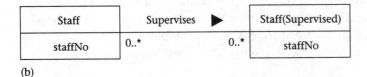

(b)

(c)

(d)

Re-examine one-to-one (1:1) relationships

1:1 relationships defined in Section 5.5.1

In the identification of entities, you may have identified two entities that represent the same object in the company. For example, you may have identified two entities named Branch and Outlet that are actually the same; in other words, Branch is a synonym for Outlet. In this case, the two entities should be merged together. If the primary keys are different, choose one of them to be the primary key and leave the other as an alternate key.

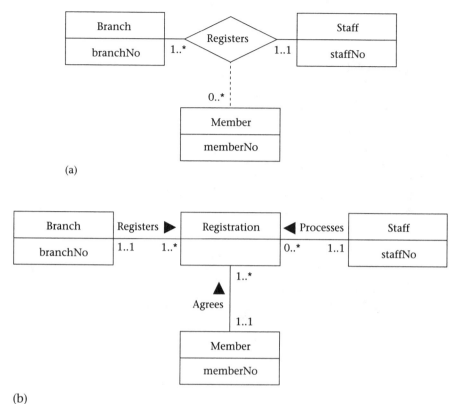

Figure 8.12

(a) The ternary
Registers relationship.
(b) Decomposing
the *Registers* ternary
relationship into
three 1:*
relationships
(*Registers, Processes,*
and *Agrees*) and
introducing the
weak entity
Registration.

Remove redundant relationships

A relationship is redundant if the same information can be obtained via other
relationships. You're trying to develop a minimal data model and, as redundant
relationships are unnecessary, they should be removed. It's relatively easy to
identify whether there is more than one path between two entities. However,
this does not necessarily imply that one of the relationships is redundant, as
they may represent different associations in the company.

For example, having decomposed the ternary *Registers* relationship into three
separate binary relationships, let's examine the relationships between Branch,
Staff, and Registration, as shown in Figure 8.14. In this model, there are two ways
to access Registration from Branch (using the Branch *Registers* Registration relationship
and using the combination of Branch *Has* Staff and Staff *Processes* Registration relationships). This type of recursive structure should always make you consider
whether there is redundancy present. Let's examine the *Has* and *Registers* relationships in turn to identify if any redundancy exists.

Figure 8.13

(a) The Branch entity with a multi-valued attribute called telNo. (b) Decomposing telNo into a 1:3 relationship called *Provides* between Branch and a new entity called Telephone with a simple (primary key) attribute telNo.

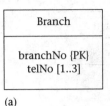

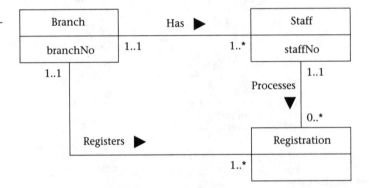

Figure 8.14

Branch, Staff, and Registration entities with three relationships.

(a) *Has* Can we identify where staff work using just the *Registers* and *Processes* relationships? For each registration, we can determine the branch associated with the registration using the *:1 *Registers* relationship. Further, for each registration, we can identify the member of staff who processed the registration using the *Processes* relationship, and from that can deduce the branch where the member of staff works. However, the participation of Staff in the *Processes* relationship is optional; in other words, not every member of staff processes registrations, and so we cannot deduce the branch for all members of staff. Therefore, you can conclude that the *Has* relationship is not redundant.

(b) *Registers* Can we identify which branch a registration is for using just the *Has* and *Processes* relationships? For each member of staff, we can determine the member's branch using the *:1 *Has* relationship. Further, for each member of staff, we can identify the registrations that this member of staff has made using the 1:* *Processes* relationship, and so can deduce the branch the registration is for from the staff's branch. This time, the participation of the Registration entity in the *Processes* relationship is mandatory, so there must be a member of staff for every registration.

Based on this examination, you might conclude that the *Registers* relationship is redundant. However, when you consider how the company operates, it's possible that staff will work at more than one branch during their time at *StayHome*. When you take this into consideration, you conclude that all relationships are required to model this situation correctly.

Examine the time dimension when assessing redundancy

The time dimension of relationships is also important when assessing redundancy. For example, consider the situation where you wish to model the relationships between the entities Man, Woman, and Child, as illustrated in Figure 8.15. Clearly, there are two paths between Man and Child: one via the direct relationship *FatherOf* and the other via the relationships *MarriedTo* and *MotherOf*. Consequently, you may think that the relationship *FatherOf* is unnecessary. However, this would be incorrect for two reasons:

(1) The father may have children from a previous marriage, and you're modeling only the father's current marriage through a 1:1 relationship.

(2) The father and mother may not be married, or the father may be married to someone other than the mother (or the mother may be married to someone who is not the father).

In either case, the required relationship could not be modeled without the *FatherOf* relationship.

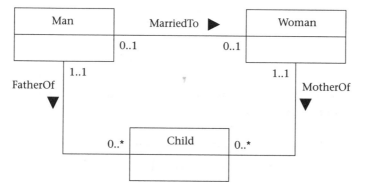

Figure 8.15

Non-redundant relationships.

> **TIP** The message here is that it's important you examine the meaning of each relationship between entities when assessing redundancy.

Draw revised local logical data model

At the end of this step, you have simplified the local logical data model by removing the data structures that are difficult to implement in relational databases. You should update the local logical data model and the data dictionary to reflect any changes introduced during this step. Incorporating the changes identified above, you get the revised local logical data model shown in Figure 8.16.

Step 1.8 Check model supports user transactions

Objective
To ensure that the local logical data model supports the transactions required by the view.

You now have a local data model that represents a specific view of the company. The objective of this step is to check the local logical data model to ensure that the model supports the transactions required by this view. In our case, the transaction requirements for the Branch view of *StayHome* are listed in Section 4.4.4.

Using the logical data model and the data dictionary, you attempt to perform the operations manually. If you can resolve all transactions in this way, you have checked that the logical data model supports the required transactions. However, if you're unable to perform a transaction manually, there must be a problem with the data model, which must be resolved. In this case, it's likely that you've omitted an entity, a relationship, or an attribute from the data model.

We examine two possible approaches to ensuring that the local logical data model supports the required transactions.

Figure 8.16

Revised local logical data model for the Branch view of *StayHome*.

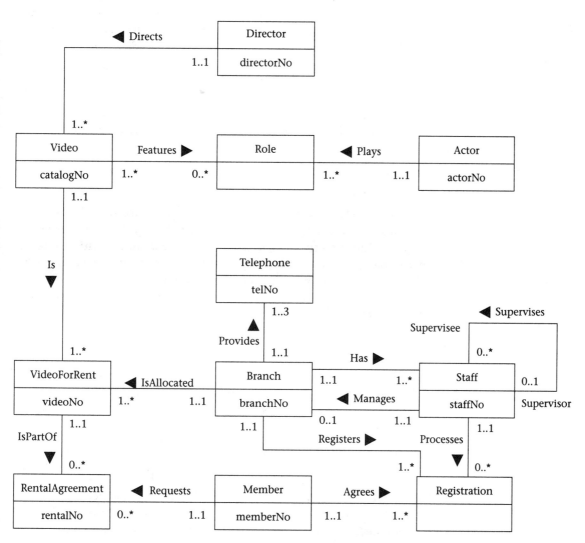

Describing the transaction

Using the first approach, you check that all the information (entities, relationships, and their attributes) required by each transaction is provided by the model, by documenting a description of each transaction's requirements. Let's examine the requirements for an example transaction for *StayHome*:

> Transaction (o) List the name of each manager at each branch, ordered by branch number

The name of each manager is held in the Staff entity and branch details are held in the Branch entity. In this case, you can use the Staff *Manages* Branch relationship to find the name of each manager for each branch.

Using transaction pathways

The second approach to validating the data model against the required transactions involves diagrammatically representing the pathway taken by each transaction directly on the ER model. An example of this approach using the data queries listed in Section 4.4.4 is shown in Figure 8.17. Clearly, the more transactions that exist, the more complex this diagram would become, so for readability you may need several such diagrams to cover all the transactions.

> **TIP** This may look like a lot of hard work and it certainly can be. As a result, you may be tempted to omit this step. However, it's very important that you do these checks now rather than later when you'll find it much more difficult and costly to resolve any errors in your data model.

At the end of this step, you've checked that the local logical data model will support the required transactions. You are now ready to proceed to the next major step, which maps the data model to a set of tables and validates the model.

Figure 8.17

Using pathways to check that the local logical data model supports the user transactions.

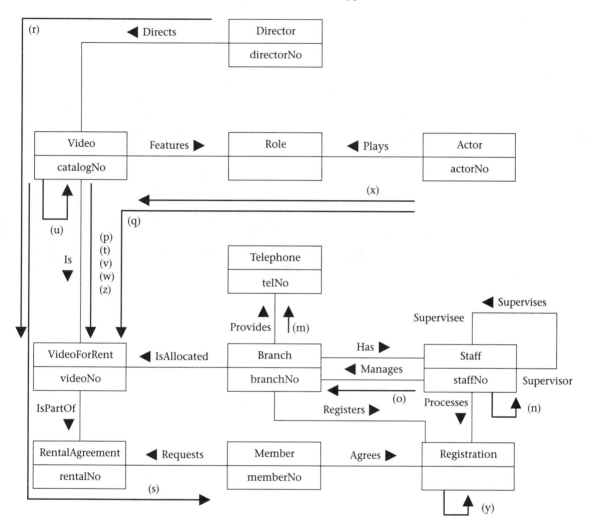

Chapter summary

✓ The main objective of Step 1 of the methodology is to build a local logical data model for each view of the company.

✓ Each local logical data model comprises: entities, relationships, attributes, attribute domains, candidate keys, primary keys, and integrity constraints.

✓ Each local logical data model is supported by documentation, such as a data dictionary, which is produced throughout the development of the model.

✓ Each logical model should be refined to: remove *:* binary relationships, remove *:* recursive relationships, remove complex relationships, remove multi-valued attributes, re-examine 1:1 relationships, and remove redundant relationships.

✓ Each logical model should be checked to ensure that it supports the transactions required by the users.

Chapter 9

Logical database design – Step 2

In this chapter you will learn:

How to create tables for a logical data model. ◄

How to check that the tables are well structured using normalization. ◄

How to check that the tables are capable of supporting the transactions required by the user. ◄

How to define and document integrity constraints. ◄

This chapter covers the second step of our logical database design methodology. In this step, you create a set of tables for each local logical data model. You then check that the tables are well structured using normalization, and that they support the user transactions. Finally, you define and document the integrity constraints for the local logical data model.

Methodology summarized in Appendix B

Step 2 Create and check tables for each local logical data model

Objective
To create tables for each local logical data model and to check the structure of the tables.

The main purpose of this step is to produce a description of the tables for each local logical data model created in Step 1 of the methodology. The set of tables produced should represent the entities, relationships, attributes, and constraints in the logical data model. The structure of each table is then checked to ensure that no errors have been introduced in creating the tables. If errors exist in the tables this may indicate that errors were introduced during the process of creating the tables or that the ER model still has errors that have not yet been identified. The tasks involved in Step 2 are:

- Step 2.1 Create tables for local logical data model
- Step 2.2 Check table structures using normalization
- Step 2.3 Check tables support user transactions
- Step 2.4 Define integrity constraints
- Step 2.5 Review local logical data model with users

Integrity constraints defined in Section 2.3

We demonstrate Step 2 of the methodology using the local logical data model created in Step 1 in the last chapter for the Branch view of the *StayHome* database application. This view represented the Manager, Supervisor, and Assistant user views.

Step 2.1 Create tables for local logical data model

> **Objective**
> To create tables for the local logical data model.

In this step, you create tables for the local logical data model to represent the entities, relationships, attributes, and constraints described in this view of the company. The structure of the tables is derived from the information that describes the logical data model, which includes the ER model, data dictionary, and any other supporting documentation. To describe the composition of each table you use a Database Definition Language (DBDL) for relational databases. Using the DBDL, you first specify the name of the table, followed by a list of the names of the table's simple attributes enclosed in brackets. You then identify the primary key and any alternate and/or foreign key(s) of the table. For each foreign key, the table containing the referenced primary key is also given.

Relational keys defined in Section 2.2.3

We illustrate this process using the ER model for the Branch view of the *StayHome* database application shown in Figure 8.16. However, in some cases it's necessary to add examples not shown in this model to illustrate particular points.

How to represent entities

For each entity in the ER model, create a table that includes all the entity's simple attributes. For composite attributes, include only the simple attributes that make up the composite attribute in the table. For example, for the composite address attribute, you would include its simple attributes street, city, state, and zipCode. Where possible, identify the column(s) that make up the primary key in each table. For the entities shown in Figure 8.16, you should create the initial table structures shown in Figure 9.1.

In some cases, you have not yet identified the full set of columns that make up the tables. The reason for this is that you have still to represent the relationships between entities. In particular, this means that you cannot identify the columns that make up the primary key for weak entities such as Role and Registration until you have represented the relationships in the ER model. We discuss the identification of primary key columns for weak entities at the end of this step.

Simple and composite attributes defined in Section 5.3.1

Weak entities defined in Section 5.4

Figure 9.1

Initial table structures representing the entities shown in Figure 8.16.

Actor (actorNo, actorName) **Primary Key** actorNo	**Branch** (branchNo, street, city, state, zipCode) **Primary Key** branchNo **Alternate Key** zipCode
Director (directorNo, directorName) **Primary Key** directorNo	**Member** (memberNo, fName, lName, address) **Primary Key** memberNo
Registration (dateJoined) **Primary Key** unknown	**RentalAgreement** (rentalNo, dateOut, dateReturn) **Primary Key** rentalNo
Role (character) **Primary Key** unknown	**Staff** (staffNo, name, position, salary) **Primary Key** staffNo
Telephone (telNo) **Primary Key** telNo	**Video** (catalogNo, title, category, dailyRental, price) **Primary Key** catalogNo
VideoForRent (videoNo, available) **Primary Key** videoNo	

How to represent relationships

Relationships discussed
in Section 5.2

The relationship that an entity has with another entity is represented by the primary key/foreign key mechanism. In deciding where to *post* (or place) the foreign key attribute(s), you must first identify the 'parent' and 'child' entities involved in the relationship. The parent entity refers to the entity that posts a copy of its primary key into the table that represents the child entity, to act as the foreign key.

We consider the identification of parent/child entities for the following types of relationships:

(a) One-to-many (1:*) binary relationships

(b) One-to-many (1:*) recursive relationships

(c) One-to-one (1:1) binary relationships

(d) One-to-one (1:1) recursive relationships

Note that you removed many-to-many (*:*) and complex relationships in Step 1.7 of the methodology covered in the last chapter.

1:* relationships defined
in Section 5.5.2

One-to-many (1:*) binary relationships

For each 1:* binary relationship, the entity on the 'one side' of the relationship is designated as the parent entity and the entity on the 'many side' is designated as the child entity. To represent this relationship, a copy of the primary key of the parent entity is placed into the table representing the child entity, to act as a foreign key.

Let's consider the Branch *Has* Staff relationship shown in Figure 8.16 to illustrate how to represent a 1:* relationship as tables. In this example, Branch is on the 'one side' and represents the parent entity, and Staff is on the 'many side' and represents the child entity. The relationship between these entities is established by placing a copy of the primary key of the Branch (parent) entity, namely branchNo, into the Staff (child) table. Figure 9.2(a) shows the Branch *Has* Staff ER model and Figure 9.2(b) shows the corresponding tables.

There are several other examples of 1:* relationships in Figure 8.16 such as Director *Directs* Video and Member *Requests* RentalAgreement. You should repeat the rules given above for every 1:* relationship in the local logical data model.

> In the case where a 1:* relationship has one or more attributes, these attributes should follow the posting of the primary key to the child table. For example, if the **Branch** *Has* **Staff** relationship had an attribute called **dateStart** representing when a member of staff started at the branch, this attribute should also be posted to the **Staff** table along with the copy of the primary key of the **Branch** table, namely **branchNo**.

Figure 9.2

The 1:* Branch *Has* Staff relationship: (a) ER model; (b) representation as tables using the DBDL.

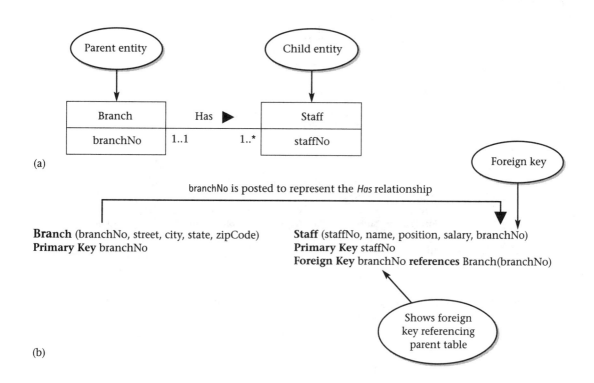

(a)

(b)

One-to-many (1:*) recursive relationships

The representation of a 1:* recursive relationship is similar to that described above. In Figure 8.16, there is a 1:* recursive relationship Staff *Supervises* Staff. In this case, both the parent and child entity is Staff. Following the rules given above, you represent the *Supervises* relationship by posting a copy of the primary key of the Staff (parent) entity, staffNo, to the Staff (child) table, creating a second copy of this column, to act as the foreign key. This copy of the column is renamed supervisorStaffNo to give a better indication of its purpose. Figure 9.3(a) shows the Staff *Supervises* Staff ER model and Figure 9.3(b) shows the corresponding table (with the Branch *Has* Staff relationship included for completeness).

Recursive relationships defined in Section 5.2.2

One-to-one (1:1) binary relationships

Creating tables to represent 1:1 relationships is slightly more complex as you cannot use the cardinality to help identify the parent and child entities in a

1:1 relationships defined in Section 5.5.1

Figure 9.3

The 1:* Staff *Supervises* Staff recursive relationship: (a) ER model; (b) representation as a table using the DBDL.

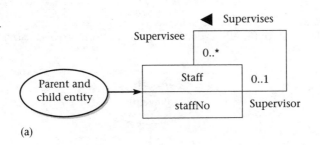

(a)

staffNo is posted to represent the *Supervises* relationship
(and renamed supervisorStaffNo)

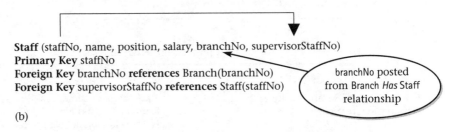

Staff (staffNo, name, position, salary, branchNo, supervisorStaffNo)
Primary Key staffNo
Foreign Key branchNo **references** Branch(branchNo)
Foreign Key supervisorStaffNo **references** Staff(staffNo)

branchNo posted
from Branch *Has* Staff
relationship

(b)

Participation defined in Section 5.5.5

relationship. Instead, you need to use participation to help decide whether it's best to represent the relationship by combining the entities involved into one table or by creating two tables and posting a copy of the primary key from one table to the other. We consider how to create tables to represent the following participation constraints:

(1) *Mandatory* participation on *both* sides of 1:1 relationship

(2) *Mandatory* participation on *one* side of 1:1 relationship

(3) *Optional* participation on *both* sides of 1:1 relationship.

Mandatory participation on both sides of 1:1 relationship
In this case, you should combine the entities involved into one table and choose one of the primary keys of the original entities to be the primary key of the new table, while the other is used as an alternate key.

We don't have an example of such a relationship in Figure 8.16. However, let's consider how to represent a 1:1 relationship called Staff *Uses* Car with mandatory participation for both entities, as shown in Figure 9.4(a). The primary key for the Car entity is the vehicle license number (vehLicenseNo), and the other attributes include make and model. In this example, you place all the attributes for the Staff and Car entities into one table. You choose one of the primary keys to be the primary key of the new table, staffNo say, and the other becomes an alternate key, as shown in Figure 9.4(b).

Figure 9.4

The 1:1 Staff *Uses* Car relationship with mandatory participation for both entities: (a) ER model; (b) representation as a table using the DBDL.

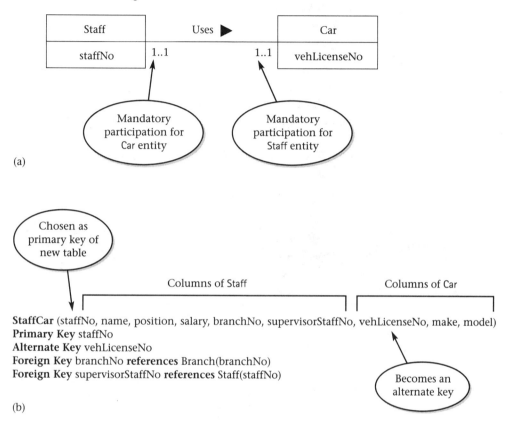

(a)

StaffCar (staffNo, name, position, salary, branchNo, supervisorStaffNo, vehLicenseNo, make, model)
Primary Key staffNo
Alternate Key vehLicenseNo
Foreign Key branchNo **references** Branch(branchNo)
Foreign Key supervisorStaffNo **references** Staff(staffNo)

(b)

In the case where a 1:1 relationship with mandatory participation on both sides has one or more attributes, these attributes should also be included in the table that represents the entities and relationship. For example, if the **Staff** *Uses* **Car** relationship had an attribute called **dateStart**, this attribute would also appear as a column in the **StaffCar** table.

Note that it is only possible to merge two entities into one table when there are no other relationships between these entities that would prevent this, such as a 1:* relationship. If this were the case, you would need to represent the Staff *Uses* Car relationship using the primary key/foreign key mechanism. We discuss how to designate the parent and child entities in this type of situation in part (3) shortly.

Mandatory participation on one side of a 1:1 relationship

In this case, you are able to identify the parent and child entities for the 1:1 relationship using the participation constraints. The entity that has optional participation in the relationship is designated as the parent entity, and the entity that has mandatory participation in the relationship is designated as the child entity. As described above, a copy of the primary key of the parent entity is placed in the table representing the child entity.

Let's now consider how you would represent the 1:1 Staff *Uses* Car relationship with mandatory participation only for the Car entity, as shown in Figure 9.5(a). The entity that has optional participation in the relationship (Staff) is designated as the parent entity, and the entity that has mandatory participation in the relationship (Car) is designated as the child entity. Therefore, a copy of the primary key of the Staff (parent) entity, staffNo, is placed in the Car (child) table, as shown in Figure 9.5(b). In this case, staffNo also becomes an alternate key for the Car table.

Figure 9.5

The 1:1 Staff *Uses* Car relationship with mandatory participation for the Car entity and optional participation for the Staff entity: (a) ER model; (b) representation as tables using the DBDL.

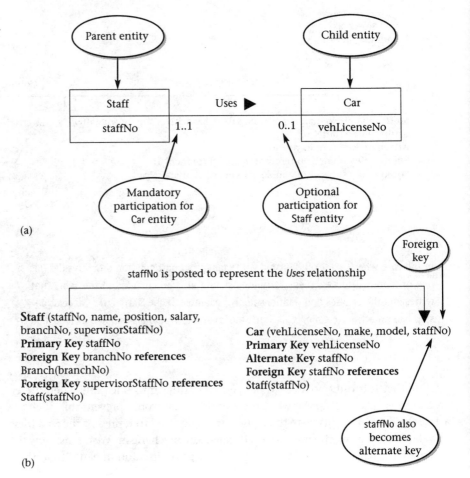

Figure 8.16 has a second example of a 1:1 relationship with mandatory participation on only one side, namely Staff *Manages* Branch with mandatory participation only for the Branch entity. Following the rules given above, the Staff entity is designated as the parent entity and the Branch entity is designated as the child entity. Therefore, a copy of the primary key of the Staff (parent) entity, staffNo, is placed in the Branch (child) table and renamed as mgrStaffNo, to more clearly indicate the purpose of the foreign key in the Branch table. Figure 9.6(a) shows the Staff *Manages* Branch ER model and Figure 9.6(b) shows the corresponding tables.

> In the case where a 1:1 relationship with only mandatory participation for one entity in a relationship has one or more attributes, these attributes should follow the posting of the primary key to the child table. For example, if the **Staff *Manages* Branch** relationship had an attribute called **dateStart**, this attribute would appear as a column in the **Branch** table along with a copy of **staffNo** (renamed **mgrStaffNo**).

Optional participation on both sides of a 1:1 relationship
In this case, the designation of the parent and child entities is arbitrary unless you can find out more about the relationship that can help you reach a decision one way or the other.

Let's consider how you would represent the 1:1 Staff *Uses* Car relationship, with optional participation on both sides of the relationship, as shown in Figure 9.7(a). (Note that the discussion that follows is also relevant for 1:1 relationships with mandatory participation for both entities where you cannot select the option to put everything into a single table.) If you don't have any additional information to help you select the parent and child entities, your choice is arbitrary. In other words, you have the choice to post a copy of the primary key of the Staff entity to the Car entity, or vice versa.

However, let's assume you find that the majority of cars, but not all, are used by staff and only a minority of staff use cars. Now you can say that the Car entity, although optional, is closer to being mandatory than the Staff entity. You can therefore designate Staff as the parent entity and Car as the child entity, and post a copy of the primary key of the Staff entity (staffNo) into the Car table, as shown in Figure 9.7(b). (The composition of the Staff and Car tables is the same as the example used in the discussion above on 1:1 relationships with mandatory participation on only one side.)

Figure 9.6

The 1:1 Staff *Manages* Branch relationship with mandatory participation for the Branch entity and optional participation for the Staff entity: (a) ER model; (b) representation as tables using the DBDL.

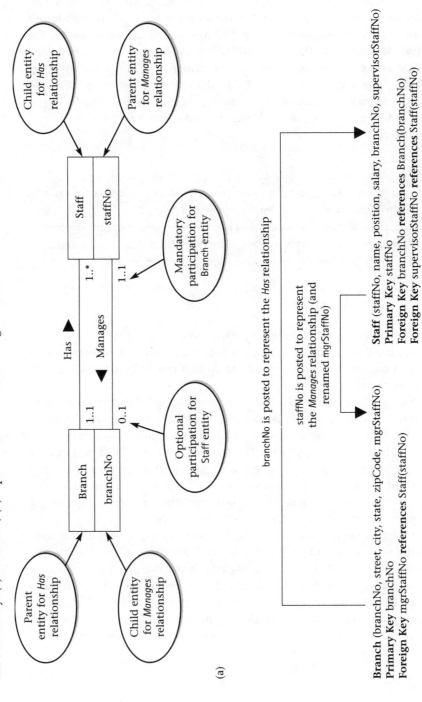

Figure 9.7

The 1:1 **Staff** *Uses* **Car** relationship with optional participation for both entities: (a) ER model; (b) representation as tables using the DBDL.

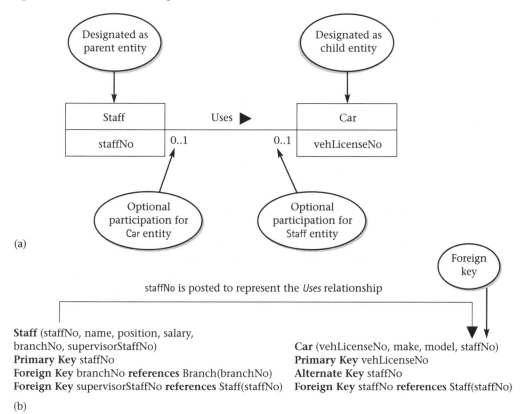

(a)

staffNo is posted to represent the *Uses* relationship

Staff (staffNo, name, position, salary,
branchNo, supervisorStaffNo)
Primary Key staffNo
Foreign Key branchNo **references** Branch(branchNo)
Foreign Key supervisorStaffNo **references** Staff(staffNo)

Car (vehLicenseNo, make, model, staffNo)
Primary Key vehLicenseNo
Alternate Key staffNo
Foreign Key staffNo **references** Staff(staffNo)

(b)

One-to-one (1:1) recursive relationships

For a 1:1 recursive relationship, you should follow the rules for participation as described above for a 1:1 relationship. However, in this special case of a 1:1 relationship, the entity on both sides of the relationship is the same. For a 1:1 recursive relationship with mandatory participation on both sides, you should represent the recursive relationship as a single table with two copies of the primary key. As before, one copy of the primary key represents a foreign key and should be renamed to indicate the relationship it represents.

For a 1:1 recursive relationship with mandatory participation on only one side, you have the option to create a single table with two copies of the primary key as described above, or to create a new table to represent the relationship. The new table would have only two columns, both copies of the primary key. As before, the copies of the primary keys act as foreign keys and have to be renamed to indicate the purpose of each in the table.

For a 1:1 recursive relationship with optional participation on both sides, you should create a new table as described above.

Summary of how to identify parent and child entities in a relationship

Table 9.1 gives a summary of how to identify the parent and child entities in a relationship.

Document tables and foreign key attributes

At the end of Step 2.1, you document the full composition of the tables created from the logical data model. The tables for the Branch view of the *StayHome* database application are shown in Figure 9.8.

Now that each table has its full set of columns, you're in a position to identify any new primary and/or alternate keys. This is particularly important for weak entities that rely on the posting of the primary key from the parent entity (or entities) to form a primary key of their own. For example, the weak entity Role now has a composite primary key made up of a copy of the primary key of the Video entity (catalogNo) and a copy of the primary key of the Actor entity (actorNo). Similarly, the weak entity Registration has a composite primary key made up of two foreign keys (branchNo and memberNo).

The DBDL syntax can be extended to show integrity constraints on the foreign keys, as you'll see in Step 2.4. The data dictionary should also be updated to indicate the presence of any new primary and alternate keys identified in this step. For example, following the posting of primary keys, the

Table 9.1 Summary of how to identify the parent and child entities in a relationship.

Relationship	Identification
1:* binary relationship	**parent:** 1 side; **child:** * side
1:* recursive relationship	**parent:** 1 side; **child:** * side
1:1 binary relationship:	
a) mandatory participation on both sides	combine tables into one table
b) mandatory participation on one side	**parent:** optional side; **child:** mandatory side
c) optional participation on both sides	arbitrary without further information
1:1 recursive relationship:	
a) mandatory participation on both sides	combine tables into one with two copies of primary key
b) mandatory participation on one side	as for a), or create new table to represent relationship
c) optional participation on both sides	create new table to represent relationship

Figure 9.8

Tables for the Branch view of the *StayHome* database application.

Actor (actorNo, actorName) **Primary Key** actorNo	**Branch** (branchNo, street, city, state, zipCode, mgrStaffNo) **Primary Key** branchNo **Alternate Key** zipCode **Foreign Key** mgrStaffNo **references** Staff(staffNo)
Director (directorNo, directorName) **Primary Key** directorNo	**Member** (memberNo, fName, lName, address) **Primary Key** memberNo
Registration (branchNo, memberNo, staffNo, dateJoined) **Primary Key** branchNo, memberNo **Foreign Key** branchNo **references** Branch(branchNo) **Foreign Key** memberNo **references** Member(memberNo) **Foreign Key** staffNo **references** Staff(staffNo)	**RentalAgreement** (rentalNo, dateOut, dateReturn, memberNo, videoNo) **Primary Key** rentalNo **Alternate Key** memberNo, videoNo, dateOut **Foreign Key** memberNo **references** Member(memberNo) **Foreign Key** videoNo **references** VideoForRent(videoNo)
Role (catalogNo, actorNo, character) **Primary Key** catalogNo, actorNo **Foreign Key** catalogNo **references** Video(catalogNo) **Foreign Key** actorNo **references** Actor(actorNo)	**Staff** (staffNo, name, position, salary, branchNo, supervisorStaffNo) **Primary Key** staffNo **Foreign Key** branchNo **references** Branch(branchNo) **Foreign Key** supervisorStaffNo **references** Staff(staffNo)
Telephone (telNo, branchNo) **Primary Key** telNo **Foreign Key** branchNo **references** Branch(branchNo)	**Video** (catalogNo, title, category, dailyRental, price, directorNo) **Primary Key** catalogNo **Foreign Key** directorNo **references** Director(directorNo)
VideoForRent (videoNo, available, catalogNo, branchNo) **Primary Key** VideoNo **Foreign Key** catalogNo **references** Video(catalogNo) **Foreign Key** branchNo **references** Branch(branchNo)	

RentalAgreement table has gained a new alternate key, which is a combination of memberNo, videoNo, and dateOut.

Step 2.2 Check table structures using normalization

Objective

To check, using normalization, that each table has an appropriate structure.

Normalization discussed in Chapter 6

The purpose of this step is to examine the groupings of columns in each table created in Step 2.1. You check the composition of each table using the rules of normalization, to avoid unnecessary duplication of data.

You should ensure that each table created in Step 2.1 is in at least third normal form (3NF). If you identify tables that are not in 3NF, this may indicate that part of the ER model is incorrect, or that you have introduced an error while creating the tables from the model. If necessary, you may need to restructure the data model and/or tables.

Step 2.3 Check tables support user transactions

Objective
To ensure that the tables support the transactions required by the view.

The objective of this step is to check that the tables created in Step 2.1 support the transactions required by the view, as documented in the users' requirements specification. This type of check was carried out in Step 1.8 to ensure that the local logical data model supported the required transactions. In this step, you check that the tables created in the previous steps also support these transactions, and thereby ensure that no error has been introduced while creating tables.

One approach to checking that the tables support a transaction is to examine the transaction's data requirements to ensure that the data is present in one or more tables. Also, if a transaction requires data in more than one table you should check that these tables can be linked through the primary key/foreign key mechanism. We demonstrate this approach by examining the transactions given in Section 4.4.4. Table 9.2(a) presents the data entry and update/deletion transactions and Table 9.2(b) presents the query transactions for the Branch view of *StayHome*, together with the tables required by each. In each case, we highlight the columns required by the transaction including, where necessary, those involved in joining tables.

From this analysis, you conclude that the tables shown in Figure 9.8 support all the transactions for the Branch view of *StayHome*. In Chapter 17, we'll demonstrate the implementation of some of the query transactions shown in Table 9.2(b) using the Microsoft Access DBMS.

Table 9.2(a) The tables required by the data entry and update/delete transactions of the Branch view of *StayHome*.

Transaction	Table(s) required
(a) Enter the details of a new branch. (g) Update/delete the details of a branch.	**Branch (branchNo, street, city, state, zipCode, mgrStaffNo)** **Telephone (telNo, branchNo)** Foreign Key branchNo references Branch(branchNo)
(b) Enter the details of a new member of staff at a branch (h) Update/delete the details of a member of staff at a branch	**Staff (staffNo, name, position, salary, branchNo, supervisorStaffNo)**
(c) Enter the details for a newly released video (i) Update/delete the details of a given video	**Video (catalogNo, title, category, dailyRental, price, directorNo)** Foreign Key directorNo references Director (directorNo) **Director (directorNo, directorName)** **Role (catalogNo, actorNo, character)** Foreign Key catalogNo references Video(catalogNo) Foreign Key actorNo references Actor(actorNo) **Actor (actorNo, actorName)**
(d) Enter the details of copies of a new video at a given branch (j) Update/delete the details of a copy of a video	**VideoForRent (videoNo, available, catalogNo, branchNo)**
(e) Enter the details of a new member registering at a given branch (k) Update/delete the details of a given member	**Member (memberNo, fName, lName, address)** **Registration (branchNo, memberNo, staffNo, dateJoined)** Foreign Key memberNo references Member(memberNo)
(f) Enter the details of a rental agreement for a member renting a video (l) Update/delete the details of a given rental agreement for a member renting a video	**RentalAgreement (rentalNo, dateOut, dateReturn, memberNo, videoNo)**

Table 9.2(b) The tables required by the query transactions of the Branch view of StayHome.

Transaction	Table(s) required
(m) List the details of branches in a given city.	**Branch (branchNo**, street, city, state, zipCode, **mgrStaffNo)** **Telephone (telNo**, branchNo) Foreign Key branchNo references Branch(branchNo)
(n) List the name, position, and salary of staff at a given branch, ordered by staff name.	**Staff (staffNo**, **name, position, salary**, branchNo, supervisorStaffNo)
(o) List the name of each Manager at each branch, ordered by branch number.	**Branch (branchNo**, street, city, state, zipCode, **mgrStaffNo)** Foreign Key mgrStaffNo references Staff (staffNo) **Staff (staffNo**, **name**, position, salary, branchNo, supervisorStaffNo)
(p) List the title, category, and availability of all videos at a specified branch, ordered by category.	**Video (catalogNo**, **title, category**, dailyRental, price, directorNo) **VideoForRent (videoNo**, **available**, catalogNo, **branchNo)** Foreign Key catalogNo references Video (catalogNo)
(q) List the title, category, and availability of all videos for a given actor's name at a specified branch, ordered by title.	**Actor (actorNo**, **actorName)** **Role (catalogNo**, **actorNo**, character) Foreign Key catalogNo references Video(catalogNo) Foreign Key actorNo references Actor(actorNo) **Video (catalogNo**, **title, category**, dailyRental, price, directorNo) **VideoForRent (videoNo**, **available**, catalogNo, **branchNo)** Foreign Key catalogNo references Video (catalogNo)
(r) List the title, category, and availability of all videos for a given director's name at a specified branch, ordered by title.	**Director (directorNo**, **directorName)** **Video (catalogNo**, **title, category**, dailyRental, price, **directorNo)** Foreign Key directorNo references Director (directorNo) **VideoForRent (videoNo**, **available**, catalogNo, **branchNo)** **Foreign Key catalogNo** references Video (catalogNo)
(s) List the details of all videos a specified member currently has on rent.	**Video (catalogNo**, **title**, category, **dailyRental, price**, directorNo) **VideoForRent (videoNo**, **available**, catalogNo, branchNo) Foreign Key catalogNo references Video (catalogNo) **RentalAgreement (rentalNo**, **dateOut, dateReturn, memberNo, videoNo)** Foreign Key videoNo references VideoForRent (videoNo) Foreign Key memberNo references Member (memberNo) **Member (memberNo**, **fName, lName**, address)
(t) List the details of copies of a given video at a specified branch.	**Video (catalogNo**, **title, category, dailyRental, price**, directorNo) **VideoForRent (videoNo**, **available**, catalogNo, **branchNo)** Foreign Key videoNo references VideoForRent (videoNo)

Table 9.2(b) *Continued*

Transaction	Table(s) required
(u) List the titles of all videos in a specified category, ordered by title.	**Video** (<u>catalogNo</u>, **title**, **category**, dailyRental, price, directorNo)
(v) List the total number of videos in each video category at each branch, ordered by branch number.	**Video** (<u>catalogNo,</u> title, **category**, dailyRental, price, directorNo) **VideoForRent** (<u>videoNo,</u> available, **catalogNo**, **branchNo**) Foreign Key catalogNo references Video (catalogNo)
(w) List the total cost of the videos at all branches.	**Video** (<u>catalogNo</u>, title, category, dailyRental, **price**, directorNo) **VideoForRent** (<u>videoNo</u>, available, **catalogNo**, branchNo) Foreign Key catalogNo references Video (catalogNo)
(x) List the total number of videos featuring each actor, ordered by actor name.	**Video** (<u>catalogNo</u>, title, category, dailyRental, price, directorNo) **Role** (<u>catalogNo</u>, <u>actorNo</u>, character) Foreign Key catalogNo references Video(catalogNo) Foreign Key actorNo references Actor(actorNo) **Actor** (<u>actorNo</u>, **actorName**)
(y) List the total number of members at each branch who joined in 1999, ordered by branch number.	**Registration** (<u>branchNo</u>, <u>memberNo</u>, staffNo, **dateJoined**)
(z) List the total possible daily rental for videos at each branch, ordered by branch number.	**Video** (<u>catalogNo</u>, title, category, **dailyRental**, price, directorNo) **VideoForRent** (videoNo, available, **catalogNo**, **branchNo**) Foreign Key catalogNo references Video(catalogNo)

TIP

As with Step 1.8 covered in the last chapter, this may look like a lot of hard work and it certainly can be. As a result, you may be tempted to omit this step. However, it's very important that you do these checks now rather than later when you'll find it much more difficult and costly to resolve any errors in your data model.

Step 2.4 Define integrity constraints

Objective
To define the integrity constraints given in the view of the company.

Integrity constraints are the constraints that you wish to impose in order to protect the database from becoming inconsistent. Although DBMS controls on integrity may or may not exist, this is not the question here. At this stage, you are concerned only with high-level design, that is, specifying *what* integrity constraints are required, irrespective of *how* this might be achieved. Having identified the integrity constraints, you will have a local logical data model that is a complete and accurate representation of the view. If necessary, you could produce a physical database design from the local logical data model, for example, to prototype the system for the user.

Prototyping discussed in Section 3.10

We consider the following five types of integrity constraints:

- required data,
- column domain constraints,
- entity integrity,
- referential integrity,
- business rules.

Required data

Nulls defined in Section 2.3.1

Some columns must always contain a value; in other words, they are not allowed to hold nulls. For example, every member of staff must have a job position (such as Manager or Supervisor). These constraints should have been identified when you documented the columns (attributes) in the data dictionary in Step 1.3.

Column domain constraints

Domains defined in Section 2.2.1

Every column has a domain (a set of values that are legal for it). For example, the position of a member of staff is Director, Manager, Supervisor, Assistant, or Buyer so the domain of the position column consists of these and only these values. These constraints should have been identified when you chose the column (attribute) domains for the data in Step 1.4.

Entity integrity

Entity integrity defined in Section 2.3.2

The primary key of an entity cannot hold nulls. For example, each record of the Staff table must have a value for the primary key column, staffNo. These constraints should have been considered when you identified the primary keys for each entity in Step 1.5.

Referential integrity

A foreign key links each record in the child table to the record in the parent table containing the matching primary key value. Referential integrity means that, if the foreign key contains a value, that value must refer to an existing record in the parent table. For example, the branchNo column in the Staff table links the member of staff to the record in the Branch table where he or she works. If branchNo is not null, it must contain a value that exists in the branchNo column of the Branch table, or the member of staff will be assigned to a non-existent branch.

Referential integrity defined in Section 2.3.3

There are two issues regarding foreign keys that must be addressed.

(1) Are nulls allowed for the foreign key?

For example, can you store the details of a member of staff without having a branch number for the employee? The issue is not whether the branch number exists, but whether a branch number must be specified. In general, if the participation of the child table in the relationship is mandatory, then the strategy is that nulls are not allowed. On the other hand, if the participation of the child table is optional, then nulls should be allowed.

Participation defined in Section 5.5.5

(2) How to ensure referential integrity

To do this, you specify **existence constraints**, which define conditions under which a primary key or foreign key may be inserted, updated, or deleted. Consider the 1:* relationship Branch *Has* Staff. The primary key of the Branch table (branchNo) is a foreign key in the Staff table. Let's consider the following six cases.

Case 1: Insert record into child table (Staff)
To ensure referential integrity, check that the foreign key column (branchNo) of the new Staff record is set to null or to a value of an existing Branch record.

Case 2: Delete record from child table (Staff)
If a record of a child table is deleted, referential integrity is unaffected.

Case 3: Update foreign key of child record (Staff)
This is similar to Case 1. To ensure referential integrity, check that the foreign key column (branchNo) of the updated Staff record is set to null or to a value of an existing Branch record.

Case 4: Insert record into parent table (Branch)
Inserting a record into the parent table (Branch) does not affect referential integrity; it simply becomes a parent without any children – in other words, a branch without members of staff.

Case 5: Delete record from parent table (Branch)

If a record of a parent table is deleted, referential integrity is lost if there is a child record referencing the deleted parent record. In other words, referential integrity is lost if the deleted branch currently has one or more members of staff working at it. There are several actions you can consider in this case:

- ■ NO ACTION Prevent a deletion from the parent table if there are any referenced child records. In our example, 'You cannot delete a branch if there are currently members of staff working there.'

- ■ CASCADE When the parent record is deleted, automatically delete any referenced child records. If any deleted child record also acts as a parent record in another relationship then the delete operation should be applied to the records in this child table, and so on in a cascading manner. In other words, deletions from the parent table cascade to the child table. In our example, 'Deleting a branch automatically deletes all members of staff working there.' Clearly, in this situation, this strategy would not be wise.

- ■ SET NULL When a parent record is deleted, the foreign key values in all related child records are automatically set to null. In our example, 'If a branch is deleted, indicate that the current branch for those members of staff previously working there is unknown.' You can only consider this strategy if the columns comprising the foreign key can accept nulls, as defined in Step 1.3.

- ■ SET DEFAULT When a parent record is deleted, the foreign key values in all related child records are automatically set to their default values. In our example, 'If a branch is deleted, indicate that the current assignment of members of staff previously working there is being assigned to another (default) branch.' You can only consider this strategy if the columns comprising the foreign key have default values, as defined in Step 1.3.

- ■ NO CHECK When a parent record is deleted, do nothing to ensure that referential integrity is maintained. This strategy should only be considered in extreme circumstances.

Case 6: Update primary key of parent record (Branch)

If the primary key value of a parent table record is updated, referential integrity is lost if there exists a child record referencing the old primary key value: that is, if the updated branch currently has staff working there. To ensure referential integrity, the strategies described above can be used. In the case of CASCADE, the updates to the primary key of the parent record are reflected in any referencing child records, and so on in a cascading manner.

The referential integrity constraints for the tables that have been created for the Branch view of *StayHome* are shown in Figure 9.9.

Business rules

Finally, you consider constraints known as business rules. Updates to entities may be constrained by business rules governing the 'real world' transactions that are represented by the updates. For example, *StayHome* has a business rule that prevents a member from renting more than 10 videos at any one time.

Document all integrity constraints

Document all integrity constraints in the data dictionary for consideration during physical database design.

Figure 9.9

The referential integrity constraints for the tables in the Branch view of *StayHome*.

Branch
Foreign Key mgrStaffNo **references** Staff(staffNo) ON UPDATE CASCADE ON DELETE NO ACTION

Registration
Foreign Key branchNo **references** Branch(branchNo) ON UPDATE CASCADE ON DELETE NO ACTION
Foreign Key memberNo **references** Member(memberNo) ON UPDATE CASCADE ON DELETE NO ACTION
Foreign Key staffNo **references** Staff(staffNo) ON UPDATE CASCADE ON DELETE NO ACTION

RentalAgreement
Foreign Key memberNo **references** Member(memberNo) ON UPDATE CASCADE ON DELETE NO ACTION
Foreign Key videoNo **references** VideoForRent(videoNo) ON UPDATE CASCADE ON DELETE NO ACTION

Role
Foreign Key catalogNo **references** Video(catalogNo) ON UPDATE CASCADE ON DELETE CASCADE
Foreign Key actorNo **references** Actor(actorNo) ON UPDATE CASCADE ON DELETE NO ACTION

Staff
Foreign Key branchNo **references** Branch(branchNo) ON UPDATE CASCADE ON DELETE NO ACTION
Foreign Key supervisorStaffNo **references** Staff(staffNo) ON UPDATE CASCADE ON DELETE SET NULL

Telephone
Foreign Key branchNo **references** Branch(branchNo) ON UPDATE CASCADE ON DELETE CASCADE

Video
Foreign Key directorNo **references** Director(directorNo) ON UPDATE CASCADE ON DELETE NO ACTION

VideoForRent
Foreign Key catalogNo **references** Video(catalogNo) ON UPDATE CASCADE ON DELETE NO ACTION
Foreign Key branchNo **references** Branch(branchNo) ON UPDATE CASCADE ON DELETE NO ACTION

Step 2.5 Review local logical data model with users

> **Objective**
> To ensure that the local logical data model and documentation that describes the model is a true representation of the view.

The local logical data model for the view should now be complete and fully documented. However, to finish this step you should review the data model and the supporting documentation with the users.

If you're designing a database that has only a single view, then you are ready to proceed to physical database design, which we'll describe in Chapters 12 to 16. If, however, you're designing a database that has multiple views and you're using the view integration approach then you should move on to Step 3 of the methodology, which we describe in the following chapter.

View integration approach discussed in Sections 3.5 and 4.4

Chapter summary

✓ The main purpose of this step is to produce a description of the tables for each local logical data model created in Step 1 of the methodology. The set of tables produced should represent the entities, relationships, attributes, and constraints in the data model.

✓ **Tables** are created for the local logical data model, and their structures are checked using normalization.

✓ The table structures are also checked to ensure that they support the transactions defined by the view.

✓ **Integrity constraints** are the constraints that you wish to impose in order to protect the database from becoming inconsistent. There are five types of integrity constraints: required data, column domain constraints, entity integrity, referential integrity, and business rules.

✓ To ensure referential integrity, you specify *existence constraints*, which define conditions under which a primary key or foreign key may be inserted, updated, or deleted.

✓ There are several strategies to consider when a child record references the parent record that you're attempting to delete/update: NO ACTION, CASCADE, SET NULL, SET DEFAULT, and NO CHECK.

Chapter 10

Logical database design – Step 3

In this chapter you will learn:

◀ How to merge the local logical data models into a global logical data model of the company.

◀ How to ensure that the resultant global model is a true and accurate representation of the company (or part of the company) being modeled.

This chapter covers the third step of our logical database design methodology. This step is optional and is only required when you're creating a reasonably complex database application with several views and you have chosen to manage these views (wholly or partly) using the **view integration** approach. So assuming that you're using this approach, you should have created data models representing each view in Steps 1 and 2 of the methodology. You should now be ready to begin this step with two or more local logical data models.

Methodology summarized in Appendix B

View integration approach discussed in Sections 3.5 and 4.4.4

In Chapter 4, we identified several user views for the *StayHome* database application, namely Director, Manager, Supervisor, Assistant, and Buyer. Following analysis of the requirements for each user view, we decided to manage these views using a mixture of the centralized and view integration approaches. We used the centralized approach to merge the requirements for the Manager, Supervisor, and Assistant user views into a view called *Branch* and merged the requirements for the Director and Buyer user views into a view called *Business*. In Chapters 8 and 9, we used the Branch view to demonstrate the building of a local logical data model using Steps 1 and 2 of the methodology. The ER model was shown in Figure 8.16 and a description of the tables was shown in Figure 9.8.

In this chapter, we first present the users' requirements specification for the Business view of *StayHome*. We don't demonstrate the building of the local logical data model for this view but instead present important components of the logical model, namely the ER model and a description of the tables based on this model. We then use the local logical data models for the Branch and Business views to demonstrate Step 3 of the methodology.

10.1 The Business view of *StayHome*

In this section, we present the users' requirements specification for the Business view of *StayHome* and the corresponding local logical data model.

> **TIP** It may be useful if you read the requirements in the following section and then attempt Steps 1 and 2 of the methodology yourself. You can then check your solution against our sample solution.

10.1.1 Users' requirements specification

The requirements specification for the Business view is listed in two sections: one that describes the data used by the Business view and one that provides examples of how the data is used (that is, the transactions that staff associated with the Business view have to perform on the data).

Data requirements

The details held on a branch of *StayHome* are the branch address and the telephone number. Each branch is given a branch number, which is unique throughout the company.

Each branch of *StayHome* has staff, which includes a Manager. The details held on a member of staff are his or her name, position, and salary. Each member of staff is given a staff number, which is unique throughout the company.

Each branch of *StayHome* is allocated a stock of videos. The details held on a video are the catalog number, video number, title, category, daily rental rate, and purchase price. The catalog number uniquely identifies each video. However, in most cases there are several copies of each video at a branch, and the individual copies are identified using the video number.

Each branch of *StayHome* receives videos from video suppliers. The details held on video suppliers are the supplier number, name, address, telephone number, and status. Orders for videos are placed with these suppliers and the details held on a video order are the order number, supplier number, supplier address, video catalog number, video title, video purchase price, quantity, date order placed, date order received, and the address of the branch receiving the order.

A customer of *StayHome* must first register as a member of a local branch of *StayHome*. The details held on a member are name, address, and the date that the member registered at a branch. Each member is given a member number, which is unique throughout all branches of the company and is used even when a member chooses to register at more than one branch.

The details held on each video rented are the rental number, full name and member number, the video number, title, and daily rental rate, and the dates the video is rented out and returned. The rental number is unique throughout the company.

Transaction requirements

Data entry

(a) Enter the details for a newly released video (such as details of a video called *Independence Day*).

(b) Enter the details of a video supplier (such as a supplier called *WorldView Videos*).

(c) Enter the details of a video order (such as ordering 10 copies of *Saving Private Ryan* for branch B002).

Data update/deletion

(d) Update/delete the details of a given video.

(e) Update/delete the details of a given video supplier.

(f) Update/delete the details of a given video order.

Data queries

(g) List the name, position, and salary of staff at all branches, ordered by branch number.

(h) List the name and telephone number of the Manager at a given branch.

(i) List the catalog number and title of all videos at a given branch, ordered by title.

(j) List the number of copies of a given video at a given branch.

(k) List the number of members at each branch, ordered by branch number.

(l) List the number of members who joined this year at each branch, ordered by branch number.

(m) List the number of video rentals at each branch between certain dates, ordered by branch number.

(n) List the number of videos in each category at a given branch, ordered by category.

(o) List the name, address, and telephone number of all video suppliers, ordered by supplier number.

(p) List the name and telephone number of a video supplier.

(q) List the details of all video orders placed with a given supplier, ordered by the date of order.

(r) List the details of all video orders placed on a certain date.

(s) List the total daily rentals for videos at each branch between certain dates, ordered by branch number.

10.1.2 Local logical data model

As we've just mentioned, rather than go through the process of building the local logical data model for the Business view of *StayHome*, we assume instead that this model was produced using Steps 1 and 2 of the methodology and present the important components of the logical model, namely:

■ the ER model, shown in Figure 10.1

■ the tables, shown in Figure 10.2.

Let's now use the Branch and Business local logical data models to build a global logical data model for the *StayHome* database application.

Step 3   Build and check global logical data model

Objective
To combine the individual local logical data models into a single global logical data model that represents the company (or part of the company) that is being modeled.

In this step, you build a global logical data model by merging together the individual local logical data models produced for each view. Recall that a local logical data model can represent a single user view or more than one user view (given a collective name and referred to simply as a **view**), whereas the global logical data model represents *all* user views. Having combined the

Figure 10.1

ER model for the Business view of *StayHome.*

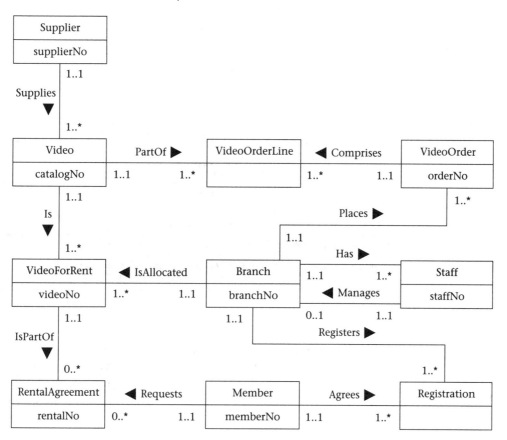

models together, it may be necessary to check that the global model is appropriately normalized and that the global model still supports the required transactions, as you did in Steps 2.2 and 2.3 covered in the last chapter. However, you need only check those areas of the model that resulted in any change during the merging process. In a large system, this will significantly reduce the amount of rechecking that needs to be performed.

Although each local logical data model should be correct, comprehensive, and unambiguous, each model is only a representation of a view of the

Figure 10.2

Tables for the Business view of *StayHome*.

Branch (branchNo, address, telNo, mgrStaffNo) **Primary Key** branchNo **Alternate Key** telNo **Foreign Key** mgrStaffNo **references** Staff(staffNo)	**Member** (memberNo, name, address) **Primary Key** memberNo
Registration (branchNo, memberNo, dateJoined) **Primary Key** branchNo, memberNo **Foreign Key** branchNo **references** Branch(branchNo) **Foreign Key** memberNo **references** Member(memberNo)	**RentalAgreement** (rentalNo, dateOut, dateReturn, memberNo, videoNo) **Primary Key** rentalNo **Alternate Key** memberNo, videoNo, dateOut **Foreign Key** memberNo **references** Member(memberNo) **Foreign Key** videoNo **references** Video(videoNo)
Staff (staffNo, name, position, salary, branchNo) **Primary Key** staffNo **Foreign Key** branchNo **references** Branch(branchNo)	**Supplier** (supplierNo, sName, sAddress, sTelNo, status) **Primary Key** supplierNo **Alternate Key** sTelNo
Video (catalogNo,title, category, dailyRental, price, supplierNo) **Primary Key** catalogNo **Foreign Key** supplierNo **references** Supplier(supplierNo)	**VideoForRent** (videoNo, available, catalogNo, branchNo) **Primary Key** videoNo **Foreign Key** catalogNo **references** Video(catalogNo) **Foreign Key** branchNo **references** Branch(branchNo)
VideoOrder (orderNo, dateOrdered, dateReceived, branchNo) **Primary Key** orderNo **Foreign Key** branchNo **references** Branch(branchNo)	**VideoOrderLine** (orderNo, catalogNo, quantity) **Primary Key** orderNo, catalogNo **Foreign Key** orderNo **references** VideoOrder(orderNo) **Foreign Key** catalogNo **references** Video(catalogNo)

company. In other words, the model is not strictly a model of the function of the company, but it's a model of one or more views and hence may not be complete. This may mean that there may be inconsistencies as well as overlaps when you look at the complete set of views. Thus, when you merge the local logical data models into a single global model, you must resolve conflicts between the views and any overlaps that exist.

The tasks involved in Step 3 are:

■ Step 3.1 Merge local logical data models into global model

■ Step 3.2 Check global logical data model

■ Step 3.3 Check for future growth

■ Step 3.4 Review global logical data model with users

Step 3.1 Merge local logical data models into global model

Objective
To merge the individual local logical data models into a single global logical data model.

Up to this point, for each local logical data model you have produced an ER model, a set of tables, a data dictionary, and supporting documentation that describes the constraints on the model. In this step, you use these components to identify the similarities and differences between the models, to help merge the models.

For simple database applications with a relatively small number of entities/tables, it's an easy task to compare the local models, merge them together, and resolve any differences that exist. However, in a large system, a more systematic approach must be taken. We present one approach that may be used to merge the local models together and resolve any inconsistencies found. Some typical tasks of this approach are:

(1) Review the names of entities/tables and their primary keys.

(2) Review the names of relationships.

(3) Merge entities/tables from the local data models.

(4) Include (without merging) entities/tables unique to each local data model.

(5) Merge relationships from the local data models.

(6) Include (without merging) relationships unique to each local data model.

(7) Check for missing entities/tables and relationships.

(8) Check foreign keys.

(9) Check integrity constraints.

(10) Draw the global logical data model.

(11) Update the documentation.

In some of the above tasks, we have used the term 'entities/tables'. We have done this because you may prefer to examine the ER models and their supporting documentation or you may prefer to examine the tables that have been produced from the ER models, or even use a combination of both approaches.

> **TIP** Perhaps the easiest way to merge several local data models together is to first merge two of the data models to produce a new model, and then to successively merge the remaining local data models until all the local models are represented in the final global data model. This may prove a simpler approach than trying to merge all the local data models at the same time.

To ensure that you are comparing like with like, it's important that each local model has been created following Steps 1 and 2 of the methodology. For example, it may be difficult to compare models if you have removed complex and redundant relationships from one model, but have left them in other models.

Review the names of entities/tables and their primary keys

It may be worthwhile reviewing the names of entities/tables that appear in the local data models by inspecting the data dictionary. Problems can arise when two or more entities/tables:

■ have the same name but are, in fact, different (homonyms);

■ are the same but have different names (synonyms).

It may be necessary to compare the data content of each entity/table to resolve these problems. In particular, you may use the primary keys to help identify equivalent entities/tables that may be named differently across views. A comparison of the entities/tables and primary keys in the Branch and Business views of *StayHome* are shown in Table 10.1. The entities/tables that are distinct to each view are highlighted.

Review the names of relationships

This activity is the same as that described for entities/tables. A comparison of the relationships in the Branch and Business views of *StayHome* is shown in Table 10.2. The relationships that are distinct to each view are again highlighted.

Table 10.1 Comparison of entities/tables and primary keys for the Branch and Business views of *StayHome.*

Branch view		Business view	
Table	Primary key	Table	Primary key
Branch	branchNo	Branch	branchNo
Staff	staffNo	Staff	staffNo
Telephone	**telNo**		
Video	catalogNo	Video	catalogNo
VideoForRent	videoNo	VideoForRent	videoNo
		Supplier	**supplierNo**
		VideoOrder	**orderNo**
		VideoOrderLine	**orderNo, catalogNo**
RentalAgreement	rentalNo	RentalAgreement	rentalNo
Member	memberNo	Member	memberNo
Registration	branchNo, memberNo	Registration	branchNo, memberNo
Actor	**actorNo**		
Role	**catalogNo, actorNo**		
Director	**directorNo**		

Merge entities/tables from the local data models

You should examine the name and content of each entity/table in the models to be merged to determine whether entities/tables represent the same thing and can therefore be merged. Typical activities involved in this task include:

- Merge entities/tables with the same name and the same primary key.
- Merge entities/tables with the same name using different primary keys.
- Merge entities/tables with different names using the same or different primary keys.

Table 10.2 Comparison of relationships for the Branch and Business views of *StayHome*.

Branch view			Business view		
Entity	Relationship	Entity	Entity	Relationship	Entity
Branch	Has	Staff	Branch	Has	Staff
Branch	IsAllocated	VideoForRent	Branch	IsAllocated	VideoForRent
Branch	**Provides**	**Telephone**			
Branch	Registers	Member	Branch	Registers	Member
			Branch	**Places**	**VideoOrder**
			VideoOrder	**Comprises**	**VideoOrderLine**
			Supplier	**Supplies**	**Video**
Staff	Manages	Branch	Staff	Manages	Branch
Staff	**Supervises**	**Staff**			
Staff	**Processes**	**Registration**			
Video	Is	VideoForRent	Video	Is	VideoForRent
Video	**Features**	**Role**	**Video**	**PartOf**	**VideoOrderLine**
VideoForRent	IsPartOf	RentalAgreement	VideoForRent	IsPartOf	RentalAgreement
Member	Agrees	Registration	Member	Agrees	Registration
Member	Requests	RentalAgreement	Member	Requests	RentalAgreement
Actor	**Plays**	**Role**			
Director	**Directs**	**Video**			

Merge entities/tables with the same name and the same primary key Generally, entities/tables with the same primary key represent the same 'real world' object and should be merged. The merged entity/table includes the attributes/columns from the original entities/tables with duplicates removed. For example, Figure 10.3 lists the columns associated with the two Member tables defined in the Branch and Business views. As the primary key of both tables is memberNo, you should merge these two tables together by combining their columns, so that the merged Member table now has all the columns associated with the original tables.

Note that there is conflict between the views on how you should represent the name of a member. In this situation, you should (if possible) consult the users of each view to determine the final representation. In this example, the Branch view with the fName and lName columns is used in the merged global logical data model.

Figure 10.3

Merging the Member tables from the Branch and Business views.

(**Branch View**)   (**Business View**)

Member (memberNo, fName, lName, address)   **Member** (memberNo, name, address)
Primary Key memberNo   **Primary Key** memberNo

Member (memberNo, fName, lName, address)   } **Global logical**
Primary Key memberNo   **data model**

Merge entities/tables with the same name using different primary keys In some situations, you may find two entities/tables with the same name and similar candidate keys, but with different primary keys. In this case, the entities/tables should be merged together as described above. However, it's necessary to choose one key to be the primary key, with the others becoming alternate keys.

Merge entities/tables with different names using the same or different primary keys. In some cases, you may identify entities/tables that have different names but appear to have the same purpose. These equivalent entities/tables may be recognized simply by:

■ their name, which indicates their similar purpose;

■ their content and, in particular, their primary key;

■ their association with particular relationships.

Include (without merging) entities/tables unique to each local data model

The previous tasks should identify all entities/tables that are the same. All remaining entities/tables are included in the global model without change. From Table 10.1, the entities/tables unique to the Branch view are Telephone, Actor, Role, and Director, and to the Business view are Supplier, VideoOrder, and VideoOrderLine.

Merge relationships from the local data models

In this step, you examine the name and purpose of each relationship in all the data models. Before merging relationships, it's important to resolve any conflicts between the relationships such as differences in multiplicity constraints. The activities in this step include merging relationships with the same name and the same purpose, and then merging relationships with different names but the same purpose. For example, the Branch *Has* Staff relationship occurs in both the Branch and Business views. We continue the process of merging the relationships that are common between the views shown in Table 10.2.

Include (without merging) relationships unique to each local data model

Again, the previous task should identify relationships that are the same (by definition, they must be between the same entities/tables, which would have been merged together earlier). All remaining relationships are included in the global model without change. From Table 10.2, the relationships unique to the Branch view include Branch *Provides* Telephone, Staff *Supervises* Staff, Staff *Processes* Registration, Video *Features* Role, Actor *Plays* Role, and Director *Directs* Video. The relationships unique to the Business view include Branch *Places* VideoOrder, VideoOrder *Comprises* VideoOrderLine, Supplier *Supplies* Video, and Video *PartOf* VideoOrderLine.

Check for missing entities/tables and relationships

Perhaps one of the most difficult tasks in producing the global model is identifying missing entities/tables and relationships between different local data models. If a corporate data model exists for the company, this may reveal entities/tables and relationships that do not appear in any local data model. Alternatively, as a preventative measure, when interviewing the users of a specific view, ask them to pay particular attention to the entities/tables and relationships that exist in other views. Otherwise, examine the attributes/columns of each entity/table and look for references to entities/tables in other local data models. You may find that you have an attribute/column associated with an entity/table in one local data model that corresponds to a primary key, alternate key, or even a **nonkey attribute/column** of an entity/table in another local data model.

Check foreign keys

During this step, entities/tables and relationships may have been merged, primary keys changed, and new relationships identified. Check that the foreign keys in child tables are still correct, and make any necessary modifications that are required.

Figure 10.4

The global logical data model for the *StayHome* database application.

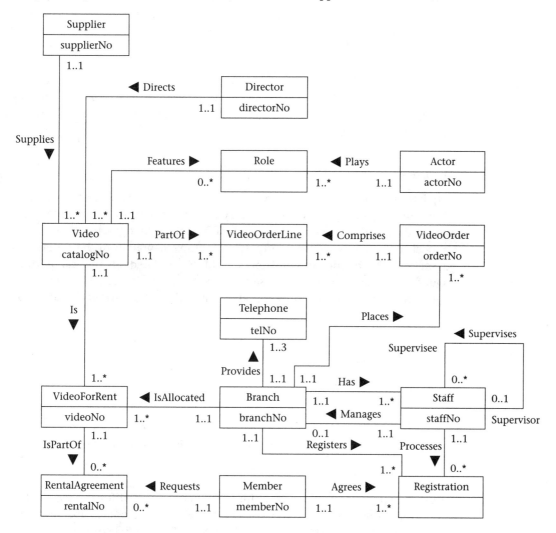

Check integrity constraints

Check that the integrity constraints for the global logical data model do not conflict with those originally specified for each user view. Any conflicts must be resolved in consultation with the users.

Draw the global logical data model

You now draw an ER model of the global data model that represents all the merged local data models. The global ER model for the *StayHome* database is shown in Figure 10.4.

Update the documentation

Update the documentation to reflect any changes made during the development of the global data model. It's very important that the documentation is up to date and reflects the current data model. If changes are made to the model subsequently, either during database implementation or during maintenance, then the documentation should be updated at the same time. Out-of-date information will cause considerable confusion at a later time. The tables that represent the global logical data model for the *StayHome* database are shown in Figure 10.5.

Step 3.2 Check global logical data model

> **Objective**
> To check that the tables created from the global logical data model are appropriately structured using normalization and support the required transactions, if necessary.

In this step you check the structure of the tables created for the global data model using normalization and also check that these tables are capable of supporting all user transactions, as you did in Steps 2.2 and 2.3 covered in the last chapter. However, you need only check those areas of the model that resulted in any change during the merging process. In a large system, this will significantly reduce the amount of rechecking that needs to be performed.

Figure 10.5

Table structures for the global logical data model of *StayHome*.

Actor (actorNo, actorName) **Primary Key** actorNo	**Branch** (branchNo, street, city, state, zipCode, mgrStaffNo) **Primary Key** branchNo **Alternate Key** zipCode **Foreign Key** mgrStaffNo **references** Staff(staffNo)
Director (directorNo, directorName) **Primary Key** directorNo	**Member** (memberNo, fName, lName, address) **Primary Key** memberNo
Registration (branchNo, memberNo, staffNo, dateJoined) **Primary Key** branchNo, memberNo **Foreign Key** branchNo **references** Branch(branchNo) **Foreign Key** memberNo **references** Member(memberNo) **Foreign Key** staffNo **references** Staff(staffNo)	**RentalAgreement** (rentalNo, dateOut, dateReturn, memberNo, videoNo) **Primary Key** rentalNo **Alternate Key** memberNo, videoNo, dateOut **Foreign Key** memberNo **references** Member(memberNo) **Foreign Key** videoNo **references** Video(videoNo)
Role (catalogNo, actorNo, character) **Primary Key** catalogNo, actorNo **Foreign Key** catalogNo **references** Video(catalogNo) **Foreign Key** actorNo **references** Actor(actorNo)	**Staff** (staffNo, name, position, salary, branchNo, supervisorStaffNo) **Primary Key** staffNo **Foreign Key** branchNo **references** Branch(branchNo) **Foreign Key** supervisorStaffNo **references** Staff(staffNo)
Supplier (supplierNo, name, address, telNo, status) **Primary Key** supplierNo **Alternate Key** telNo	**Telephone** (telNo, branchNo) **Primary Key** telNo **Foreign Key** branchNo **references** Branch(branchNo)
Video (catalogNo, title, category, dailyRental, price, directorNo, supplierNo) **Primary Key** catalogNo **Foreign Key** directorNo **references** Director(directorNo) **Foreign Key** supplierNo **references** Supplier(supplierNo)	**VideoForRent**(videoNo, available, catalogNo, branchNo) **Primary Key** videoNo **Foreign Key** catalogNo **references** Video(catalogNo) **Foreign Key** branchNo **references** Branch(branchNo)
VideoOrder (orderNo, dateOrdered, dateReceived, branchNo) **Primary Key** orderNo **Foreign Key** branchNo **references** Branch(branchNo)	**VideoOrderLine** (orderNo, catalogNo, quantity) **Primary Key** orderNo, catalogNo **Foreign Key** orderNo **references** VideoOrder(orderNo) **Foreign Key** catalogNo **references** Video(catalogNo)

Objective

To determine whether there are any significant changes likely in the foreseeable future and to assess whether the global logical data model can accommodate these changes.

Step 3.3 Check for future growth

It's important that the global logical data model can be easily expanded. If the model can sustain current requirements only, then the life of the model may be relatively short and significant reworking may be necessary to accommodate new requirements. It's important to develop a model that is *extensible*, and has the ability to evolve to support new requirements with minimal effect on existing users. Of course, this can be very difficult to achieve, as the company may not know what it wants to do in the future. Even if it does, it may be prohibitively expensive both in time and money to accommodate possible future enhancements now. Therefore, you may have to be very selective in what you accommodate.

Step 3.4   Review global logical data model with users

Objective
To ensure that the global logical data model is a true representation of the company.

The global logical data model for the company should now be complete and accurate. The model and the documentation that describes the model should be reviewed with the users to ensure that it's a true representation of the company.

You are now ready to translate the logical design into a physical design. This is covered in Steps 4 to 8 of the methodology, which we describe in Chapters 12 to 16.

Chapter summary

 Step 3 of the logical database design methodology is optional and only required when creating a reasonably complex database application with multiple views that are to be managed using the **view integration** approach.

Chapter 11

Advanced modeling techniques

In this chapter you will learn:

The limitations of the basic ER modeling concepts and the ◄ requirements to model more complex applications using enhanced data modeling concepts.

The main concepts associated with the Enhanced Entity-Relationship ◄ (EER) model called specialization/generalization.

A diagrammatic technique for displaying specialization/generalization ◄ in an EER model.

How to create tables that represent specialization/generalization ◄ in an EER model.

We covered the basic concepts associated with Entity-Relationship (ER) modeling in Chapter 5, and used these concepts in the construction of ER models in the logical database design methodology presented in Chapters 8 to 10. These basic concepts are normally adequate for the representation of the majority of data models for traditional, administrative-based database applications. However, for more complex database applications the basic ER concepts can be limiting. This stimulated the need to develop additional 'semantic' modeling concepts. The original ER model with additional semantic concepts is referred to as the **Enhanced Entity-Relationship** (EER) model. In this chapter, we describe one of the most useful concepts associated with the EER model called specialization/generalization and show how it can be used.

The database design methodology presented in this book provides an option to use the additional concepts of the EER model in Step 1.6. The choice of

Methodology summarized in Appendix B

whether to use this step is dependent on the complexity of the company (or part of the company) being modeled and whether using these additional modeling concepts will help the process of database design.

11.1 Specialization/Generalization

The concept of specialization/generalization is associated with special types of entities known as **superclasses** and **subclasses**, and the process of **attribute inheritance**. We begin this section by defining what superclasses and subclasses are and examining superclass/subclass relationships. We describe the process of attribute inheritance and contrast the process of specialization with generalization. We also show how to represent specialization/generalization diagrammatically using the UML (Unified Modeling Language) notation.

Superclass
An entity that holds common attributes and relationships for all occurrences in the entity.

Subclass
An entity that has a distinct role and holds specific attributes and relationships for some occurrences in the (superclass) entity.

1:1 relationships defined in Section 5.5.1

11.1.1 Superclasses and subclasses

A general entity called a superclass includes more specific kinds of entities called subclasses. For example, an entity that may have many distinct subclasses is Staff. The entities that are members of the Staff entity may be classified as Manager, Secretary, and SalesPersonnel. In other words, the Staff entity is the superclass of the Manager, Secretary, and SalesPersonnel subclasses.

11.1.2 Superclass/Subclass relationships

The relationship between a superclass and any one of its subclasses is one-to-one (1:1) and is called a superclass/subclass relationship. For example, Staff/Manager forms a superclass/subclass relationship. Each member of a subclass is also a member of the superclass but has a distinct role.

We can use superclasses and subclasses to avoid describing different types of entities with possibly different attributes within a single entity. For example, SalesPersonnel may have special attributes such as salesArea and carAllowance, and so on. If all staff attributes and those specific to particular jobs are represented by a single Staff entity, this may result in a lot of nulls for the job-specific attributes. Clearly, Sales Personnel have common attributes with other staff, such as staffNo, name, position, and salary, but it's the unshared attributes that cause problems when we try to represent all members of staff within a single entity. Defining superclasses/subclasses can also allow us to show relationships that are only associated with particular subclasses of staff and not with staff in general. For example, Sales Personnel may have distinct relationships that are not appropriate for all staff, such as SalesPersonnel *Requires* Car.

To illustrate the points being made above, let's consider the table called AllStaff in Figure 11.1. This table holds the details of all members of staff no matter what

Figure 11.1

The AllStaff table holding details of all members of staff.

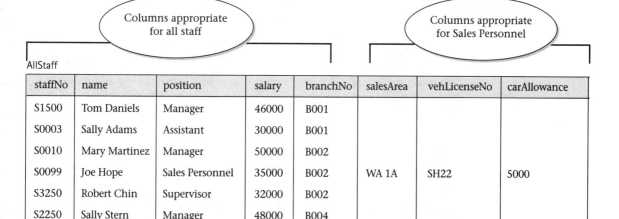

AllStaff

staffNo	name	position	salary	branchNo	salesArea	vehLicenseNo	carAllowance
S1500	Tom Daniels	Manager	46000	B001			
S0003	Sally Adams	Assistant	30000	B001			
S0010	Mary Martinez	Manager	50000	B002			
S0099	Joe Hope	Sales Personnel	35000	B002	WA 1A	SH22	5000
S3250	Robert Chin	Supervisor	32000	B002			
S2250	Sally Stern	Manager	48000	B004			
S2345	Linda Haven	Sales Personnel	37500	B002	WA 2B	SH34	5000
S0415	Art Peters	Manager	41000	B003			

position they hold. A consequence of holding the details of all members of staff in one table is that while the columns appropriate to all staff are filled (namely, staffNo, name, position, salary, and branchNo), those that are applicable only to particular job roles will be only partially filled. For example, the columns associated with the SalesPersonnel subclass (namely salesArea, vehLicenseNo, and carAllowance) have no values for those members of staff not in this subclass.

> There are two important reasons for introducing the concepts of superclasses and subclasses into an ER model. The first is that it avoids describing similar concepts more than once, thereby saving you time and making the ER model more readable. The second reason is that it adds more semantic information to the design in a form that is familiar to many people. For example, the assertions that 'Manager IS-A member of staff' and 'van IS-A type of vehicle' communicate significant semantic content in an easy-to-follow form.

11.1.3 Attribute inheritance

As mentioned above, an entity occurrence in a subclass represents the same 'real world' object as in the superclass. Hence, a member of a subclass inherits those attributes associated with the superclass, but may also have subclass-specific attributes. For example, a member of the SalesPersonnel subclass has subclass-specific attributes, salesArea, vehLicenseNo, and carAllowance, and all the attributes of the Staff superclass, namely staffNo, name, position, salary, and branchNo.

A subclass is an entity in its own right and so it may also have one or more subclasses. A subclass with more than one superclass is called a *shared subclass*. In other words, a member of a shared subclass must be a member of the associated superclasses. As a consequence, the attributes of the superclasses are inherited by the shared subclass, which may also have its own additional attributes. This process is referred to as *multiple inheritance*.

> An entity and its subclasses and their subclasses, and so on, is called a **type hierarchy**. Type hierarchies are known by a variety of names including: **specialization hierarchy** (for example, **Manager** is a specialization of **Staff**), **generalization hierarchy** (for example, **Staff** is a generalization of **Manager**), and **IS-A hierarchy** (for example, **Manager** IS-A (member of) **Staff**). We describe the process of specialization and generalization in the following sections.

11.1.4 Specialization process

Specialization
The process of maximizing the differences between members of an entity by identifying their distinguishing characteristics.

Specialization is a top-down approach to defining a set of superclasses and their related subclasses. The set of subclasses is defined on the basis of some distinguishing characteristics of the entities in the superclass. When we identify a subclass of an entity, we then associate attributes specific to the subclass (where necessary), and also identify any relationships between the subclass and other entities or subclasses (where necessary).

11.1.5 Generalization process

Generalization
The process of minimizing the differences between entities by identifying their common features.

The process of generalization is a bottom-up approach, which results in the identification of a generalized superclass from the original subclasses. The process of generalization can be viewed as the reverse of the specialization process. For example, consider a model where Manager, Secretary, and SalesPersonnel are represented as distinct entities. If we apply the process of generalization on these entities, we attempt to identify any similarities between them such as common attributes and relationships. As stated earlier, these entities share attributes common to all staff, and therefore we would identify Manager, Secretary, and SalesPersonnel as subclasses of a generalized Staff superclass.

Diagrammatic representation

UML has a special notation for representing subclasses and superclasses. For example, consider the specialization/generalization of the Staff entity into subclasses that represent job roles. The Staff superclass and the Manager, Secretary, and SalesPersonnel subclasses can be represented diagrammatically in the EER model illustrated in Figure 11.2. Note that the Staff superclass and the subclasses, being entities, are represented as rectangles. Specialization/generalization subclasses are attached by lines to a triangle that points towards the superclass. The label below the triangle, shown as {Optional, And}, describes the constraints on the specialization/generalization relationship. These constraints are discussed in more detail in the following section.

Attributes that are specific to a given subclass are listed in the lower section of the rectangle representing that subclass. For example, the salesArea, vehLicenseNo, and carAllowance attributes are associated only with the SalesPersonnel subclass, and are not applicable to the Manager or Secretary subclasses. Similarly, we show attributes that are specific to the Manager (bonus) and Secretary (typingSpeed) subclasses.

Figure 11.2 also shows relationships that are applicable to specific subclasses or to just the superclass. For example, the Manager subclass is related to the

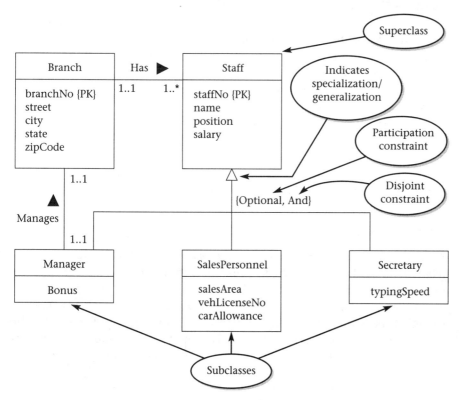

Figure 11.2

Specialization/ generalization of the **Staff** entity into subclasses representing job roles.

Branch entity through the *Manages* relationship, whereas the Staff entity is related to the Branch entity through the *Has* relationship.

> Note that the multiplicity of **Manager** in the *Manages* relationship is 1..1, whereas previously the multiplicity of **Staff** in the *Manages* relationship was 0..1 (in other words, **Manager** has mandatory participation whereas **Staff** had optional participation).

In Figure 11.3, the Staff specialization/generalization has been expanded to show a shared subclass called SalesManager and a subclass called Secretary with its own subclass called AssistantSecretary. In other words, a member of the SalesManager shared subclass must be a member of the SalesPersonnel and Manager subclasses and Staff superclass. As a consequence, the attributes of the Staff superclass (staffNo, name, position, salary), and the attributes of the subclasses SalesPersonnel (salesArea, vehLicenseNo, carAllowance) and Manager (bonus) are inherited by the SalesManager subclass, which also has its own additional attribute called salesTarget.

AssistantSecretary is a subclass of Secretary, which is a subclass of Staff. This means that a member of the AssistantSecretary subclass must be a member of the Secretary subclass and the Staff superclass. As a consequence, the attributes of the Staff superclass (staffNo, name, position, salary) and the attribute of the Secretary subclass (typingSpeed) are inherited by the AssistantSecretary subclass, which also has its own additional attribute called startDate.

11.1.6 Constraints on superclass/subclass relationships

There are two constraints that may apply to a superclass/subclass relationship called participation constraints and disjoint constraints.

Participation constraints

Participation constraint
Determines whether every occurrence in the superclass must participate as a member of a subclass.

A **participation constraint** may be *mandatory* or *optional*. A superclass/subclass relationship with a *mandatory* participation specifies that every entity occurrence in the superclass must also be a member of a subclass. To represent mandatory participation, a 'Mandatory' is placed in curly brackets below the triangle that points towards the superclass. For example, in Figure 11.4 the Vehicle specialization/generalization (Van, Bus, and Car) has mandatory participation, which means that every vehicle must be a van, bus, or car.

A superclass/subclass relationship with *optional* participation specifies that a member of a superclass need not belong to any of its subclasses. To represent optional participation, an 'Optional' is placed in curly brackets below the trian-

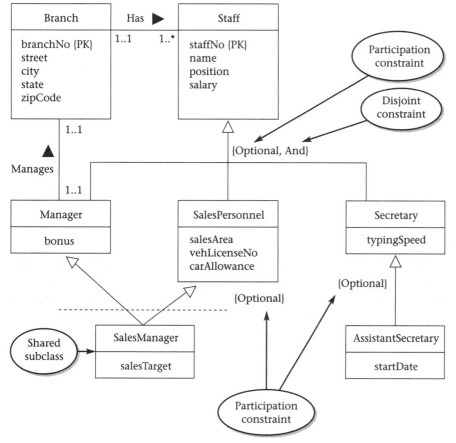

Figure 11.3

Specialization/
generalization of the
Staff entity
including a shared
subclass called
SalesManager and a
subclass called
Secretary with its
own subclass called
AssistantSecretary.

gle that points towards the superclass. For example, in Figure 11.2 the job role specialization/generalization has optional participation, which means that a member of staff need not have an additional job role such as a Manager, Secretary, or Sales Personnel.

Disjoint constraints

The **disjoint constraint** only applies when a superclass has more than one subclass. If the subclasses are disjoint, then an entity occurrence can be a member of only one of the subclasses. To represent a disjoint superclass/subclass relationship, an 'Or' is placed next to the participation constraint within the curly brackets. For example, in Figure 11.4 the subclasses of the Vehicle specialization/generalization (Van, Bus, and Car) are disjoint, which means that a vehicle is a van, bus, or car.

Disjoint constraint
Describes the relationship between members of the subclasses and indicates whether it's possible for a member of a superclass to be a member of one, or more than one, subclass.

Figure 11.4

Specialization/
generalization of
the Vehicle entity
into vehicle types.

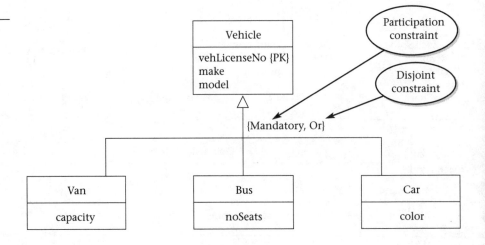

If subclasses of a specialization/generalization are not disjoint (called *nondis-joint*), then an entity occurrence may be a member of more than one subclass. To represent a nondisjoint superclass/subclass relationship, an 'And' is placed next to the participation constraint within the curly brackets. For example, in Figure 11.2 (and Figure 11.3) the subclasses of the job role specialization/generalization (Manager, Secretary, SalesPersonnel) are nondisjoint, which means that an entity occurrence can be a member of both the Manager and SalesPersonnel subclasses. This is also confirmed by the presence of the shared subclass called SalesManager.

The participation and disjoint constraints of specialization/generalization are distinct giving the following four categories: mandatory and nondisjoint, optional and nondisjoint, mandatory and disjoint, and optional and disjoint.

11.2 Creating tables to represent specialization/ generalization

In Chapter 9, we described how to create tables from a data model built using the basic concepts of the ER model. In this section, we show how to create tables for a specialization/generalization hierarchy. We illustrate this process for the EER models shown in Figures 11.2 and 11.4. As before, we describe each table using the Database Definition Language (DBDL) for relational databases.

DBDL defined in Step 2.1 in Chapter 9

Parent/child entities covered in Step 2.1 in Chapter 9

For each superclass/subclass relationship in the EER model, you identify the superclass as the parent entity and the subclass as the child entity. There are various options on how you may best represent such a relationship as one or more tables. The selection of the most appropriate option is dependent on the participation and disjoint constraints on the superclass/subclass relationship, as shown in Table 11.1.

Table 11.1 Options available for the representation of a superclass/subclass relationship based on the participation and disjoint constraints.

Participation constraint	Disjoint constraint	Tables required
Mandatory	Nondisjoint {And}	Single table
Optional	Nondisjoint {And}	Two tables: one table for superclass and one table for all subclasses
Mandatory	Disjoint {Or}	Many tables: one table for each combined superclass/subclass
Optional	Disjoint {Or}	Many tables: one table for superclass and one for each subclass

We use the Staff specialization/generalization in Figure 11.2 as our first example. The relationship that the Staff superclass has with its subclasses (Manager, SalesPersonnel, or Secretary) is **optional,** as a member of staff may not belong to any of the subclasses, and **nondisjoint,** as a member of staff may belong to more than one subclass. Based on the options given in Table 11.1, you should represent the Staff superclass/subclass relationship by creating a table for the superclass and a table for all of the subclasses, as shown in Figure 11.5. For clarification, we also include a table to represent the Branch entity and its relationship with Staff.

We use the Vehicle specialization/generalization in Figure 11.4 as our second example. The relationship that the Vehicle superclass has with its subclasses (Van, Bus, or Car) is *mandatory,* as all members of the Vehicle superclass must belong to one of the subclasses, and *disjoint,* as a member of the Vehicle superclass can

Figure 11.5

Tables to represent the Staff specialization/generalization and the Branch entity shown in Figure 11.2.

Staff Superclass
staff (staffNo, name, position, salary, branchNo)
Primary Key staffNo
Foreign Key branchNo **references** Branch(branchNo)

Staff Subclasses
AllStaffSubclasses (subclassStaffNo, bonus, salesArea, vehLicenseNo, carAllowance, typingSpeed)
Primary Key subclassStaffNo
Foreign Key subclassStaffNo **references** Staff(staffNo)

Branch
Branch (branchNo, street, city, state, zipCode, mgrStaffNo)
Primary Key branchNo
Foreign Key mgrStaffNo **references** AllStaffSubclasses(subclassStaffNo)

Figure 11.6

Tables to represent the Vehicle specialization/generalization shown in .Figure 11.4.

Van Subclass
Van (vehLicenseNo, make, model, capacity)
Primary Key vehLicenseNo

Bus Subclass
Bus (vehLicenseNo, make, model, noSeats)
Primary Key vehLicenseNo

Car Subclass
Car (vehLicenseNo, make, model, color)
Primary Key vehLicenseNo

belong to only one subclass. Based on the options given in Table 11.1, you should represent the Vehicle superclass/subclass relationship by creating a table for each combined superclass/subclass, as shown in Figure 11.6.

Although the options described in Table 11.1 provide some guidelines for how best to represent a superclass/subclass relationship, there are other factors that may influence the final selection such as:

■ whether the subclasses are involved in distinct relationships;

■ the number of attributes that are distinct to each subclass;

■ the relative number of entity occurrences represented by the superclass and by each subclass.

Chapter summary

✔ A **superclass** is an entity that holds common attributes and relationships for all occurrences in the entity.

✔ A **subclass** is an entity that has a distinct role and holds specific attributes and relationships for some occurrences in the (superclass) entity.

✔ **Attribute inheritance** is the process by which a member of a subclass may possess subclass-specific attributes, and inherit those attributes associated with the superclass.

✔ **Specialization** is the process of maximizing the differences between members of an entity by identifying their distinguishing characteristics.

✔ **Generalization** is the process of minimizing the differences between entities by identifying their common features.

✓ The constraints that may apply on a superclass/subclass relationship are called participation and disjoint constraints.

✓ A **participation constraint** determines whether every occurrence in the superclass must participate as a member of a subclass.

✓ A **disjoint constraint** describes the relationship between members of the subclasses and indicates whether it's possible for a member of a superclass to be a member of one, or more than one, subclass.

Part Four

Physical database design

Chapter 12

Physical database design – Step 4

In this chapter you will learn:

The purpose of physical database design. ◄

How to map the logical database design to a physical database design. ◄

How to design base tables for the target DBMS. ◄

How to design business rules for the target DBMS. ◄

In this chapter and the following four chapters, we describe and illustrate by example a physical database design methodology for relational databases. The starting point for this chapter is the global logical data model and the documentation that describes the model created in Steps 1–3 of the method-ology. The methodology started by producing local logical data models in Step 1 and then used the logical models to derive a set of tables in Step 2. The logical models and derived tables were checked to ensure they were cor-rectly structured using the technique of normalization, and to ensure they supported the transactions the users require. The logical database design phase concluded in Step 3 by merging together the local data models (which represent each view of the company) to create a global data model (which represents the entire company).

Steps 1–3 covered in Chapters 8–10

In the second phase of the database design methodology, namely **physical database design**, you must decide how to translate the logical database struc-ture (that is, the entities, attributes, relationships, and constraints) into a physical database design that can be implemented using the target DBMS. As many parts of physical database design are highly dependent on the target DBMS, you may find that there may be more than one way of implementing any given part of the database. Therefore to do this work properly, you need to be fully aware of the functionality of the target DBMS, and you need to understand the advantages and disadvantages of each alternative for a particular implementation. For some systems, you may also need to select a suitable storage strategy that takes account of intended database usage. PC RDBMSs, such as Microsoft Access, generally have a fixed storage structure and so, if you are using such a system, you probably won't have to worry about this step.

In this chapter, we show you how to convert the tables derived from the global logical data model into a specific database implementation. In Chapter 13, we'll give you guidelines for choosing file organizations for the base tables and deciding when to create indexes. In Chapter 14, we'll give you guidelines for deciding when to denormalize the physical data model and introduce redundancy. In Chapter 15, we'll look at how you can ensure the database is secure, and finally in Chapter 16, we'll discuss the ongoing process of monitoring and tuning the operational system.

In places, we'll show physical implementation details to clarify the discussion. To show the differences between DBMSs, for the *StayHome* case study we've worked through so far in this book, we'll use Microsoft Access to illustrate implementation issues. In contrast, we'll use the Oracle DBMS for the second case study we'll work through in Chapters 18 and 19.

Before we present the methodology for physical database design, we briefly review the design process.

12.1 Comparison of logical and physical database design

Logical database design is largely independent of implementation details, such as the specific functionality of the target DBMS, application programs, programming languages, or any other physical considerations. The output of this process is a global logical data model and documentation that describes this model, such as a data dictionary and a set of relational tables. Together, these represent the sources of information for the physical design process, and they provide you with a vehicle for making trade-offs that are so important to an efficient database design.

Whereas logical database design is concerned with the *what*, physical database design is concerned with the *how*. In particular, as the physical database designer you must know how the computer system hosting the DBMS operates, and you must be fully aware of the functionality of the target DBMS. As the functionality provided by current systems varies widely, physical design must be tailored to a specific DBMS system. However, physical database design is not an isolated activity – there is often feedback between physical, logical, and application design. For example, decisions taken during physical design to improve performance, such as merging tables together, might affect the logical data model.

Application design discussed in Section 3.9

12.2 Overview of the physical database design methodology

The steps for physical database design are shown in Figure 12.1. We've divided the physical database design methodology into four main steps, numbered consecutively from 4 to fit in with the three steps of the logical database design methodology. The chapter in which the step will be discussed is noted in the adjacent column.

Step 4 of physical database design involves the design of the base tables and integrity constraints using the available functionality of the target DBMS.

Step 5 involves choosing the file organizations and indexes for the base tables. Typically, PC DBMSs have a fixed storage structure but other DBMSs tend to provide a number of alternative file organizations for data. From the user's viewpoint, the internal storage representation for tables should be invisible – the user should be able to access tables and records without having to specify where or how the records are stored. As the physical database designer, you must provide the physical design details to both the DBMS and the operating system. For the DBMS, you must specify the file organizations that are to be used to represent each table; for the operating system, you must specify details such as the location and protection for each file.

Physical database design
The process of producing a description of the implementation of the database on secondary storage; it describes the base tables, file organizations and indexes used to achieve efficient access to the data, and any associated integrity constraints and security restrictions.

	Chapter
Step 4 Translate global logical data model for target DBMS	12
Step 4.1 Design base tables for target DBMS	
Step 4.2 Design business rules for target DBMS	
Step 5 Design physical representation	13
Step 5.1 Analyze transactions	
Step 5.2 Choose file organizations	
Step 5.3 Choose indexes	
Step 6 Consider the introduction of controlled redundancy	14
Step 6.1 Consider derived data	
Step 6.2 Consider duplicating columns or joining tables together	
Step 7 Design security mechanisms	15
Step 7.1 Design user views	
Step 7.2 Design access rules	
Step 8 Monitor and tune the operational system	16

Figure 12.1

Steps in the physical database design methodology.

Step 6 considers relaxing the normalization constraints imposed on the logical data model to improve the overall performance of the system. This is a step that you should undertake only if necessary, because of the inherent problems involved in introducing redundancy while still maintaining consistency.

Step 7 involves designing the security measures to protect data from unauthorized access. This involves deciding how each user view should be implemented, and the access controls that are required on the base tables.

Step 8 is an ongoing process of monitoring the operational system to identify and resolve any performance problems resulting from the design, and to implement new or changing requirements.

Appendix B presents a summary of the methodology for those of you who are already familiar with database design and simply require an overview of the main steps. In the remainder of this chapter, we examine Step 4 of the database design methodology. In this and the following four chapters, we demonstrate the close association between physical database design and implementation by describing how alternative designs can be implemented.

Step 4   Translate global logical data model for target DBMS

Objective
To produce a basic working relational database from the global logical data model.

The first activity of physical database design involves the translation of the tables you derived from the global logical data model into a form that you can implement in the target relational DBMS. The first part of this process entails collating the information you gathered during logical database design and documented in the data dictionary. The second part of the process uses this information to produce the design of the base tables. This process requires intimate knowledge of the functionality offered by the target DBMS. For example, you will need to know:

Base tables: Section 2.3.2

■ how to create base tables;

Keys: Section 2.2.3

■ whether the system supports the definition of primary keys, foreign keys, and alternate keys;

Nulls: Section 2.3.1

■ whether the system supports the definition of required data (that is, whether the system allows columns to be defined as NOT NULL);

Domains: Section 2.2.1

■ whether the system supports the definition of domains;

Rules: Section 2.3

■ whether the system supports relational integrity rules;

■ whether the system supports the definition of business rules.

The two tasks in Step 4 are:

- Step 4.1 Design base tables for target DBMS
- Step 4.2 Design business rules for target DBMS

Step 4.1 Design base tables for target DBMS

Objective
To decide how to represent the base tables identified in the global logical data model in the target DBMS.

To start the physical design process, you first need to collate and assimilate the information about the tables that you produced during logical database design. The necessary information can be obtained from the data dictionary and the definition of the tables that you defined using the Database Design Language (DBDL). For each table you identified in the global logical data model, you should have a definition consisting of:

DBDL defined in Step 2.1 in Chapter 9

- the name of the table;
- a list of simple columns in brackets;
- the primary key and, where appropriate, alternate keys and foreign keys;
- referential integrity constraints for any foreign keys identified.

From the data dictionary, you should also have for each column:

- its domain, consisting of a data type, length, and any constraints on the domain;
- an optional default value for the column;
- whether the column can hold nulls;
- whether the column is derived and, if so, how it should be computed.

To represent the design of the base tables, we use an extended form of the DBDL to define domains, default values, and null indicators. For example, for the Branch table of the *StayHome* database application defined in Figure 10.5, you may produce the design shown in Figure 12.2.

Implementing base tables

The next step is to decide how to implement the base tables. As we've already said, this decision is dependent on the target DBMS; some systems provide more facilities than others for defining base tables and integrity constraints. To

Figure 12.2

The physical design of the Branch table using an extended DBDL.

domain Branch_Numbers	fixed length character string length 4
domain Street_Names	variable length character string maximum length 30
domain City_Names	variable length character string maximum length 20
domain State_Codes	fixed length character string length 2
domain Zip_Codes	fixed length character string length 5
domain Staff_Numbers	fixed length character string length 5

```
branch(  branchNo      Branch_Numbers    NOT NULL,
         street        Street_Names      NOT NULL,
         city          City_Names        NOT NULL,
         state         State_Names       NOT NULL,
         zipCode       Zip_Codes         NOT NULL,
         mgrStaffNo    Staff_Numbers     NOT NULL)
         Primary Key branchNo
         Alternate Key zipCode
         Foreign Key mgrStaffNo References Staff(staffNo) ON UPDATE CASCADE ON DELETE NO ACTION
```

illustrate this process, we show two particular ways to create tables and integrity constraints using:

(1) the 1992 ISO SQL standard (SQL2),

(2) Microsoft Access 97.

   We cover SQL2 because it's the standard language for relational DBMSs, and can be viewed as a baseline that many systems will try to become compliant with (at least to some extent) although many will provide additional functionality as well.

The 1992 ISO SQL Standard (SQL2)

SQL discussed in Section 2.4 and Chapter 17

If the target DBMS is compliant with the 1992 ISO SQL standard, then it's relatively easy to design the base implementation. For example, to create the Branch table from the design above, you could use the SQL2 statements shown in Figure 12.3.

   The table has the same column names and domain types as identified in the DBDL in Figure 12.2. The primary key of the table is the branch number, branchNo, defined using the PRIMARY KEY clause. SQL2 automatically enforces uniqueness on this column. The alternate key, zipCode, has been defined using the combination of:

Figure 12.3

SQL2 to create Branch table.

```
CREATE DOMAIN Branch_Numbers AS CHAR(4)
CREATE DOMAIN Street_Names AS VARCHAR(30)
CREATE DOMAIN City_Names AS VARCHAR(20)
CREATE DOMAIN State_Codes AS CHAR(2)
CREATE DOMAIN Zip_Codes AS CHAR(5)
CREATE DOMAIN Staff_Numbers AS CHAR(5)
        CHECK(VALUE IN (SELECT staffNo FROM staff)

CREATE TABLE branch( branchNo                   Branch_Numbers      NOT NULL,
                     street                     Street_Names        NOT NULL,
                     city                       City_Names          NOT NULL,
                     state                      State_Names         NOT NULL,
                     zipCode                    Zip_Codes           NOT NULL UNIQUE,
                     mgrStaffNo                 Staff_Numbers       NOT NULL,
                     PRIMARY KEY (branchNo),
                     FOREIGN KEY (mgrStaffNo) REFERENCES Staff ON UPDATE CASCADE
                                                         ON DELETE NO ACTION

                  )
```

■ the NOT NULL constraint, to ensure that a value is always supplied, and

■ the UNIQUE constraint, to ensure that no two records in the table may have the same values.

One foreign key has been identified using the FOREIGN KEY clause with appropriate referential integrity constraints, which are:

Referential constraints discussed in Step 2.4 in Chapter 9

■ an update rule (ON UPDATE CASCADE), which ensures that when a value in the staffNo column in the Staff table is updated, then any corresponding value(s) in the mgrStaffNo column in the Branch table are set to the new value (that is, the update 'cascades');

■ a deletion rule (ON DELETE NO ACTION), which prevents a record being deleted from the Staff table if the corresponding member of staff is a manager of a branch.

> Note that the domain for staff numbers has a check associated with it to ensure that the specified staff number exists in the **Staff** table. It's not possible to create a similar check here for the domain of branch numbers as this domain is being used to create the new record in the first instance. However, it would be a good idea to create a second domain for any branch number that is used as a foreign key with a check that the specified branch number exists in the **Branch** table.

Microsoft Access 97

In some systems that do not fully comply with the SQL2 standard, there is no support for one or more of the clauses PRIMARY KEY, FOREIGN KEY, UNIQUE, NOT NULL, DEFAULT, and CHECK. Similarly, many systems do not support domains. For example, in Microsoft Access 97 you can define:

- primary keys,
- default values,
- not null (called *required*) fields. (Note, Microsoft uses the term 'field' instead of column.)

However, there is no specific FOREIGN KEY clause within the table creation facility, but it is possible to define foreign key clauses via relationships, as you'll see shortly. In addition, the data types are slightly different from the SQL2 standard, as shown in Table 12.1. We now illustrate how to create the Branch table with the constraints specified above in Microsoft Access.

Creating a blank table in Microsoft Access

Microsoft Access provides four ways to create a blank (empty) table. You can:

- Use the Database Wizard to create in one operation all the tables, forms, and reports that you require for the entire database. The Database Wizard creates a new database, although it can't be used to add new tables, forms, or reports to an existing database.
- Use the Table Wizard to choose the fields for your table from a variety of pre-defined tables such as business contacts, household inventory, or medical records.
- Enter data directly into a blank table (called a *datasheet*). When you save the new datasheet, Access will analyze your data and automatically assign the appropriate data type and format for each field.
- Use Design view to specify all your table details from scratch.

Figure 12.4 shows the Design View for the creation of the Branch table. Regardless of which method you use to create a table, you can use table Design View at any time to customize your table further, such as adding new fields, setting default values, or creating input masks.

Creating a relationship between two tables in Access

Relationships are created in the Relationships window. To create a relationship, you display the tables you want to create the relationships between, and then

Table 12.1 Microsoft Access data types.

Data type	Use	Size
Text	Text or text/numbers. Also numbers that do not require calculations, such as phone numbers.	Up to 255 characters
Memo	Lengthy text and numbers, such as notes or descriptions.	Up to 64 000 characters
Number	Numeric data to be used for mathematical calculations, except calculations involving money (use Currency type).	1, 2, 4, or 8 bytes
Date/Time	Dates and times.	8 bytes
Currency	Currency values. Use the Currency data type to prevent rounding off during calculations.	8 bytes
Autonumber	Unique sequential (incrementing by 1) or random numbers automatically inserted when a record is added.	4 bytes
Yes/No	Fields that will contain only one of two values, such as Yes/No, True/False, On/Off.	1 bit
OLE Object	Objects (such as Microsoft Word documents, Microsoft Excel spreadsheets, pictures, sounds, or other binary data), created in other programs using the OLE protocol, that can be linked to, or embedded in, a Microsoft Access table.	Up to 1 gigabyte
Hyperlink	Field that will store hyperlinks.	Up to 64 000 characters
Lookup Wizard	Creates a field that allows you to choose a value from another table or from a list of values using a combo box. Choosing this option in the data type list starts a wizard to define this for you.	Typically 4 bytes

drag the primary key attribute of the parent table to the foreign key attribute of the child table. At this point, Access will display a window allowing you to specify the referential integrity constraints.

Figure 12.5(a) shows the referential integrity dialog box that is displayed when creating the one-to-one (1:1) relationship Staff *Manages* Branch, and Figure 12.5(b) shows the Relationships window after the relationship has been created.

1:1 relationship defined in Section 5.5.1

There are a couple of things to note about setting referential integrity constraints in Microsoft Access:

1:* relationships defined in Section 5.5.2

(1) A one-to-many (1:*) relationship is created if only one of the related fields is a primary key or has a unique index; a 1:1 relationship is created if both the related fields are primary keys or have unique indexes. Therefore, to ensure that the *Manages* relationship is 1:1, you must not only ensure that the staffNo field in the Staff table has been set as the primary key, but you must also ensure that the mgrStaffNo field in the Branch table has the Indexed property set to Yes (No Duplicates), as shown in Figure 12.4.

Figure 12.4

Design view showing creation of the Branch table.

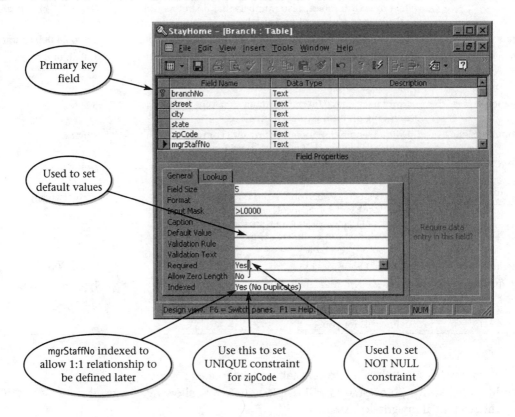

(2) There are only two referential integrity actions for update and delete that correspond to NO ACTION and CASCADE. Therefore, if you have identified other actions during Step 2.4 Define Integrity Constraints, you must consider whether to modify these constraints to fit in with the constraints available in Access, or you must investigate how to implement these constraints in application code. You'll see an example of how to implement referential integrity constraints that are not directly supported by the target DBMS in Chapter 19.

Step 2.4 covered in Chapter 9

Document design of base tables

The design of the base tables should be fully documented along with the reasons for selecting the proposed design. In particular, document the reasons for selecting one approach where many alternatives exist.

Figure 12.5

(a) Setting the referential integrity constraints for the 1:1 Staff *Manages* Branch relationship.

(b) Relationship window with the 1:1 Staff *Manages* Branch relationship displayed.

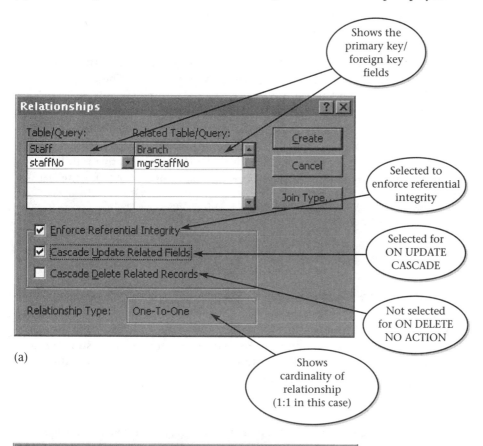

(a)

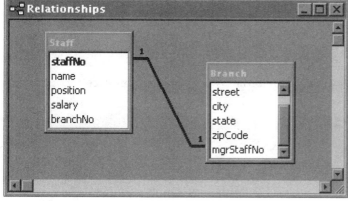

(b)

Step 4.2 Design business rules for target DBMS

Objective
To design the business rules for the target DBMS.

Updates to tables may be constrained by business rules governing the 'real world' transactions that are represented by the updates. The design of such rules is again dependent on the choice of DBMS; some systems provide more facilities than others for defining business rules. As in the previous step, if the system is compliant with the SQL2 standard, some rules may be easy to implement. For example, *StayHome* has a rule that prevents a member from renting more than 10 videos at any one time. You could design this rule into the SQL2 Create Table statement for the RentalAgreement table, using the following clause:

```
CONSTRAINT member_not_renting_too_many
      CHECK (NOT EXISTS  (SELECT memberno
                          FROM rentalagreement
                          GROUP BY memberno
                          HAVING COUNT(*) >= 10))
```

Alternatively, in some systems a *trigger* could be used to enforce some constraints. For the previous example, in some systems we could create the trigger shown in Figure 12.6 to enforce this integrity constraint. This trigger is invoked before a record is inserted into the RentalAgreement table or an existing record is updated. If the member is currently renting 10 videos, the system displays a message and aborts the transaction.

Don't worry too much about the details of this trigger. We'll discuss triggers in more detail in Step 4.2 in Chapter 19.

Creating business rules in Microsoft Access 97

There are several ways to create business rules in Microsoft Access 97 using, for example:

(a) validation rules for fields;

(b) validation rules for records;

(c) validation for forms using Access Basic.

We illustrate each of these below with some simple examples.

Figure 12.6

Trigger to enforce constraint that member cannot rent more than 10 videos at any one time.

```
CREATE TRIGGER member_not_renting_too_many
BEFORE INSERT OR UPDATE ON rentalagreement
FOR EACH ROW
DECLARE
      x   NUMBER;
BEGIN
      SELECT COUNT(*) INTO x
            FROM rentalagreement r
            WHERE r.memberno = :new.memberno;
      IF x  >= 10 THEN
            raise_application_error(-20000,('Member' ||:new.memberno||
'already renting 10 videos');
      END IF;
END;
```

Validation rules for fields

You can ensure that data is entered correctly into a field by defining a field validation rule. A field validation rule is used to check the value entered into a field as the user leaves the field. A message you define is displayed if the value breaks the validation rule.

For example, *StayHome* has a simple constraint that all return dates for video rentals cannot be earlier than the current date, although the date may initially be left unspecified. You can implement this constraint at the field level in the RentalAgreement table using the function Date(), which returns the current date, as shown in Figure 12.7.

Validation rules for records

A record validation rule controls when an entire record can be saved. Unlike field validation rules, record validation rules can refer to other fields. This makes them useful when you want to compare values from different fields in a table. For example, *StayHome* may have a constraint that the maximum rental period for videos is five days, although the date may initially be left unspecified. You can implement this constraint at the record level in the RentalAgreement table using the validation rule:

```
[dateReturn] Is Null OR [dateReturn] <= [dateOut] + 5
```

Figure 12.7

Example of field validation in Microsoft Access.

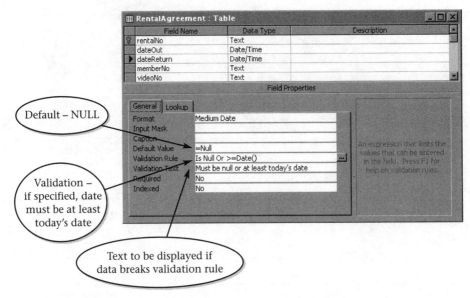

Figure 12.8 shows the Validation Rule property box for the table with this rule set.

Figure 12.8

Example of record validation in Microsoft Access.

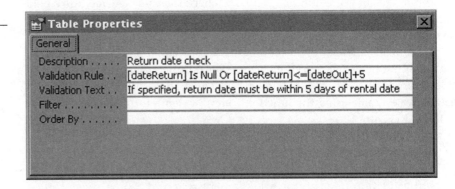

Validation for forms using Access Basic

As we've just mentioned, *StayHome* has a constraint that members are not allowed to rent more than 10 videos at any one time. This is a more complex constraint, which requires you to check how many rentals the member currently has. One way to implement this constraint in Access is to use an event procedure (BeforeUpdate), as shown in Figure 12.9. The BeforeUpdate event is triggered before a record is updated, and you can associate code with this event on a form.

Figure 12.9

Access Basic code to check member does not have more than 10 videos currently rented.

```
Private Sub Form_BeforeUpdate(Cancel As Integer)
Dim MyDB As Database
Dim MySet As Recordset
Dim MyQuery As String


'Set up query to select all records for specified member'
MyQuery = "SELECT rentalno FROM rentalagreement WHERE memberno ='"+ memberNoField +"'"


'Open the database and run the query'
Set MyDB = DBEngine.Workspaces(0).Databases(0)
Set MySet = MyDB.OpenRecordset(MyQuery)


'Check if any records have been returned, then move to the end of the file to allow RecordCount'
'property to be correctly set'
If (NOT MySet.EOF) Then
        MySet.MoveLast
        If (MySet.RecordCount >= 10) Then 'If currently 10 - cannot rent any more'
                MsgBox "Member currently has 10 videos out"
                Me.Undo
        End If
End If

MySet.Close
MyDB.Close
End Sub
```

Name of field on form

In some systems, there will be no support for some or all of the business rules and it will be necessary to design the rules into the application, as we've shown with the last example, which has built the constraint into the application's Visual Basic code. Implementing a business rule in application code is, of course, potentially dangerous and can lead to duplication of effort and, worse still, to inconsistencies if the rule is not implemented everywhere it should be.

Document design of business rules

The design of business rules should be fully documented. In particular, document the reasons for selecting one approach where many alternatives exist.

Chapter summary

✓ **Physical database design** is the process of producing a description of the implementation of the database on secondary storage. It describes the base tables, file organizations and indexes used to access this data effectively, and any associated integrity constraints and security restrictions. The design of the base tables can be undertaken only once you are fully aware of the facilities offered by the target DBMS.

✓ In the initial step (Step 4) of physical database design, you translate the global logical data model into a form that can be implemented in the target relational DBMS.

✓ In the next step (Step 5), you design the file organizations and indexes that will be used to store the base tables. This involves analyzing the transactions that will run on the database, choosing suitable file organizations based on this analysis, and adding indexes.

✓ In Step 6, you consider the introduction of controlled redundancy to improve performance.

✓ A database represents an essential corporate resource, and so security of this resource is extremely important. The objective of Step 7 is to design how the security measures identified during logical database design will be realized. This may include the creation of user views and the use of access control mechanisms, such as those provided by SQL.

✓ The final step (Step 8) is the ongoing process of monitoring and tuning the operational system to achieve maximum performance.

Chapter 13

Physical database design – Step 5

In this chapter you will learn:

How system resources affect performance. ◀

How to analyze the users' transactions to determine characteristics that ◀
may impact performance.

How to select appropriate file organizations based on an analysis of the ◀
transactions.

When to select indexes to improve performance. ◀

This chapter covers the second step of our physical database design methodology. In the previous step, we showed how to translate the logical design into a basic set of tables. However, even for the simplest database, there are additional considerations required to achieve acceptable performance. In this chapter, we consider the next step of physical database design, which considers those aspects of performance that you can influence by the appropriate choice of file organizations and indexes.

Methodology summarized in Appendix B

> If you are unfamiliar with file organization and indexing concepts, we **TIP** strongly recommend reading Appendix C before reading this chapter.

As with logical design, physical design must be guided by the nature of the data and its intended use. In particular, you must understand the typical workload that the database must support. During the analysis phase, you may also have found that some users have requirements about how fast certain transactions must run or how many transactions must be processed per second. This information forms the basis for a number of decisions that you'll need to make during this step.

As we mentioned previously, to undertake physical database design, you must understand the workings of the target DBMS, particularly the file organizations, indexing, and query processing techniques that it supports. For example, there may be circumstances where the DBMS would not use a secondary index, even if one were available. Thus, adding a secondary index would not improve the performance of the query, and the resultant overhead would be unjustified.

Secondary indexes defined in Appendix C.5.1

> You may recall from Section 2.4 that SQL and QBE are *non-procedural* data manipulation languages (DMLs). Such languages hide the low-level details of how to access the data on secondary storage. This is the responsibility of the DBMS, or to be more precise, the DBMS's *query optimizer*. Typically, the query optimizer will analyze a number of different strategies for carrying out the user's request and select the one it believes will give optimal performance. This analysis will be based on the estimated cost of database operations using database statistics, such as the number of records in a table, the size of each record, and the availability of indexes.
>
> This might suggest that you have no influence over the final strategy that the DBMS will choose. In fact, you'll see that you can define some of the storage structures that will be available to the query optimizer to select the optimal strategy.

Before going on to discuss the activities in this step, let's briefly examine how the various system components interact and affect DBMS performance.

13.1 Understanding system resources

To improve performance, you must be aware of how the four basic hardware components interact and affect system performance:

■ *Main memory* Main memory accesses are significantly faster than secondary storage accesses, sometimes tens or even hundreds of thousands of times faster. In general, the more main memory available to the DBMS and the database applications, the faster the application programs will run. However, it's sensible always to have a minimum of 5 per cent of main memory available. Equally well, it's advisable not to have any more than 10 per cent available, otherwise main memory is not being used optimally. When there is insufficient memory to accommodate all processes, the operating system transfers pages of processes to disk to free up memory. When one of these pages is next required, the operating system has to transfer it back from disk. Sometimes, it's necessary to swap entire processes from main memory to disk and back again, to free up memory. Problems occur with main memory when paging (also called swapping) becomes excessive.

■ *CPU* The CPU controls the tasks of the other system resources and executes user processes. The main objective for this component is to prevent CPU contention in which processes are waiting for the CPU. CPU bottlenecks occur when either the operating system or application programs make too many demands on the CPU. This is often a result of excessive paging.

■ *Disk I/O* With any large DBMS, there's a significant amount of disk I/O involved in storing and retrieving data. The way in which data is organized on disk can have a major impact on the overall disk performance. It's recommended that storage should be evenly distributed across available drives to reduce the likelihood of performance problems occurring. Figure 13.1 illustrates the basic principles of distributing the data across disks:
  - The operating system files should be separated from the database files.
  - The main database files should be separated from the index files.
  - The recovery log file, if available and if used, should be separated from the rest of the database.

■ *Network* When the amount of data being transferred across the network is too great, network bottlenecks occur.

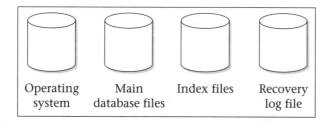

Figure 13.1

Typical disk configuration.

Each of these resources may affect other system resources. Equally well, an improvement in one resource may effect an improvement in other system resources. For example:

■ Adding more main memory should result in less paging. This should help avoid CPU bottlenecks.

■ More effective use of main memory may result in less disk I/O.

With these objectives in mind, let's now discuss the activities in Step 5.

13.2   Step 5 Design physical representation

Objective
To determine the optimal file organizations to store the base tables, and the indexes that are required to achieve acceptable performance.

We provide a brief introduction to file organizations and indexes in Appendix C for those readers who are unfamiliar with these terms. To recap, a **file organization** is a way of arranging the records in a file when the file is stored on disk; an **index** allows the DBMS to locate particular records in a file more quickly, and thereby increase the response to user queries.

The types of file organization available are dependent on the target DBMS; some systems provide more choice of file organizations than others. It's important that you fully understand the structures that are available, and how the target system uses these structures.

You also can't make meaningful physical design decisions until you understand in detail the transactions that have to be supported. In analyzing the transactions, you're attempting to identify performance criteria, such as:

■ the transactions that run frequently and will have a significant impact on performance;

■ the transactions that are critical to the operation of the business;

■ the times during the day/week when there will be a high demand made on the database (called the *peak load*).

You'll use this information to identify the parts of the database that may cause performance problems. At the same time, you need to identify the high-level functionality of the transactions, such as the columns that are updated in an update transaction or the columns that are retrieved in a query. You'll use this information to select appropriate file organizations and indexes.

As a result, we've broken the tasks in Step 5 into:

■ Step 5.1 Analyze transactions

■ Step 5.2 Choose file organizations

■ Step 5.3 Choose indexes

Step 5.1 Analyze transactions

> **Objective**
> To understand the functionality of the transactions that will run on the database and to analyze the important transactions.

To carry out physical database design effectively, you need to have a good understanding of the transactions that will run on the database.

> **TIP**
>
> In many situations it would be far too time-consuming to analyze all the expected transactions, so you should at least investigate the '*most important*' ones. It has been suggested that the most active 20 per cent of user queries account for 80 per cent of the total data access. You may find this 80/20 rule is a useful guideline when carrying out the analysis.

To help identify which transactions to investigate, you could use a *transaction usage map*, which diagrammatically indicates which tables are potentially heavily used, and/or a *transaction/table cross-reference matrix*, which shows the tables each transaction accesses. To focus on areas that may be problematic, one way to proceed is to:

(1) Map all transaction paths to tables.

(2) Determine which tables are most frequently accessed by transactions.

(3) Analyze selected transactions that involve these tables.

Map all transaction paths to tables

In Steps 1.8, 2.3, and 3.2 of the logical database design methodology, you checked that the model supported the transactions that the users require by mapping the transaction paths to entities/tables. If you used a transaction pathway diagram similar to the one shown in Figure 8.17, you'll be able to use this diagram to determine the tables that are most frequently accessed. On the other hand, if you checked the transactions in some other way, you may find it useful to create a transaction/table cross-reference matrix. The matrix shows the transactions that are required and the tables they access. For example, Table 13.1 shows a transaction/table cross-reference matrix for the following selection of entry, update/delete, and query transactions for *StayHome*:

StayHome transactions listed in Section 4.4.4

(e) Enter the details of a new member registering at a given branch.

Table 13.1 Cross-referencing transactions and tables.

Transaction/ Table	(e)				(k)				(p)				(q)				(r)				(s)			
	I	R	U	D	I	R	U	D	I	R	U	D	I	R	U	D	I	R	U	D	I	R	U	D
Branch																								
Staff		X																						
Video										X				X				X				X		
VideoForRent										X				X				X				X		
RentalAgreement																						X		
Member	X					X	X	X														X		
Registration	X																							
Actor														X										
Role														X										
Director																		X						

I = Insert; R = Read; U = Update; D = Delete

(k) Update/delete the details of a given member.

(p) List the title, category, and availability of all videos at a specified branch, ordered by category.

(q) List the title, category, and availability of all videos for a given actor's name at a specified branch, ordered by title.

(r) List the title, category, and availability of all videos for a given director's name at a specified branch, ordered by title.

(s) List the details of all videos a specified member currently has on rent.

The matrix summarizes, in a visual way, the access patterns of the transactions that will run on the database. For example, the matrix indicates that transaction (e) reads the Staff table and also inserts records into the Member and Registration tables. To be more useful, you should indicate the number of accesses over some time interval (for example, hourly, daily, weekly) in each cell. However, to keep the matrix simple, we do not show this information. This matrix shows that the Video and VideoForRent tables are accessed by the four query transactions.

Determine frequency information

In discussion with the *StayHome* branch managers it's estimated that there are about 20 000 video titles and 400 000 videos for rent distributed over 100 branch offices, with an average of 4000 and a maximum of 10 000 videos for rent at each branch. In addition, *StayHome* holds data for about 10 000 directors and 30 000 main actors in 60 000 roles. Figure 13.2 shows a reduced logical data model with these numbers added.

Figure 13.3 shows the transaction usage map for transactions (p), (q), and (r), which all access the VideoForRent and Video tables. Owing to the size of the VideoForRent table, it will be important that access to this table is as efficient as possible. You may now decide that a closer analysis of transactions involving these tables would be useful.

In considering each transaction, it's important that you know not only the average and maximum number of times it runs per hour, but also the day and time that the transaction is run, including when the peak load is likely. For example, some transactions may run at the average rate for most of the time, but have a peak loading between 14.00 and 16.00 on a Thursday prior to a meeting on Friday morning. Other transactions may run only at specific times, for example 18.00–21.00 on Friday/Saturdays, which is also their peak loading.

Where transactions require frequent access to particular tables, then their pattern of operation is very important. If these transactions operate in a mutually exclusive manner, the risk of likely performance problems is reduced. However, if their operating patterns conflict, potential problems may be alleviated by examining the transactions more closely to determine whether changes can be made to the structure of the tables to improve performance, as we'll discuss in Step 6 in the next chapter.

Data usage analysis

Having identified the important transactions, you now need to analyze each one in more detail. For each transaction, you should determine:

(a) The tables and columns accessed by the transaction and the type of access; that is, whether it's an insert, update, delete, or retrieval (also known as a query) transaction.
   – For an update transaction, note the columns that are updated, as these columns may be candidates for avoiding an access structure (such as a secondary index).

(b) The columns used in any *search conditions* (in SQL, these are the conditions specified in the WHERE clause). Check whether the conditions involve:
   (i)   pattern matching; for example: (name LIKE '%Smith%');
   (ii) range searches; for example: (salary BETWEEN 30000 AND 40000);
   (iii) exact-match key retrieval; for example: (salary = 30000).

Figure 13.2

Simplified logical data model showing expected occurrences.

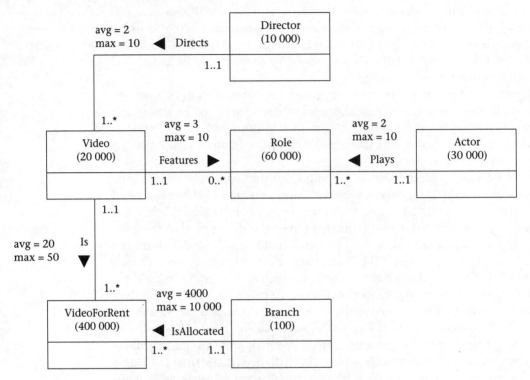

This applies not only to queries but also to update and delete transactions, which can restrict the records to be updated/deleted in a table.

– These columns may be candidates for access structures.

(c) For a query, the columns that are involved in the join of two or more tables.

– Again, these columns may be candidates for access structures.

(d) The expected frequency at which the transaction will run; for example, the transaction will run approximately 50 times per day.

(e) The performance goals for the transaction; for example, the transaction must complete within 1 second.

– The columns used in any search conditions for very frequent or critical transactions should have a higher priority for access structures.

Figure 13.4 shows an example of a transaction analysis form for transaction (p). This form shows that the average frequency of this transaction is 50 times per hour, with a peak loading of 100 times per hour between 18.00

Figure 13.3

Transaction usage map for sample transactions.

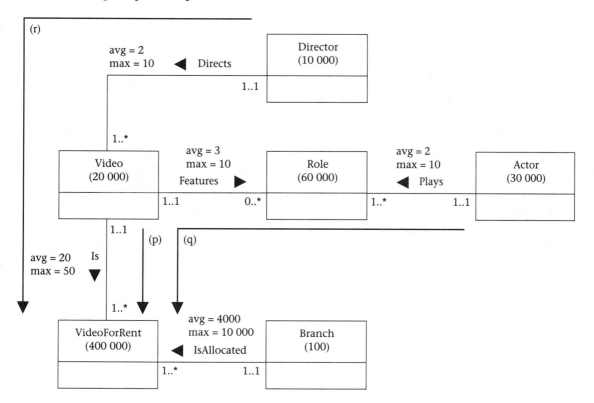

and 21.00. In other words, typically half the branches will run this transaction per hour and at peak time all branches will run this transaction once per hour.

The form also shows the required SQL statement and the transaction usage map. At this stage, the full SQL statement may be too detailed but you should at least identify the types of details that are shown adjacent to the SQL statement, namely:

■ any search conditions that will be used;

■ any columns that will be required to join tables together (for retrieval transactions);

■ columns used to order results (for retrieval transactions);

■ columns used to group data together (for retrieval transactions);

■ any built-in functions that may be used (such as AVG, SUM);

■ any columns that will be updated by the transaction.

Figure 13.4

Example transaction analysis form.

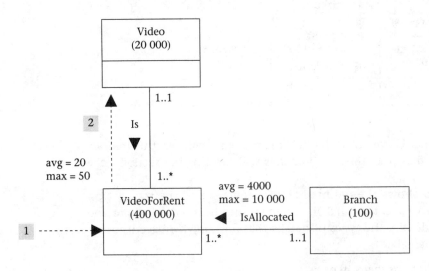

| | Transaction Analysis Form | 1-Jan-2000 |

Transaction (p) List the title, category, and availability of all videos at at specified branch, ordered by category.

Transaction volume
  Average: 50 per hour
  Peak: 100 per hour (between 18.00 and 21.00 every day of the week)

SELECT title, category, availability
FROM video v INNER JOIN videoforrent vfr ON
        vfr.catalogno = v.catalogno
WHERE vfr.branchNo = 'B001'
ORDER BY title;

Search condition: branchno = 'B001'
Join columns: vfr.catalogno = v.catalogno
Ordering column: title
Grouping column: none
Built-in functions: none
Columns updated: none

Transaction usage map

Access	Entity	Type of access	No. of references		
			Per transaction	Avg per hour	Peak per hour
1	VideoForRent (entry)	R	4000–10 000	200 000–500 000	400 000–1 000 000
2	Video	R	4000–10 000	200 000–500 000	400 000–1 000 000
Total references			8000–20 000	400 000–1 000 000	800 000–2 000 000

You'll use this information to determine the indexes that are required, which we'll discuss shortly. Below the transaction usage map, there is a detailed breakdown documenting:

■ how each table is accessed (reads in this case);

■ how many records will be accessed each time the transaction is run;

■ how many records will be accessed per hour on average and at peak loading times.

> Note, for an update transaction, there will be two accesses made on a table: one to read the data and one to update the data.

The frequency information will identify the tables that will need careful consideration to ensure that appropriate access structures are used. As mentioned above, the search conditions used by transactions that have time constraints become higher priority for access structures.

Step 5.2 Choose file organizations

> **Objective**
> To determine an efficient file organization for each base table.

One of the main objectives of physical database design is to store data in an efficient way. For example, if you want to retrieve staff records in alphabetical order of name, sorting the file by staff name is a good file organization. However, if you want to retrieve all staff whose salary is in a certain range, a file ordered by staff name would not be a good file organization.

To complicate matters, some file organizations are efficient for bulk-loading data into the database but inefficient after that. In other words, you may want to use an efficient storage structure to set up the database and then change it for normal operational use.

The objective of this step therefore is to choose an optimal file organization for each table, if the target DBMS allows this. In many cases, you may find that a relational DBMS gives you little or no choice for choosing file organizations, although some may be established as you specify indexes. However, as an aid to understanding file organizations and indexes more fully, we provide guidelines for selecting a file organization based on the following types of files:

■ heap

■ hash

■ Indexed Sequential Access Method (ISAM)

■ B$^+$-Tree.

If your target DBMS does not allow you to choose the file organization, you can omit this step and move on to the next step, Step 5.3.

<table>
<tr><td>Heap discussed in
Appendix C.2</td><td>

Heap (unordered)

Heap is a good storage structure in the following situations:

(1) When data is being bulk-loaded into the table. For example, you may want to insert a batch of records into a table after it has been created. If you choose heap as the initial file organization, it may be more efficient to restructure the file after you've completed the insertions.

(2) The table is only a few pages long. In this case, the time to locate any record is short, even if the entire table has to be searched sequentially.

(3) When every record in the table has to be retrieved (in any order) every time the table is accessed. For example, retrieve the addresses of all members of *StayHome*.

(4) When the table has an additional access structure, such as an index key, heap storage can be used to conserve space.

Heap files are inappropriate when only selected records of a table are to be accessed.

</td></tr>
<tr><td>Hash discussed in
Appendix C.4</td><td>

Hash

Hash is a good storage structure when records are retrieved based on an exact match on the hash field value, particularly if the access order is random. For example, if the Member table is hashed on memberNo, retrieval of the record with memberNo equal to M250178 is efficient. However, hash is not a good storage structure in the following situations:

(1) When records are retrieved based on a pattern match of the hash field value. For example, retrieve all members whose member number (memberNo) begins with the characters 'M2'.

</td></tr>
</table>

(2) When records are retrieved based on a range of values for the hash field. For example, retrieve all members with a member number between 'M200000' and 'M200100'.

(3) When records are retrieved based on a column other than the hash column. For example, if the Member table is hashed on memberNo, then hashing could not be used to search for a record based on the lName column. In this case, it would be necessary to perform a linear search to find the record, or add lName as a secondary index (see Step 5.3).

(4) When records are retrieved based on only part of the hash field. For example, if the Role table is hashed on catalogNo and actorNo, then hashing could not be used to search for a record based on the catalogNo column alone. Again, it would be necessary to perform a linear search to find the record.

(5) When the hash column is frequently updated. When a hash column is updated, the DBMS must delete the entire record and possibly relocate it to a new address (if the hash function results in a new address). Thus, frequent updating of the hash column impacts performance.

Indexed Sequential Access Method (ISAM)

ISAM is a more versatile storage structure than hash; it supports retrievals based on exact key match, pattern matching, range of values, and part key specification. However, the ISAM index is static, created when the file is created. Thus, you'll find that the performance of an ISAM file deteriorates as the table is updated. Updates also cause an ISAM file to lose the access key sequence, so that retrievals in order of the access key will become slower. These two problems are overcome by the B^+-Tree file organization.

ISAM discussed in Appendix C.5.3

B^+-Tree

Again, B^+-Tree is a more versatile storage structure than hashing. It supports retrievals based on exact key match, pattern matching, range of values, and part key specification. The B^+-Tree index is dynamic, growing as the table grows. Thus, unlike ISAM, the performance of a B^+-Tree file does not deteriorate as the table is updated. The B^+-Tree also maintains the order of the access key even when the file is updated, so retrieval of records in the order of the access key is more efficient than ISAM. However, if the table is not frequently updated, the ISAM structure may be more efficient as it has one less level of index than the B^+-Tree, whose leaf nodes contain pointers to the actual records of the table rather than the actual records themselves.

B^+-Tree discussed in Appendix C.5.4

Indexes discussed in Appendix C.5

Document choice of file organizations

The choice of file organizations should be fully documented, along with the reasons for the choice. In particular, document the reasons for selecting one file organization where many alternatives exist.

Step 5.3   Choose indexes

> **Objective**
> To determine whether adding indexes will improve the performance of the system.

One approach to selecting an appropriate file organization for a table is to keep the records unordered and create as many **secondary indexes** as you need. Another approach is to order the records in the table by specifying a **primary** or **clustering index**. In this case, you should choose the column for ordering or clustering the records as:

- ■ the column that is used most often for join operations, as this makes the join operation more efficient, or
- ■ the column that is used most often to access the records in a table in order of that column.

If the ordering column chosen is a key of the table, the index will be a primary index; if the ordering column is not a key, the index will be a clustering index. Remember that you can only have either a primary index or a clustering index for each file.

Specifying indexes

> The initial version of the SQL standard had statements for creating and dropping indexes. However, these statements were removed from the second major release of the standard in 1992 because they were considered to be a physical concept rather than a logical concept. The statements also do not appear in the draft of the revised standard, generally referred to as SQL3, due for release within the next year or so. Having said that, most of the major relational DBMSs support these statements in one form or another. The SQL statements we use below are typical of what current products support.

To create an index in SQL, typically you use the CREATE INDEX statement. For example, to create a primary index on the Video table based on the catalogNo column, you might use the following SQL statement:

```
CREATE UNIQUE INDEX catalogno_index
    ON video(catalogno);
```

If you wanted to create a clustering index on the VideoForRent table based on the catalogNo column, you might use the following SQL statement:

```
CREATE INDEX catalogno_index
    ON videoforrent(catalogno) CLUSTER;
```

As we've already mentioned, in some systems the file organization is fixed. For example, until recently Oracle has only supported B^+-Trees, but has now added support for hash clusters. On the other hand, INGRES offers a wide set of different index structures that you can choose using the optional clause in the CREATE INDEX statement:

Oracle discussed in Chapter 19

```
[STRUCTURE = BTREE | ISAM | HASH | HEAP|];
```

To drop an index in SQL, typically you use the DROP INDEX statement. For example, to drop the clustering index catalogNo_Index, you might use the following SQL statement:

```
DROP INDEX catalogno_index;
```

Choosing secondary indexes

Secondary indexes provide a mechanism for specifying an additional key for a base table that can be used to retrieve data more efficiently. For example, the Member table may be hashed on the member number, memberNo, the *primary index*. However, there may be frequent access to this table based on the lName (last name) column. In this case, you may decide to add lName as a *secondary index*.

However, there is an overhead involved in the maintenance and use of secondary indexes that you have to balance against the performance improvement gained when retrieving data. This overhead includes:

■ adding an index record to every secondary index whenever a record is inserted in the table;

■ updating a secondary index when the corresponding record in the table is updated;

■ the increase in disk space needed to store the secondary index;

■ possible performance degradation during query optimization, as the query optimizer may consider all secondary indexes before selecting an optimal execution strategy.

Guidelines for choosing a 'wish–list' of indexes

One approach to determining which secondary indexes you need is to produce a 'wish-list' of columns you think are candidates for indexing, and then to consider the impact of maintaining each of these indexes. We provide the following guidelines to help you produce such a 'wish-list':

(1) In general, index the primary key of a table if it's not a key of the file organization. Although the SQL2 standard provides a clause for the specification of primary keys as discussed in Step 4.1 covered in the last chapter, it should be noted that this does not guarantee that the primary key will be indexed.

(2) Do not index small tables. It may be more efficient to search the table in memory than to store an additional index structure.

(3) Add a secondary index to any column that is heavily used for data retrieval (for example, add a secondary index to the Member table based on the column lName, as discussed above).

(4) Add a secondary index to a foreign key if there is frequent access based on it. For example, you may frequently join the VideoForRent and Branch tables on the column branchNo (the branch number). Therefore, it may be more efficient to add a secondary index to the VideoForRent table based on branchNo.

(5) Add a secondary index on columns that are frequently involved in:
    (a) selection or join criteria;
    (b) ORDER BY;
    (c) GROUP BY;
    (d) other operations involving sorting (such as UNION or DISTINCT).

(6) Add a secondary index on columns involved in built-in functions, along with any columns used to aggregate the built-in functions. For example, to find the average staff salary at each branch, you could use the following SQL query:

```
SELECT branchno, AVG(salary)
FROM staff
GROUP BY branchno;
```

From the previous guideline, you could consider adding an index to the branchNo column by virtue of the GROUP BY clause. However, it may be more efficient to consider an index on both the branchNo column and the salary column. This may allow the DBMS to perform the entire query from data in the index alone, without having to access the data file. This is sometimes called an *index-only plan*, as the required response can be produced using only data in the index.

(7) As a more general case of the previous guideline, add a secondary index on columns that could result in an index-only plan.

(8) Avoid indexing a column or table that is frequently updated.

(9) Avoid indexing a column if the query will retrieve a significant proportion (for example, 25 per cent) of the records in the table, even if the table is large. In this case, it may be more efficient to search the entire table than to search using an index.

(10) Avoid indexing columns that consist of long character strings.

TIP

If the search criteria involve more than one condition, and one of the terms contains an OR clause, and the term has no index/sort order, then adding indexes for the other columns is not going to help improve the speed of the query, because a linear search of the table will still be required. For example, assume that only the **category** and **dailyRental** columns of the **Video** table are indexed, and you need to use the following query:

```
SELECT *
FROM video
WHERE (category = 'Action' OR dailyrental > 3 OR price >
15);
```

Although the two indexes could be used to find the records where (category = 'Action' or dailyRental > 3), the fact that the **price** column is not indexed will mean that these indexes cannot be used for the full WHERE clause. Thus, unless there are other queries that would benefit from having the **category** and **dailyRental** columns indexed, there would be no benefit gained in indexing them for this query.

On the other hand, if the search conditions in the WHERE clause were AND'ed together, the two indexes on the **category** and **dailyRental** columns could be used to optimize the query.

Removing indexes from the 'wish–list'

Having drawn up your 'wish-list' of potential indexes, you should now consider the impact of each of these on update transactions. If the maintenance of the index is likely to slow down important update transactions, then consider dropping the index from the list. Note, however, that a particular index may also make update operations more efficient. For example, if you want to update a member of staff's salary given the member's staff number, staffNo, and you have an index on staffNo, then the record to be updated can be found more quickly.

> **TIP** It's a good idea to experiment when possible to determine whether an index is improving performance, providing very little improvement, or adversely impacting performance. In the last case, clearly you should remove this index from the 'wish-list'. If there is little observed improvement with the addition of the index, further examination may be necessary to determine under what circumstances the index will be useful, and whether these circumstances are sufficiently important to warrant the implementation of the index.

Some systems allow you to inspect the optimizer's strategy for executing a particular query or update, sometimes called the Query Execution Plan (QEP). For example, Oracle has an EXPLAIN PLAN diagnostic utility, Microsoft Access has a Performance Analyzer, DB2 has an EXPLAIN utility, and INGRES has an online QEP-viewing facility. When a query runs slower than expected, it's worth using such a facility to determine the reason for the slowness, and to find an alternative strategy that may improve the performance of the query.

> **TIP** If a large number of records are being inserted into a table with one or more indexes, it may be more efficient to drop the indexes first, perform the inserts, and then re-create the indexes afterwards. As a rule of thumb, if the insert will increase the size of the table by at least 10 per cent, drop the indexes temporarily.

Updating the database statistics

Earlier we mentioned that the query optimizer relies on database statistics held in the system catalog to select the optimal strategy. Whenever you create an index, the DBMS automatically adds the presence of the index to the system catalog. However, you may find that the DBMS requires you to run a utility to update the statistics in the system catalog relating to the table and the index.

System catalog defined in Section 1.2.1

Document choice of indexes

The choice of indexes should be fully documented, along with the reasons for the choice. In particular, if there are performance reasons why some columns should not be indexed, these should also be documented.

13.3 File organizations and indexes for *StayHome* with Microsoft Access 97

Like most, if not all, PC DBMSs, Microsoft Access uses a fixed file organization, so if you're using Access, Step 5.2 can be omitted.

13.3.1 Guidelines for choosing indexes

Microsoft Access does, however, support indexes as we now briefly discuss. In Access, the primary key of a table is automatically indexed, but a field whose data type is Memo, Hyperlink, or OLE Object can't be indexed. For other fields, Microsoft advise that you should consider indexing a field if all the following apply:

■ the field's data type is Text, Number, Currency, or Date/Time;

■ you anticipate searching for values stored in the field;

■ you anticipate sorting values in the field;

■ you anticipate storing many different values in the field. If many of the values in the field are the same, the index may not significantly speed up queries.

In addition, Microsoft advise that:

■ you should consider indexing fields on both sides of a join or create a relationship between these fields, in which case Access will automatically create an index on the foreign key field, if one does not exist already;

■ when grouping records by the values in a joined field, you should specify GROUP BY for the field that's in the same table as the field you're calculating the aggregate on.

Microsoft Access can optimize simple and complex search conditions (called *expressions* in Access). For certain types of complex expressions, Microsoft Access uses a data access technology called Rushmore, to achieve a greater level of optimization. A complex expression is formed by combining two simple expressions with the AND or OR operator, such as:

```
branchno = 'B001' AND available = Yes
category = 'Action' OR dailyrental > 3
```

In Access, a complex expression is fully or partially optimizable depending on whether one or both simple expressions are optimizable, and which operator was used to combine them. A complex expression is *Rushmore-optimizable* if all three of the following conditions are true:

■ The expression uses AND or OR to join two conditions.

■ Both conditions are made up of simple optimizable expressions.

■ Both expressions contain indexed fields. The fields can be indexed individually or they can be part of a multiple-field index.

Creating indexes in Access

You create an index in Access by setting the Indexed property of a table in the Field Properties section in table Design View. The Indexed property has the following values:

No	No index (the default).
Yes (Duplicates OK)	The index allows duplicates.
Yes (No Duplicates)	The index doesn't allow duplicates.

We saw an example of setting an index in Figure 12.4 in the previous chapter.

13.3.2 Indexes for *StayHome*

Based on the guidelines provided above, you should ensure that you create the primary key for each table, which will cause Access to automatically index this column. Secondly, you should ensure that you've correctly created all relationships in the Relationships window, which will cause Access to automatically index the foreign key columns.

From the *StayHome* transactions listed in Section 4.4.4, you may decide to create the additional indexes shown in Figure 13.5. This figure shows the columns in each table that should be indexed, the transaction(s) that use the column, and the reason for adding the index (either because the column has been used in a *search condition*, as an *ordering column*, or as a *grouping column*). We show the implementation of some of these transactions in both Access QBE and SQL in Chapter 17, so you may want to look at these implementations as a cross-check. You could perform a similar exercise for the transactions in the Business view documented in Chapter 10.

Note that the **available** column in the **VideoForRent** table is used as a search condition by transaction (s). However, this column can only take on two values (Y or N) and so from guideline (9) above, it is not worthwhile indexing this column.

Table	Column	Transaction	Reason
Branch	city	(m)	search condition
Staff	name	(n)	ordering
Video	category	(p)	ordering
		(u)	search condition
		(v)	grouping
	title	(q), (r), (u)	ordering
		(t)	search condition
Actor	actorName	(q)	search condition
		(x)	grouping, ordering
Director	directorName	(r)	search condition
Member	fName/lName	(s)	search condition
RentalAgreement	dateReturn	(s)	search condition
Registration	dateJoined	(y)	search condition

Figure 13.5

Additional indexes for *StayHome*.

Chapter summary

✓ In Step 5, you select the optimal file organizations to store the base tables, and the indexes that are required to achieve acceptable performance. This involves analyzing the transactions that will run on the database, choosing suitable file organizations based on this analysis, and adding indexes.

✓ It's not possible to make meaningful physical design decisions until you understand in detail the transactions that have to be supported. This involves analyzing the most important transactions, that is, the transactions that run most frequently or are critical to the operation of the business.

✓ **Heap files** are good for inserting a large number of records into the file. They are inappropriate when only selected records are to be retrieved.

✓ **Hash files** are good when retrieval is based on an exact key match. They are not good when retrieval is based on pattern matching, range of values, part keys, or when retrieval is based on a column other than the hash field.

✓ ISAM is more versatile than hashing, supporting retrievals based on exact key match, pattern matching, range of values, and part key specification. However, the ISAM index is static and so performance deteriorates as the table is updated. Updates also cause the ISAM file to lose the access key sequence, so that retrievals in order of the access key will become slower.

✓ These two problems are overcome by the B^+-Tree file organization, which has a dynamic index. If a table is not frequently updated or not very large nor likely to be, the ISAM structure may be more efficient as it has one less level of index than the B^+-Tree, whose leaf nodes contain record pointers.

✓ **Secondary indexes** provide a mechanism for specifying an additional key for a base table that can be used to retrieve data more efficiently. However, there is an overhead involved in the maintenance and use of secondary indexes that has to be balanced against the performance improvement gained when retrieving data.

✓ One approach to selecting an appropriate file organization for a table is to keep the records unordered and create as many secondary indexes as you need. Another approach is to order the records in the table by specifying a primary or clustering index.

✓ One approach to determining which secondary indexes you need is to produce a 'wish-list' of columns you think are candidates for indexing, and then to consider the impact of maintaining each of these indexes.

Chapter 14

Physical database design – Step 6

In this chapter you will learn:

How to handle derived data. ◀

When to denormalize to improve performance. ◀

This chapter covers the third step of our physical database design methodology. In the previous two chapters, we showed how to translate the logical design into a basic set of tables and select suitable file organizations and indexes based on an analysis of the transactions the database has to support. In some instances, additional performance improvements can be achieved by relaxing the normalization rules, which is what we consider in this chapter.

Methodology summarized in Appendix B

Normalization covered in Chapter 6

Step 6 Consider the introduction of controlled redundancy

> **Objective**
> To decide how to handle derived data and to determine whether introducing redundancy in a controlled manner by relaxing the normalization rules will improve the performance of the system.

Normalization is a procedure for deciding which columns belong together in a table. One of the basic aims of relational database design is to group columns

Functional dependency defined in Section 5.4

together in a table because there is a direct relationship (called a **functional dependency**) between them. The result of performing normalization on data is a logical database design that is structurally consistent and has minimal redundancy.

However, a normalized database design may not provide maximum processing efficiency. In these circumstances, you may wish to accept the loss of some of the benefits of a fully normalized design to achieve better performance. You should only consider this when you have estimated that the system will not be able to meet its performance requirements.

We are not advocating that normalization should be omitted from logical database design: normalization forces you to completely understand each column in each table in the database. Undertaking this process may be the most important factor that contributes to the overall success of the system. The following factors have to be considered if you're considering denormalization:

■ Denormalization makes implementation more complex.

■ Denormalization often sacrifices flexibility.

■ Denormalization may speed up retrievals but it slows down updates.

Formally, the term **denormalization** refers to a change to the structure of a base table, such that the new table is in a lower normal form than the original table. However, we also use the term more loosely to refer to situations where we combine two tables into one new table, where the new table is in the same normal form but contains more nulls than the original tables.

TIP As a general rule of thumb, if performance is unsatisfactory and a table has a low update rate and a very high query rate, denormalization may be a viable option.

The transaction/table cross-reference matrix that you may have produced in Step 5.1 provides useful information for this step. This matrix summarizes, in a visual way, the access patterns of the transactions that will run on the database. You can use it to highlight possible candidates for denormalization, and to assess the effects this would have on the rest of the model.

The two tasks in this step are:

■ Step 6.1 Consider derived data

■ Step 6.2 Consider duplicating columns or joining tables together

Step 6.1 Consider derived data

Derived attributes
defined in Section 5.3.3

> **Objective**
> To decide how to handle derived data.

A column whose value can be found by examining the values of other columns is known as a *derived* or *calculated* column. For example, the following are all derived columns:

- the number of staff who work at a particular branch;
- the total monthly salaries of all staff at a particular branch;
- the number of videos that a member currently has on rental.

As we mentioned in Step 1.3 in Chapter 8, derived columns often do not appear in the logical data model, but are instead documented in the data dictionary. If a derived column is shown in the model, the name is preceded by a '/' to indicate it's derived. The first step, then, is to examine the logical data model and the data dictionary, and produce a list of all derived columns.

From a physical database design perspective, whether a derived column is stored in the database or calculated every time it's needed is a trade-off. To decide, you should calculate:

- the additional cost to store the derived data and keep it consistent with operational data from which it is derived, and
- the cost to calculate it each time it's required,

and choose the less expensive option subject to performance constraints. For the last example given above, you could store an additional column in the Member table representing the number of rentals that each member currently has. The RentalAgreement table and the Member table with the new derived column are shown in Figure 14.1.

The additional storage overhead for this new derived column would not be particularly significant. However, the noOfRentals column would need to be updated every time a member rented or returned a video. You would need to ensure that this change was made consistently to maintain the correct count, and thereby ensure the integrity of the database. By storing the data in this way, when a query requires this information, the value is immediately available and does not have to be calculated.

On the other hand, if the column is not stored directly in the Member table, it must be calculated each time it's needed. This involves a join of the Member and RentalAgreement tables. For example, to calculate the number of videos that member 'Don Nelson' currently has on rental, you could use the following SQL query:

Figure 14.1

The RentalAgreement table and the Member table with the additional derived column noOfRentals.

RentalAgreement

rentalNo	dateOut	dateReturn	memberNo	videoNo
R753461	4-Feb-00	6-Feb-00	M284354	245456
R753462	4-Feb-00	6-Feb-00	M284354	243431
R668256	5-Feb-00	7-Feb-00	M115656	199004
R668189	2-Feb-00	4-Feb-00	M115656	178643

Member

memberNo	fName	lName	address	noOfRentals
M250178	Bob	Adams	57 – 11th Avenue, Seattle, WA, 98105	0
M166884	Art	Peters	89 Redmond Rd, Portland, OR, 97117	0
M115656	Serena	Parker	22 W. Capital Way, Portland, OR, 97201	2
M284354	Don	Nelson	123 Suffolk Lane, Seattle, WA, 98117	2

```
SELECT COUNT(*) AS noofrentals
FROM member m INNER JOIN rentalagreement ra
     ON m.memberno = ra.memberno
WHERE m.fname = 'Don' AND m.lname = 'Nelson';
```

If this type of query is frequent or is considered to be critical for performance purposes, it may be more appropriate to store the derived column rather than calculate it each time. In our example, *StayHome* would want to run this type of query every time a member attempted to rent a new video. Through discussion with *StayHome* staff, it's estimated that the size of the RentalAgreement table is 400 000 records, assuming records are archived from RentalAgreement whenever videos are returned. Therefore, as the RentalAgreement table is likely to be large and the query frequent, you may decide that it would be more efficient to add the derived column to the Member table. The same query could now be written as follows:

```
SELECT noofrentals
FROM member m
WHERE m.fname = 'Don' AND m.lname = 'Nelson';
```

TIP It may also be more appropriate to store derived columns whenever the system's query language cannot easily cope with the algorithm to calculate the derived column. For example, SQL has a limited set of aggregate functions and cannot easily handle recursive queries.

Step 6.2   Consider duplicating columns or joining tables together

Objective
To determine whether introducing redundancy in a controlled manner by relaxing the normalization rules will improve the performance of the system.

The next step is to consider duplicating certain columns or joining tables together to reduce the number of joins needed to perform a query. Indirectly, you've encountered an implicit example of denormalization when dealing with addresses. For example, consider the definition of the Branch table:

Branch   (branchNo, street, city, state, zipCode, mgrStaffNo)

Strictly speaking, this table is not in third normal form (3NF): zipCode functionally determines city and state; in other words, if you know the zip code, you also know the city and state. Therefore, to normalize the table it would be necessary to split the table into two, as follows:

3NF defined in Section 6.5

Branch   (branchNo, street, zipCode, mgrStaffNo)

ZipCode   (zipCode, city, state)

However, you rarely wish to access the branch address without the city and state columns. This would mean that you would have to perform a join whenever you wanted a complete address for a branch. As a result, we would normally implement the original Branch table and settle for second normal form (2NF).

Unfortunately, there are no fixed rules for determining when to denormalize tables. Let's however discuss some of the more common situations for considering denormalization to speed up frequent or critical transactions:

■ Step 6.2.1 Combining one-to-one (1:1) relationships

■ Step 6.2.2 Duplicating nonkey columns in one-to-many (1:*) relationships to reduce joins

■ Step 6.2.3 Duplicating foreign key columns in one-to-many (1:*) relationships to reduce joins

■ Step 6.2.4 Duplicating columns in many-to-many (*:*) relationships to reduce joins

■ Step 6.2.5 Introducing repeating groups

■ Step 6.2.6 Merging lookup tables with base tables

■ Step 6.2.7 Creating extract tables

1:1 relationships defined
in Section 5.5.1

Step 6.2.1 Combining one-to-one (1:1) relationships

Re-examine one-to-one (1:1) relationships to determine the effects of combining the tables into a single table. You should only consider this for tables that are frequently referenced together and infrequently referenced separately. Let's consider a potential 1:1 relationship between Staff and NOK, as shown in Figure 14.2(a). The Staff entity contains information on staff and the NOK entity contains information about a member of staff's next of kin. The resulting tables are shown in Figure 14.2(b).

Participation defined in
Section 5.5.5

The relationship between Staff and NOK is 1:1 and the participation is optional. Since the participation is optional, when the two tables are combined together a number of the columns have nulls appearing within them for some records, as shown in Figure 14.3. If the Staff table is large and the proportion of records involved in the participation is small, there will be a significant amount of wasted space. The amount of wastage has to then be balanced against any performance improvements gained by combining the tables.

1:* relationships defined
in Section 5.5.2

Step 6.2.2 Duplicating nonkey columns in one-to-many (1:*) relationships to reduce joins

With the specific aim of reducing or removing joins from frequent or critical queries, you should consider the benefits that may result in duplicating one or more nonkey columns of the parent table in the child table, in a one-to-many

Figure 14.2

Staff and NOK: (a) original ER model; (b) original tables.

Staff	RelatedTo ▶		NOK
staffNo {PK}	1..1	0..1	

(a)

Staff

staffNo	name	position	salary	branchNo
S1500	Tom Daniels	Manager	46000	B001
S0003	Sally Adams	Assistant	30000	B001
S0010	Mary Martinez	Manager	50000	B002
S3250	Robert Chin	Supervisor	32000	B002
S2250	Sally Stern	Manager	48000	B004
S0415	Art Peters	Snr Assistant	41000	B003

NOK

staffNo	nokName	nokTelNo
S1500	Jane Daniels	207-878-2751
S0003	John Adams	518-474-5355
S3250	Michelle Chin	206-655-9867
S0415	Amy Peters	718-507-7923

(b)

Figure 14.3

Combining Staff and NOK: (a) revised ER model; (b) combined table.

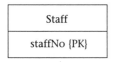

Staff
staffNo {PK}

(a)

Staff

staffNo	name	position	salary	nokName	nokTelNo	branchNo
S1500	Tom Daniels	Manager	46000	Jane Daniels	207-878-2751	B001
S0003	Sally Adams	Assistant	30000	John Adams	518-474-5355	B001
S0010	Mary Martinez	Manager	50000			B002
S3250	Robert Chin	Supervisor	32000	Michelle Chin	206-655-9867	B002
S2250	Sally Stern	Manager	48000			B004
S0415	Art Peters	Snr Assistant	41000	Amy Peters	718-507-7923	B003

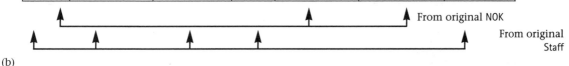

From original NOK

From original Staff

(b)

(1:*) relationship. For example, whenever the VideoForRent table is accessed, it's very common for the video's daily rental rate to be accessed at the same time. A typical SQL query would be:

```
SELECT vfr.*, v.dailyrental
FROM videoforrent vfr INNER JOIN video v
    ON vfr.catalogno = v.catalogno
WHERE branchno = 'B001';
```

based on the original ER model and resulting tables shown in Figure 14.4.

If you duplicate the dailyRental column in the VideoForRent table, you can remove the Video table from the query, which in SQL would now be:

```
SELECT vfr.*
FROM videoforrent vfr
WHERE branchno = 'B001';
```

based on the revised VideoForRent table shown in Figure 14.5.

Figure 14.4

Video and VideoForRent: (a) original ER model; (b) original tables.

Video	Is ▶	VideoForRent
catalogNo {PK}	1..1 1..*	videoNo {PK} catalogNo {FK}

(a)

Video

catalogNo	title	category	dailyRental	price	directorNo
207132	Tomorrow Never Dies	Action	5.00	21.99	D1001
902355	Primary Colors	Comedy	4.50	14.50	D7834
330553	Face/Off	Thriller	5.00	31.99	D4576
781132	101 Dalmatians	Children	4.00	18.50	D0078
445624	The Rock	Action	4.00	29.99	D5743
634817	Independence Day	Sci-Fi	4.50	32.99	D3765

VideoForRent

videoNo	available	catalogNo	branchNo
199004	N	207132	B001
245456	Y	207132	B002
178643	N	634817	B001
243431	N	634817	B002

(b)

Figure 14.5

Duplicating the dailyRental column in the VideoForRent table.

dailyRental column duplicated in VideoForRent

VideoForRent

videoNo	available	catalogNo	dailyRental	branchNo
199004	N	207132	5.00	B001
245456	Y	207132	5.00	B002
178643	N	634817	4.50	B001
243431	N	634817	4.50	B002

The benefits that result from this change have to be balanced against the problems that may arise. For example, if you change the duplicated data in the parent table, you must also update it in the child table. Further, for a 1:* relationship, there may be multiple occurrences of each data item in the child table (for example, videos 207132 and 634817 with rental rates 5.00 and 4.50, respectively, both appear twice in the revised VideoForRent table). Thus, you also have to maintain consistency of the multiple copies. If the update of the dailyRental column in the Video and VideoForRent table cannot be automated, the potential for loss of integrity is considerable. Even if this process can be automated, additional time will be required to maintain consistency every time a record is inserted, updated, or deleted. In our case, it's likely that the daily rental rate will be reduced as the video becomes older, so the duplication may be unwarranted.

Another problem to consider is the increase in storage space resulting from the duplication. Again, with the relatively low cost of secondary storage nowadays, this may be less of a problem. However, this is not a justification for arbitrary duplication.

Step 6.2.3 Duplicating foreign key columns in one-to-many (1:*) relationships to reduce joins

Again, with the specific aim of reducing or removing joins from frequent or critical queries, you should consider the benefits that may result in duplicating one or more of the foreign key columns in a relationship. For example, a frequent query for *StayHome* is to list all rental agreements at a branch, using the following SQL query:

```
SELECT ra.*
FROM rentalagreement ra INNER JOIN videoforrent vfr
    ON ra.videono = vfr.videono
WHERE vfr.branchno = 'B001';
```

based on the original ER model and tables shown in Figure 14.6.

As can be seen from this query, to get the list of rental agreements you have to use the VideoForRent table to gain access to the required branch number, branchNo. You can remove the need for this join by duplicating the foreign key branchNo in the RentalAgreement table; that is, you introduce a direct relationship between the Branch and RentalAgreement tables. In this case, you can simplify the SQL query to:

```
SELECT *
FROM rentalagreement
WHERE branchno = 'B001';
```

based on the revised ER model and RentalAgreement table shown in Figure 14.7. If this change is made, it will be necessary to introduce additional foreign key constraints, as discussed in Step 2.3.

Figure 14.6

RentalAgreement and
VideoForRent: (a)
original ER model;
(b) original tables.

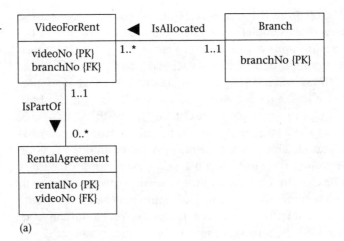

(a)

RentalAgreement

rentalNo	dateOut	dateReturn	memberNo	videoNo
R753461	4-Feb-00	6-Feb-00	M284354	245456
R753462	4-Feb-00	6-Feb-00	M284354	243431
R668256	5-Feb-00	7-Feb-00	M115656	199004
R668189	2-Feb-00	4-Feb-00	M115656	178643

VideoForRent

videoNo	available	catalogNo	branchNo
199004	N	207132	B001
245456	Y	207132	B002
178643	N	634817	B001
243431	N	634817	B002

(b)

: relationships defined
in Section 5.5.3

Note that this only works because the new relationship between **Branch** and
RentalAgreement is 1:*. In other words, for any one rental agreement there is one
and only one associated branch. If the relationship was many-to-many (*:*), the
above change would not work. For example, another frequent query might be to list
the video titles in stock at a branch using the following SQL query:

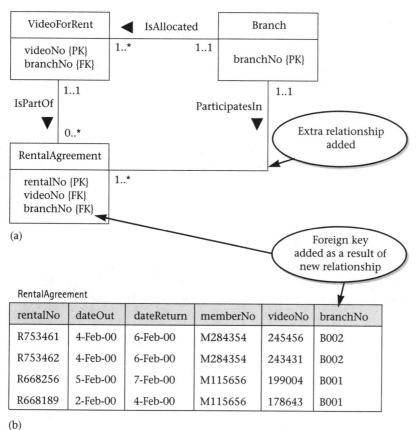

Figure 14.7

Duplicating the foreign key branchNo in the RentalAgreement table: (a) revised ER model; (b) revised RentalAgreement table.

(a)

RentalAgreement

rentalNo	dateOut	dateReturn	memberNo	videoNo	branchNo
R753461	4-Feb-00	6-Feb-00	M284354	245456	B002
R753462	4-Feb-00	6-Feb-00	M284354	243431	B002
R668256	5-Feb-00	7-Feb-00	M115656	199004	B001
R668189	2-Feb-00	4-Feb-00	M115656	178643	B001

(b)

```
SELECT v.title
FROM video v INNER JOIN videoforrent vfr
    ON v.catalogno = vfr.catalogno
WHERE vfr.branchno = 'B001';
```

This query cannot be simplified by adding the **branchNo** column to the **Video** table, as the relationship between **Branch** and **Video** is *:*; that is, a video title is stocked by many branches, and a branch can have many video titles. However, in this case you could consider duplicating the **title** column of the **Video** table in the **VideoForRent** table, although the increased storage may be more significant in this case.

Step 6.2.4 *Duplicating columns in many-to-many (*:*) relationships to reduce joins*

In Step 1.7, you transformed each *:* relationship into two 1:* relationships. This transformation introduced a third, intermediate entity. Now, if you wish to produce information from the *:* relationship, you have to join three tables: the two tables derived from the original entities and the new table representing the relationship between the two entities. In some circumstances, you may be able to reduce the number of tables to be joined by duplicating columns from one of the original entities in the intermediate table.

For example, a *:* relationship exists between Video and Actor, with Role acting as an intermediate entity. Consider the query that lists the video titles and roles that each actor has starred in:

```
SELECT v.title, a.*, r.*
FROM video v INNER JOIN (role r INNER JOIN actor a
    ON r.actorno = a.actorno) ON v.catalogno = r.catalogno;
```

based on the ER model and tables shown in Figure 14.8.

If you duplicate the title column in the Role table, you can remove the Video table from the query, giving the following revised SQL query:

```
SELECT a.*, r.*
FROM role r INNER JOIN actor a ON r.actorno = a.actorno;
```

based on the revised Role table shown in Figure 14.9.

Step 6.2.5 *Introducing repeating groups*

Repeating groups were eliminated from the logical data model as a result of the requirement that all entities be in first normal form (1NF). Repeating groups were separated out into a new table, forming a 1:* relationship with the original (parent) table. Occasionally, reintroducing repeating groups is an effective way to improve system performance.

For example, each *StayHome* branch office has a maximum of three telephone numbers, although not all offices necessarily have the same number of lines. In the logical data model, you created a Telephone entity with a three-to-one (3:1) relationship with Branch. This resulted in two tables, as shown in Figure 14.10.

If access to this information is important or frequent, it may be more efficient to combine the tables and store the telephone details in the original Branch table, with one column for each telephone number, as shown in Figure 14.11.

In general, you should only consider this type of denormalization in the following circumstances:

Telephone entity created in Step 1.7 in Chapter 8

Figure 14.8

Video, Actor, and Role:
(a) original ER
model; (b) original
tables.

Video	Features ▶	Role	◀ Plays	Actor
	1..1 0..*		1..* 1..1	
catalogNo {PK}		catalogNo {PK} actorNo {PK/FK}		actorNo {PK}

(a)

Video

catalogNo	title	category	dailyRental	price	directorNo
207132	Tomorrow Never Dies	Action	5.00	21.99	D1001
902355	Primary Colors	Comedy	4.50	14.50	D7834
330553	Face/Off	Thriller	5.00	31.99	D4576
781132	101 Dalmatians	Children	4.00	18.50	D0078
445624	The Rock	Action	4.00	29.99	D5743
634817	Independence Day	Sci-Fi	4.50	32.99	D3765

Actor

actorNo	actorName
A1002	Pierce Brosnan
A3006	John Travolta
A2019	Nicolas Cage
A7525	Will Smith
A4343	Glenn Close

Role

actorNo	catalogNo	character
A1002	207132	James Bond
A3006	330553	Sean Archer
A3006	902355	Jack Stanton
A2019	330553	Castor Troy
A2019	445624	Stanley Goodspeed
A7525	634817	Captain Steve Hiller
A4343	781132	Cruella De Vil

(b)

■ The absolute number of items in the repeating group is known (in this example, there is a maximum of three telephone numbers).

■ The number is static and will not change over time (the maximum number of telephone lines in a branch is fixed by *StayHome* and is not anticipated to change).

■ The number is not very large, typically not greater than 10, although this is not as important as the first two conditions.

Sometimes, it may be only the most recent or current value in a repeating group, or just the fact that there is a repeating group, that is needed most frequently. In the above example, you may choose to store one telephone number

Figure 14.9

Duplicating the title
column from the
Video table in the
Role table.

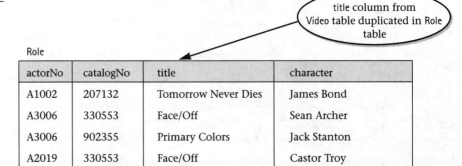

title column from
Video table duplicated in Role
table

Role

actorNo	catalogNo	title	character
A1002	207132	Tomorrow Never Dies	James Bond
A3006	330553	Face/Off	Sean Archer
A3006	902355	Primary Colors	Jack Stanton
A2019	330553	Face/Off	Castor Troy
A2019	445624	The Rock	Stanley Goodspeed
A7525	634817	Independence Day	Captain Steve Hiller
A4343	781132	101 Dalmatians	Cruella De Vil

Figure 14.10

Branch and Telephone:
(a) original ER
model; (b) original
tables.

Branch — Provides ▶ — Telephone

Branch — branchNo {PK} — 1..1 — 1..3 — Telephone — telNo {PK} branchNo {FK}

(a)

Branch

branchNo	street	city	state	zipCode	mgrStaffNo
B001	8 Jefferson Way	Portland	OR	97201	S1500
B002	City Center Plaza	Seattle	WA	98122	S0010
B003	14 – 8th Avenue	New York	NY	10012	S0415
B004	16 – 14th Avenue	Seattle	WA	98128	S2250

Telephone

telNo	branchNo
503-555-3618	B001
503-555-2727	B001
503-555-6534	B001
206-555-6756	B002
206-555-8836	B002
212-371-3000	B003
206-555-3131	B004
206-555-4112	B004

(b)

Figure 14.11

Branch incorporating repeating group: (a) revised ER model; (b) revised table.

Branch
branchNo {PK} telNo1 {AK}

(a)

Branch

branchNo	street	...	telNo1	telNo2	telNo3	mgrStaffNo
B001	8 Jefferson Way	...	503-555-3618	503-555-2727	503-555-6534	S1500
B002	City Center Plaza	...	206-555-6756	206-555-8836		S0010
B003	14 – 8th Avenue	...	212-371-3000			S0415
B004	16 – 14th Avenue	...	206-555-3131	206-555-4112		S2250

from original
Telephone table

(b)

in the Branch table and leave the remaining numbers for the Telephone table. This would remove the presence of nulls from the Branch table, as each branch must have at least one telephone number.

Step 6.2.6 Merging lookup tables with base tables

Lookup tables, sometimes called reference tables or pick lists, are a special case of one-to-many (1:*) relationships. Typically, a lookup table contains a code and a description. For example, you may define a lookup table for video category and modify the Video table, as shown in Figure 14.12.

The advantages of using a lookup table are:

■ Reduction in the size of the child table (in this case, the Video table); the category code occupies 1 byte as opposed to 8 bytes for the category description.

■ If the description can change (which would generally not be the case in this particular example), it's easier changing it once in the lookup table (VideoCategory) as opposed to changing it many times in the child table (Video).

■ The lookup table can be used to validate user input.

If lookup tables are used in frequent or critical queries, and the description is unlikely to change, you should also consider duplicating the description column in the child table, as shown in Figure 14.13. The original lookup table is not

Figure 14.12

Lookup table for video category: (a) original ER model; (b) original tables.

VideoCategory	CategoryFor ▶	Video
categoryID {PK}	1..1 1..*	catalogNo {PK} categoryID {FK}

(a)

VideoCategory

categoryID	description
1	Action
2	Comedy
3	Children
4	Sci-Fi
5	Thriller

Video

catalogNo	title	categoryID	dailyRental	price	directorNo
207132	Tomorrow Never Dies	1	5.00	21.99	D1001
902355	Primary Colors	2	4.50	14.50	D7834
330553	Face/Off	5	5.00	31.99	D4576
781132	101 Dalmatians	3	4.00	18.50	D0078
445624	The Rock	1	4.00	29.99	D5743
634817	Independence Day	4	4.50	32.99	D3765

lookup list

(b)

Figure 14.13

Modified Video table with duplicated description column.

description column from VideoCategory table duplicated in Video table

Video

catalogNo	title	categoryID	description	dailyRental	price	directorNo
207132	Tomorrow Never Dies	1	Action	5.00	21.99	D1001
902355	Primary Colors	2	Comedy	4.50	14.50	D7834
330553	Face/Off	5	Thriller	5.00	31.99	D4576
781132	101 Dalmatians	3	Children	4.00	18.50	D0078
445624	The Rock	1	Action	4.00	29.99	D5743
634817	Independence Day	4	Sci-Fi	4.50	32.99	D3765

redundant – it can still be used to validate user input. However, by duplicating the description column in the child table, you've eliminated the need to join the child table to the lookup table.

Step 6.2.7 Creating extract tables

There may be situations where you have to run certain reports at peak times during the day. These reports access derived data and perform multi-table joins on the same set of base tables. However, the data the report is based on may be relatively static or, in some cases, may not have to be current (that is, if the data were a few hours old, the report would be perfectly acceptable). In this case, it may be possible to create a single, highly denormalized extract table based on the tables required by the reports, and allow the users to access the extract table directly instead of the base tables. The most common technique for producing extract tables is to create and populate the tables in an overnight batch run when the system is lightly loaded.

Consider implications of denormalization

You should consider the implications of denormalization on the previous steps in the methodology. For example, you may have to reconsider the choice of indexes on the tables you have denormalized to check whether existing indexes should be removed or additional indexes added.

Document introduction of redundancy

The introduction of redundancy should be fully documented, along with the reasons for introducing it. In particular, document the reasons for selecting one approach where many alternatives exist. Update the logical data model and supporting documentation to reflect any changes made as a result of denormalization.

Chapter summary

✓ In Step 6, you consider the introduction of controlled redundancy to improve performance.

✓ There may be circumstances where it may be necessary to accept the loss of some of the benefits of a fully normalized design in favor of performance. This should be considered only when it's estimated that the system will not be able to meet its performance requirements. As a rule of thumb, if performance is unsatisfactory and a table has a low update rate and a very high query rate, **denormalization** may be a viable option.

✓ From a physical database design perspective, whether a derived column is stored in the database or calculated every time it's needed is a trade-off. Consider the additional cost to store the derived data and keep it consistent and the cost to calculate it each time it's required and choose the less expensive option.

✓ Consider denormalization in the following situations, specifically to speed up frequent or critical transactions: combining 1:1 relationships; duplicating nonkey columns in 1:* relationships to reduce joins; duplicating foreign key columns in 1:* relationships to reduce joins; duplicating columns in *:* relationships to reduce joins; introducing repeating groups; merging lookup tables with base tables; creating extract tables.

Chapter 15

Physical database design – Step 7

In this chapter you will learn:

A database represents an essential corporate resource that must be made secure. ◄

How to design security mechanisms to satisfy user requirements ◄

This chapter covers the fourth step of our physical database design methodology. In the previous three chapters, we translated the logical design into a basic set of tables, selected appropriate file organizations and indexes based on an analysis of the most important transactions, and then considered the introduction of controlled redundancy to achieve additional performance improvements.

Methodology summarized in Appendix B

In this chapter, we examine how to make the database secure. As with the other steps of physical database design, the implementation of the security mechanisms will be dependent on the target DBMS.

Step 7 Design security mechanisms

Objective
To design the security measures for the database as specified by the users.

A database represents an essential corporate resource, and so security of this resource is extremely important. There may have been specific security requirements documented during the Requirements Collection and Analysis phase of the database application lifecycle. The objective of this step is to decide how

Security requirements covered in Section 4.4.4

these security measures will be realized. Some systems offer different security facilities than others. Again, you must be aware of the facilities offered by the target DBMS. The two tasks in this step are:

■ Step 7.1 Design user views

■ Step 7.2 Design access rules

User views defined in
Section 3.5

Step 7.1   Design user views

Objective
To design the user views that were identified during the analysis phase of the relational database application lifecycle.

The first step of the database design methodology involved the production of a *local logical data model* for each view identified during the database analysis phase. Each view consisted of one or more *user views*. In Section 4.4.4, we identified two views for *StayHome*:

■ *Branch,* consisting of the Manager, Supervisor, and Assistant user views;

■ *Business,* consisting of the Director and Buyer user views.

In Step 3, these local logical models were merged into one *global logical data model*. The objective of this step is to design all the user views identified previously. In a standalone DBMS on a personal computer, views are usually a convenience, defined to simplify queries. However, in a multi-user DBMS views play a central role in defining the structure of the database and enforcing security. As with the design of base tables discussed in Chapter 12, to illustrate this process we show two particular ways to create views using:

(1) the 1992 ISO SQL standard (SQL2),

(2) Microsoft Access 97.

The 1992 ISO SQL Standard (SQL2)

Base tables defined in
Section 2.3.2

Normally, views are created using SQL or a QBE-like facility. For example, for Supervisors and Assistants at branch B001 you may wish to create a view of the base table Staff that excludes salary information. The SQL statement to create this view would be:

```
CREATE VIEW staff1_view
AS   SELECT staffno, name, position
     FROM staff
     WHERE branchno = 'B001';
```

Staff1_View

staffNo	name	position
S1500	Tom Daniels	Manager
S0003	Sally Adams	Assistant

Figure 15.1

List of the
Staff1_View view.

This creates a view called Staff1_View with the same columns as the Staff table, but excluding the salary and branchNo columns. If you list this view you would get the data shown in Figure 15.1.

To ensure that only the branch manager can see the salary column, Supervisors and Assistants should not be given access to the base table Staff. Instead, they should be given *access privilege* to the view Staff1_View, thereby denying them access to sensitive salary data. We'll discuss access privileges further in Step 7.2.

Creating views in Microsoft Access 97

Microsoft Access does not support the SQL CREATE VIEW statement. Instead, you can create a (stored) query using QBE or SQL. For example, you could create the Staff1_View view using the QBE query shown in Figure 15.2(a) or using the SQL statement shown in Figure 15.2(b). This query can now be used to create other queries, or insert/update/delete records in the base table Staff, and can be used as the basis for creating forms and reports.

Figure 15.2

Creating a (stored) query in Microsoft Access: (a) using QBE; (b) using SQL.

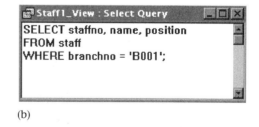

(b)

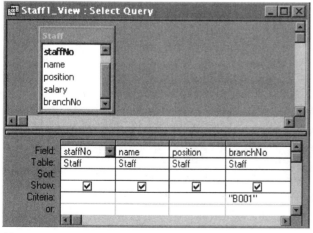

(a)

Step 7.2 Design access rules

> **Objective**
> To design the access rules to the base tables and user views.

Relational DBMSs generally provide two types of database security:

■ system security,

■ data security.

System security covers access and use of the database at the system level, such as a username and password. **Data security** covers access and use of database objects (such as tables and views) and the actions that users can have on the objects.

As we've already said, the design of access rules is dependent on the target DBMS; some systems provide more facilities than others for designing access rules. As before, to illustrate this process we show two particular ways to design access rules using:

(1) the 1992 ISO SQL standard (SQL2),

(2) Microsoft Access 97.

> In Chapter 17, we'll show how to design access rules in Oracle 8 using a different worked example.

The 1992 ISO SQL Standard (SQL2)

One way to provide data security is to use the access control facilities of SQL. As we've just mentioned, typically, users should not be given direct access to the base tables. Instead, they should be given access to the base tables through the user views designed in Step 7.1. This provides a large degree of data independence and insulates users from changes in the database structure. We briefly review the access control mechanisms of SQL2. For additional information, the interested reader is referred to Connolly and Begg (1999).

Data independence defined section 1.2.1

Each database user is assigned an *authorization identifier* by the Database Administrator (DBA); usually, the identifier has an associated password, for obvious security reasons. Every SQL statement that is executed by the DBMS is performed on behalf of a specific user. The authorization identifier is used to determine which database objects that user may reference, and what operations may be performed on those objects. Each object that is created in SQL has an owner, who is identified by the authorization identifier. By default, the owner is the only person who may know of the existence of the object and perform any operations on the object.

Privileges are the actions that a user is permitted to carry out on a given base table or view. For example, SELECT is the privilege to retrieve data from a table and UPDATE is the privilege to modify records of a table. When a user creates a table using the SQL CREATE TABLE statement, he or she automatically becomes the owner of the table and receives full privileges for the table. Other users initially have no privileges on the newly created table. To give them access to the table, the owner must explicitly grant them the necessary privileges using the SQL GRANT statement. A WITH GRANT OPTION clause can be specified with the GRANT statement to allow the receiving user(s) to pass the privilege(s) on to other users. Privileges can be revoked using the SQL REVOKE statement.

When a user creates a view with the CREATE VIEW statement, he or she automatically becomes the owner of the view, but does not necessarily receive full privileges on the view. To create the view, a user must have SELECT privilege to all the tables that make up the view. However, the owner will only get other privileges if he or she holds those privileges for every table in the view.

For example, to allow the user MANAGER to retrieve records from the Staff table and to insert, update, and delete data from the Staff table, you could use the following SQL statement:

```
GRANT ALL PRIVILEGES
ON staff
TO manager WITH GRANT OPTION;
```

In this case, MANAGER will also be able to reference the table and all the columns in any table he or she creates subsequently. The clause WITH GRANT OPTION is specified so that MANAGER can pass these privileges on to other users that he or she sees fit. As another example, you could give the user with authorization identifier ADMIN the privilege SELECT on the Staff table using the following SQL statement:

```
GRANT SELECT
ON staff
TO admin;
```

The clause WITH GRANT OPTION is omitted this time so that ADMIN will not be able to pass this privilege on to other users.

Security in Microsoft Access 97

Microsoft Access 97 does not support the SQL GRANT and REVOKE statements. Instead, Access provides the following two methods for securing a database:

(a) setting a password for opening a database (system security);

(b) user-level security, which can be used to limit the parts of the database that a user can read or update (data security).

Setting a password

The simpler method is to set a password for opening the database. Once a password has been set (from the *Tools*, *Security* menu), a dialog box requesting the password will be displayed whenever the database is opened. The dialog box to set the password and the dialog box requesting the password whenever the database is opened are shown in Figure 15.3.

Only users who type the correct password will be allowed to open the database. This method is secure as Microsoft Access encrypts the password so that it cannot be accessed by reading the database file directly. However, once a database is open, all the objects contained within the database are available to the user.

User-level security

User-level security in Microsoft Access is similar to methods used in most network systems. Users are required to identify themselves and type a password when they start Microsoft Access. Within the workgroup information file, users are identified as members of a *group*. Access provides two default groups: administrators (*Admins* group) and users (*Users* group), but additional groups can be defined. Figure 15.4 displays the dialog box used to define the security level for user and

Figure 15.3

Securing the *StayHome* database using a password: (a) the Set Database Password dialog box; (b) the Password dialog box shown at startup.

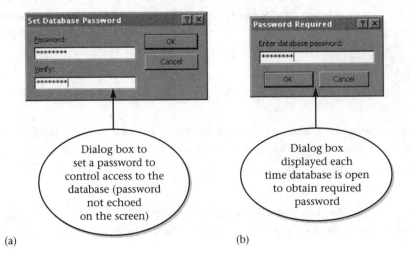

(a)   (b)

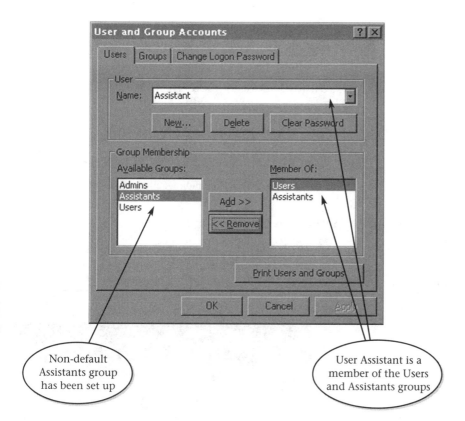

Figure 15.4

The User and Group Accounts dialog box for the *StayHome* database.

group accounts. It shows a non-default group called Assistants, and a user called Assistant who is a member of the Users and Assistants groups.

Permissions are granted to groups and users to regulate how they are allowed to work with each object in the database using the User and Group Permissions dialog box. Table 15.1 shows the permissions that can be set in Microsoft Access. For example, Figure 15.5 shows the dialog box for a user called Assistant in *StayHome* who has only read access to the Staff1_View created previously. In a similar way, all access to the base table Staff would be removed so that the Assistant user could only view the data in the Staff table using this view.

Document design of user views and security measures

The design of the individual user views and associated security mechanisms should be fully documented. If the physical design affects the individual local logical data models, these models should also be updated.

Table 15.1 Microsoft Access permissions.

Permission	Description
Open/Run	Open a database, form, report, or run a macro.
Open Exclusive	Open a database with exclusive access.
Read Design	View objects in Design view.
Modify Design	View and change database objects, and delete them.
Administer	For databases, set database password, replicate database, and change startup properties.
	Full access to database objects including ability to assign permissions.
Read Data	View data.
Update Data	View and modify data (but not insert or delete data).
Insert Data	View and insert data (but not update or delete data).
Delete Data	View and delete data (but not insert or update data).

Figure 15.5

User and Group Permissions dialog box showing the Assistant user only has read access to the Staff1_View query.

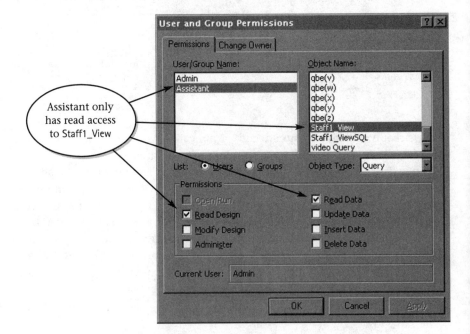

Chapter summary

✓ A database represents an essential corporate resource, and so security of this resource is extremely important.

✓ In Step 7, you design how the security measures identified during the analysis phase will be realized. This may include the creation of user views and the use of access control mechanisms, such as those provided by SQL.

✓ Relational DBMSs generally provide two types of database security: system security and data security. **System security** covers access and use of the database at the system level, such as a username and password. **Data security** covers access and use of database objects (such as tables and views) and the actions that users can have on the objects.

Chapter 16

Physical database design – Step 8

In this chapter you will learn:

➤ The importance of monitoring and tuning the operational system.

Methodology summarized in Appendix B

This chapter covers the fifth and final step of our physical database design methodology. In the previous four chapters, we translated the logical design into a basic set of tables, selected appropriate file organizations and indexes based on an analysis of the most important transactions, considered the introduction of controlled redundancy to achieve additional performance improvements, and examined how to make the database secure.

As user requirements evolve, it's usually necessary to *tune*, or adjust, the database to continue to achieve acceptable performance. In addition, you'll probably find that the requirements change, either as a result of the success of the system and users wanting more functionality, or as a result of the business evolving and adapting. In this chapter, we consider the remaining step of physical database design that takes these aspects into consideration.

Step 8   Monitor and tune the operational system

Objective
To monitor the operational system and improve the performance of the system to correct inappropriate design decisions or reflect changing requirements.

You should not regard the initial physical database design as static, but as an estimate of how the operational system might perform. Once the initial design has been implemented, you should monitor the system and tune it as a result of observed performance and changing requirements. Many DBMSs provide the Database Administrator (DBA) with utilities to monitor the operation of the system and tune it.

There are many benefits to be gained from tuning the database:

■ It can avoid the procurement of additional hardware.

■ It may be possible to downsize the hardware configuration. This results in less, and cheaper, hardware and potentially less expensive maintenance.

■ A well-tuned system produces faster response times and better throughput, which in turn makes the users, and hence the company, more productive.

■ Improved response times can improve staff morale.

■ Improved response times can increase customer satisfaction.

These last two benefits are more intangible than the others. However, we can certainly state that slow response times demoralize staff and potentially lose customers.

Tuning is an activity that is never complete. Throughout the life of the system, you'll need to monitor performance, particularly to account for changes in the environment and user requirements. However, making a change to one area of an operational system to improve performance may have an adverse effect on another area. For example, adding an index to a table may improve the performance of one application, but it may adversely affect another, perhaps more important, application. Therefore, care must be taken when making changes to an operational system. If possible, test the changes either on a test database, or alternatively, when the system is not being fully used (for example, out of working hours).

New requirement from *StayHome*

It has been decided that the Video table should hold a picture of the video cover together with a brief story line, in preparation for making the video catalog available over the Web. You can accommodate this new requirement in Microsoft Access using the OLE (Object Linking and Embedding) data type, which is used to store data such as Microsoft Word or Excel documents, pictures, sound, and other types of binary data created in other programs. OLE objects can be linked to, or embedded in, a field in a Microsoft Access table and then displayed in a form or report.

To satisfy this new requirement, you can restructure the Video table to add:

(1) a column called videoCover specified as an OLE Object data type, and

(2) a column called storyLine specified as a Memo data type, capable of storing lengthy text.

Figure 16.1

Form based on a
revised Video table
with the new
videoCover and
storyLine columns
added.

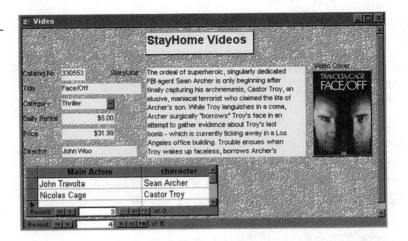

A form using these new columns is shown in Figure 16.1. The main problem
with the addition of these two extra columns is the potentially large amount of
disk space that will be required to store the graphics files and the large amounts
of text for the story line. You will therefore need to continue to monitor the
performance of the *StayHome* database to ensure that satisfying this new
requirement does not compromise the system's performance.

Now that you have gone through all the steps in the methodology, you might like
to look back at Section 7.1.4 to revisit the factors that we said were critical for
successful database design. Possibly when you first read this section, it may have
been difficult to see the relevance of some of these factors, but hopefully now you
will see the importance of them all.

Chapter summary

 Step 8, the final step of physical database design, involves the ongoing
process of monitoring and tuning the operational system to achieve
maximum performance or to reflect changing requirements.

Chapter 17

Sample *StayHome* queries using SQL and QBE

In this chapter you will learn:

How to implement the *StayHome* queries using SQL. ◄

How to implement the *StayHome* queries using QBE. ◄

In this chapter, we show how some of the *StayHome* data queries listed in Section 4.4.4 can be implemented in Microsoft SQL and Microsoft QBE. However, this chapter is not intended to be a review of SQL or QBE, but instead shows how the preceding design can lead to implementation. For a more complete discussion of SQL and QBE, the interested reader is referred to Connolly and Begg (1999).

17.1 Introduction to Microsoft SQL and QBE

The two main languages that have emerged for relational DBMSs are:

- SQL (Structured Query Language)
- QBE (Query-by-Example).

17.1.1 SQL

SQL is the most widely used commercial relational database language, designed to be used by professionals and non-professionals alike. It consists of standard English words such as SELECT, INSERT, UPDATE, and DELETE. It was originally developed in the SEQUEL and System-R projects at IBM's research laboratory in San José between 1974 and 1977. Today, many people still pronounce SQL as 'See-Quel', although the official pronunciation is 'S-Q-L'. Starting with Oracle in the late 1970s, there have been many commercial RDBMSs based on SQL, and with an ANSI/ISO standard, it's now the standard language for defining and manipulating relational databases.

Unfortunately, no RDBMS currently conforms fully to the most recent release of the standard, which was in 1992. For example, some systems will provide additional data types over and above those specified in the standard (such as the non-standard Autonumber, OLE-Object, and Currency data types provided by Microsoft Access). While this does look as though the vendor is providing additional functionality, it's at the cost of portability. In the examples we go through in this chapter, we highlight those parts of the SQL queries that are not standard SQL. Let's first examine the format of the SELECT statement, which we'll concentrate on in this chapter.

The SELECT statement

The purpose of the SELECT statement is to retrieve and display data from one or more tables. It's an extremely powerful command and is also the most frequently used command in SQL. The general form of the SELECT statement is:

```
SELECT   [DISTINCT ¦ ALL]
         {* ¦ [column_expression [AS new_name]] [, ... ]}
FROM    table_name [alias] [, ... ]
[WHERE condition]
[GROUP BY column_list]      [HAVING condition]
[ORDER BY column_list]
```

The square brackets [ ] indicate optional elements, and the curly brackets { } indicate that the element can be repeated zero or more times. In addition:

- *column_expression* represents a column name or an expression;
- *new_name* is a name you can give the column as a display heading;
- *table_name* is the name of an existing database table or view that you have access to;
- *alias* is an optional abbreviation for *table_name*;
- *column_list* is a list of one or more columns.

The sequence of processing in a SELECT statement is:

FROM	Specifies the table or tables to be used.
WHERE	Filters the records subject to some condition.
GROUP BY	Forms groups of records with the same field value.
HAVING	Filters the groups subject to some condition.
SELECT	Specifies which columns are to appear in the output.
ORDER BY	Specifies the order of the output.

The order of the clauses in the SELECT statement *cannot* be changed. The only two mandatory clauses are the first two, SELECT and FROM; the remainder are optional.

17.1.2 Query–By–Example (QBE)

QBE is an alternative, graphical-based, 'point-and-click' way of querying the database. QBE has acquired the reputation of being one of the easiest ways for non-technical users to obtain information from a database. QBE provides a visual means for querying the data through the use of templates. Querying the database is achieved by illustrating the query to be answered. The screen display is used instead of typing in field names and formats; however, you must indicate the columns (called *fields* in Access) you want to see and specify data values that you want to use to restrict the query. Languages like QBE can be a highly productive way to interactively query or update the database.

Like SQL, QBE was developed at IBM (in fact, QBE is an IBM trademark), but a number of other vendors, including Microsoft, sell QBE-like interfaces. Often vendors provide both SQL and QBE facilities, with QBE serving as a more intuitive interface for simple queries and the full power of SQL available for more complex queries.

Once you have read this chapter, you will see that the QBE version of the queries is more straightforward, perhaps with the exception of those queries that involve a single table and do not require the use of groupings or aggregate functions.

17.2 Sample queries for *StayHome*

In this section, we consider some of the data queries listed in Section 4.4.4 for *StayHome*. We adopt the transaction numbering scheme used in that section.

(m) List the details of branches in a given city

Branch details are spread over two tables. Most branch details are stored in the Branch table, but branch telephone numbers are stored in the Telephone table. To access both sets of details, we need to join the two tables together based on the join column, branchNo.

In addition, we are asked to restrict the list to branches in a given city. If the city was Seattle, for example, we could use the criterion (city = 'Seattle'). To allow the user to specify the city at runtime, Microsoft Access provides an extension to standard SQL called *parameters*, which can be created by typing a prompt enclosed in square brackets as the criteria expression, for example '[Enter name of city]'. Microsoft Access displays a dialog box with the specified prompt for each parameter that forms part of the query. The QBE query for this transaction is illustrated in Figure 17.1(a) and the dialog box for the city parameter in Figure 17.1(b). The equivalent SQL query is shown in Figure 17.1(c).

Note that we have used aliases in the FROM clause as abbreviations. If you were to examine the SQL view of a QBE query, you would find that Microsoft Access does not use aliases but instead uses the expanded form of each table. However, the SQL standard does allow aliases, as does Microsoft Access if you type in the SQL query in SQL view. Access SQL also uses the INNER JOIN form of the SELECT statement when two or more tables have to be joined together. We also show an alternative form of the SQL statement in Figure 17.1(d), which some of you may be more familiar with, and is still perfectly acceptable if you were to enter the query in SQL view.

Figure 17.1(e) shows the output from running the query.

Note that in both versions of the SQL query we have to specify how to join the **Branch** and **Telephone** tables. However, QBE does this automatically for us. You'll see this in the other queries we discuss in this chapter. See how much easier this makes QBE to use than SQL.

Figure 17.1

Transaction (m): (a) QBE; (b) parameter dialog box for city;
(c) equivalent SQL with inner join; (d) alternative form of SQL;
(e) resulting datasheet showing output from query.

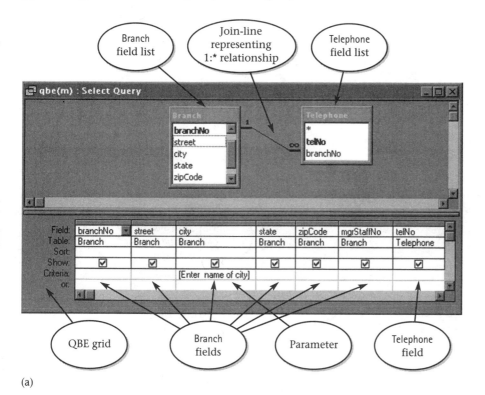

(a)

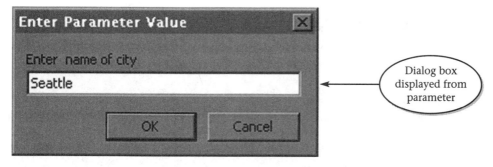

(b)

Figure 17.1

Continued

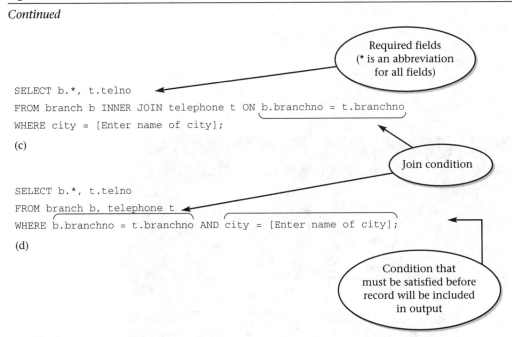

(c)

(d)

(e)

Having shown an example of the two alternative versions of SQL, we'll just show the INNER JOIN version in the remainder of this chapter.

(n)   List the name, position, and salary of staff at a given branch, ordered by staff name

All the required information for this query is part of the Staff table. Again, we can use a parameter query to allow the user to specify a branch number at run-

Figure 17.2

Transaction (n): (a) QBE; (b) equivalent SQL.

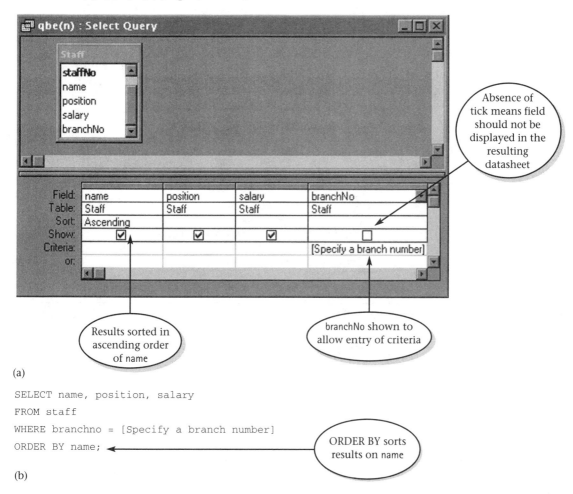

(a)

```
SELECT name, position, salary
FROM staff
WHERE branchno = [Specify a branch number]
ORDER BY name;
```

(b)

time. To output the data in order of staff name, we select Ascending from the drop-down list in the *Sort* cell for the name field. The QBE query is illustrated in Figure 17.2(a) and the equivalent SQL query in Figure 17.2(b).

(p) List the title, category, and availability of all videos at a specified branch, ordered by category

The title and category fields are part of the Video table; the available and branchNo fields are part of the VideoForRent table. The two tables are joined on the catalogNo field, and the resulting output sorted on the category field. The QBE query is illustrated in Figure 17.3(a) and the equivalent SQL query in Figure 17.3(b).

Figure 17.3

Transaction (p):
(a) QBE; (b)
equivalent SQL.

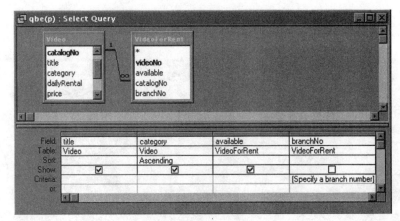

(a)

```
SELECT title, category, available
FROM video v INNER JOIN videoforrent vfr ON v.catalogno = vfr.catalogno
WHERE vfr.branchno = [Specify a branch number]
ORDER BY category;
```

(b)

Figure 17.4

Transaction (q): (a) QBE; (b) equivalent SQL.

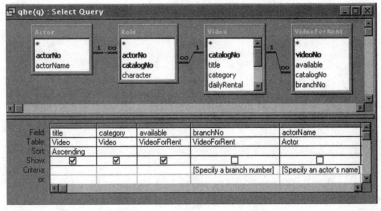

(a)

```
SELECT title, category, available
FROM (video v INNER JOIN (actor a INNER JOIN role r ON a.actorno = r.actorno)
      ON v.catalogno = r.catalogno) INNER JOIN videoforrent vfr
      ON v.catalogno = vfr.catalogno
WHERE vfr.branchno = [Specify a branch number] AND
      a.actorname = [Specify an actor's name]
ORDER BY title;
```

(b)

(q) List the title, category, and availability of all videos for a given actor's name at a specified branch, ordered by title

As with the previous query, the title and category fields are part of the Video table; the available and branchNo fields are part of the VideoForRent table, with the two tables joined on the catalogNo field. The actor's name is part of the Actor table. To join the Actor table to the Video table we have to use the Role table. The Actor and Role tables are joined on the actorNo field and the Role table is joined to the Video table on the catalogNo fields. The QBE query is illustrated in Figure 17.4(a) and the equivalent SQL query in Figure 17.4(b).

(v) List the total number of videos in each video category at each branch, ordered by branch number

The category field is part of the Video table and the information about copies of each video is part of the VideoForRent table. This time, however, rather than list the details of each copy, we want to calculate the total number of copies. To do this, we use the aggregate function *Count*, which is accessed by changing the query type to *Totals*. This results in the display of an additional row called *Total* in the QBE grid. When you select *Totals*, all fields that you have selected will automatically be set to Group By in the *Total* row. We wish to group the information based on the category and the branch number (we're looking for totals for each category at each branch), so make sure these fields are set to Group By, but change the *Total* row for the catalogNo field to *Count* from the drop down list. To make the output more meaningful, we change the name of the field heading in the resulting datasheet to Total Videos. When a totals query is run, the resulting datasheet is a *snapshot*, a set of records that is not updatable.

The QBE query is illustrated in Figure 17.5(a) and the equivalent SQL query in Figure 17.5(b).

> Note that the Count function can be applied to any field in the resulting table. In SQL, this is generally written as COUNT(*). However, in QBE the function has to be applied to a specific field.

(x) List the total number of videos featuring each actor, ordered by actor name

The required information is part of the Video, Role, and Actor tables. To find the total number of videos featuring each actor, we want to group the data on actorName and then apply the *Count* function to any of the fields in the Video table (catalogNo, say). The QBE query is illustrated in Figure 17.6(a) and the equivalent SQL query in Figure 17.6(b).

Figure 17.5

Transaction (v): (a) QBE; (b) equivalent SQL.

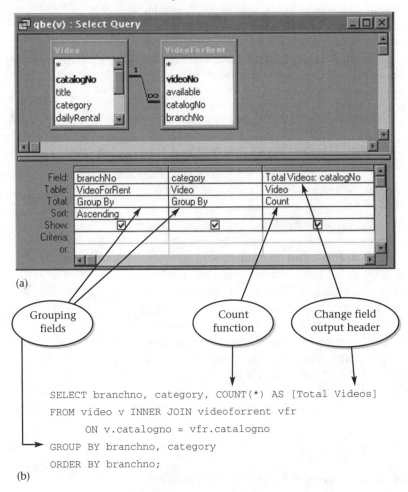

(a)

```
SELECT branchno, category, COUNT(*) AS [Total Videos]
FROM video v INNER JOIN videoforrent vfr
     ON v.catalogno = vfr.catalogno
GROUP BY branchno, category
ORDER BY branchno;
```

(b)

Note, we could have used **actorNo** as the grouping field, but as we have to sort the results by **actorName**, we also use **actorName** as the grouping field.

(z) List the total possible daily rental for videos at each branch, ordered by branch number

The data we require for this query is part of the Video and VideoForRent tables. To sum the daily rental prices for videos at each branch, we first use a *Totals* query

Figure 17.6

Transaction (x): (a) QBE; (b) equivalent SQL.

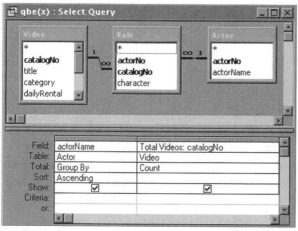

(a)

```
SELECT actorname, COUNT(*) AS [Total Videos]
FROM video v INNER JOIN (actor a INNER JOIN role r ON a.actorno = r.actorno)
     ON v.catalogno = r.catalogno
GROUP BY actorname
ORDER BY actorname;
```

(b)

Figure 17.7

Transaction (z): (a) QBE; (b) equivalent SQL.

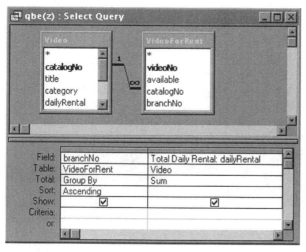

(a)

Figure 17.7

Continued

```
SELECT branchno, SUM(dailyrental) as [Total Daily Rental]
FROM video v INNER JOIN videoforrent vfr ON v.catalogno = vfr.catalogno
GROUP BY branchno
ORDER BY branchno;
```

(b)

to group the data by the branchNo field in the VideoForRent table. We then use the *Sum* function to add all the daily rental prices together to get the total in each group. The resulting output is sorted on the branchNo field. The QBE query is illustrated in Figure 17.7(a) and the equivalent SQL query in Figure 17.7(b).

Chapter summary

✓ SQL is a non-procedural language, consisting of standard English words such as SELECT, INSERT, DELETE, that can be used by professionals and non-professionals alike. It's the standard language for defining and manipulating relational databases.

✓ The purpose of the SELECT statement is to retrieve and display data from one or more database tables. It's an extremely powerful command and is also the most frequently used command in SQL.

✓ QBE is an alternative, graphical-based, 'point-and-click' way of querying the database. QBE has acquired the reputation of being one of the easiest ways for non-technical computer users to obtain information from a database.

Part Five

Second worked example

Chapter 18

Perfect Pets – Logical database design

In this chapter, we provide a second case study to help reinforce the methodology we've presented in Chapters 8 to 16. We go through the steps of the logical database design methodology in this chapter and then the steps of physical database design in the next chapter. To demonstrate some of the physical implementation aspects we also use a different relational DBMS, this time Oracle 8. It may be useful if you read the case study in the following section and then attempt the steps in the methodology yourself. You can then check your solution against our sample solution. You may find the summary of the methodology given in Appendix B helpful.

18.1 *Perfect Pets*

A practice called *Perfect Pets* provides private health care for domestic pets throughout America. This service is provided through various clinics located in the main cities of America. The Director of *Perfect Pets* is concerned that there is a lack of communication within the practice and particularly in the sharing of information and resources across the various clinics. To resolve this problem the Director has requested the creation of a centralized database system to assist in the more effective and efficient running of the practice. The Director has provided the following description of the current system.

18.1.1 Data requirements

Veterinary clinics

Perfect Pets has many veterinary clinics located in the main cities of America. The details of each clinic include the clinic number, clinic address (consisting of the street, city, state, and zipcode), and the telephone and fax numbers. Each clinic has a Manager and a number of staff (for example, vets, nurses, secretaries, cleaners). The clinic number is unique throughout the practice.

Staff

The details stored on each member of staff include the staff number, name (first and last), address (street, city, state, and zipcode), telephone number, date of birth, sex, social security number (SSN), position, and current annual salary. The staff number is unique throughout the practice.

Pet owners

When a pet owner first contacts a clinic of *Perfect Pets* the details of the pet owner are recorded, which include an owner number, owner name (first name and last name), address (street, city, state, and zipcode), and home telephone number. The owner number is unique to a particular clinic.

Pets

The details of the pet requiring treatment are noted, which include a pet number, pet name, type of pet, description, date of birth (if unknown, an approximate date is recorded), date registered at clinic, current status (alive/deceased), and the details of the pet owner. The pet number is unique to a particular clinic.

Examinations

When a sick pet is brought to a clinic, the vet on duty examines the pet. The details of each examination are recorded and include an examination number, the date and time of the examination, the name of the vet, the pet number, pet name, and type of pet, and a full description of the examination results. The examination number is unique to a particular clinic. As a result of the examination, the vet may propose treatment(s) for the pet.

Treatments

Perfect Pets provides various treatments for all types of pets. These treatments are provided at a standard rate across all clinics. The details of each treatment include a treatment number, a full description of the treatment, and the cost to the pet owner. For example, treatments include:

T123	Penicillin antibiotic course	$50.00
T155	Feline hysterectomy	$200.00
T112	Vaccination course against feline flu	$70.00
T56	Small dog – stay in pen per day (includes feeding)	$20.00

A standard rate of $20.00 is charged for each examination, which is recorded as a type of treatment. The treatment number uniquely identifies each type of treatment and is used by all *Perfect Pets* clinics.

Pet treatments

Based on the results of the examination of a sick pet, the vet may propose one or more types of treatment. For each type of treatment, the information recorded includes the examination number and date, the pet number, name and type, treatment number, description, quantity of each type of treatment, and date the treatment is to begin and end. Any additional comments on the provision of each type of treatment are also recorded.

Pens

In some cases, it's necessary for a sick pet to be admitted to the clinic. Each clinic has 20–30 animal pens, each capable of holding between one and four pets. Each pen has a unique pen number, capacity, and status (an indication of availability). The sick pet is allocated to a pen and the details of the pet, any treatment(s) required by the pet, and any additional comments about the care of the pet are recorded. The details of the pet's stay in the pen are also noted, which include a pen number, and the date the pet was put into and taken out of the pen. Depending on the pet's illness, there may be more than one pet in a pen at the same time. The pen number is unique to a particular clinic.

Invoices

The pet owner is responsible for the cost of the treatment given to a pet. The owner is invoiced for the treatment arising from each examination, and the details recorded on the invoice include the invoice number, invoice date, owner number, owner name and full address, pet number, pet name, and the details of the treatment given. The invoice provides the cost for each type of treatment and the total cost of all treatments given to the pet.

Additional data is also recorded on the payment of the invoice, including the date the invoice was paid and the method of payment (for example, check, cash, Visa). The invoice number is unique throughout the practice.

Surgical, non-surgical, and pharmaceutical supplies

Each clinic maintains a stock of surgical supplies (for example, syringes, sterile dressings, bandages) and non-surgical supplies (for example, plastic bags, aprons, litter trays, pet name tags, pet food). The details of surgical and non-surgical supplies include the item number and name, item description, quantity in stock (this is ascertained on the last day of each month), reorder level, reorder quantity, and cost. The item number uniquely identifies each type of surgical or non-surgical supply. The item number is unique for each surgical or non-surgical item and used throughout the practice.

Each clinic also maintains a stock of pharmaceutical supplies (for example, antibiotics, pain killers). The details of pharmaceutical supplies include a drug number and name, description, dosage, method of administration, quantity in stock (this is ascertained on the last day of each month), reorder level, reorder quantity, and cost. The drug number uniquely identifies each type of pharmaceutical supply. The drug number is unique for each pharmaceutical supply and used throughout the practice.

Appointments

If the pet requires to be seen by the vet at a later date, the owner and pet are given an appointment. The details of an appointment are recorded and include an appointment number, owner number, owner name (first name and last name), home telephone number, the pet number, pet name, type of pet, and the appointment date and time. The appointment number is unique to a particular clinic.

18.1.2 Transaction requirements

Listed below are the transactions that should be supported by the *Perfect Pets* database application.

(1) Maintenance transactions

(a) Create and maintain records recording the details of *Perfect Pets* clinics and the members of staff at each clinic.

(b) Create and maintain records recording the details of pet owners.

(c) Create and maintain the details of pets.

(d) Create and maintain records recording the details of the types of treatments available for pets.

(e) Create and maintain records recording the details of examinations and treatments given to pets.

(f) Create and maintain records recording the details of invoices to pet owners for treatment to their pets.

(g) Create and maintain records recording the details of surgical, non-surgical, and pharmaceutical supplies at each clinic.

(h) Create and maintain records recording the details of pens available at each clinic and the allocation of pets to pens.

(i) Create and maintain pet owner/pet appointments at each clinic.

(2) Query transactions

(a) Present a report listing the Manager's name, clinic address, and telephone number for each clinic, ordered by clinic number.

(b) Present a report listing the names and owner numbers of pet owners with the details of their pets.

(c) List the historic details of examinations for a given pet.

(d) List the details of the treatments provided to a pet based on the results of a given examination.

(e) List the details of an unpaid invoice for a given pet owner.

(f) Present a report on invoices that have not been paid by a given date, ordered by invoice number.

(g) List the details of pens available on a given date for clinics in the New York area, ordered by clinic number.

(h) Present a report that provides the total monthly salary for staff at each clinic, ordered by clinic number.

(i) List the maximum, minimum, and average cost for treatments.

(j) List the total number of pets in each pet type, ordered by pet type.

(k) Present a report of the names and staff numbers for all vets and nurses over 50 years old, ordered by staff name.

(l) List the appointments for a given date and for a particular clinic.

(m) List the total number of pens in each clinic, ordered by clinic number.

(n) Present a report of the details of invoices for pet owners between 1997 and 1999, ordered by invoice number.

(o) List the pet number, name, and description of pets owned by a particular owner.

(p) Present a report listing the pharmaceutical supplies that need to be reordered at each clinic, ordered by clinic number.

(q) List the total cost of the non-surgical and surgical supplies currently in stock at each clinic, ordered by clinic number.

18.2 Using the logical database design methodology

In this section, we're going to work through the steps in the logical database design methodology to come up with an acceptable logical data model that satisfies the above requirements for *Perfect Pets*. We will assume that the Requirements Collection and Analysis stage has identified only one user view.

Methodology summarized in Appendix B

Step 1.1 Identify entities

The first step in logical database design is to identify the main entities that you have to represent in the database. From the description of the practice given above, you may identify the following entities:

Entities defined in Section 5.1

Clinic   Staff
PetOwner   Pet
Examination   Treatment
Pen   PetTreatment
Invoice   Appointment
Stock (with specializations Surgical, NonSurgical, and Pharmaceuticals)

Document entities

As you identify entities, assign them names that are meaningful and obvious to the user, and record this information in a data dictionary. Figure 18.1 shows an extract from the data dictionary that documents the entities for *Perfect Pets*.

Step 1.2   Identify relationships

Relationships defined in Section 5.2

Having identified the entities, your next step is to identify all the relationships that exist between these entities. For *Perfect Pets*, you may identify the relationships shown in Figure 18.2.

Determine the multiplicity constraints of relationships

Multiplicity defined in Section 5.5

Having identified the relationships you wish to model, you now want to determine the multiplicity of each relationship. For *Perfect Pets*, you should identify the multiplicity constraints shown in Figure 18.3.

Figure 18.1

Extract from the data dictionary for *Perfect Pets* showing descriptions of entities

Entity name	Description	Aliases	Occurrence
Clinic	Veterinary clinics.	Surgery	One or more *Perfect Pet* clinics located in main cities throughout the US.
Staff	General term describing all staff employed by *Perfect Pets*.	Vet, Nurse, Secretary	Each member of staff works at a particular clinic.
PetOwner	Owners of pets taken to *Perfect Pets*.		Owner takes his/her pet to a particular clinic.

Entity	Relationship	Entity
Clinic	Has	Staff
	Holds	Stock
	Registers	Pet
	Provides	Pen
	Schedules	Appointment
	IsContactedBy	PetOwner
Staff	Manages	Clinic
	Performs	Examination
PetOwner	Owns	Pet
	Pays	Invoice
	Attends	Appointment
Pet	Undergoes	Examination
	IsAllocatedTo	Pen
	Attends	Appointment
Examination	ResultsIn	PetTreatment
Treatment	UsedIn	PetTreatment
Invoice	ResultsFrom	Examination

Figure 18.2

First draft of the relationships for *Perfect Pets*.

Entity	Multiplicity	Relationship	Entity	Multiplicity
Clinic	1..*	Has	Staff	1..1
	1..*	Holds	Stock	1..*
	1..*	Registers	Pet	1..1
	20..30	Provides	Pen	1..1
	1..*	Schedules	Appointment	1..1
	1..*	IsContactedBy	PetOwner	1..1
Staff	0..1	Manages	Clinic	1..1
	0..*	Performs	Examination	1..1
PetOwner	1..*	Owns	Pet	1..1
	1..*	Pays	Invoice	1..1
	1..*	Attends	Appointment	1..1
Pet	1..*	Undergoes	Examination	1..1
	0..*	IsAllocatedTo	Pen	1..*
	1..*	Attends	Appointment	1..1
Examination	1..*	ResultsIn	PetTreatment	1..1
Treatment	1..*	UsedIn	PetTreatment	1..1
Invoice	1..1	ResultsFrom	Examination	1..1

Figure 18.3

Multiplicity constraints for relationships identified above.

Use Entity-Relationship (ER) modeling

Throughout the database design phase, you'll create several versions of the ER model representing *Perfect Pets*. Figure 18.4 shows the first draft ER model for *Perfect Pets*.

Step 1.3 Identify and associate attributes with entities or relationships

Attributes defined in
Section 5.3

The next step is to identify the attributes that are associated with the entities and relationships that you've identified. For *Perfect Pets*, you should identify the attributes with the associated entities, as shown in Figure 18.5(a).

However, when examining the information on pens, you may have difficulty associating the attributes dateIn/dateOut, representing the date a pet was put in/taken out of a pen, and the attribute comments with either the Pen or Pet entity. Similarly, you may have difficulty associating the attribute inStock, representing the amount of quantity in stock for the different categories of supplies, and the attributes reorderLevel/reorderQty with either the Clinic or Stock entities. In both these cases, you should identify a new entity or associate the attributes with the corresponding relationships, as shown in Figure 18.5(b).

You should also be careful not to include the same attribute in two entities, when the occurrence of the attribute actually represents a relationship between the entities. For example, in the requirements specification given in Section 18.1.1, under Examinations it states that the details of each examination includes 'the name of the vet'. You might be misled here to include the name of the vet in both the Staff and Examination entities. However, this would be incorrect: the appearance of the vet's name in this situation represents a relationship and you should not include it as an attribute of the Examination entity. If you were to do this, it would subsequently result in the Examination table not conforming to third normal form (3NF).

3NF disscussed in
Section 6.5

> **TIP** This is quite a common mistake for inexperienced designers to make, so you should look out for it.

Figure 18.4

First draft ER model for *Perfect Pets*

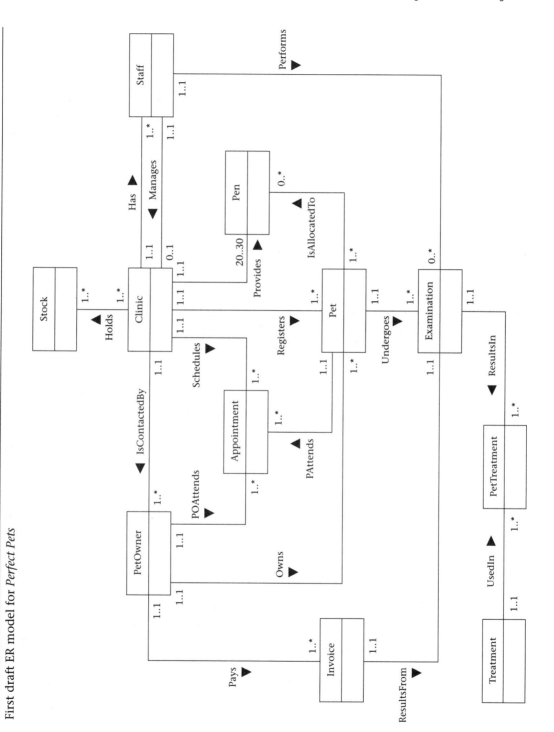

Figure 18.5

Attributes for *Perfect Pets*: (a) attributes associated with entities; (b) attributes associated with relationships.

Entity	Attributes
Clinic	clinicNo, address (street, city, state, zipCode), telNo, faxNo
Staff	staffNo, sName (sFName, sLName), sAddress (sStreet, sCity, sState, sZipCode), sTelNo, DOB, sex, SSN, position, salary
PetOwner	ownerNo, oName (oFName, oLName), oAddress (oStreet, oCity, oState, oZipCode), oTelNo
Pet petStatus	petNo, petName, petType, petDescription, pDOB, dateRegistered,
Examination	examNo, examDate, examTime, examResults
Treatment	treatNo, description, cost
Pen	penNo, penCapacity, penStatus
Invoice	invoiceNo, invoiceDate, datePaid, paymentMethod
Stock: Item	itemNo, itemName, itemDescription, itemCost
Stock: Pharmacy drugCost	drugNo, drugName, drugDescription, dosage, methodAdmin,
Appointment	appNo, aDate, aTime
PetTreatment	startDate, endDate, quantity, ptComments

(a)

Relationship	Attributes
IsAllocatedTo	dateIn, dateOut, comments
Holds	inStock, reorderLevel, reorderQty

(b)

Document attributes

As you identify attributes, assign them names that are meaningful and obvious to the user, and record their details in a data dictionary, as discussed in Step 1.3 in Chapter 8.

Domains defined in Section 2.2.1

Step 1.4 Determine attribute domains

You should now add the necessary domains to support the attributes you identified in the previous step to your data dictionary.

Step 1.5 Determine candidate and primary key attributes

This step is concerned with identifying the candidate key(s) for an entity and then selecting one to be the primary key. In the process of identifying primary keys, note whether an entity is strong or weak.

Keys defined in Section 2.2.3

In trying to identify candidate keys, you should observe that the clinic number for the Clinic entity, the staff number for the Staff entity, the treatment number for the Treatment entity, the invoice number for the Invoice entity, and the item/drug number for the Stock entities are unique for the entire practice. On the other hand, the owner number for the PetOwner entity, the pet number for the Pet entity, and the pen number for the Pen entity are unique only for a particular clinic. It's not uncommon for a company to give different offices a degree of local autonomy. However, in a centralized database system it is sometimes more appropriate to have uniqueness throughout the company. In discussion with the *Perfect Pets* management, it is agreed that all numbers should be allocated across the entire practice, as opposed to each clinic. If this had not been the decision, it would have been necessary to add the clinic number to those numbers only unique within each clinic to gain uniqueness across the practice.

Strong and weak entities defined in Section 5.4

With this in mind, you should now identify the primary keys shown in Figure 18.6 (other alternate keys are shown in Figure 18.9). In particular, you should identify PetTreatment as a weak entity.

Step 1.6 Specialize/Generalize entities (optional step)

The identification of the Stock entity in its current form is perfectly acceptable to continue with the logical database design methodology. However, there is additional information given that you may wish to add, to model the practice more accurately. The requirements specification states that there are surgical and non-surgical supplies that have a unique item number to distinguish them. There are also pharmaceutical supplies that have a unique drug number to distinguish them. In addition, these two types of supplies have slightly different attributes associated with them. Therefore, we could consider Surgical/Non-Surgical Stock and Pharmaceuticals to be particular types of the Stock entity. This specialization/generalization is shown in Figure 18.6. For simplicity, we have renamed Surgical/Non-Surgical Stock as Item and Pharmaceuticals as Pharmacy.

Specialization/ Generalization covered in Chapter 11

You may also identify Vet, Nurse, Secretary, and Cleaner as particular types of Staff. Although these job titles would all have the same attributes, only the Vet entity would participate in the *Performs* relationship with Examination. This would be a perfectly valid way of modeling staff. However, to keep the model simple, we omit this specialization/generalization.

Figure 18.6

ER model for *Perfect Pets* with primary keys shown and specialization/generalization of stock.

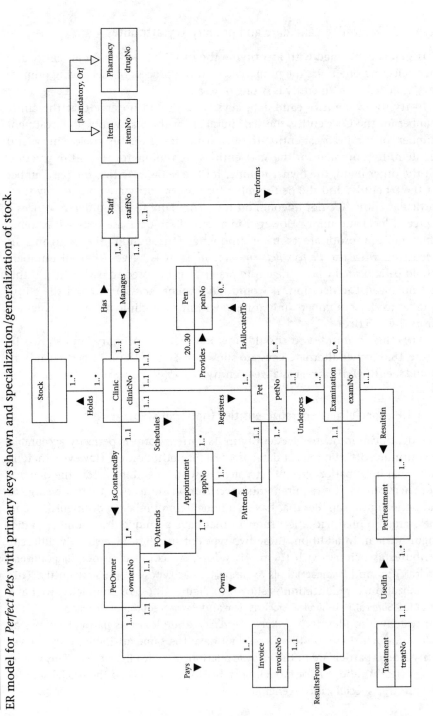

Step 1.7 Remove features not compatible with the relational model

At this point, you now have a local logical data model for *Perfect Pets*. However, the data model contains some data structures that are not easily modeled by relational DBMSs. In this step, you transform such data structures into a form that is more easily handled by relational systems. More specifically, you have to:

(1) Remove many-to-many (*:*) binary relationships.

(2) Remove many-to-many (*:*) recursive relationships.

(3) Remove complex relationships.

(4) Remove multi-valued attributes.

(5) Re-examine one-to-one (1:1) relationships.

(6) Remove redundant relationships.

Many-to-many (*:*) binary relationships

From Figure 18.6, there are two *:* relationships: Clinic *Holds* Stock and Pet *IsAllocatedTo* Pen. In both cases, the relationships also have attributes associated with them, as shown in Figure 18.5(b). To model these situations correctly in the relational model, you have to introduce intermediate entities, which we have called ClinicStock and PetPen, as shown in Figure 18.7.

: relationships defined in Section 5.5.3

One-to-one (1:1) relationships

From Figure 18.4, there are two 1:1 relationships: Staff *Manages* Clinic and Invoice *ResultsFrom* Examination. However, in both cases the two entities are clearly distinct and should not be merged together.

1:1 relationships defined in Section 5.5.1

Redundant relationships

From Figure 18.6, there are a number of relationships between PetOwner, Pet, Clinic, and Appointment, and a closer examination would be useful to identify any redundant relationships. First of all, note that the PetOwner/Pet entities have mandatory participation in the *POAttends/PAttends/Owns* relationships, and that a PetOwner may own many pets. Therefore, for any given Appointment we can identify the Owner through the *POAttends* relationship, but we cannot then identify the Pet through the *Owns* relationship. However, for any given Appointment, we can identify the Pet through the *PAttends* relationship and for any given Pet we can identify the PetOwner through the *Owns* relationship, which would suggest that the *POAttends* relationship is redundant. In a similar way, through the *PAttends* relationship we can identify the Pet, and through the *Registers* relationship we can identify the Clinic involved in the Appointment, which would suggest the *Schedules* relationship is also redundant.

Participation defined in Section 5.5.5

Note that the *IsContactedBy* relationship between Clinic and PetOwner also appears to be redundant. However, *Perfect Pets* note the details of pet owners when they first make contact and only obtain the details of pets at the first appointment, and so the *IsContactedBy* relationships is retained. The revised logical data model is shown in Figure 18.7.

Step 1.8 Check model supports user transactions

In this step, you check that the local logical data model you have developed will support the transactions identified by the users. This involves checking that:

■ the required attributes are present in the data model, and

■ where attributes have to be taken from more than one entity, that there is a pathway between the two entities; in other words, there is an identified relationship, either direct or indirect, between the two entities.

The transaction pathway diagram for the query transactions identified in Section 18.1.2 is shown in Figure 18.8, and you can readily check that the required attributes are available from an individual entity or from multiple entities via one or more relationships.

Step 2.1 Create tables for local logical data model

In this step, you create tables from the local logical data model to represent the entities and relationships described in the user's view of the practice, using a Database Design Language (DBDL) for relational databases.

DBDL discussed in Step 2.1 in Chapter 9

Document tables and foreign key attributes

At the end of Step 2.1, you document the full composition of the tables created from the local logical data model. Each table is described using the DBDL, as shown in Figure 18.9.

Step 2.2 Check model using normalization

Normalization covered in Chapter 6

In this step, you want to ensure that each table created in the previous step is in at least third normal form (3NF). If you identify tables that are not in 3NF, this may indicate that part of the logical data model is incorrect, or you have introduced an error when deriving the tables from the model. However, you can readily check that the tables identified in Figure 18.9 are in 3NF.

Figure 18.7

Revised local logical data model for *Perfect Pets* after removing features not compatible with the relational model.

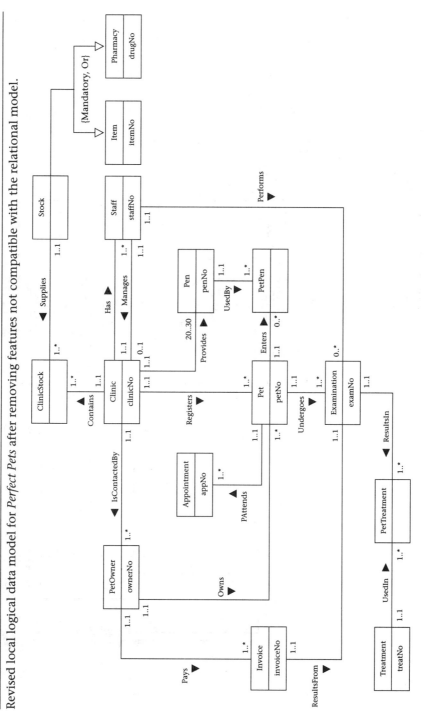

Figure 18.8

Transaction pathway diagram for *Perfect Pets*.

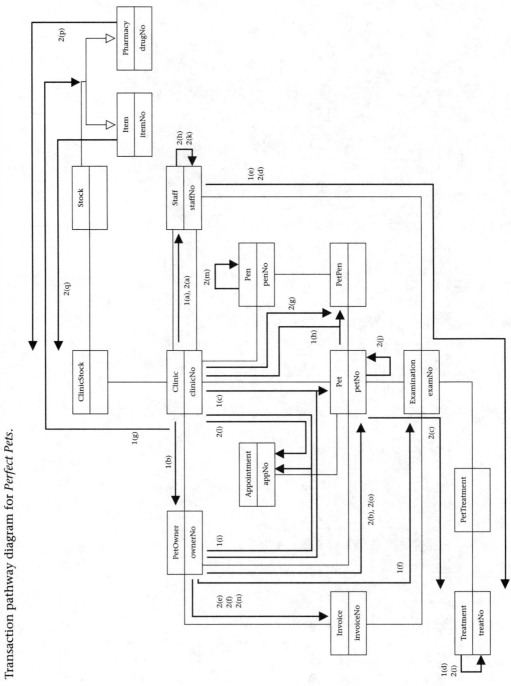

Figure 18.9

Tables created from local logical data model for *Perfect Pets*.

Clinic (clinicNo, street, city, state, zipcode, telNo, faxNo, mgrStaffNo) **Primary Key** clinicNo **Alternate Key** zipCode **Alternate Key** telNo **Alternate Key** faxNo **Foreign Key** mgrStaffNo **references** Staff(staffNo)	**Staff** (staffNo, sFName, sLName, sStreet, sCity, sState, sZipCode, sTelNo, DOB, sex, SSN, position, salary, clinicNo) **Primary Key** staffNo **Alternate Key** SSN **Foreign Key** clinicNo **references** Clinic(clinicNo)
PetOwner (ownerNo, oFName, oLName, oState, oZipCode, oTelNo, clinicNo) **Primary Key** ownerNo **Foreign Key** clinicNo **references** Clinic(clinicNo)	**Pet** (petNo, petName, petType, petDescription, pDOB, dateRegistered, petStatus, ownerNo, clinicNo) **Primary Key** petNo **Foreign Key** ownerNo **references** Owner(ownerNo) **Foreign Key** clinicNo **references** Clinic(clinicNo)
Examination (examNo, examDate, examTime, examResults, petNo, staffNo) **Primary Key** examNo **Alternate Key** staffNo, examDate, examTime **Foreign Key** petNo **references** Pet(petNo) **Foreign Key** staffNo **references** Staff(staffNo)	**Treatment** (treatNo, description, cost) **Primary Key** treatNo
Pen (penNo, penCapacity, penStatus, clinicNo) **Primary Key** penNo **Foreign Key** clinicNo **references** Clinic(clinicNo)	**PetPen** (penNo, petNo, dateIn, dataOut, comments) **Primary Key** penNo, petNo, dateIn **Alternate Key** penNo, petNo, dateOut **Foreign Key** penNo **references** Pen(penNo) **Foreign Key** petNo **references** Pet(petNo)
PetTreatment (examNo, treatNo, startDate, endDate, quantity, ptComments) **Primary Key** examNo, treatNo **Foreign Key** examNo **references** Examination(examNo) **Foreign Key** treatNo **references** Treatment(treatNo)	**Item** (itemNo, itemName, itemDescription, itemCost) **Primary Key** itemNo
Pharmacy (drugNo, drugName, drugDescription, dosage, methodAdmin, drugCost) **Primary Key** drugNo	**ItemClinicStock** (itemNo, clinicNo, inStock, reorderLevel, reorderQty) **Primary Key** itemNo, clinicNo **Foreign Key** itemNo **references** Item(itemNo) **Foreign Key** clinicNo **references** Clinic(clinicNo)
PharmClinicStock (drugNo, clinicNo, inStock, reorderLevel, reorderQty) **Primary Key** drugNo, clinicNo **Foreign Key** drugNo **references** Pharmacy(drugNo) **Foreign Key** clinicNo **references** Clinic(clinicNo)	**Invoice** (invoiceNo, invoiceDate, datePaid, paymentMethod, ownerNo, examNo) **Primary Key** invoiceNo **Foreign Key** ownerNo **references** Owner(ownerNo) **Foreign Key** examNo **references** Examination(examNo)
Appointment (appNo, aDate, aTime, petNo) **Primary Key** appNo **Foreign Key** petNo **references** Pet(petNo)	

Step 2.3 Check model against user transactions

This step is similar to Step 1.8, except in this step you're checking that the mapping from entities to tables and the posting of primary keys to act as foreign keys have been undertaken correctly. In this case, you can again readily check the mapping has been performed correctly and the tables do support the user transactions identified in Section 18.1.2.

Step 2.4 Define integrity constraints

Integrity constraints
defined in Section 2.3

Integrity constraints are the constraints that you wish to impose in order to protect the database from becoming inconsistent. Of the five types of integrity constraints, three should have been identified in a previous step and documented in the data dictionary, namely: required data, attribute domain constraints, and entity integrity. We consider the remaining two here: referential integrity and business rules.

Referential integrity

There are two issues to consider here:

Participation defined in
Section 5.5.5

(1) *Identify whether nulls are allowed for the foreign key.* In general, if the participation of the child table in the relationship is mandatory, then the strategy is that nulls are not allowed. On the other hand, if the participation of the child table is optional, then nulls should be allowed.

(2) *Identify the existence constraints under which a foreign key may be inserted, updated, or deleted.* In general, this involves specifying two actions for each foreign key: an ON UPDATE action and an ON DELETE action, relating to what should happen to maintain referential integrity if a record in the parent table is updated/deleted. Figure 18.10 shows the necessary actions for the foreign keys identified in Figure 18.9.

Business rules

Finally, consider whether there are any other types of constraints that *Perfect Pets* has defined that have not been covered elsewhere in the data model. Such constraints are more generally called **business rules**.

Document all integrity constraints

All constraints should be documented in the data dictionary for consideration during physical database design.

Figure 18.10

The referential integrity constraints for the *Perfect Pets* tables.

<table>
<tr><td>

Clinic
Foreign Key mgrStaffNo **references** Staff(staffNo) ON UPDATE CASCADE ON DELETE NO ACTION
</td></tr>
<tr><td>

Staff
Foreign Key clinicNo **references** Clinic(clinicNo) ON UPDATE CASCADE ON DELETE NO ACTION
</td></tr>
<tr><td>

PetOwner
Foreign Key clinicNo **references** Clinic(clinicNo) ON UPDATE CASCADE ON DELETE NO ACTION
</td></tr>
<tr><td>

Pet
Foreign Key ownerNo **references** Owner(ownerNo) ON UPDATE CASCADE ON DELETE CASCADE
Foreign Key clinicNo **references** Clinic(clinicNo) ON UPDATE CASCADE ON DELETE NO ACTION
</td></tr>
<tr><td>

Examination
Foreign Key petNo **references** Pet(petNo) ON UPDATE CASCADE ON DELETE CASCADE
Foreign Key staffNo **references** Staff(staffNo) ON UPDATE CASCADE ON DELETE NO ACTION
</td></tr>
<tr><td>

Pen
Foreign Key clinicNo **references** Clinic(clinicNo) ON UPDATE CASCADE ON DELETE CASCADE
</td></tr>
<tr><td>

PetPen
Foreign Key penNo **references** Pen(penNo) ON UPDATE CASCADE ON DELETE CASCADE
Foreign Key petNo **references** Pet(petNo) ON UPDATE CASCADE ON DELETE CASCADE
</td></tr>
<tr><td>

PetTreatment
Foreign Key treatNo **references** Treatment(treatNo) ON UPDATE CASCADE ON DELETE NO ACTION
</td></tr>
<tr><td>

ItemClinicStock
Foreign Key itemNo **references** Item(itemNo) ON UPDATE CASCADE ON DELETE NO ACTION
Foreign Key clinicNo **references** Clinic(clinicNo) ON UPDATE CASCADE ON DELETE NO ACTION
</td></tr>
<tr><td>

PharmClinicStock
Foreign Key drugNo **references** Pharmacy(drugNo) ON UPDATE CASCADE ON DELETE NO ACTION
Foreign Key clinicNo **references** Clinic(clinicNo) ON UPDATE CASCADE ON DELETE NO ACTION
</td></tr>
<tr><td>

Invoice
Foreign Key ownerNo **references** Owner(ownerNo) ON UPDATE CASCADE ON DELETE NO ACTION
Foreign Key examNo **references** Examination(examNo) ON UPDATE CASCADE ON DELETE NO ACTION
</td></tr>
<tr><td>

Appointment
Foreign Key petNo **references** Pet(petNo) ON UPDATE CASCADE ON DELETE CASCADE
</td></tr>
</table>

Step 2.5 Review local logical data model with users

The local logical data model should now be complete and fully documented. At this point, you should review the model and supporting documentation with the users. We'll assume that this does not identify any major deficiencies in the design. As stated at the start of this chapter, we have assumed that there is only one user view and so Step 3 is unnecessary. Therefore, this completes the logical database design methodology for *Perfect Pets*. In the next chapter, we'll proceed to the physical database design phase.

Chapter 19

Perfect Pets – Physical database design

In this chapter, we go through the steps of physical database design for the *Perfect Pets* case study introduced in the previous chapter. To demonstrate some of the physical implementation aspects we use Oracle 8. As we mentioned at the start of the last chapter, it may be useful if you attempt the steps in the methodology yourself before reading this chapter. You can then check your solution against our sample solution. If you are unfamiliar with file organizations and indexes, you may want to read Appendix C first. You may also find the summary of the methodology in Appendix B helpful.

19.1 Using the physical database design methodology

In this section, we're going to work through the steps in the physical database design methodology to come up with a suitable physical design and implementation for the *Perfect Pets* database.

Step 4.1 Design base tables for target DBMS

During logical database design you created a number of **base tables** to represent the entities and relationships in the logical data model. Along with these tables you produced a set of supporting documentation, detailing:

Base tables defined in Section 2.3.2

- for each table, its attributes, the primary, alternate, and foreign keys, and integrity constraints;
- for each attribute, its domain, an optional default value, whether it can hold nulls, and whether it's derived.

To represent the design of the base tables, you use this information to define domains, default values, and null indicators. For example, for the Pen table of

DBDL discussed in Step
2.1 in Chapter 9

Perfect Pets, you may produce the design shown in Figure 19.1 using an extended Database Design Language (DBDL). You use this information to determine how to implement the base tables in the target DBMS, which for this case study will be Oracle 8.

Creating base tables in Oracle 8

In some systems that do not fully comply with the 1992 SQL standard (SQL2), there is no support for one or more of the clauses PRIMARY KEY, FOREIGN KEY, DEFAULT. Similarly, many systems do not support domains. However, Oracle 8 supports many of the SQL2 CREATE TABLE clauses, so you can define:

- primary keys, using the PRIMARY KEY clause;
- alternate keys, using the UNIQUE keyword;
- default values, using the DEFAULT clause;
- not null columns, using the NOT NULL keyword;
- foreign keys, using the FOREIGN KEY clause;
- other column or table constraints using the CHECK and CONSTRAINT clauses.

However, there is no facility to create domains, although Oracle 8 does allow user-defined types to be created. In addition, the data types are slightly different from the SQL standard, as shown in Table 19.1.

In Chapter 12, we saw that Microsoft Access had an Autonumber data type that created a new sequential number for a column value whenever a record was inserted. Oracle does not have such a data type but it does have a similar facility through the (non-standard) SQL CREATE SEQUENCE statement. For example, the statement:

Figure 19.1

DBDL for the Pen table.

domain Pen_Numbers	fixed length character string length 4
domain Pen_Capacity	integer value, between 1 and 4
domain Pen_Status	one character, indicating whether pen is available (A) or not available (N)
domain Clinic_Numbers	fixed length character string length 5

```
pen(   penNo         Pen_Numbers     NOT NULL,
       penCapacity   Pen_Capacity    NOT NULL DEFAULT 2,
       penStatus     Pen_Status      NOT NULL DEFAULT 'A',
       clinicNo      Clinic_Numbers  NOT NULL)
       Primary Key penNo
       Foreign Key clinicNo References Clinic(clinicNo)ON UPDATE CASCADE ON DELETE NO ACTION
```

Table 19.1 Partial list of Oracle data types.

Data type	Use	Size
char(size)	Stores fixed-length character data (default size is 1).	Up to 2000 bytes
nchar(size)	Same as char data type, except the maximum length is determined by the character set of the database (for example, American English, Eastern European, or Korean).	
varchar2(size)	Stores variable length character data.	Up to 4000 bytes
nvarchar2(size)	Same as varchar2 with the same caveat as for nchar data type.	
varchar	Currently the same as char. However, use of varchar2 is recommended as varchar might become a separate data type with different comparison semantics in a later release.	Up to 2000 bytes
number(l, d)	Stores fixed-point or floating-point numbers, where l stands for length and d stands for the number of decimal digits. For example, number(5,2) could contain nothing larger than 999.99 without an error.	1.0E-130 .. 9.99E125
decimal(l, d), dec(l, d), or numeric(l, d)	Same as number. Provided for compatibility with SQL standard.	
integer, int, or smallint	Provided for compatibility with SQL standard. Converted to number(38).	
date	Stores dates from 1 Jan 4712 B.C. to 31 Dec A.D. 4712.	
blob	A binary large object.	Up to 4 Gigabytes
clob	A character large object.	Up to 4 Gigabytes
raw(size)	Raw binary data, such as a sequence of graphics characters or a digitized picture.	Up to 2000 bytes

```
CREATE SEQUENCE appnoseq
    START WITH 1 INCREMENT BY 1 CACHE 30;
```

creates a sequence, called appNoSeq, that starts with the initial value one and increases by one each time. The CACHE 30 clause specifies that Oracle should preallocate 30 sequence numbers and keep them in memory for faster access.

Once a sequence has been created, you can access its values in SQL statements with the following pseudocolumns:

CURRVAL   which returns the current value of the sequence
NEXTVAL   which increments the sequence and returns the new value.

For example, the SQL statement:

```
INSERT INTO appointment(appno, adate, atime, petno)
     VALUES (appnoseq.NEXTVAL, SYSDATE, '12.00', '010090');
```

inserts a new record into the Appointment table with the value for column appNo (the appointment number) set to the next available number in the sequence.

Creating a blank table in Oracle 8 using SQL*Plus

To illustrate the process of creating a blank table in Oracle, we first use SQL*Plus, which is an interactive, command-line driven, SQL interface to the Oracle database. Figure 19.2 shows the creation of the Pen table using the Oracle SQL CREATE TABLE statement.

Oracle allows named constraints to be enabled (the default setting) and disabled. In certain situations, it may be desirable to disable constraints temporarily for performance reasons, for example:

- when loading large amounts of data into a table using SQL*Loader;
- when performing batch operations that make a significant number of changes to a table;
- when importing or exporting one table at a time.

Referential actions discussed in Step 2.4 in Chapter 9

By default, Oracle enforces referential integrity on the named foreign keys. Thus, it enforces the referential actions ON DELETE NO ACTION and ON UPDATE NO ACTION. It also allows the additional clause ON DELETE CASCADE to be specified to allow deletions from the parent table to cascade to the child table. However, it does not support the ON UPDATE CASCADE action,

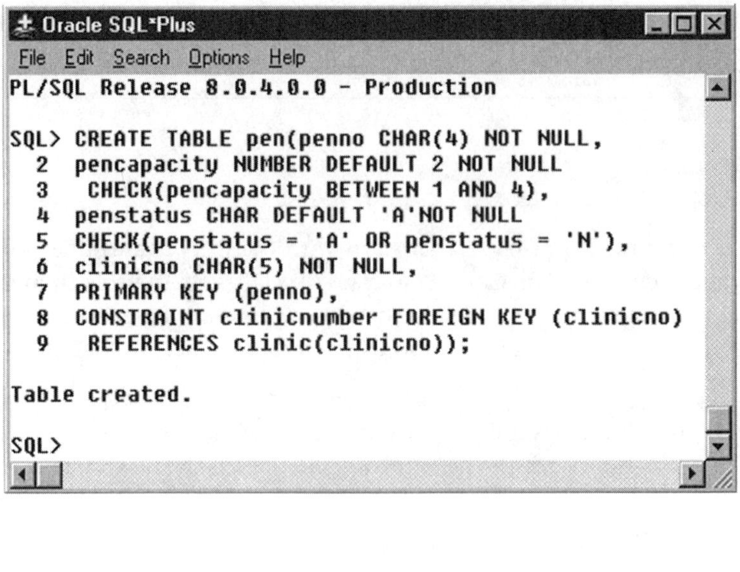

Figure 19.2

Creation of the Pen table using the Oracle SQL CREATE TABLE statement.

```
± Oracle SQL*Plus                                      _ □ ✕
File  Edit  Search  Options  Help
PL/SQL Release 8.0.4.0.0 - Production

SQL> CREATE TABLE pen(penno CHAR(4) NOT NULL,
   2   pencapacity NUMBER DEFAULT 2 NOT NULL,
   3    CHECK(pencapacity BETWEEN 1 AND 4),
   4   penstatus CHAR DEFAULT 'A'NOT NULL
   5   CHECK(penstatus = 'A' OR penstatus = 'N'),
   6   clinicno CHAR(5) NOT NULL,
   7   PRIMARY KEY (penno),
   8   CONSTRAINT clinicnumber FOREIGN KEY (clinicno)
   9    REFERENCES clinic(clinicno));

Table created.

SQL>
```

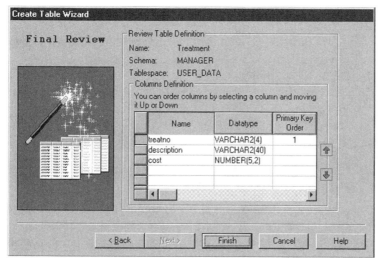

Figure 19.3

Treatment table created using the Oracle Create Table Wizard.

nor the SET DEFAULT or SET NULL actions. If any of these actions are required, you will have to consider implementing them as triggers or within the application code. We'll consider this in Step 4.2 shortly.

Creating a table using the Table Wizard

An alternative approach in Oracle 8 is to use the Create Table Wizard that is part of the Schema Manager. Using a series of interactive forms, the Create Table Wizard takes you through the process of defining each of the columns with its associated data type, defining any constraints on the columns and/or constraints on the table that you may require, and defining the key fields. Figure 19.3 shows the final form of the Create Table Wizard used to create the Treatment table.

Document design of base tables

The design of the base tables should be fully documented along with the reasons for selecting the proposed design. In particular, document the reasons for selecting one approach where many alternatives exist.

Step 4.2 Design business rules for target DBMS

Updates to tables may be constrained by business rules. The design of such rules is again dependent on the target DBMS; some systems provide more facilities than others for defining business rules. In Chapter 12, we saw that if the system is compliant with the 1992 SQL standard, some rules may be easy to implement. As we've seen above, Oracle 8 allows constraints to be defined as part of the SQL CREATE TABLE statement using the CHECK and CONSTRAINT clauses, and also allows additional constraints to be defined using *before triggers* and *after triggers*. For more flexibility, Oracle 8 also allows procedures to be created and invoked from SQL.

For example, from Figure 19.1 the foreign key clinicNo in the Pen table should have the action ON UPDATE CASCADE. Unfortunately, as we've already noted, the Oracle CREATE TABLE statement does not support this action. However, this action can be implemented using the triggers shown in Figure 19.4.

Trigger 1 (Pen_Clinic_Check_Before)

The trigger in Figure 19.4(a) is *fired* whenever the clinicNo column in the Pen table is updated. The trigger checks *before* the update takes place that the new value specified exists in the Clinic table. If an Invalid_Clinic exception is raised, the trigger issues an error message and prevents the change from occurring. The following points should be noted:

■ The *BEFORE* keyword indicates that the trigger should be executed before the update to the clinicNo column is applied to the Pen table.

■ The *FOR EACH ROW* keyword indicates that this is a row-level trigger, which executes for each row of the Pen table that is updated in the transaction. The alternative type of trigger is a statement-level trigger, which executes once for each transaction. We'll see examples of statement-level triggers shortly.

■ The *WHEN* clause specifies a condition that must be met for the trigger to fire.

■ The *new* keyword is used to refer to the new value of the column and the *old* keyword is used to refer to the old value of the column.

Changes to support triggers on the Clinic table

The three triggers shown in Figure 19.4(b) are fired whenever the clinicNo column in the Clinic table is updated. Before the definition of the triggers, a sequence number updateSequence is created along with a public variable updateSeq (which is accessible to the three triggers through the seqPackage package). In addition, the Pen table is modified to add a column called updateId, which is used to flag whether a record has been updated, to prevent it from being updated more than once during the cascade operation.

Trigger 2 (Cascade_ClinicNo_Update1)

The (statement-level) trigger, Cascade_ClinicNo_Update1, fires before the update to the column clinicNo in the Clinic table to set a new sequence number for the update.

Figure 19.4

Oracle triggers to enforce ON UPDATE CASCADE on the foreign key clinicNo in the Pen table when the primary key clinicNo is updated in the Clinic table: (a) trigger for the Pen table; (b) triggers for the Clinic table.

```
--Before the clinicNo column is updated in the Pen table, fire this trigger
--to verify that the new foreign key value is present in the Clinic table.
CREATE TRIGGER Pen_Clinic_Check_Before                              Before trigger
    BEFORE UPDATE OF clinicno ON pen
    FOR EACH ROW WHEN (new.clinicno IS NOT NULL)
DECLARE
    dummy CHAR(5);                                                  Condition for
    invalid_clinic EXCEPTION;                                       trigger to fire
    valid_clinic EXCEPTION;
    mutating_table EXCEPTION;
    PRAGMA EXCEPTION_INIT (mutating_table,-4091);
--Use cursor to verify parent key value exists.                    Row-level
--Use FOR UPDATE OF to lock parent key's record so that it cannot be deleted  trigger
--by another transaction before this transaction completes.
CURSOR update_cursor (sn CHAR(5)) IS
    SELECT clinicno FROM clinic
    WHERE clinicno = sn
    FOR UPDATE OF clinicno;
    BEGIN
        OPEN update_cursor (:new.clinicno);
        FETCH update_cursor INTO dummy;
--Verify parent key. Raise exceptions as appropriate.
        IF update_cursor%NOTFOUND THEN
            RAISE invalid_clinic;
        ELSE
            RAISE valid_clinic;
        END IF;                                                    Invalid clinicNo
        CLOSE update_cursor;                                        specified
    EXCEPTION
    WHEN invalid_clinic THEN
        CLOSE update_cursor;
        raise_application_error(-20000, 'Invalid Clinic Number'||:new.clinicno);
    WHEN valid_clinic THEN
        CLOSE update_cursor;
--A mutating table is a table that is currently being modified by an INSERT, UPDATE,
--or DELETE statement, or one that might need to be updated by the effects of a declarative
--DELETE CASCADE referential integrity constraint.
--This error would raise an exception, but in this case the exception is OK, so trap it,
--but don't do anything.
    WHEN mutating_table THEN
        NULL;
    END;
```

(a)

Figure 19.4

Continued

```
--Create a sequence number and a public variable UPDATESEQ.
CREATE SEQUENCE updatesequence INCREMENT BY 1 MAXVALUE 500 CYCLE;
CREATE PACKAGE seqpackage AS
    updateseq NUMBER;
END seqpackage;
CREATE or REPLACE PACKAGE BODY seqpackage AS END seqpackage;


--Add a new column to the Pen table to flag changed records.
ALTER TABLE pen ADD updateid NUMBER;


--Before updating the Clinic table using this statement trigger, generate a new
--sequence number and assign it to the public variable UPDATESEQ.
CREATE TRIGGER Cascade_ClinicNo_Update1
    BEFORE UPDATE OF clinicno ON clinic
    DECLARE
        dummy NUMBER;
        BEGIN
            SELECT updatesequence.NEXTVAL
            INTO dummy FROM dual;
            seqpackage.updateseq :=dummy;
        END;


--Create a row after-trigger that cascades the update to the Pen table.
--Only cascade the update if the child row has not already been updated by the trigger.
CREATE TRIGGER Cascade_ClinicNo_Update2
    AFTER UPDATE OF clinicno ON clinic
    FOR EACH ROW
    BEGIN
        UPDATE pen SET clinicno = :new.clinicno, updateid = seqpackage.updateseq
        WHERE pen.clinicno = :old.clinicno AND updateid IS NULL;
    END;


--Create a final statement after-trigger to reset the updateid flags
CREATE TRIGGER Cascade_ClinicNo_Update3
    AFTER UPDATE OF clinicno ON clinic
    BEGIN
        UPDATE pen SET updateid = NULL
        WHERE updateid = seqpackage.updateseq;
    END;
```

Package to hold sequence number

Add extra column to Pen table

Statement-level before trigger

Set new sequence number for update

Row-level after trigger

Update Pen table and set updated flag for these records

Statement-level after trigger; resets flags for updated records

(b)

Trigger 3 (Cascade_ClinicNo_Update2)

The (row-level) trigger, Cascade_ClinicNo_Update2, fires to update all records in the Pen table that have the old clinicNo value (:old.clinicno) to the new value (:new.clinicno), and to flag the record as having been updated.

Trigger 4 (Cascade_ClinicNo_Update3)

The final (statement-level) trigger, Cascade_ClinicNo_Update3, fires after the update to reset the flagged records back to unflagged.

> Don't worry too much about the detail of how these triggers work. What is important to note is the significant amount of programming effort required to implement these actions. Put another way, think how much effort can be saved if the DBMS provides this functionality instead!

Step 5.1 Analyze transactions

Having set up the base tables, integrity constraints, and business rules, the next step is to analyze the transactions to help determine appropriate file organizations and indexes for each base table. Let's assume that the transactions identified in Section 18.1.2 are the most important transactions for *Perfect Pets*. To focus on areas that may be problematic, we suggested in Chapter 13 that one way to proceed is to:

(1) Map all transaction paths to tables.

(2) Determine which tables are most frequently accessed by transactions.

(3) Analyze selected transactions that involve these tables.

The first step has already been carried out in Steps 1.8 and 2.3 (see Figure 18.9). To carry out the second step, you need to estimate the frequency with which tables will be accessed. If possible, you could add the frequency information to the transaction path diagram. This sometimes makes the diagram very cluttered and difficult to interpret, and you may prefer to keep the information separate. In discussion with the staff of *Perfect Pets*, the frequency information shown in Figure 19.5 is obtained.

In addition, you have to estimate the likely frequency of each transaction. All this information has to be analyzed to identify those areas that may require special consideration.

Figure 19.5

Logical data model for *Perfect Pets* showing expected occurrences.

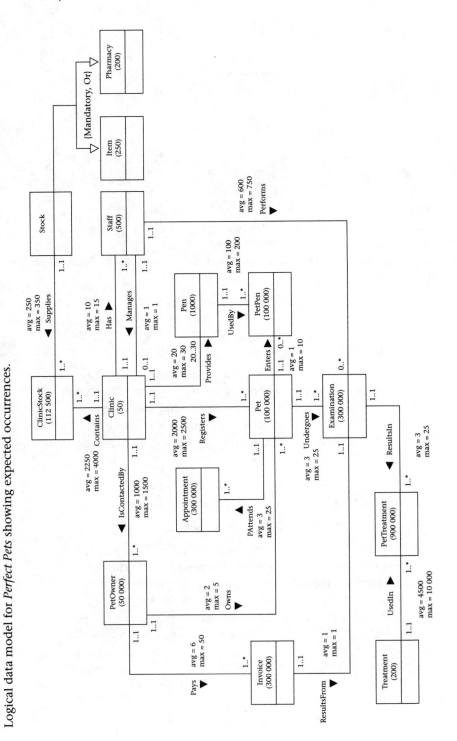

Step 5.2 Choose file organizations

The objective of this step is to choose an optimal file organization for each table, if the target DBMS allows this. To undertake this step, you need to understand how the target DBMS operates at both the logical and physical levels. In this step, we examine how Oracle stores data and we discuss:

■ clustered tables

■ space management parameters.

The discussion is fairly technical but it should give you a feel for the type of knowledge you'll need to undertake this step in practice.

Oracle's logical database structure

At the logical level, Oracle maintains tablespaces, schemas, and data blocks and extents/segments, as we now explain.

Tablespaces

An Oracle database is divided into logical storage units called tablespaces. A tablespace is used to group related logical structures together. For example, tablespaces commonly group all the application's objects to simplify some administrative operations.

Every Oracle database contains a tablespace named SYSTEM, which is created automatically when the database is created. The SYSTEM tablespace always contains the system catalog tables for the entire database. A small database might need only the SYSTEM tablespace; however, it's recommended that you create at least one additional tablespace to store user data separate from the system catalog, to reduce contention among dictionary objects and schema objects for the same datafiles (see Figure 13.1). Figure 19.6 illustrates an Oracle database consisting of the SYSTEM tablespace and a USER_DATA tablespace.

System catalog defined in Section 1.2.1

A new tablespace can be created using the CREATE TABLESPACE command; for example:

```
CREATE TABLESPACE user_data
DATAFILE 'DATA3.ORA' SIZE 100K;
```

A table can then be associated with a specific tablespace using the CREATE TABLE or ALTER TABLE statement; for example:

```
CREATE TABLE pen (penno char(4) NOT NULL, ...)
    TABLESPACE user_data;
```

If no tablespace is specified when creating a new table, the default tablespace associated with the user when the user account was set up is used. We'll see how this can be specified in Step 7.2.

Figure 19.6

Relationship
between an Oracle
database,
tablespaces, and
datafiles.

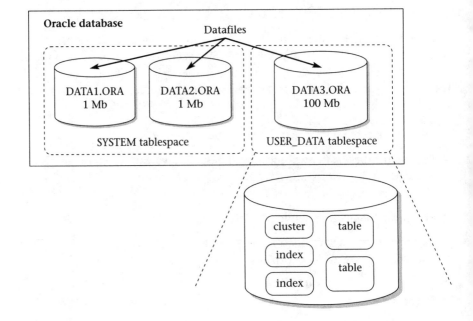

Users, schemas, and schema objects

A *user* (sometimes called a *username*) is a name defined in the database that can connect to, and access, objects. A *schema* is a named collection of objects, such as tables, views, clusters, and procedures, associated with a particular user. Schemas and users help DBAs manage database security.

To access a database, a user must run a database application (such as an Oracle form or SQL*Plus) and connect using a username defined in the database. When a database user is created, a corresponding schema of the same name is created for the user. By default, once a user connects to a database, the user has access to all objects contained in the corresponding schema. As a user is associated only with the schema of the same name, the terms user and schema are often used interchangeably.

Note there is no relationship between a tablespace and a schema; objects in the same schema can be in different tablespaces, and a tablespace can hold objects from different schemas.

Data blocks, extents, and segments

The *data block* is the smallest unit of storage that Oracle can use or allocate. One data block corresponds to a specific number of bytes of physical disk space. You

Figure 19.7

Relationship between Oracle data blocks, extents, and segments.

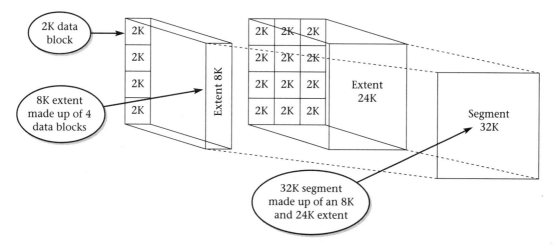

set the data block size for each Oracle database when you create the database. This data block size should be a multiple of the operating system's block size (within the system's maximum operating limit) to avoid unnecessary I/O.

The next level of logical database space is called an *extent*. An extent is a specific number of contiguous data blocks allocated for storing a specific type of information. The level above an extent is called a *segment*. A segment is a set of extents allocated for a certain logical structure. For example, each table's data is stored in its own data segment, while each index's data is stored in its own index segment. Figure 19.7 shows the relationship between data blocks, extents, and segments.

Oracle dynamically allocates space when the existing extents of a segment become full. Because extents are allocated as needed, the extents of a segment may or may not be contiguous on disk.

Oracle's physical database structure

The main physical database structures in Oracle are datafiles, redo log files, and control files.

Datafiles

Every Oracle database has one or more physical datafiles. The data of logical database structures (such as tables and indexes) is physically stored in these datafiles. One or more datafiles form a tablespace. The simplest Oracle database would have one tablespace and one datafile. A more complex database might have four tablespaces, each consisting of two datafiles, giving a total of eight datafiles. The architecture for datafiles and tablespaces is shown in Figure 19.6.

Recovery briefly discussed in Section 1.3

Redo log files

Every Oracle database has a set of two or more redo log files, which record all changes made to data, for recovery purposes. Should a failure prevent modified data from being permanently written to the datafiles, the changes can be obtained from the redo log, thus preventing work from being lost.

Control files

Every Oracle database has a control file, which contains entries that specify the physical structure of the database, such as:

- the database name
- the names and locations of a database's datafiles and redo log files
- the time stamp of database creation.

Clustered and non-clustered tables

Oracle 8 supports *clustered* and *non-clustered* tables. The choice of whether to use a clustered or non-clustered table depends on the analysis of the transactions undertaken previously, but the choice can have an impact on performance. In this section, we'll examine both types of structures and provide guidelines for their use.

Clusters are groups of one or more tables physically stored together because they share common columns and are often used together. With related records being physically stored together, disk access time is improved. The related columns of the tables in a cluster are called the *cluster key*. The cluster key is stored only once, and so clusters store a set of tables more efficiently than if the tables were stored individually (not clustered).

Figure 19.8 illustrates how the Clinic and Pen tables would be stored if we clustered the tables based on the column clinicNo. When these two tables are clustered, each unique clinicNo value is stored only once, in the cluster key. To each clinicNo value are attached the columns from both these tables.

Oracle supports two types of clusters:

(a) indexed clusters,

(b) hash clusters.

Indexed files discussed in Appendix C.5

Indexed clusters

In an *indexed cluster,* records with the same cluster key are stored together. Oracle suggests using indexed clusters when:

- queries retrieve records over a range of cluster key values;
- clustered tables may grow unpredictably.

Figure 19.8

How the Clinic and Pen tables would be stored clustered on clinicNo.

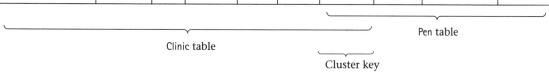

street	city	state	zipCode	telNo	faxNo	clinicNo	penNo	penCapacity	status
121-32nd Avenue	New York	NY	10012	...	...	C1000	1201	1	N
							1202	3	A
Roosevelt Center	Seattle	WA	98122	...	...	C1001	1405	2	N
							1406	4	N

Clinic table

Pen table

Cluster key

Clusters can improve performance of data retrieval, depending on the data distribution and what SQL operations are most often performed on the data. In particular, tables that are joined in a query benefit from the use of clusters because the records common to the joined tables are retrieved with the same I/O operation.

To create an indexed cluster in Oracle called Staff_Cluster with the cluster key column staffNo, you could use the following SQL statement:

```
CREATE CLUSTER staff_cluster
    (staffno CHAR(5))
SIZE 512
STORAGE (INITIAL 100K NEXT 50K PCTINCREASE 10);
```

The SIZE parameter specifies the amount of space (in bytes) to store all records with the same cluster key value. The size is optional and, if it is omitted, Oracle reserves one data block for each cluster key value. The INITIAL parameter specifies the size (in bytes) of the cluster's first extent, and the NEXT parameter specifies the size (in bytes) of the next extent to be allocated. The PCTINCREASE parameter specifies the percentage by which the third and subsequent extents grow over the preceding extent (default 50). In our example, we've specified that each subsequent extent should be 10 per cent larger than the preceding extent.

Guidelines for using indexed clusters

You may find the following guidelines helpful when deciding whether to cluster tables:

■ Consider clustering tables that are often accessed in join statements.

■ Do not cluster tables if they are joined only occasionally or if their common column values are modified frequently. (Modifying a record's cluster key value takes longer than modifying the value in an unclustered table, because Oracle may have to migrate the modified record to another block to maintain the cluster.)

■ Do not cluster tables if a full search of one of the tables is often required. (A full search of a clustered table can take longer than a full search of an unclustered table. Oracle is likely to read more blocks because the tables are stored together.)

1:* Relationships defined in Section 5.5.2

■ Consider clustering tables involved in one-to-many (1:*) relationships if you often select a record from the parent table and then the corresponding records from the child table. (Child records are stored in the same data block(s) as the parent record, so they are likely to be in memory when you select them, requiring Oracle to perform less I/O.)

■ Consider storing a child table alone in a cluster if you often select many child records of the same parent. (This measure improves the performance of queries that select child records of the same parent but does not decrease the performance of a full search of the parent table.)

■ Do not cluster tables if the data from all tables with the same cluster key value exceeds more than one or two Oracle blocks. (To access a record in a clustered table, Oracle reads all blocks containing records with that value. If these records occupy multiple blocks, accessing a single record could require more reads than accessing the same record in an unclustered table.)

Hash clusters

Hash files discussed in Appendix C.4

Hash clusters also cluster table data in a manner similar to index clusters. However, a record is stored in a hash cluster based on the result of applying a hash function to the record's cluster key value. All records with the same hash key value are stored together on disk. Oracle suggests using hash clusters when:

■ queries retrieve records based on equality conditions involving all cluster key columns (for example, return all records for clinic S1000);

■ clustered tables are static or you can determine the maximum number of records and the maximum amount of space required by the cluster when you create it.

To create a hash cluster in Oracle called Exams_Cluster clustered by the column examNo, you could use the following SQL statement:

```
CREATE CLUSTER exams_cluster
    (examno NUMBER(6, 0))
HASH IS examno HASHKEYS 300000;
```

Once you've created the hash cluster, you can create the tables that will be part of the structure. For example:

```
CREATE TABLE examination
     (examno NUMBER(6, 0) PRIMARY KEY,
…)
CLUSTER exams_cluster (examno);
```

Guidelines for using hash clusters

You may find the following guidelines helpful when deciding whether to use hash clusters:

■ Consider using hash clusters to store tables that are frequently accessed using a search clause containing equality conditions with the same column(s). Designate these column(s) as the cluster key.

■ Store a table in a hash cluster if you can determine how much space is required to hold all records with a given cluster key value, both now and in the future.

■ Do not use hash clusters if space is scarce and you cannot afford to allocate additional space for records to be inserted in the future.

■ Do not use a hash cluster to store a constantly growing table if the process of occasionally creating a new, larger hash cluster to hold that table is impractical.

■ Do not store a table in a hash cluster if a search of the entire table is often required and you must allocate a significant amount of space to the hash cluster in anticipation of the table growing. (Such full searches must read all blocks allocated to the hash cluster, even though some blocks may contain few records. Storing the table alone would reduce the number of blocks read by a full table search.)

■ Do not store a table in a hash cluster if your application frequently modifies the cluster key values.

■ Storing a single table in a hash cluster can be useful, regardless of whether the table is often joined with other tables, provided that hashing is appropriate for the table based on the previous guidelines.

PCTFREE and PCTUSED

The two space management parameters, PCTFREE and PCTUSED, may also have a significant affect on performance. You specify these parameters when creating or altering a table or cluster (which has its own data segment). You can also specify the storage parameter PCTFREE when creating or altering an index (which has its own index segment). The parameters are used as follows:

■ *PCTFREE* sets the minimum percentage of a data block to be reserved as free space for possible updates to records that already exist in that block (default value is 10);

■ *PCTUSED* sets the minimum percentage of a block that can be used for record data plus any overhead required by Oracle before new records will be added to the block (default value is 40). After a data block is filled to the limit determined by PCTFREE, Oracle considers the block unavailable for the insertion of new records until the percentage of that block falls below the parameter PCTUSED. Until this value is achieved, Oracle uses the free space of the data block only for updates to records already contained in the data block.

A lower value for PCTFREE reserves less space for updates to existing records, and allows inserts to fill the block more completely. This might save you space but it increases processing costs because blocks frequently need to be reorganized as their free space area becomes filled with new/updated records. A lower value for PCTUSED increases the unused space in a database but reduces processing costs during insert/update operations.

Clearly the sum of PCTFREE and PCTUSED can be no greater than 100. If the sum is less than 100, the optimum setting to balance use of space and I/O is a sum of the two parameters that differs from 100 by the percentage of space occupied by a record. For example, if the block size is 2048 bytes with a 100 byte overhead, and the record size is 390 bytes, which is 20 per cent of the available block size, then a good value for the sum of PCTFREE and PCTUSED would be 80 per cent to make best use of space. On the other hand, if the sum equals 100, Oracle would attempt to keep no more than PCTFREE free space, which would result in the highest processing costs. The combined use of PCTFREE and PCTUSED is illustrated in Figure 19.9.

The above descriptions of the logical and physical database structures used by Oracle are not intended to be detailed. Rather, they have been included to give you a feel for the type of knowledge of the target DBMS you need to acquire to allow you to successfully undertake some aspects of physical database design. We have also included them to emphasize the differences between systems. For example, having read this step, look back at Step 5.2 in Chapter 13, which dealt with Microsoft Access. You'll see in that step that there was really nothing to do – the file organization in Microsoft Access 97 is fixed. For PC RDBMSs, this is not unusual. If you were to look now at another multi-user RDBMS, such as Ingres or SQL Server, you'd find that the logical and physical structures used by these systems are different again.

Before we can decide on the file organizations for the *Perfect Pets* database, we need to examine what indexes we want to add to enhance performance.

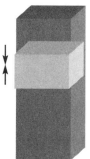

Records are inserted until the block is 80 per cent full, because PCTFREE specifies that 20 per cent of the block must remain available for updates to existing records.

Updates to existing records use the free space reserved in the block. No new records can be inserted into the block until the amount of used space is less than 40 per cent.

Figure 19.9

Combined use of PCTFREE and PCTUSED with PCTFREE = 20 per cent and PCTUSED = 40 per cent.

Step 5.3 Choose indexes

Oracle automatically adds an index for each primary key. In addition, Oracle recommends that you do not explicitly define UNIQUE indexes on tables but instead define UNIQUE integrity constraints on the desired columns. Oracle enforces UNIQUE integrity constraints by automatically defining a unique index on the unique key. Exceptions to this recommendation are usually performance related. For example, using a CREATE TABLE ... AS SELECT with a UNIQUE constraint is slower than creating the table without the constraint and then manually creating a UNIQUE index.

Let's assume that the tables will be created with the identified primary, alternate, and foreign keys specified. What you have to do now is identify whether any clusters are required and whether any additional indexes are required. In Chapter 13, we suggested creating a 'wish-list' and then considering each potential index in the wish-list to determine whether the increase in query performance outweighs the performance degradation when updates occur. Before creating the wish-list, it's a good idea to ignore small tables from further consideration, as small tables can usually be processed in memory without requiring additional indexes. From Figure 19.5, we can see that the small tables in the *Perfect Pets* database are Clinic, Staff, Pen, Treatment, Item, and Pharmacy. We therefore exclude these tables from further consideration. If we now consider the remaining tables, we can produce a summary of interactions between the base tables for the retrieval transactions listed in Section 18.1.2, as shown in Table 19.2.

Based on the guidelines given above for clusters, there would appear to be no real benefit in using clusters. However, there may be performance benefits in adding the indexes shown in Table 19.3.

Table 19.2 Interactions between tables and retrieval transactions.

Table	Transaction	Access	Frequency (per day)
Appointment	2(l)	join: petNo	250
		search condition: aDate	
Examination	2(c), 2(d)	join: Pet on petNo	100
	2(d)	join: Staff on staffNo	
Invoice	2(e), 2(f)	join: PetOwner on ownerNo	10
		search condition: datePaid IS NULL	
	2(n)	join: PetOwner on ownerNo	1 per month
		search condition: invoiceDate	
ItemClinicStock	2(q)	search condition: inStock < reorderLevel	50 per month
Pet	2(b)	join: PetOwner on ownerNo	50
	2(j)	group: petType	1
		order by: petType	
		aggregate: count on petType	
	2(l)	join: Clinic on clinicNo	250
	2(o)	join: PetOwner on ownerNo	1500
PharmClinicStock	2(p)	search condition: inStock < reorderLevel	50 per month

Table 19.3 Additional indexes for the *Perfect Pets* database.

Table	Index
Pet	clinicNo
	ownerNo
Appointment	aDate
	petNo
Invoice	ownerNo
	invoiceDate

Note that the search condition used by transaction 2(e) (datepaid IS NULL) would suggest creating an index on the **datePaid** column. However, Oracle does not use an index when the search condition involves an IS NULL/IS NOT NULL condition. Further, because transaction 2(j) only runs once a day and there are not many pet types, an index on **petType** in the Pet table is unwarranted.

Step 6.1 Consider derived data

The requirements given in Section 18.1.1 indicate only one derived item, namely that the total cost of all treatments given to a pet should be recorded on the invoice. The algorithm to derive this information can be written using the following SQL statement:

```
SELECT SUM(pt.quantity*t.cost)
FROM invoice i INNER JOIN (examination e INNER JOIN
     (treatment t INNER JOIN pettreatment pt
     ON t.treatno = pt.treatno) ON e.examno = pt.examno)
     ON i.examno = e.examno;
```

If access to the Invoice table is frequent, there may be performance benefits to be gained by storing the total cost in the Invoice table. However, from the expected frequency data given in Table 19.2, you can see that the access to the Invoice table is not particularly frequent, and so you may decide in this case just to calculate the total whenever it's required.

Step 6.2 Consider duplicating columns or joining tables together

In Step 1.7, the relationship Clinic *Schedules* Appointment was considered to be redundant. However, this causes a potential performance problem. For example, the Pet table has to be accessed just to determine an available time for an appointment at a clinic. In this case, it may be preferable to reinstate the *Schedules* relationship and add the primary key of the Clinic table (clinicNo) to the Appointment table to act as a foreign key.

Consider implications of denormalization

Owing to the addition of the column clinicNo to the Appointment table, it would probably be worthwhile considering the creation of an index on this column to improve the performance of transaction 2(l).

Step 7.1 Design user views

Oracle 8 supports the SQL CREATE VIEW statement, so views can be created easily for each user view. In addition, using the Oracle Forms Builder, you can create forms based on one or more tables or based on a view. For example, you may decide to create a view for clinic manager details. Figure 19.10(a) illustrates the creation of a view called Clinic_Managers using the Schema Manager, and Figure 19.10(b) shows a form built from this view.

Figure 19.10

Creating and using user views: (a) creation of a view using the Oracle Schema Manager; (b) form built from this view.

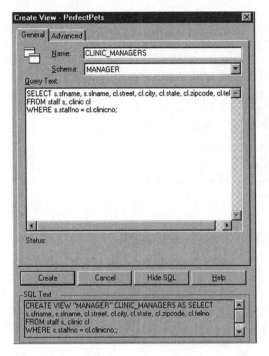

(a)

(b)

Step 7.2 Design access rules

As part of the database analysis phase, you need to determine the types of users who'll be working with the system and the level of access that they must be given to accomplish their designated tasks. As we mentioned in Step 7.2 in Chapter 15, database security usually involves both system security and data security. One form of system security used by Oracle is the standard username and password mechanism, whereby a user has to provide a valid username and password before access can be gained to the database, although the responsibility to authenticate users can be devolved to the operating system. Figure 19.11 illustrates the creation of a new user called ADAMS with password authentication set. Whenever user ADAMS tries to connect to the database, this user will be presented with a Connect or Log On dialog box similar to the one illustrated in Figure 19.12, prompting for a username and password to access the specified database.

Privileges

A **privilege** is a right to execute a particular type of SQL statement or to access another user's objects. Some examples of privileges include the right to:

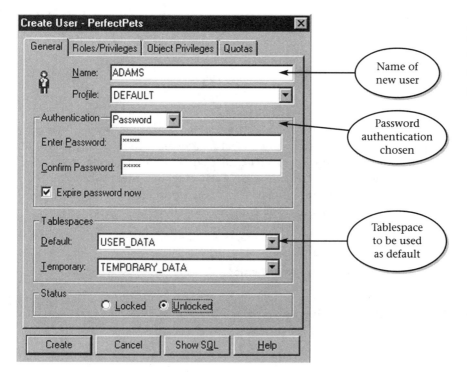

Figure 19.11

Creation of a new user called ADAMS, with password authentication set.

Figure 19.12

Connect dialog box requesting user name, password, and database to connect to.

■ connect to the database (create a session);

■ create a table;

■ select rows from another user's table.

You grant privileges to users so these users can accomplish the tasks required for their jobs. As excessive granting of unnecessary privileges can compromise security, you should grant a privilege only to a user who absolutely requires the privilege to accomplish his or her work. In Oracle, there are two distinct categories of privileges:

(a) system privileges

(b) object privileges.

System privileges

Roles discussed shortly

A system privilege is the right to perform a particular action or to perform an action on any schema objects of a particular type. For example, the privileges to create tablespaces and to create users in a database are system privileges. There are over 80 distinct system privileges. System privileges are granted to, or revoked from, users and *roles* using either of the following:

- Grant System Privileges/Roles dialog box and Revoke System Privileges/Roles dialog box of the Oracle Security Manager;
- SQL GRANT and REVOKE statements.

However, only users who have been granted a specific system privilege with the ADMIN OPTION or users with the GRANT ANY PRIVILEGE system privilege can grant or revoke system privileges.

Object privileges

An object privilege is a privilege or right to perform a particular action on a specific table, view, sequence, procedure, function, or package. Different object privileges are available for different types of objects. For example, the privilege to delete rows from the table Pen is an object privilege.

Some schema objects (such as clusters, indexes, and triggers) do not have associated object privileges; their use is controlled with system privileges. For example, to alter a cluster, a user must own the cluster or have the ALTER ANY CLUSTER system privilege.

A user automatically has all object privileges for schema objects contained in his or her schema. A user can grant any object privilege on any schema object he or she owns to any other user or role. If the grant includes the WITH GRANT OPTION (of the GRANT statement), the grantee can further grant the object privilege to other users; otherwise, the grantee can use the privilege but cannot grant it to other users.

The object privileges for tables and views are shown in Table 19.4.

Roles

A user can receive a privilege in two different ways:

- You can grant privileges to users explicitly. For example, you can explicitly grant the privilege to insert records into the Clinic table to the user ADAMS.

Table 19.4 What each object privilege allows a grantee to do with tables and views.

Object/ Privilege	Table	View
ALTER	Change the table definition with the ALTER TABLE statement.	N/A
DELETE	Remove rows from the table with the DELETE statement. Note: you must grant the SELECT privilege on the table along with the DELETE privilege.	Remove rows from the view with the DELETE statement.
INDEX	Create an index on the table with the CREATE INDEX statement.	N/A
INSERT	Add new rows to the table with the INSERT statement.	Add new rows to the view with the INSERT statement.
REFERENCES	Create a constraint that refers to the table. You cannot grant this privilege to a role.	N/A
SELECT	Query the table with the SELECT statement.	Query the view with the SELECT statement.
UPDATE	Change data in the table with the UPDATE statement. Note: you must grant the SELECT privilege on the table along with the UPDATE privilege.	Change data in the view with the UPDATE statement.

For example:

```
GRANT INSERT ON clinic TO ADAMS;
```

■ You can also grant privileges to a *role* (a named group of privileges), and then grant the role to one or more users. For example, you can grant the privileges to select, insert, update, and delete records from the Clinic table to the role named DEPUTYMANAGER, which in turn you can grant to the users ADAMS and GLENN. A user can have access to several roles, and several users can be assigned the same roles. Figure 19.13 illustrates the granting of these privileges to the role DEPUTYMANAGER using the Oracle Security Manager.

Because roles allow for easier and better management of privileges, you should normally grant privileges to roles and not to specific users.

Figure 19.13

Setting the Select, Insert, Update, and Delete privileges on the Clinic table to the role DEPUTYMANAGER.

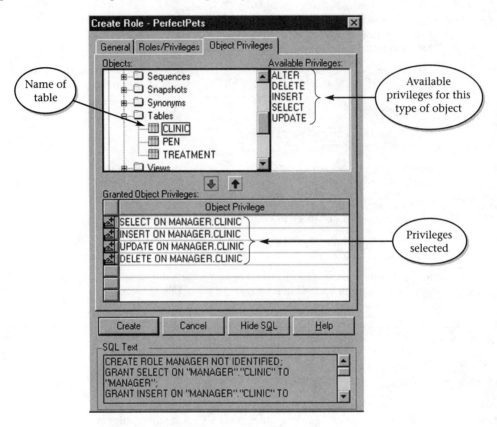

Implementation

You're now in a position to start implementing the base tables, file organizations, indexes, views, and security mechanisms, and thereafter, to start populating the database. However, as discussed in Chapter 16, this is not the end of database design – the ongoing monitoring and tuning of the operational system is a vital activity to achieve continued success for the system. In addition, it's highly likely that once the system goes live, changes will be required as a result of user feedback and changing requirements. In some cases, the changes will be cosmetic, requiring alterations to the user interface, with no impact on the database itself. In others, however, there will be a need to modify the structure of the database, and in these cases, you will have to go through some of the steps in both the logical and physical design methodology again to ensure that the changes are designed and implemented correctly.

What next?

You have now worked through two case studies and hopefully you have now acquired a reasonable amount of experience of database design, and picked up a number of tips that you will find helpful. As we have mentioned a number of times in this book, you will become more competent at database design with experience. With competence will come confidence, and the skill to know how to carry out the analysis stages of the database application lifecycle professionally.

To help you further, we have included additional database solutions in Appendix D (with corresponding SQL scripts included on the accompanying CD-ROM). Each solution has a small introduction, which you may like to read and then try to produce the ER model and matching base tables yourself before looking at our sample solution.

We have also included on the CD-ROM a full implementation of the *StayHome* case study in Microsoft Access 97 and the SQL scripts to create the base tables for the *Perfect Pets* case study. Also included is easy access to demonstration versions of Rational Rose, a CASE tool that will allow you to practice producing UML diagrams.

We hope this book has been useful and look forward to any comments you may have to improve its contents.

Appendices

Alternative data modeling notations

In this appendix you will learn:

Alternative data modeling notations.

In Chapter 5, you learned how to create an Entity-Relationship (ER) model using an increasingly popular notation called UML (Unified Modeling Language). In this appendix you are shown two additional notations that are often used to create ER models. The first ER notation is called the Chen notation and the second is called the Crow's Feet notation. We demonstrate each by presenting a table that shows the notation used for each of the main concepts of the ER model and then we present the notation using as an example the ER model shown in Figure 8.16.

A.1   ER Modeling using the Chen notation

Table A.1 shows the Chen notation for the main concepts of the ER model and Figure A.1 shows the ER model in Figure 8.16 redrawn using the Chen notation.

A.2   ER Modeling using the Crow's Feet notation

Table A.2 shows the Crow's Feet notation for the main concepts of the ER model and Figure A.2 shows the ER model in Figure 8.16 redrawn using the Crow's Feet notation.

Table A.1

The Chen notation for ER modeling.

Notation	Meaning
Entity name	Strong entity
Entity name	Weak entity
Relationship name	Relationship
Relationship name	Relationship associated with a weak entity
Relationship name / Role name / Role name / Entity name	Recursive relationship with role names to identify the roles played by the entity in the relationship
Attribute name	Attribute
Attribute name	Primary key attribute
Attribute name	Multi-valued attribute

(Attribute name)	Derived attribute
1 ◇ 1	One-to-one (1:1) relationship
1 ◇ M	One-to-many (1:M) relationship
M ◇ N	Many-to-many (M:N) relationship
A 1 ◇ M B	One-to-many relationship with mandatory participation for both entities A and B
A 1 ◇ M B	One-to-many relationship with optional participation for entity A and mandatory participation for entity B
A 1 ◇ M B	One-to-many relationship with optional participation for both entities A and B
Superclass — Subclass Subclass	Generalization/Specialization. If circle contains 'd' relationship is disjoint; if circle contains 'o' relationship is nondisjoint. Double lines from superclass represents mandatory participation; single line represents optional participation

Table A.1

Continued

Figure A.1

The ER model shown in Figure 8.16 redrawn using the Chen notation.

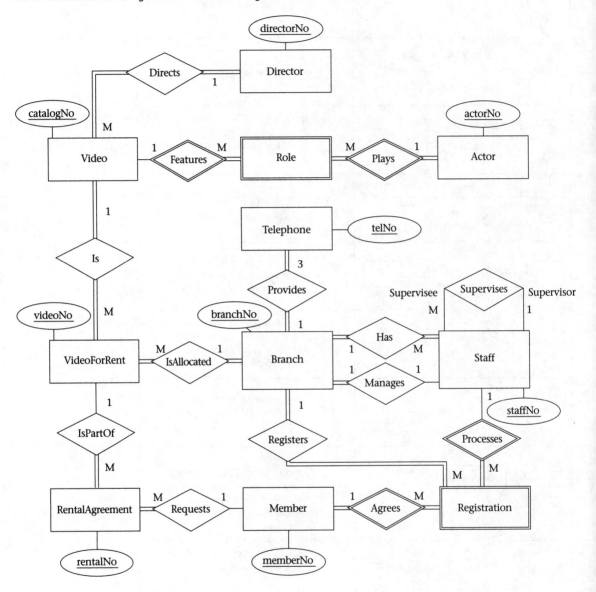

Notation	Meaning
Entity name	Entity
Relationship name	Relationship
Role name Relationship name Role name Entity name	Recursive relationship with role names to identify the roles played by the entity in the relationship
Entity name Attribute name Attribute 1 Attribute 2 Attribute n	Attributes are listed in the lower section of the entity symbol The primary key attribute is underlined Multi-valued attribute placed in curly braces { }
Relationship name	One-to-one relationship
Relationship name	One-to-many relationship
Relationship name	Many-to-many relationship

Table A.2

The Crow's Feet notation for ER modeling.

Table A.2

Continued

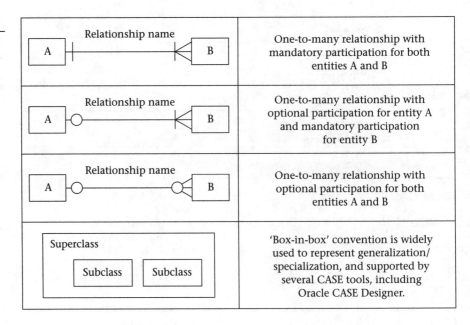

Relationship name A ⊢———⊢<⊢ B	One-to-many relationship with mandatory participation for both entities A and B
Relationship name A ⊢O———⊢< B	One-to-many relationship with optional participation for entity A and mandatory participation for entity B
Relationship name A ⊢O———O< B	One-to-many relationship with optional participation for both entities A and B
Superclass Subclass Subclass	'Box-in-box' convention is widely used to represent generalization/ specialization, and supported by several CASE tools, including Oracle CASE Designer.

Figure A.2

The ER model shown in Figure 8.16 redrawn using the Crow's Feet notation.

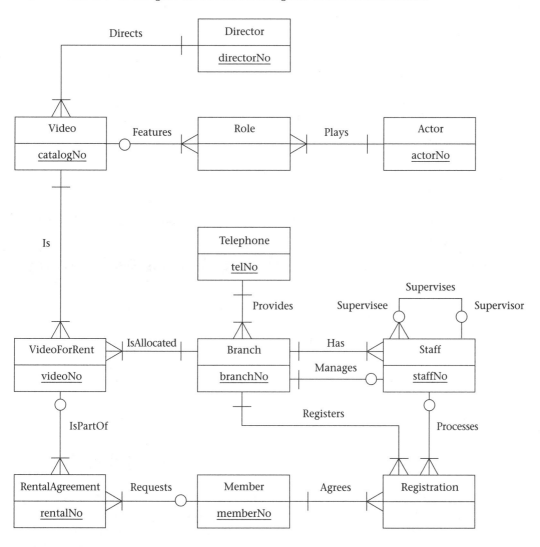

Appendix B

Summary of the database design methodology

In this appendix you will learn:

➤ Database design is composed of two main phases: logical and physical database design.

➤ The steps involved in the main phases of the database design methodology.

In this book, we present a database design methodology for relational databases. This methodology is made up of the two main phases, logical database design and physical database design, which are described in detail in Chapters 7 to 16. In this appendix, we summarize the steps involved in these phases for those readers who are already familiar with database design.

Step 1 Build local logical data model for each view

During analysis, you will have identified a number of user views. Depending on the amount of overlap, for manageability you may decide to merge some of these views. The purpose of this step is to build a local logical data model of the company (or part of the company) for each of these (possibly merged) views.

Step 1.1 Identify entities

Identify and document the main entities in the view of the company.

Step 1.2 Identify relationships

Identify the important relationships that exist between the entities that you have identified. Determine the multiplicity constraints of the relationships. Document relationships. Use Entity-Relationship (ER) modeling when necessary.

Step 1.3 Identify and associate attributes with entities or relationships

Associate attributes with the appropriate entities or relationships. Identify simple/composite attributes, single-valued/multi-valued attributes, and derived attributes. Document attributes.

Step 1.4 Determine attribute domains

Determine domains for the attributes in the local logical data model. Document attribute domains.

Step 1.5 Determine candidate and primary key attributes

Identify the candidate key(s) for each entity and, if there is more than one candidate key, choose one to be the primary key, the others becoming alternate keys. Document candidate, primary, and alternate keys for each strong entity.

Step 1.6 Specialize/Generalize entities (optional step)

Identify superclass and subclass entities, where appropriate.

Step 1.7 Remove features not compatible with the relational model

Refine the local logical data model to remove undesirable features. Remove many-to-many (*:*) binary relationships, many-to-many (*:*) recursive relationships, complex relationships, multi-valued attributes, re-examine 1:1 relationships, and remove redundant relationships.

Step 1.8 Check model supports user transactions

Ensure that the local logical data model supports the transactions required by the view.

Step 2 Create and check tables for each local logical data model

To create tables for each local logical data model, and to check the structure of the tables.

Step 2.1 Create tables for local logical data model

In this step, you create base tables for the local logical data model to represent the entities, relationships, attributes, and constraints described in the view of the company. The structure of the tables is derived from the information that describes the local logical data model. This information includes the ER model, data dictionary, and any other documentation that describes the model. Also, document any new primary or candidate keys that have been formed as a result of the process of creating tables for the local logical data model.

The basic rules for creating tables are as follows:

(a) For each entity, create a table that includes all the entity's simple attributes.

(b) Each relationship is represented by the primary key/foreign key mechanism. In deciding where to post the foreign key, you must identify the 'parent' and 'child' entities in the relationship. The parent entity then posts a copy of its primary key into the child table, to act as the foreign key. Table B.1 gives a summary of how you identify the parent and child entities in a relationship.

(c) For each superclass/subclass relationship, you identify the superclass as the parent entity and the subclass as the child entity. There are various options on how you may best represent such a relationship as one or more tables. The selection of the most appropriate option is dependent on the participation and disjoint constraints on the superclass/subclass relationship, as shown in Table B.2.

Step 2.2 Check table structures using normalization

The purpose of this step is to examine the groupings of columns in each table created in Step 2.1. You check the composition of each table using the rules of normalization. Each table should be in at least third normal form (3NF).

Step 2.3 Check that tables support user transactions

In this step, you ensure that the tables support the transactions required by the view. The transactions that are required by a view can be determined from the users' requirements specifications.

Table B.1 Summary of how to identify the parent and child entities in a relationship.

Relationship	Identification
1:* binary relationship	**parent**: 1 side; **child**: * side
1:* recursive relationship	**parent**: 1 side; **child**: * side
1:1 binary relationship:	
a) mandatory participation on both sides	combine tables into one table
b) mandatory participation on one side	**parent**: optional side; **child**: mandatory side
c) optional participation on both sides	arbitrary without further information
1:1 recursive relationship:	
a) mandatory participation on both sides	combine tables into one with two copies of primary key
b) mandatory participation on one side	as for a), or create new table to represent relationship
c) optional participation on both sides	create new table to represent relationship

Table B.2 Options available for the representation of a superclass/subclass relationship based on the participation and disjoint constraints.

Participation constraint	Disjoint constraint	Tables required
Mandatory	Nondisjoint {And}	Single table
Optional	Nondisjoint {And}	Two tables: one table for superclass and one table for all subclasses
Mandatory	Disjoint {Or}	Many tables: one table for each combined superclass/subclass
Optional	Disjoint {Or} and one for each subclass	Many tables: one table for superclass

Step 2.4 Define integrity constraints

Identify the integrity constraints given in the view of the company. These include specifying the required data, attribute domain constraints, entity integrity, referential integrity, and business rules. Document all integrity constraints.

Step 2.5 Review local logical data model with users

Ensure that the local logical data model is a true representation of the view of the company (or part of the company) being modeled.

Step 3 Build and check global logical data model

Combine the individual local logical data models into a single global logical data model that represents the company (or part of the company) that is being modeled.

Step 3.1 Merge local logical data models into global model

Merge the individual local logical data models into a single global logical data model. Some typical tasks of this step are as follows:

(1) Review the names of entities/tables and their primary keys.

(2) Review the names of relationships.

(3) Merge entities/tables from the local data models.

(4) Include (without merging) entities/tables unique to each local data model.

(5) Merge relationships from the local data model.

(6) Include (without merging) relationships unique to each local data model.

(7) Check for missing entities/tables and relationships.

(8) Check foreign keys.

(9) Check integrity constraints.

(10) Draw the global logical data model.

(11) Update the documentation.

Step 3.2 Check global logical data model

This step is equivalent to Steps 2.3 and 2.4, where you check the structure of the tables created for the global data model using normalization and then check that these tables are capable of supporting all user transactions.

Step 3.3 Check for future growth

Determine whether there are any significant changes likely in the foreseeable future and assess whether the global logical data model can accommodate these changes.

Step 3.4 Review global logical data model with users

Ensure that the global logical data model is a true representation of the company (or the part of the company being modeled).

Step 4 Translate global logical data model for target DBMS

Produce a basic working set of base tables from the global logical data model.

Step 4.1 Design base tables for target DBMS

Decide how to represent the base tables you have identified in the global logical data model in the target DBMS. Document design of tables.

Step 4.2 Design business rules for target DBMS

Design the business rules for the target DBMS. Document design of business rules.

Step 5 Design physical representation

Determine the file organizations that will be used to store the base tables; that is, the way in which tables and records will be held on secondary storage. Consider the addition of indexes to improve performance.

Step 5.1 Analyze transactions

Understand the functionality of the transactions that will run on the database and analyze the important transactions.

Step 5.2 Choose file organizations

Determine an efficient file organization for each base table.

Step 5.3 Choose indexes

Determine whether adding indexes will improve the performance of the system.

Step 6 Consider the introduction of controlled redundancy

Determine whether introducing redundancy in a controlled manner by relaxing the normalization rules will improve the performance of the system.

Step 6.1 Consider derived data

Consider how derived data will be represented. The choice is to calculate derived data each time it's needed or to introduce redundancy and store the derived data as a column in a table.

Step 6.2 Consider duplicating columns or joining tables together

Consider duplicating columns or joining tables together to achieve improved performance. In particular, consider combining one-to-one (1:1) relationships, duplicating nonkey columns in one-to-many (1:*) relationships to reduce joins, duplicating foreign key columns in one-to-many (1:*) relationships to reduce joins, duplicating columns in many-to-many (*:*) relationships to reduce joins, introducing repeating groups, merging lookup tables with base tables, and creating extract tables.

Step 7 Design security mechanisms

Design the security measures for the database implementation as specified by the users.

Step 7.1 Design user views

Design the user views that you identified during the analysis phase.

Step 7.2 Design access rules

Design the access rules to the base tables and user views. Document the design of the security measures and user views.

Step 8 Monitor and tune the operational system

Monitor the operational system and improve the performance of the system to correct inappropriate design decisions or reflect changing requirements.

File organizations and indexes

In this appendix you will learn:

The distinction between primary and secondary storage. ◄

The meanings of file organization and access method. ◄

How heap files are organized. ◄

How ordered files are organized. ◄

How hash files are organized. ◄

What an index is and how it can be used to speed up database retrievals. ◄

The distinction between primary, secondary, and clustered indexes. ◄

How multilevel indexes are organized. ◄

How B^+-Trees are organized. ◄

Steps 5.2 and 5.3 of the physical database design methodology presented in Chapter 13 concern the selection of appropriate file organizations and indexes for the base tables that have been created to represent the company (or the part of the company being modeled). In this appendix, we introduce the main concepts regarding the physical storage of the database on secondary storage devices such as magnetic disks and optical disks. The computer's primary storage, that is main memory, is inappropriate for storing the database. Although the access times for primary storage are much faster than secondary storage, primary storage is not large or reliable enough to store the quantity of data that a typical database might require. As the data stored in primary storage disappears when power is lost, we refer to primary storage as *volatile storage*. In contrast, the data on secondary storage persists through power loss, and is consequently referred to as *non-volatile storage*. Further, the cost of storage per unit of data is an order of magnitude greater for primary storage than for disk.

In the following section, we introduce the basic concepts of physical storage. In the subsequent three sections, we discuss the main types of file organization, namely heap (unsorted), sequential (sorted), and hash files. In Section C.5, we discuss how indexes can be used to improve the performance of database retrievals. In particular, we look at multilevel indexes and B$^+$-Trees.

C.1 Basic concepts

The database on secondary storage is organized into one or more *files*, where each file consists of one or more *records* and each record consists of one or more *fields*. Typically, a record corresponds to an entity/table and a field to an attribute/column. Consider the Staff table from the *StayHome* case study shown in Figure C.1.

We may expect each record in this table to map onto a record in the operating system file that holds the Staff table. Each field in a record would store one column from the Staff table. When you request a record from the DBMS, for example Staff record S0003, the DBMS maps this *logical record* onto a *physical record* and retrieves the physical record into the DBMS buffers in primary storage using the operating system file access routines.

The physical record is the unit of transfer between disk and primary storage, and vice versa. Generally, a physical record consists of more than one logical record, although depending on size, a logical record may correspond to one physical record. It is even possible for a large logical record to span more than one physical record. The terms 'block' and 'page' are generally used in place of physical record. In the remainder of this appendix we use the term 'page'. For example, the Staff records in Figure C.1 may be stored on two pages, as shown in Figure C.2.

Figure C.1

Staff table from the *StayHome* case study.

staffNo	name	position	salary	branchNo
S1500	Tom Daniels	Manager	46000	B001
S0003	Sally Adams	Assistant	30000	B001
S0010	Mary Martinez	Manager	50000	B002
S3250	Robert Chin	Supervisor	32000	B002
S2250	Sally Stern	Manager	48000	B004
S0415	Art Peters	Manager	41000	B003

staffNo	name	position	salary	branchNo	Page
S1500	Tom Daniels	Manager	46000	B001	1
S0003	Sally Adams	Assistant	30000	B001	
S0010	Mary Martinez	Manager	50000	B002	
S3250	Robert Chin	Supervisor	32000	B002	
S2250	Sally Stern	Manager	48000	B004	2
S0415	Art Peters	Manager	41000	B003	

Figure C.2

Storage of the Staff table in pages.

The order in which records are stored and accessed in the file is dependent on the *file organization*.

The main types of file organization are:

■ *Heap (unordered) files* Records are placed on disk in no particular order.

■ *Sequential (ordered) files* Records are ordered by the value of a specified field.

■ *Hash files* Records are placed on disk according to a hash function.

Along with a file organization, there is a set of **access methods**.

Since some access methods can be applied only to certain file organizations (for example, we cannot apply an indexed access method to a file without an index), the terms file organization and access method are used interchangeably. In the remainder of this appendix, we discuss the main types of file organization. In Chapter 13, we present a methodology for physical database design for relational systems, and provide guidelines for choosing appropriate indexes and file organizations.

> **File organization**
> A way of arranging the records in a file when the file is stored on disk.

> **Access method**
> The steps involved in storing and retrieving records from a file.

C.2 Heap files

An *unordered file*, sometimes called a *heap file*, is the simplest type of file organization. Records are placed in the file in the same order as they are inserted. A new record is inserted in the last page of the file; if there is insufficient space in the last page, a new page is added to the file. This makes insertion very efficient. However, as a heap file has no particular ordering with respect to field values, a *linear search* must be performed to access a record. A linear search involves reading pages from the file until the required record is found. This makes retrievals from heap files that have more than a few pages relatively slow, unless the retrieval involves a large proportion of the records in the file.

To delete a record, the required page first has to be retrieved, the record marked as deleted, and the page written back to disk. The space with deleted records is not reused. Consequently, performance progressively deteriorates as deletions occur. This means that heap files have to be periodically reorganized by the Database Administrator (DBA) to reclaim the unused space of deleted records.

Heap files are one of the best organizations for bulk-loading data into a table, as records are inserted at the end of the sequence; there is no overhead incurred in calculating what page the record should go on.

C.3 Ordered files

Keys defined in Section 2.2.3

The records in a file can be sorted on the values of one or more of the fields, forming a key-sequenced data set. The field(s) that the file is sorted on is called the *ordering field*. If the ordering field is also a key field of the file, and therefore guaranteed to have a unique value in each record, the field is also called the *ordering key* for the file. For example, consider the following SQL query:

```
SELECT *
FROM staff
ORDER BY staffno;
```

If the records of the Staff table are already ordered according to the ordering column staffNo, it should be possible to reduce the execution time for the query, as no sorting is necessary.

> Although in Section 2.2 we stated that records in the relational model are unordered, this applies as an external (logical) property, not as an implementational (physical) property. There will always be a first record, second record, and *n*th record.

If the records are ordered on staffNo, under certain conditions we can use a *binary search* to execute queries that involve a search condition based on staffNo. For example, consider the following SQL query:

```
SELECT *
FROM staff
WHERE staffno = 'S1500';
```

If we use the sample records shown in Figure C.1 and for simplicity assume there is one record per page, we would get the ordered file shown in Figure C.3. The binary search proceeds as follows:

(1) Retrieve the mid-page of the file. Check whether the required record is between the first and last record of this page. If so, the required record lies in this page and no more pages need to be retrieved.

(2) If the value of the key field in the first record on the page is greater than the required value, the required value (if it exists) occurs on an earlier page.

Page	staffNo	name	position	salary	branchNo
1	S0003	Sally Adams	Assistant	30000	B001
2	S0010	Mary Martinez	Manager	50000	B002
3	S0415	Art Peters	Manager	41000	B003
4	S1500	Tom Daniels	Manager	46000	B001
5	S2250	Sally Stern	Manager	48000	B004
6	S3250	Robert Chin	Supervisor	32000	B002

Figure C.3

Binary search on ordered *Staff* file.

Therefore, we repeat the above steps using the lower half of the file as the new search area.

(3) If the value of the key field in the last record on the page is less than the required value, the required value occurs on a later page, and so we repeat the above steps using the top half of the file as the new search area. In this way, half the search space is eliminated from the search with each page retrieved.

In our case, the middle page is page 3, and the record on the retrieved page (S0415) does not equal the one we want (S1500). The value of the key field in page 3 is less than the one we want, so we can discard the first half of the file from the search. We now retrieve the mid-page of the top half of the file, that is, page 5. This time the value of the key field (S2250) is greater than S1500, which enables us to discard the top half of this search space. We now retrieve the mid-page of the remaining search space (page 4), which is the record we want.

In general, the binary search is more efficient than a linear search. However, binary search is applied more frequently to data in primary storage than in secondary storage.

Inserting and deleting records in a sorted file are problematic because the order of records has to be maintained. To insert a new record, we must find the correct position in the ordering for the record and then find space to insert it. If there is sufficient space in the required page for the new record, then the single page can be reordered and written back to disk. If this is not the case, then it would be necessary to move one or more records onto the next page. Again, the next page may have no free space and the records on this page must be moved, and so on.

Inserting a record near the start of a large file could be very time-consuming. One solution is to create a temporary unsorted file, called an *overflow file*. Insertions are added to the overflow file and, periodically, the overflow file is merged with the main sorted file. This makes insertions very efficient, but has a detrimental effect on retrievals. If the record is not found during the binary search, the overflow file has to be searched linearly. Inversely, to delete a record we must reorganize the records to remove the now free slot.

Ordered files are rarely used for database storage unless a primary index is added to the file (see Section C.5.1).

C.4 Hash files

In a hash file, records do not have to be written sequentially to the file. Instead, a *hash function* calculates the address of the page in which the record is to be stored based on the values of one or more of the fields in the record. The base field is called the *hash field,* or if the field is also a key field of the file, it is called the *hash key*. Records in a hash file will appear to be randomly distributed across the available file space. For this reason, hash files are sometimes called *random,* or *direct, files*.

The hash function is chosen so that records are as evenly distributed as possible throughout the file. One technique, called *division-remainder hashing,* uses the MOD function, which takes the field value, divides it by some predetermined integer value, and uses the remainder of this division as the disk address.

The problem with most hashing functions is that they do not guarantee a unique address because the number of possible values a hash field can take is typically much larger than the number of available addresses for records. Each address generated by a hashing function corresponds to a page, or *bucket,* with *slots* for multiple records. Within a bucket, records are placed in order of arrival. When the same address is generated for two or more records, a *collision* is said to have occurred. In this situation, we must insert the new record in another position, since its hash address is occupied. Collision management complicates hash file management and degrades overall performance.

C.5 Indexes

Index
A data structure that allows the DBMS to locate particular records in a file more quickly, and thereby speed response to user queries.

In this section, we discuss techniques for making the retrieval of data more efficient using **indexes**.

An index in a database is similar to an index in a book. It is an auxiliary structure associated with a file that can be referred to when searching for an item of information, just like searching the index of a book, in which we look up a keyword and get a list of one of more pages the keyword appears on. An index prevents us from having to scan sequentially through the file each time we want to find the item. In the case of database indexes, the required item will be one or more records in a file. As in the book index analogy, the index is ordered, and each index entry contains the item required and one or more locations (record identifiers) where the item can be found.

While indexes are not strictly necessary to use the DBMS, they can have a significant impact on performance. As with the book index, we could find the desired keyword by looking through the entire book, but this would be tedious and time-consuming. Having an index at the back of the book in alphabetical order of keyword allows us to go directly to the page or pages we want.

An index structure is associated with a particular search key, and contains records consisting of the key value and the address of the logical record in the file containing the key value. The file containing the logical records is called the *data file* and the file containing the index records is called the *index file*. The values in the index file are ordered according to the *indexing field*, which is usually based on a single column.

C.5.1 Types of indexes

There are different types of indexes, the main ones being:

- **Primary index** The data file is sequentially ordered by an ordering key field (see Section C.3), and the indexing field is built on the ordering key field, which is guaranteed to have a unique value in each record.
- **Clustering index** The data file is sequentially ordered on a nonkey field, and the indexing field is built on this nonkey field, so that there can be more than one record corresponding to a value of the indexing field. The nonkey field is called a *clustering attribute*.
- **Secondary index**: An index that is defined on a non-ordering field of the data file.

A file can have *at most* one primary index or one clustering index, and in addition can have several secondary indexes. In addition, an index can be sparse or dense: a *sparse index* has an index record for only some of the search key values in the file; a *dense index* has an index record for every search key value in the file.

The search key for an index can consist of several fields. Figure C.4 looks at four dense indexes on the (reduced) Staff table: one based on the salary column, one based on the branchNo column, one based on the composite index (salary, branchNo), and one based on the composite index (branchNo, salary).

C.5.2 Secondary indexes

A secondary index is also an ordered file similar to a primary index. However, whereas the data file associated with a primary index is sorted on the index key, the data file associated with a secondary index may not be sorted on the indexing key. Further, the secondary index key need not contain unique values, unlike a primary index. For example, we may wish to create a secondary index on the branchNo column of the Staff table. From Figure C.1, we can see that the values in the branchNo column are not unique.

Secondary indexes improve the performance of queries that use columns other than the primary key. However, the improvement to queries has to be

Figure C.4

Index on the Staff table: (a) (salary, branchNo) and Salary; (b) (branchNo, salary) and branchNo.

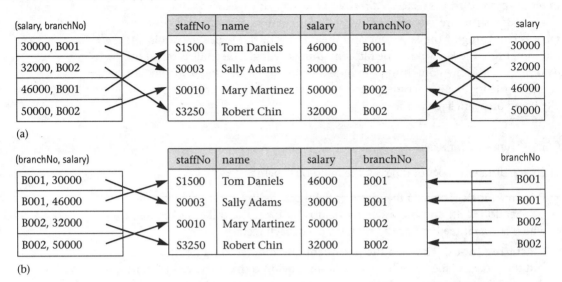

(a)

(b)

balanced against the overhead involved in maintaining the indexes while the database is being updated. This is part of physical database design, and was discussed in Chapter 13.

C.5.3 Multilevel indexes

Consider again the Staff table, this time sorted on the salary column, and the query 'Find all staff with a salary between \$32 000 and \$45 000'. We have already noted that if the file is ordered, we can perform a binary search to find the first record and then a sequential scan from that point on to find the remaining qualifying records. However, if the Staff file is large, the initial binary search could be quite slow.

One method to overcome this is to create an index file based on the salary column. If the index contains an entry for the first value of the salary column on each page of the data file, we could then perform a binary search on the index file to find the page containing the first salary value greater than \$32 000.

However, when the index file becomes large and extends over many pages, the search time for the required index increases. A *multilevel index* attempts to overcome this problem by reducing the search range. It does this by treating the index like any other file, splits the index into a number of smaller indexes, and maintains an index to the indexes. Figure C.5 shows an example of a two-level (sparse) index for the Staff table of Figure C.1. Each page in the data file can store two records. For illustration, there are also two index records per page,

Figure C.5

Example of multilevel index.

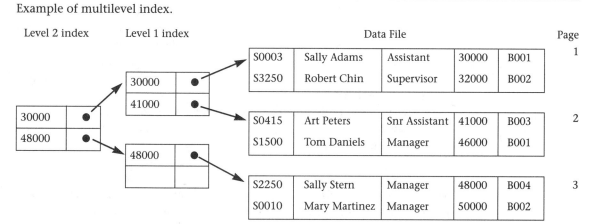

Level 2 index | Level 1 index | Data File | Page

S0003	Sally Adams	Assistant	30000	B001	1
S3250	Robert Chin	Supervisor	32000	B002	
S0415	Art Peters	Snr Assistant	41000	B003	2
S1500	Tom Daniels	Manager	46000	B001	
S2250	Sally Stern	Manager	48000	B004	3
S0010	Mary Martinez	Manager	50000	B002	

although in practice there would be many index records per page. Each index record stores an access key (salary) value and a page address. The stored access key value is the first in the addressed page.

To locate the records we require, we start from the second-level index and search the page for the last access key value that is less than or equal to 32 000, in our case 30 000. This record contains an address to the first-level index page to continue the search. Repeating the above process leads to page 1 in the data file, where the first record is stored. We can now find the remaining qualifying records by reading serially through the data file.

IBM's Indexed Sequential Access Method (ISAM) is based on a two-level index structure. Insertion is handled by overflow pages, as discussed in Section C.3. In general, an *n*-level index can be built, although three levels are common in practice; a file would have to be very large to require more than three levels. In the following section, we discuss a particular type of multilevel dense index called a B+-Tree.

C.5.4 B+-Trees

The major disadvantage of ISAM is that as the database grows, performance deteriorates rapidly due to overflows and so the DBA needs to reorganize the index periodically. Reorganization is not only expensive but makes the file unavailable while it takes place. The B+-Tree structure overcomes this problem by splitting a node whenever it overflows.

A B+-Tree is a special type of multilevel index in which the number of levels from the top of the tree (called the *root node*) to the bottom of the tree (called the leaf nodes) are the same; in other words, the tree is *balanced*. The leaf nodes contain pointers to the records of the table, rather than the records themselves.

A B^+-Tree always takes approximately the same time to access any data record by ensuring that the same number of nodes is searched: in other words, by ensuring that the tree has a constant depth. As it is a dense index, every record is addressed by the index so there is no requirement for the data file to be sorted. However, balancing can be costly to maintain as the tree contents are updated.

In practice, each node in the tree is actually a page, so we can generally store several key values on the same page. For example, if we assume that a page has 4096 bytes and the key field and its associated pointer requires 4 bytes of storage, and each page has a 4-byte pointer to the next node on the same level, we could store (4096 − 4)/(4 + 4) = 511 index records per page. The root can store 511 records and can have 512 children. Each child can also store 511 records, giving a total of 261 632 records. Each child can also have 512 children, giving a total of 262 144 children on level 2 of the tree. Each of these children can have 511 records giving a total of 133 955 584. This gives a theoretical maximum number of index records as:

root:	511
Level 1:	261 632
Level 2:	133 955 584
TOTAL	134 217 727

Thus, we could randomly access one record in the file containing 134 217 727 records within four disk accesses (in fact, the root would normally be stored in main memory, so there would be one less disk access). In practice, however, the number of records held in each page would be smaller as not all pages would be full.

Common data models

In this appendix you will learn:

More about building logical data models. ◄

About common logical data models. ◄

In this appendix, we introduce some common data models that you may find useful. In fact, it has been estimated that one-third of a data model consists of common constructs that are applicable to most companies and the remaining two-thirds are either industry-specific or company-specific. Thus, most data modeling work is re-creating constructs that have already been produced many times before in other companies.

The two mains aims of this appendix therefore are to provide you with:

(1) additional knowledge of building data models;

(2) data model templates that you may find useful in your business. The models featured here may not represent your company exactly, but they may provide a starting point from which you can develop a more suitable model that matches your company's specific requirements.

We provide models for the following common business areas:

- Customer order entry
- Inventory control
- Asset management
- Project management
- Course management
- Human resource management
- Payroll management.

We also provide the following data models that are less common but may still be useful both from a business perspective and from a learning perspective:

- Vehicle rentals
- Student accommodation
- Client transportation
- Publisher printing
- County library
- Real estate rentals
- Travel agent
- Student results.

In each case, we provide a short description of the requirements, and show an example of a typical logical data model and the mapping of the model to a set of tables. We assume that you are familiar with the modeling notation used throughout the rest of this book. If you are not, look at Chapter 5 on ER Modeling, which introduces the main concepts and notations we use in this appendix. You will also find a summary of the methodology in Appendix B.

D.1 Customer order entry

A company wishes to create a database for its order entry activities. A customer can place one or more orders, with each order for one or more products. Each order gives rise to one invoice, which can be paid by a number of methods, such as check, credit card, or cash. The name of the employee who initially processes the customer order is recorded.

An employee in the Shipping department is responsible for packaging the order and sending it to the customer. If an ordered product is not in stock, Shipping send out what is in stock, so more than one shipment may be required to fulfill the order. The logical data model is shown in Figure D.1 and the associated tables in Figure D.2.

Figure D.1

Logical data model for customer order entry.

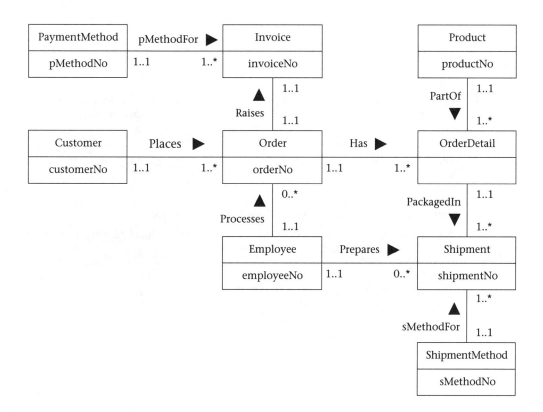

Figure D.2

Tables for customer order entry.

Customer	(<u>customerNo</u>, customerName, customerStreet, customerCity, customerState, customerZipCode, custTelNo, custFaxNo, DOB, maritalStatus, creditRating) Primary Key customerNo Alternate Key custTelNo Alternate Key custFaxNo
Employee	(<u>employeeNo</u>, title, firstName, middleName, lastName, address, workTelExt, homeTelNo, empEmailAddress, socialSecurityNumber, DOB, position, sex, salary, dateStarted) Primary Key employeeNo Alternate Key socialSecurityNumber
Invoice	(<u>invoiceNo</u>, dateRaised, datePaid, creditCardNo, holdersName, expiryDate, orderNo, pMethodNo) Primary Key invoiceNo Foreign Key orderNo references Order(orderNo) Foreign Key pMethodNo references PaymentMethod(pMethodNo)
Order	(<u>orderNo</u>, orderDate, billingStreet, billingCity, billingState, billingZipCode, promisedDate, status, customerNo, employeeNo) Primary Key orderNo Foreign Key customerNo references Customer(customerNo) Foreign Key employeeNo references Employee(employeeNo)
OrderDetail	(<u>orderNo</u>, <u>productNo</u>, quantityOrdered) Primary Key orderNo, productNo Foreign Key orderNo references Order(orderNo) Foreign Key productNo references Product(ProductNo)
PaymentMethod	(<u>pMethodNo</u>, paymentMethod) Primary Key pMethodNo
Product	(<u>productNo</u>, productName, serialNo, unitPrice, quantityOnHand, reorderLevel, reorderQuantity, reorderLeadTime) Primary Key productNo Alternate Key serialNo
Shipment	(<u>shipmentNo</u>, quantity, shipmentDate, completeStatus, orderNo, productNo, employeeNo, sMethodNo) Primary Key shipmentNo Foreign Key orderNo, productNo references OrderDetail(orderNo, productNo) Foreign Key employeeNo references Employee(employeeNo) Foreign Key sMethodNo references ShipmentMethod(sMethodNo)
ShipmentMethod	(<u>sMethodNo</u>, shipmentMethod) Primary Key sMethodNo

D.2 Inventory control

A company wishes to create a database to control its inventory, which consists of a number of products divided into a number of categories, such as clothing, food, and stationery. An employee raises a purchase order when a product has to be reordered from the supplier. The tracking records supplies received, units sold, and any wastage. The logical data model is shown in Figure D.3 and the associated tables in Figure D.4.

Figure D.3

Logical data model for inventory control.

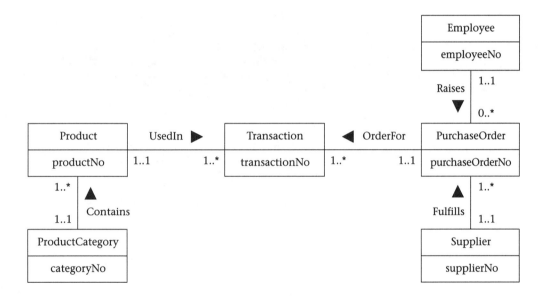

Figure D.4

Tables for inventory control.

Employee	as defined in Section D.1.2
Product	(<u>productNo</u>, productName, serialNo, unitPrice, quantityOnHand, reorderLevel, reorderQuantity, reorderLeadTime, categoryNo) Primary Key productNo Alternate Key serialNo Foreign Key categoryNo references ProductCategory(categoryNo)
ProductCategory	(<u>categoryNo</u>, categoryDescription) Primary Key categoryNo
PurchaseOrder	(<u>purchaseOrderNo</u>, purchaseOrderDescription, orderDate, dateRequired, shippedDate, freightCharge, supplierNo, employeeNo) Primary Key purchaseOrderNo Foreign Key supplierNo references Supplier(supplierNo) Foreign Key employeeNo references Employee(employeeNo)
Supplier	(<u>supplierNo</u>, supplierName, supplierStreet, supplierCity, supplierState, supplierZipCode, suppTelNo, suppFaxNo, suppEmailAddress, suppWebAddress, contactName, contactTelNo, contactFaxNo, contactEmailAddress, paymentTerms) Primary Key supplierNo Alternate Key supplierName Alternate Key suppTelNo Alternate Key suppFaxNo
Transaction	(<u>transactionNo</u>, transactionDate, transactionDescription, unitPrice, unitsOrdered, unitsReceived, unitsSold, unitsWastage, productNo, purchaseOrderNo) Primary Key transactionNo Foreign Key productNo references Product(productNo) Foreign Key purchaseOrderNo references PurchaseOrder(purchaseOrderNo)

D.3 Asset management

A company wishes to create a database to monitor each of its assets (such as PCs, printers, cars, desks, chairs). Assets are divided into a number of categories, such as computers and furniture. An asset is assigned to an employee. On a regular basis, an employee in the Finance Department checks each asset to determine its current market value, and records the date and the current value of the asset. As a result of the assessment, the company may decide to sell the asset. Also on a regular basis, maintenance is carried out on each asset. In some cases, the maintenance is carried out by an employee, but in others, the asset has to be sent to an external company for maintenance. The logical data model is shown in Figure D.5 and the associated tables in Figure D.6.

Figure D.5

Logical data model for asset management.

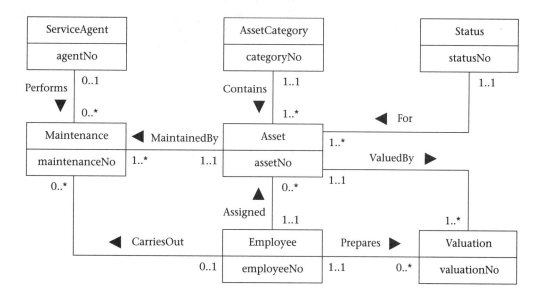

Figure D.6

Tables for asset management.

Employee   As defined in Section D.1.2

Asset
(<u>assetNo</u>, assetDescription, serialNo, dateAcquired, purchasePrice, currentValue, dateSold, nextMaintenanceDate, employeeNo, assetCategoryNo, statusNo)
Primary Key assetNo
Alternate Key serialNo
Foreign Key employeeNo references Employee(employeeNo)
Foreign Key assetCategoryNo references AssetCategory(assetCategoryNo)
Foreign Key statusNo references Status(statusNo)

AssetCategory
(<u>assetCategoryNo</u>, assetCategoryDescription)
Primary Key assetCategoryNo

Maintenance
(<u>maintenanceNo</u>, maintenanceDate, maintenanceDescription, maintenanceCost, assetNo, employeeNo, agentNo)
Primary Key maintenanceNo
Foreign Key assetNo references Asset(assetNo)
Foreign Key employeeNo references Employee(employeeNo)
Foreign Key agentNo references ServiceAgent(agentNo)

ServiceAgent
(<u>agentNo</u>, agentName, agentStreet, agentCity, agentState, agentZipCode, agentTelNo, agentFaxNo, agentEmailAddress, agentWebAddress, contactName, contactTelNo, contactFaxNo, contactEmailAddress)
Primary Key agentNo
Alternate Key agentName
Alternate Key agentTelNo
Alternate Key agentFaxNo

Status
(<u>statusNo</u>, statusDescription)
Primary Key statusNo

Valuation
(<u>valuationNo</u>, valuationDate, valuationPrice, assetNo, employeeNo)
Primary Key valuationNo
Foreign Key assetNo references Asset(assetNo)
Foreign Key employeeNo references Employee(employeeNo)

D.4 Project management

A consultancy company wishes to create a database to help manage its projects. Each project is for a specific client and has a nominated project manager. The project is divided into a number of work packages, and employees bill their time and expenses against a work package. Each employee has a specific role, which defines the charging rate for the client. Over time, an employee can work on several work packages associated with the same project. In addition, most, but not all, work packages have a number of associated documents as deliverables, each of which may be written by more than one employee. The logical data model is shown in Figure D.7 and the associated tables in Figure D.8.

Figure D.7

Logical data model for project management.

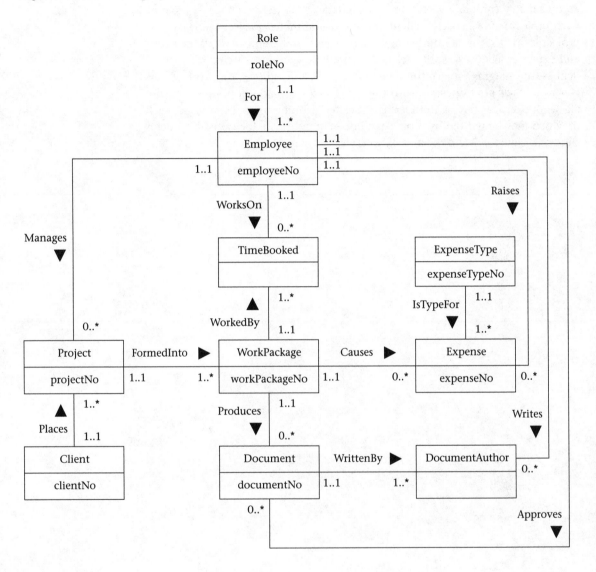

Figure D.8

Tables for project management.

Client	(<u>clientNo</u>, clientName, clientStreet, clientCity, clientState, clientZipCode, clientTelNo, clientFaxNo, clientWebAddress, contactName, contactTelNo, contactFaxNo, contactEmailAddress) Primary Key clientNo Alternate Key clientName Alternate Key clientTelNo Alternate Key clientFaxNo
Document	(<u>documentNo</u>, documentTitle, documentDate, versionNo, workPackageNo, approvedByEmployeeNo) Primary Key documentNo Foreign Key workPackageNo references WorkPackage(workPackageNo) Foreign Key approvedByEmployeeNo references Employee(employeeNo)
DocumentAuthor	(<u>documentNo</u>, <u>employeeNo</u>) Primary Key documentNo, employeeNo Foreign Key documentNo references Document(documentNo) Foreign Key employeeNo references Employee(employeeNo)
Employee	(<u>employeeNo</u>, dateStartRole, firstName, middleName, lastName, address, workTelExt, homeTelNo, empEmailAddress, socialSecurityNumber, DOB, position, sex, salary, dateStarted, roleNo) Primary Key employeeNo Alternate Key socialSecurityNumber Foreign Key roleNo references Role(roleNo)
Expense	(<u>expenseNo</u>, expenseDate, expenseDescription, expenseAmount, workPackageNo, employeeNo, expenseTypeNo) Primary Key expenseNo Alternate Key workPackageNo, employeeNo, expenseDate Foreign Key workPackageNo references WorkPackage(workPackageNo) Foreign Key employeeNo references Employee(employeeNo) Foreign Key expenseTypeNo reference ExpenseType(expenseTypeNo)
ExpenseType	(<u>expenseTypeNo</u>, expenseTypeDescription) Primary Key expenseTypeNo
Project	(<u>projectNo</u>, projectName, plannedStartDate, plannedEndDate, actualStartDate, actualEndDate, projectedCost, actualCost, clientNo, managerEmployeeNo) Primary Key projectNo Foreign Key clientNo references Client(clientNo) Foreign Key managerEmployeeNo references Employee(employeeNo)
Role	(<u>roleNo</u>, roleDescription, billingRate) Primary Key roleNo
TimeBooked	(<u>workPackageNo</u>, <u>employeeNo</u>, dateStartWork, dateStopWork, timeWorked) Primary Key workPackageNo, employeeNo Foreign Key workPackageNo references WorkPackage(workPackageNo) Foreign Key employeeNo references Employee(employeeNo)
WorkPackage	(<u>workPackageNo</u>, plannedStartDate, plannedEndDate, actualStartDate, actualEndDate, projectedCost, actualCost, projectNo) Primary Key workPackageNo Foreign Key projectNo references Project(projectNo)

D.5 Course management

A training company wishes to create a database of its course information. The company delivers a number of seminars and training courses. Each course is delivered by one member of staff at some location (such as internal seminar room S10, Hilton Hotel Suite 100). The fees vary for each course and with the number of delegates a company sends. For example, if a company sends one person, the charge may be $1000. If the company sends two people, the first may be charged $1000, but the second may be charged $750. The course can be attended by a number of delegates, subject to some upper limit for the course. A delegate can register as an individual or through his/her company. The name of the employee who registers the delegate is recorded. An invoice is sent either to the delegate or to his/her company. The logical data model is shown in Figure D.9 and the associated tables in Figure D.10.

Figure D.9

Logical data model for course management.

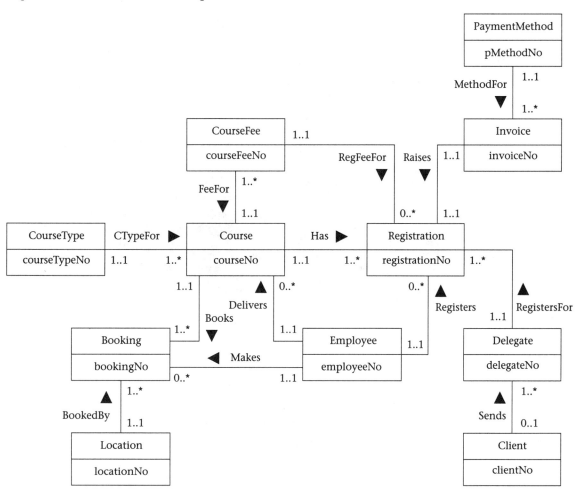

Figure D.10

Tables for course management.

Client	As defined in Section D.4.2
Employee	As defined in Section D.1.2
PaymentMethod	As defined in Section D.1.2

Delegate   (<u>delegateNo</u>, delegateTitle, delegateFName, delegateLName, delegateStreet, delegateCity, delegateState, delegateZipCode, attTelNo, attFaxNo, attEmailAddress, clientNo)
Primary Key delegateNo
Foreign Key clientNo references Client(clientNo)

Booking   (<u>bookingNo</u>, bookingDate, locationNo, courseNo, bookingEmployeeNo)
Primary Key bookingNo
Foreign Key locationNo references Location(locationNo)
Foreign Key courseNo references Course(courseNo)
Foreign Key bookingEmployeeNo references Employee(employeeNo)

Course   (<u>courseNo</u>, courseName, courseDescription, startDate, startTime, endDate, endTime, maxDelegates, confirmed, delivererEmployeeNo, courseTypeNo)
Primary Key courseNo
Foreign Key delivererEmployeeNo references Employee(employeeNo)
Foreign Key courseTypeNo references CourseType(courseTypeNo)

CourseFee   (<u>courseFeeNo</u>, feeDescription, fee, courseNo)
Primary Key courseFeeNo
Foreign Key courseNo references Course(courseNo)

CourseType   (<u>courseTypeNo</u>, courseTypeDescription)
Primary Key courseTypeNo

Invoice   (<u>invoiceNo</u>, dateRaised, datePaid, creditCardNo, holdersName, expiryDate, registrationNo, pMethodNo)
Primary Key invoiceNo
Foreign Key registrationNo references Registration(registrationNo)
Foreign Key pMethodNo references PaymentMethod(pMethodNo)

Location   (<u>locationNo</u>, locationName, maxSize)
Primary Key locationNo

Registration   (<u>registrationNo</u>, registrationDate, delegateNo, courseFeeNo, registerEmployeeNo, courseNo)
Primary Key registrationNo
Foreign Key delegateNo references Delegate(delegateNo)
Foreign Key courseFeeNo references CourseFee(courseFeeNo)
Foreign Key registerEmployeeNo references Employee(employeeNo)
Foreign Key courseNo references Course(courseNo)

D.6 Human resource management

An HRM department wishes to create a database to monitor its employees. The company is divided into a number of departments, and employees are assigned to one department. The department has a designated Manager who has overall responsibility for the department and the employees in the department. However, to help manage the department, a number of employees are nominated to supervise groups of staff. When a new employee joins the company, information on previous work history and qualifications are required. On a regular basis, each employee is required to undergo a review, which is normally carried out by the Manager, but may be delegated to a nominated representative.

The company has defined a number of position types, such as Manager, Business Analyst, Salesman, and Secretary, and each type has a number of grades associated with it, which for most non-senior positions determines the employee's salary. At a senior level, salary is negotiable. Posts are allocated to a department depending on its workload. For example, a department may be allocated two new Business Analyst posts. A post will be filled by one employee, although over time, employees will fill a number of different posts.

The logical data model is shown in Figure D.11 and the associated tables in Figure D.12.

Figure D.11

Logical data model for human resource management.

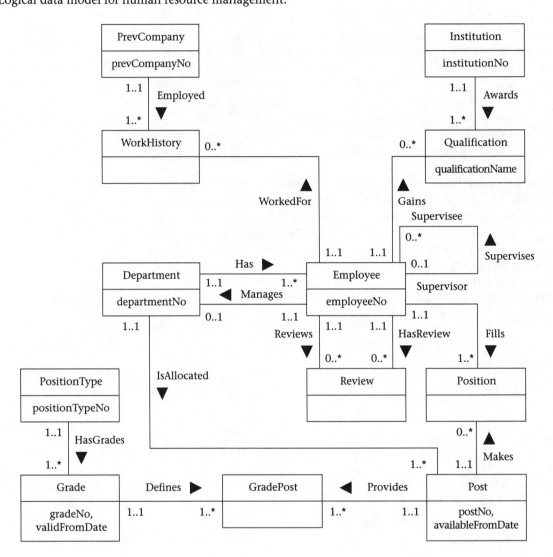

Figure D.12

Tables for human resource management.

Department (<u>departmentNo</u>, departmentName, deptLocation, managerEmployeeNo)
Primary Key departmentNo
Foreign Key managerEmployeeNo references Employee(employeeNo)

Employee (<u>employeeNo</u>, title, firstName, middleName, lastName, address, workTelExt, homeTelNo, empEmailAddress, socialSecurityNumber, DOB, position, sex, salary, dateStarted, dateLeft, departmentNo, supervisorEmployeeNo)
Primary Key employeeNo
Alternate Key socialSecurityNumber
Foreign Key departmentNo references Department(departmentNo)
Foreign Key supervisorEmployeeNo references Employee(employeeNo)

Grade (<u>gradeNo</u>, <u>validFromDate</u>, validToDate, gradeDescription, gradeSalary, noDaysLeaveEntitlement, positionTypeNo)
Primary Key gradeNo, validFromDate
Foreign Key positionTypeNo references PositionType(positionTypeNo)

GradePost (<u>gradeNo</u>, <u>validFromDate</u>, <u>postNo</u>, <u>availableFromDate</u>)
Primary Key gradeNo, validFromDate, postNo, availableFromDate
Foreign Key gradeNo, validFromDate references Grade(gradeNo, validFromDate)
Foreign Key postNo, availableFromDate references Post(postNo, availableFromDate)

Institution (<u>institutionNo</u>, institutionName, instAddress, instTelNo, instFaxNo, instWebAddress, contactName, contactTelNo, contactFaxNo, contactEmailAddress)
Primary Key institutionNo
Alternate Key institutionName
Alternate Key instTelNo
Alternate Key instFaxNo

Position (<u>employeeNo</u>, <u>postNo</u>, <u>startDate</u>, endDate)
Primary Key employeeNo, postNo, startDate
Foreign Key employeeNo references Employee(employeeNo)
Foreign Key postNo, startDate references Post(postNo, availableFromDate)

PositionType (<u>positionTypeNo</u>, positionTypeDescription)
Primary Key positionTypeNo

Post (<u>postNo</u>, <u>availableFromDate</u>, availableToDate, postDescription, salariedHourly, fullPartTime, temporaryPermanent, freeLaborStandardsActExempt, departmentNo)
Primary Key postNo, availableFromDate
Foreign Key departmentNo references Department(departmentNo)

PrevCompany (<u>prevCompanyNo</u>, pCompanyName, pCompanyStreet, pCompanyCity, pCompanyState, pCompanyZipCode, pCompanyTelNo, pCompanyFaxNo, pCompanyWebAddress, contactName, contactTelNo, contactFaxNo, contactEmailAddress)
Primary Key prevCompanyNo
Alternate Key pCompanyName
Alternate Key pCompanyTelNo
Alternate Key pCompanyFaxNo

Qualification (<u>qualificationName</u>, <u>employeeNo</u>, gradeObtained, startQualDate, endQualDate, gpa, institutionNo)
Primary Key qualificationName, employeeNo
Foreign Key employeeNo references Employee(employeeNo)
Foreign Key institutionNo references Institution(institutionNo)

Figure D.12

Continued

Review

(<u>revieweeEmployeeNo</u>, <u>reviewerEmployeeNo</u>, <u>reviewDate</u>, comments)
Primary Key revieweeEmployeeNo,
reviewerEmployeeNo, reviewDate
Foreign Key revieweeEmployeeNo references Employee(employeeNo)
Foreign Key reviewerEmployeeNo references Employee(employeeNo)

WorkHistory

(<u>prevCompanyNo</u>, <u>employeeNo</u>, prevPosition, prevGrade, prevSalary, prevLocation,
prevResponsibilities)
Primary Key prevCompanyNo, employeeNo
Foreign Key prevCompanyNo references PrevCompany(prevCompanyNo)
Foreign Key employeeNo references Employee(employeeNo)

D.7 Payroll management

A Payroll department wishes to create a database to monitor employees' salary payments. To calculate an employee's salary, Payroll need to take into consideration holidays taken against holiday entitlement, number of days' sick leave in pay period, bonuses, and deductions. An employee must specify how his/her salary should be paid, although this may change over time. Most employees are paid by electronic bank transfer, but some types of employees may be paid by cash or check. If payment is electronic, then a routing number and account type are required. Payment can only be made by one method. There are various reasons for deductions being made; for example, federal tax, state tax, medical plan, retirement plan, or cash advance.

The logical data model is shown in Figure D.13 and the associated tables in Figure D.14.

Figure D.13

Logical data model for payroll management.

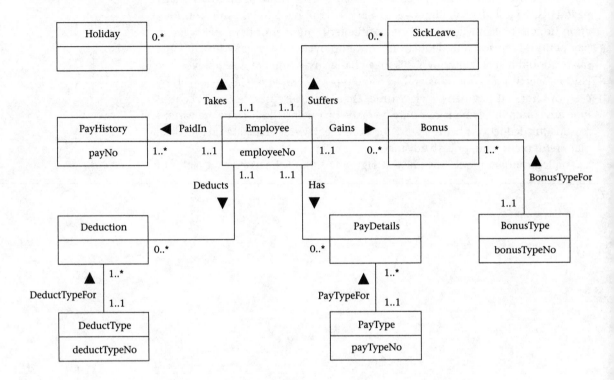

Figure D.14

Tables for payroll management.

Employee	As defined in Section D.1.2
Bonus	(<u>employeeNo</u>, <u>bonusDate</u>, bonusAmount, bonusTypeNo) Primary Key employeeNo, bonusDate Foreign Key employeeNo references Employee(employeeNo) Foreign Key bonusTypeNo references BonusType(bonusTypeNo)
BonusType	(<u>bonusTypeNo</u>, bonusDescription) Primary Key bonusTypeNo
Deduction	(<u>employeeNo</u>, <u>deductDate</u>, deductAmount, deductTypeNo) Primary Key employeeNo, deductDate Foreign Key employeeNo references Employee(employeeNo) Foreign Key deductTypeNo references DeductType(deductTypeNo)
DeductType	(<u>deductTypeNo</u>, deductDescription) Primary Key deductTypeNo
Holiday	(<u>employeeNo</u>, <u>startDate</u>, endDate) Primary Key employeeNo, startDate Foreign Key employeeNo references Employee(employeeNo)
PayDetails	(<u>employeeNo</u>, <u>startDate</u>, routingNumber, accountType, bankName, bankAddress, payTypeNo) Primary Key employeeNo, startDate Foreign Key employeeNo references Employee(employeeNo) Foreign Key payTypeNo references PayType(payTypeNo)
PayHistory	(<u>payNo</u>, employeeNo, payDate, checkNumber, payAmount) Primary Key payNo Foreign Key employeeNo references Employee(employeeNo)
PayType	(<u>payTypeNo</u>, payTypeDescription) Primary Key payTypeNo
SickLeave	(<u>employeeNo</u>, <u>startDate</u>, endDate, reason) Primary Key employeeNo, startDate Foreign Key employeeNo references Employee(employeeNo)

D.8 Vehicle rentals

A vehicle rental company wishes to create a database to monitor the renting of vehicles to clients. The company has various outlets and each outlet has staff including a Manager and several Senior Mechanics who are responsible for supervising the work of allocated groups of Mechanics. Each outlet has a stock of vehicles for rent that may be rented by clients for various periods of time from a minimum of four hours to a maximum of six months. Each rental agreement between a client and the company is uniquely identified using a rental number. A client must take out insurance cover for each vehicle rental period. Each vehicle is checked for faults after each rental. The logical data model is shown in Figure D.15 and the associated tables in Figure D.16.

Figure D.15

Logical data model for vehicle rentals.

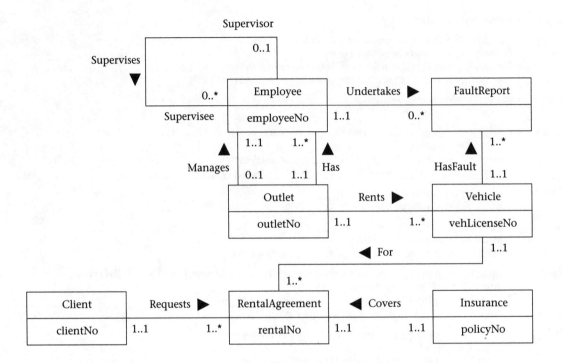

Figure D.16

Tables for vehicle rentals.

Client	As defined in Section D.4.2
Employee	(<u>employeeNo</u>, title, firstName, middleName, lastName, address, workTelExt, homeTelNo, empEmailAddress, socialSecurityNumber, DOB, position, sex, salary, dateStarted, outletNo) Primary Key employeeNo Alternate Key socialSecurityNumber Foreign Key outletNo references Outlet(outletNo)
FaultReport	(<u>vehLicenseNo</u>, <u>dateChecked</u>, timeChecked, comments, employeeNo) Primary Key vehLicenseNo, dateChecked Foreign Key vehLicenseNo references Vehicle(vehLicenseNo) Foreign Key employeeNo references Employee(employeeNo)
Outlet	(<u>outletNo</u>, outletStreet, outletCity, outletState, outletZipCode, outletTelNo, outletFaxNo, managerEmployeeNo) Primary Key outletNo Alternate Key outletTelNo Alternate Key outletFaxNo Foreign Key managerEmployeeNo references Employee(employeeNo)
RentalAgreement	(<u>rentalNo</u>, dateStart, timeStart, dateReturn, timeReturn, mileageBefore, mileageAfter, policyNo, insuranceCoverType, insurancePremium, clientNo, vehLicenseNo) Primary Key rentalNo Alternate Key policyNo Foreign Key clientNo references Client(clientNo) Foreign Key vehLicenseNo references Vehicle(vehLicenseNo)
Vehicle	(<u>vehLicenseNo</u>, vehicleMake, vehicleModel, color, noDoors, capacity, hireRate, outletNo) Primary Key vehLicenseNo Foreign Key outletNo references Outlet(outletNo)

D.9   Student accommodation

The Accommodation Office of a university wishes to create a database to monitor the allocation of accommodation to students. Each student requiring accommodation fills out an application form, which holds the student's details and an indication of the type of accommodation required and the duration. Students may rent a room in a hall of residence or student apartment. The halls provide only single rooms, which have a room number, place number, and monthly rental rate. The place number uniquely identifies each room in all the halls controlled by the Accommodation Office and is used when renting a room to a student. Each hall is managed by a member of the Accommodation Office.

The Accommodation Office also offers student apartments, each identified by a unique apartment number. These apartments are fully furnished and provide single room accommodation for groups of three, four, or five students. Each bedroom in an apartment has a monthly rental rate, a room number, and a place number. The place number uniquely identifies each room available in all student apartments and is used when renting a room to a student. Apartments are inspected by members of the Accommodation Office on a regular basis to ensure that the accommodation is well maintained.

New lease agreements are negotiated at the start of each academic year with a minimum rental period of one semester and a maximum rental period of one year. The students pay for their accommodation throughout the academic year and are sent an invoice at the start of each semester. If a student does not pay by a certain date, two reminder letters are sent. The logical data model is shown in Figure D.17 and the associated tables in Figure D.18.

Figure D.17

Logical data model for student accommodation.

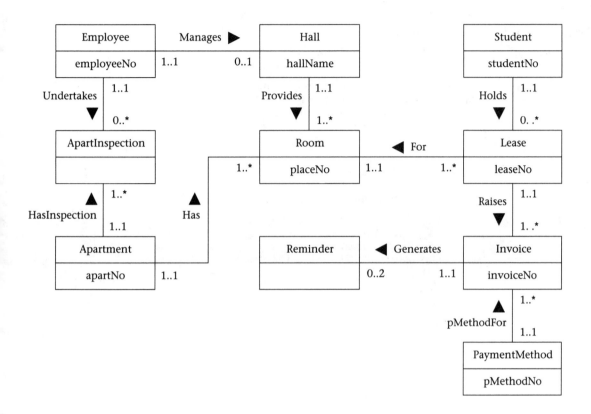

Figure D.18

Tables for student accommodation.

Employee	As defined in Section D.1.2
PaymentMethod	As defined in Section D.1.2
Apartment	(<u>apartNo</u>, apartAddress, noOfRoomsInApart) Primary Key apartNo
ApartInspection	(<u>apartNo</u>, <u>dateOfInspection</u>, comments, status, employeeNo) Primary Key apartNo, dateOfInspection Foreign Key apartNo references Apartment(apartNo) Foreign Key employeeNo references Employee(employeeNo)
Hall	(<u>hallName</u>, hallAddress, hallTelNo, hallFaxNo, noOfRoomsInHall, managerEmployeeNo) Primary Key hallName Alternate Key hallTelNo Alternate Key hallFaxNo Foreign Key managerEmployeeNo references Employee(employeeNo)
Invoice	(<u>invoiceNo</u>, semester, dateDue, datePaid, leaseNo, pMethodNo) Primary Key invoiceNo Foreign Key leaseNo references Lease(leaseNo) Foreign Key pMethodNo references PaymentMethod(pMethodNo)
Reminder	(<u>invoiceNo</u>, dateReminder1sent, dateReminder2sent, dateInterview, comments) Primary Key invoiceNo Foreign Key invoiceNo references Invoice(invoiceNo)
Lease	(<u>leaseNo</u>, duration, dateStart, dateLeave, studentNo, placeNo) Primary Key leaseNo Alternate Key placeNo, dateStart Alternate Key studentNo, dateStart Foreign Key studentNo references Student(studentNo) Foreign Key placeNo references Room(placeNo)
Room	(<u>placeNo</u>, roomNo, rentPerSemester, hallName, apartNo) Primary Key placeNo Alternate Key roomNo, hallName Alternate Key roomNo, apartNo Foreign Key hallName references Hall(hallName) Foreign Key apartNo references Apartment(apartNo)
Student	(<u>studentNo</u>, studentFirstName, studentMiddleIntial, studentLastName, studentHomeStreet, studentHomeCity, studentHomeState, studentHomeZipCode, studentHomeTelNo, studentSex, studentDOB, studentType, studentStatus, accommodationTypeRequired, accommodationDuration) Primary Key studentNo

D.10   Client transportation

A haulage company that specializes in the transportation of loads throughout the US wishes to create a database to control client orders for transportation. The company has many offices throughout the US to process client orders. A client registers with an office and can place one or more orders. Each order describes the load to be transported along with the collection address and the delivery address. The transportation requirements for each order are then calculated. The transport requirements describe the number of units and trailers required to transport the load. Each office is allocated several units and trailers. One unit can pull one or two trailers. The logical data model is shown in Figure D.19 and the associated tables in Figure D.20.

Figure D.19

Logical data model for client transportation.

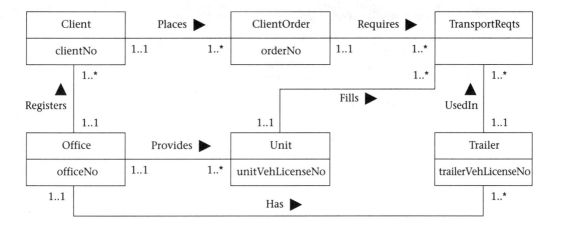

Figure D.20

Tables for client transportation.

Client (<u>clientNo</u>, clientName, clientStreet, clientCity, clientState, clientZipCode, clientTelNo, clientFaxNo, clientWebAddress, contactName, contactTelNo, contactFaxNo, contactEmailAddress, officeNo)
Primary Key clientNo
Alternate Key clientTelNo
Alternate Key clientFaxNo
Foreign Key officeNo references Office(officeNo)

Office (<u>officeNo</u>, officeAddress, officeTelNo, officeFaxNo)
Primary Key officeNo
Alternate Key officeTelNo
Alternate Key officeFaxNo

ClientOrder (<u>orderNo</u>, dateOrder, collectionDate, collectionAddress, deliveryDate, deliveryAddress, loadWeight, loadDescription, clientNo)
Primary Key orderNo
Foreign Key clientNo references Client(clientNo)

Trailer (<u>trailerVehLicenseNo</u>, trailerDescription, trailerLength, maxCarryingWeight, officeNo)
Primary Key trailerVehLicenseNo
Foreign Key officeNo references Office(officeNo)

TransportReqts (<u>orderNo</u>, <u>transportReqPartNo</u>, unitVehLicenseNo, trailerVehLicenseNo1, trailerVehLicenseNo2)
Primary Key orderNo, transportReqPartNo
Foreign Key unitVehLicenseNo references Unit(unitVehLicenseNo)
Foreign Key trailerVehLicenseNo1 references Trailer(trailerVehLicenseNo)
Foreign Key trailerVehLicenseNo2 references Trailer(trailerVehLicenseNo)

Unit (<u>unitVehLicenseNo</u>, unitDescription, maxPayLoad, officeNo)
Primary Key unitVehLicenseNo
Foreign Key officeNo references Office(officeNo)

D.11   Publisher printing

A printing company that handles print jobs for book publishers wishes to create a database to control client requests for printing. A book publisher submits an order that describes the printing job. A print job requires the use of materials, such as paper and ink, which are assigned to a job through one or more purchase orders. Each print job is assigned to a Print Manager, who has the responsibility to ensure that the job is carried out correctly. For larger print jobs, additional employees are normally allocated to help with the printing. The logical data model is shown in Figure D.21 and the associated tables in Figure D.22.

Figure D.21

Logical data model for publisher printing.

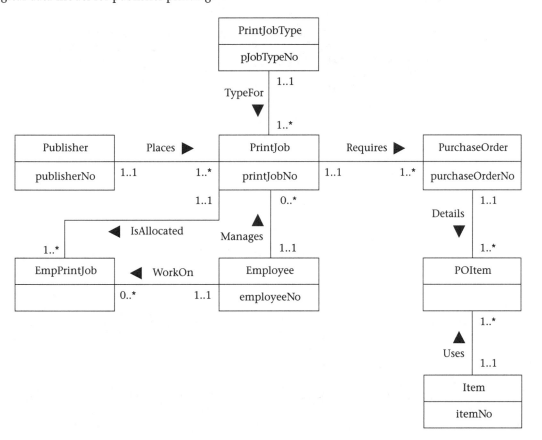

Figure D.22

Tables for publisher printing.

Employee	As defined in Section D.1.2
EmpPrintJob	(<u>employeeNo</u>, <u>printJobNo</u>, jobDate) Primary Key employeeNo, printJobNo Foreign Key employeeNo references Employee(employeeNo) Foreign Key printJobNo references PrintJob(printJobNo)
Item	(<u>itemNo</u>, itemDescription, itemPrice, itemQuantityInStock, itemReorderLevel, itemReorderQuantity, itemReorderLeadTime) Primary Key itemNo
PrintJob	(<u>printJobNo</u>, printJobDescription, printJobDateReceived, printJobDateCompleted, managerEmployeeNo, publisherNo, printJobTypeNo) Primary Key printJobNo Foreign Key managerEmployeeNo references Employee(employeeNo) Foreign Key publisherNo references Publisher(publisherNo) Foreign Key printJobTypeNo references PrintJobType(printJobTypeNo)
Publisher	(<u>publisherNo</u>, publisherName, publisherStreet, publisherCity, publisherState, publisherZipCode, pubTelNo, pubFaxNo, pubWebAddress, contactName, contactTelNo, contactFaxNo, contactEmailAddress, creditRating) Primary Key publisherNo Alternate Key publisherName Alternate Key pubTelNo Alternate Key pubFaxNo
POItem	(<u>purchaseOrderNo</u>, <u>itemNo</u>, quantity) Primary Key purchaseOrderNo, itemNo Foreign Key purchaseOrderNo references PurchaseOrder (purchaseOrderNo) Foreign Key itemNo references Item(itemNo)
PrintJobType	(<u>printJobTypeNo</u>, printJobTypeDescription) Primary key printJobTypeNo
PurchaseOrder	(<u>purchaseOrderNo</u>, <u>printJobNo</u>, purchaseOrderDate) Primary Key purchaseOrderNo Foreign Key printJobNo references PrintJob(printJobNo)

D.12   County library

A county wishes to create a database to control its local libraries. Each library has a number of employees, one of whom is designated as the manager of the library and is responsible for supervising employees and the general day-to-day management of the library. Each library stores a number of books and CDs. A citizen has to become a member of a library before he/she is allowed to borrow any books, but thereafter can borrow books from any county library. Books are stored on shelves and CDs are stored in a number of racks in the centre of the library. Generally, a library stocks a number of copies of each book title and each CD. Details of book publishers are maintained but not CD publishers. To find an item, searches can be performed based on the book/CD title, the author/artist's name, the category of the book/CD, or the publisher's name. The logical data model is shown in Figure D.23 and the associated tables in Figure D.24.

Figure D.23

Logical data model for county library.

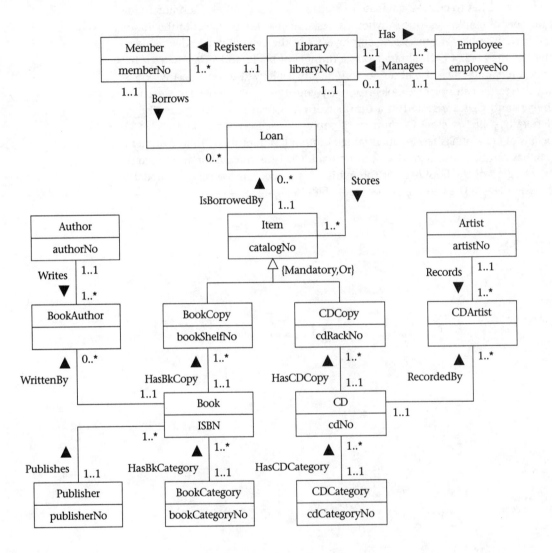

Figure D.24

Tables for county library.

Publisher	As defined in Section D.11.2
Artist	(artistNo, name) Primary Key artistNo
Author	(authorNo, name) Primary Key authorNo
Book	(ISBN, title, year, publisherNo, bookCategoryNo) Primary Key ISBN Foreign Key publisherNo references Publisher(publisherNo) Foreign Key bookCategoryNo references BookCategory(bookCategoryNo)
BookAuthor	(ISBN, authorNo) Primary Key ISBN, authorNo Foreign Key ISBN references Book(ISBN) Foreign Key authorNo references Author(authorNo)
BookCategory	(bookCategoryNo, bookCatDescription) Primary Key bookCategoryNo
BookCopy	(catalogNo, bookShelfNo, ISBN, dateInStock, libraryNo) Primary Key catalogNo Alternate Key bookShelfNo Foreign Key ISBN references Book(ISBN) Foreign Key libraryNo references Library(libraryNo)
CD	(cdNo, title, releaseDate, cdCategoryNo) Primary Key cdNo Foreign Key cdCategoryNo references CDCategory(cdCategoryNo)
CDArtist	(cdNo, artistNo) Primary Key cdNo, artistNo Foreign Key cdNo references CD(cdNo) Foreign Key artistNo references Artist(artistNo)
CDCategory	(cdCategoryNo, cdCatDescription) Primary Key cdCategoryNo
CDCopy	(catalogNo, cdRackNo, cdNo, dateInStock, libraryNo) Primary Key catalogNo Alternate Key cdRackNo Foreign Key cdNo references CD(cdNo) Foreign Key libraryNo references Library(libraryNo)
Employee	(employeeNo, title, firstName, middleName, lastName, address, workTelExt, homeTelNo, empEmailAddress, socialSecurityNumber, DOB, position, sex, salary, dateStarted, libraryNo) Primary Key employeeNo Alternate Key socialSecurityNumber Foreign Key libraryNo references Library(libraryNo)
Library	(libraryNo, libStreet, libCity, libState, libZipCode, libTelNo, libFaxNo, libWebAddress, managerEmployeeNo) Primary Key libraryNo Alternate Key libTelNo Alternate Key libFaxNo

Figure D.24

Continued

<table>
<tr><td></td><td>Foreign Key managerEmployeeNo references Employee(employeeNo)</td></tr>
<tr><td>Loan</td><td>(<u>catalogNo</u>, <u>memberNo</u>, dateOut, dateReturn)
Primary Key catalogNo, memberNo
Foreign Key catalogNo references BookCopy(catalogNo) and CDCopy(catalogNo)
Foreign Key memberNo references Member(memberNo)</td></tr>
<tr><td>Member</td><td>(<u>memberNo</u>, memTitle, memFirstName, memMiddleName, memLastName, memAddress, memWorkTelExt, memHomeTelNo, memDOB, memSex, dateJoined, libraryNo)
Primary Key memberNo
Foreign Key libraryNo references Library(libraryNo)</td></tr>
</table>

D.13 Real estate rentals

A real estate agency with branches throughout the US wishes to create a database to control the properties it rents out on behalf of owners, who are classified as Business and Private owners. Within each branch, staff oversee the rental of properties, and are responsible for handling property viewings and lease agreements. Some staff are also given the role Supervisor, responsible for overseeing a group of staff and ensuring the efficient management of the branch. The administrative work of each group of staff is supported by a secretary. The logical data model is shown in Figure D.25 and the associated tables in Figure D.26.

Figure D.25

Logical data model for real estate rentals.

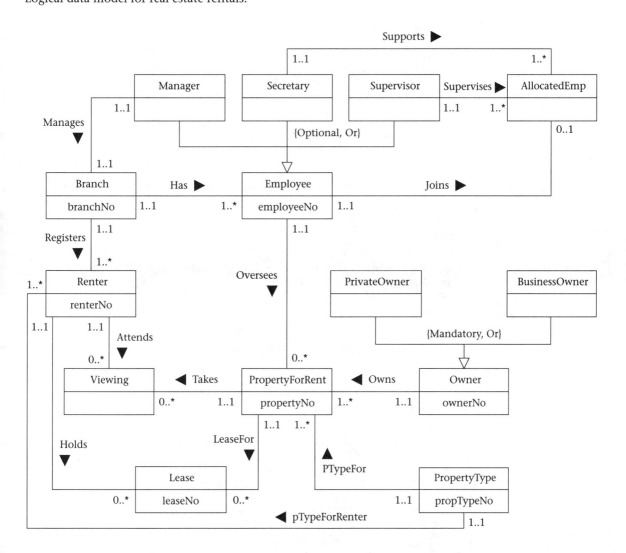

Figure D.26

Tables for real estate rentals.

AllocatedEmp	(<u>superviseeEmployeeNo</u>, supervisorEmployeeNo, secretaryEmployeeNo) Primary Key superviseeEmployeeNo Foreign Key superviseeEmployeeNo references Employee(employeeNo) Foreign Key supervisorEmployeeNo references Employee(employeeNo) Foreign Key secretaryEmployeeNo references Employee(employeeNo)
Branch	(<u>branchNo</u>, branchStreet, branchCity, branchState, branchZipCode, branchTelNo, branchFaxNo, managerEmployeeNo) Primary Key branchNo Alternate Key branchTelNo Alternate Key branchFaxNo Foreign Key managerEmployeeNo references Employee(employeeNo)
BusinessOwner	(<u>ownerNo</u>, businessName, businessAddress, businessTelNo, businessFaxNo, contactName, contactTelNo, contactFaxNo, contactEmailAddress) Primary Key ownerNo Alternate Key businessName Alternate Key businessTelNo Alternate Key businessFaxNo
Employee	(<u>employeeNo</u>, title, firstName, middleName, lastName, address, workTelExt, homeTelNo, empEmailAddress, socialSecurityNumber, DOB, position, sex, salary, typingSpeed, dateStarted, branchNo) Primary Key employeeNo Alternate Key socialSecurityNumber Foreign Key branchNo references Branch(branchNo)
Lease	(<u>leaseNo</u>, rentStart, rentFinish, depositPaid, renterNo, propertyNo) Primary Key leaseNo Foreign Key renterNo references Renter(renterNo) Foreign Key propertyNo references PropertyForRent(propertyNo)
PrivateOwner	(<u>ownerNo</u>, ownerName, ownerAddress, ownerTelNo) Primary Key ownerNo
PropertyForRent	(<u>propertyNo</u>, propStreet, propCity, propState, propZipCode, noRooms, rent, propTypeNo, ownerNo, employeeNo, branchNo) Primary Key propertyNo Foreign Key propTypeNo references PropertyType(propTypeNo) Foreign Key ownerNo references PrivateOwner(ownerNo) and BusinessOwner(ownerNo) Foreign Key employeeNo references Employee(employeeNo) Foreign Key branchNo references Branch(branchNo)
PropertyType	(<u>propTypeNo</u>, propTypeDescription) Primary Key propTypeNo
Renter	(<u>renterNo</u>, rFName, rLName, rAddress, rTelNo, maxRent, prefTypeNo) Primary Key renterNo Foreign Key prefTypeNo references PropertyType(propTypeNo)
Viewing	(<u>propertyNo</u>, <u>renterNo</u>, <u>dateView</u>, comments) Primary Key propertyNo, renterNo, dateView Foreign Key propertyNo references PropertyForRent(propertyNo) Foreign Key renterNo references Renter(renterNo)

D.14 Travel agent

A travel agent wishes to create a database for its customer holiday booking activities. The travel agent has numerous branches spread through the major cities in the US. A customer can call into, or contact by telephone, any branch and book a holiday. A holiday normally includes a flight and accommodation, although sometimes customers require only a flight or accommodation. Once the travel agent has found a suitable holiday for a customer, the flight and accommodation requirements are reserved for the customer. However, the reservation can only be held for up to 24 hours by which time the customer must accept or decline the booking. Once the booking is accepted, the customer is invoiced for the holiday and must pay the invoice in full, a minimum of four weeks before the departure date. The name of the employee who initially processes the customer booking is recorded. The logical data model is shown in Figure D.27 and the associated tables in Figure D.28.

Figure D.27

Logical data model for travel agent.

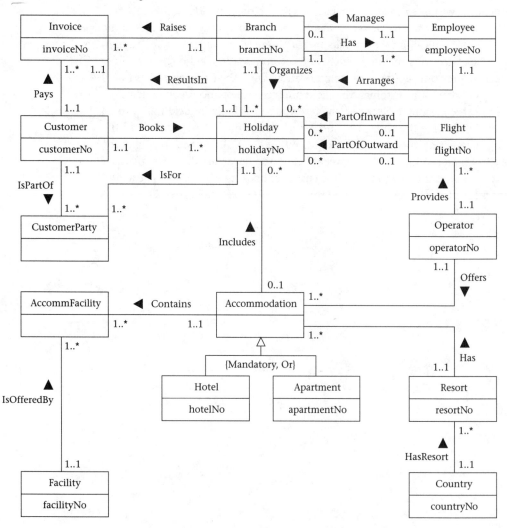

Figure D.28

Tables for travel agent.

Branch	As defined in Section D.13.2
ApartFacility	(<u>apartmentNo</u>, <u>facilityNo</u>, comments) Primary Key apartmentNo, facilityNo Foreign Key apartmentNo references Apartment(apartmentNo) Foreign Key facilityNo references Facility(facilityNo)
Apartment	(<u>apartmentNo</u>, apartmentName, apartmentType, apartmentDescription, apartmentRating, apartmentStreet, apartmentCity, apartmentState, apartmentCountry, apartmentZipCode, noOfRooms, operatorNo, resortNo) Primary Key apartmentNo Foreign Key operatorNo references Operator(operatorNo) Foreign Key resortNo references Resort(resortNo)
Country	(<u>countryNo</u>, countryName) Primary Key countryNo Alternate Key countryName
Customer	(<u>customerNo</u>, customerName, customerStreet, customerCity, customerState, customerZipCode, custTelNo, custFaxNo, nationality, sex, DOB, passportNo) Primary Key customerNo Alternate Key custTelNo Alternate Key custFaxNo Alternate Key passportNo
CustomerParty	(<u>customerNo</u>, <u>holidayNo</u>) Primary Key customerNo, holidayNo Foreign Key customerNo references Customer(customerNo) Foreign Key holidayNo references Holiday(holidayNo)
Employee	(<u>employeeNo</u>, title, firstName, middleName, lastName, address, workTelExt, homeTelNo, empEmailAddress, socialSecurityNumber, DOB, position, sex, salary, dateStarted, branchNo) Primary Key employeeNo Alternate Key socialSecurityNumber Foreign Key branchNo references Branch(branchNo)
Facility	(<u>facilityNo</u>, description, additionalCharge) Primary Key facilityNo
Flight	(<u>flightNo</u>, planeType, seatCapacity, airportDepart, departTime, airportArrive, arriveTime, operatorNo) Primary Key flightNo Foreign Key operatorNo references Operator(operatorNo)
Hotel	(<u>hotelNo</u>, hotelName, hotelStreet, hotelCity, hotelState, hotelCountry, hotelZipCode, hotelTelNo, hotelFaxNo, hotelType, hotelDescription, hotelRating, hotelManagerName, operatorNo, resortNo) Primary Key hotelNo Foreign Key operatorNo references Operator(operatorNo) Foreign Key resortNo references Resort(resortNo)
HotelFacility	(<u>hotelNo</u>, <u>facilityNo</u>, comments) Primary Key hotelNo, facilityNo Foreign Key hotelNo references Hotel(hotelNo) Foreign Key facilityNo references Facility(facilityNo)

Figure D.28

Continued

Holiday	(<u>holidayNo</u>, status, dateBooked, cateringType, startDate, finishDate, invoiceNo, totalCost, dateSent, datePaid, bookCustomerNo, hotelNo, apartmentNo, inwardFlightNo, inwardNoOfSeats, outwardFlightNo, outwardNoOfSeats, employeeNo, branchNo) Primary Key holidayNo Foreign Key bookCustomerNo references customer(customerNo) Foreign Key hotelNo references Hotel(hotelNo) Foreign Key apartmentNo references Apartment(apartmentNo) Foreign Key inwardFlightNo references Flight(flightNo) Foreign Key outwardFlightNo references Flight(flightNo) Foreign Key employeeNo references Employee(employeeNo) ForeignKey branchNo references Branch(branchNo)
Operator	(<u>operatorNo</u>, operatorName, operatorType, operatorStreet, operatorCity, operatorState, operatorZipCode, operTelNo, operFaxNo, contactName, contactTelNo, contactFaxNo, contactEmailAddress) Primary Key operatorNo Alternate Key operTelNo Alternate Key operFaxNo
Resort	(<u>resortNo</u>, resortName, distanceFromAirport, timeFromAirport, countryNo) Primary Key resortNo Foreign Key countryNo references Country(countryNo)

D.15 Student results

A university wishes to create a database for recording the results of students. When a student joins the university he or she registers with a particular course. Each student is also assigned an Advisor of Studies. Each year of each course is made up of modules. The minimum and maximum number of modules that make up a year of a course is 6 and 8, respectively. A student must take and pass each module in a given year before he or she is allowed to move into the next year of the course or to graduate. A student is normally allowed three attempts to pass a module; however, additional attempts are allowed at the discretion of the university. A particular module can be offered as part of one or more courses.

The university has several departments, each of which offers a portfolio of courses. Each department has a Head of Department (HOD) and each course has a Course Leader. Each module is assigned to a member of staff called a Module Coordinator, who has the responsibility to oversee the teaching and the assessment of the module. The logical data model is shown in Figure D.29 and the associated tables in Figure D.30.

Figure D.29

Logical data model for student results

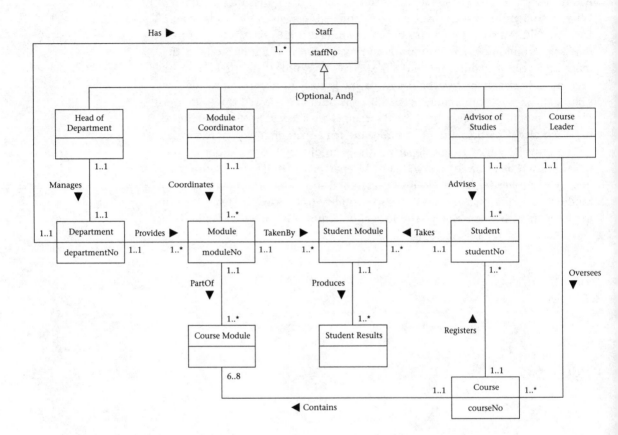

Figure D.30

Tables for student results.

Course	(<u>courseNo</u>, courseName, level, entranceRequirements, maxNumber, departmentNo, courseLeaderNo) Primary Key courseNo Alternate Key courseName Foreign Key departmentNo references Department(departmentNo) Foreign Key courseLeaderNo references Department(courseLeaderNo)
CourseModule	(<u>courseNo</u>, <u>moduleNo</u>) Primary Key courseNo, moduleNo Foreign Key courseNo references Course(courseNo) Foreign Key moduleNo references Module(moduleNo)
Department	(<u>departmentNo</u>, departmentName, location, HODstaffNo) Primary Key departmentNo Alternate Key departmentName Foreign Key HODstaffNo references Staff(staffNo)
Module	(<u>moduleNo</u>, moduleName, semesterDelivered, moduleAims, moduleObjectives, moduleSyllabus, moduleResources, moduleModeOfAssessment, moduleCoordinatorStaffNo, departmentNo) Primary Key moduleNo Alternate Key moduleName Foreign Key moduleCoordinatorStaffNo references Staff(staffNo) Foreign Key departmentNo references Department(departmentNo)
Staff	(<u>staffNo</u>, title, firstName, lastName, address, homeTelNo, workTelExt, empEmailAddress, socialSecurityNumber, DOB, position, sex, salary, dateStarted, departmentNo) Primary Key staffNo Alternate Key socialSecurityNumber Foreign Key departmentNo references Department(departmentNo)
Student	(<u>studentNo</u>, studentFirstName, studentMiddleName, studentLastName, studentHomeStreet, studentHomeCity, studentHomeState, studentHomeZipCode, studentHomeTelNo, familyHomeStreet, familyHomeCity, familyHomeState, familyHomeZipCode, familyHomeTelNo, studentDOB, studentSex, nationality, courseNo, advisorStaffNo) Primary Key studentNo Foreign Key courseNo references Course(courseNo) Foreign Key advisorStaffNo references Staff(staffNo)
StudentModule	(<u>studentNo</u>, <u>moduleNo</u>) Primary key studentNo, moduleNo Foreign Key studentNo references Student(studentNo) Foreign Key moduleNo references Module(moduleNo)
StudentResult	(<u>studentNo</u>, <u>moduleNo</u>, <u>attempt</u>, attemptDate, mark, proposal, additionalComments) Primary key studentNo, moduleNo, attempt Foreign Key studentNo, moduleNo references StudentModule(studentNo, moduleNo)

Glossary

Access method. The steps involved in storing and retrieving records from a file.

Alias. An alternative name given to an attribute. In SQL, you may substitute an alias for a table name.

Alternate keys (ER/relational model). The candidate keys that are not selected as the primary key of the entity/table.

Anomalies. See *Update anomalies*.

Application design. A stage of the database application lifecycle that involves designing the user interface and the application programs that use and process the database.

Application server. Handles the business logic and data processing layer in a three-tier architecture.

Attribute (relational model). An attribute is a named column of a relation.

Attribute (ER model). A property of an entity or a relationship.

Attribute inheritance. The process by which a member of a subclass may possess subclass-specific attributes, and inherit those attributes associated with the superclass.

Base table. A named table whose records are physically stored in the database.

Binary relationship. An ER term used to describe a relationship between two entities. For example, Branch *Has* Staff.

Bottom-up approach (to database design). A design philosophy that begins by identifying individual design components and then aggregates these components into larger units. In database design, you start at the bottom level by identifying the attributes, and then group the attributes together to form tables that represent entities and relationships.

Business rules. Additional rules specified by the users or database administrators of a database.

Candidate key (ER/relational model). A superkey that contains only the minimum number of attributes/columns necessary for unique identification.

Cardinality. Describes the number of possible relationships for each participating entity.

Centralized approach (to database design). Requirements for each user view are merged into a single set of requirements for the new database application.

Chasm trap. Suggests the existence of a relationship between entities, but the pathway does not exist between certain entity occurrences.

Client. A software application that requests services from one or more servers. See also *two-tier/three-tier client–server architecture*.

Clustering field. Any nonkey field in a record that is used to cluster (group together) the rows that have a common value for this field.

Clustering index. An index defined on a clustering field of a file. A file can have at most one primary index or one clustering index.

Column. Same as *attribute*.

Complex relationship. A relationship where the degree is higher than binary.

Composite attribute. An attribute composed of multiple single components.

Composite key. A primary key that contains more than one column.

Concurrency control. A DBMS service that coordinates the simultaneous execution of transactions in a multi-user environment while preserving data integrity.

Constraint. A consistency rule that the database is not permitted to violate.

Data conversion and loading. A stage of the database application lifecycle that involves transferring any existing data into the new database and converting any existing applications to run on the new database.

Data dictionary. See *system catalog*.

Data independence. The separation of data descriptions from the applications that use the data. This means that if new data structures are added to the database or existing structures in the database are modified then the application programs that use the database are unaffected, provided they don't directly depend upon what has been modified.

Data model. An integrated collection of concepts for describing data, relationships between data, and constraints on the data used by a company.

Data redundancy. Same as *redundant data*.

Data security. Covers access and use of database objects (such as tables and views) and the actions that users can have on the objects.

Database. A shared collection of logically related data (and a description of this data), designed to meet the information needs of a company.

Database design. A stage of the database application lifecycle that involves creating a design for a database that will support the company's operations and objectives.

Database integrity. Refers to the correctness and consistency of stored data. Integrity is usually expressed in terms of constraints.

Database Management Systems (DBMS). A software system that enables users to define, create, and maintain the database, and provides controlled access to this database.

Database planning. The management activities that allow the stages of the database application to be realized as efficiently and effectively as possible.

Database server. Same as *server* (see *two-tier/three-tier client–server architecture*).

DBMS engine. Same as *server* (see *two-tier client–server architecture*).

DBMS selection. A stage of the database application lifecycle that involves the selection of an appropriate DBMS to support the database application.

Degree of a relationship. The number of participating entities in a relationship.

Denormalization. Formally, the term refers to a change to the structure of a base table, such that the new table is in a lower normal form than the original table. However, we also use the term more loosely to refer to situations where we combine two tables into one new table, where the new table is in the same normal form but contains more nulls than the original tables.

Derived attribute. An attribute that represents a value that is derivable from the value of a related attribute, or a set of attributes, not necessarily in the same entity.

Design methodology. A structured approach that uses procedures, tools and documentation aids to support and facilitate the process of design.

Disjoint constraint. Describes the relationship between members of the subclasses and indicates whether it's possible for a member of a superclass to be a member of one, or more than one, subclass.

Domain. The set of allowable values for one or more attributes.

Entity. A set of objects with the same properties that are identified by a user or company as having an independent existence.

Entity integrity. In a base table, no column of a primary key can be null.

Entity occurrence. A uniquely identifiable object in an entity.

Entity-Relationship model. A detailed logical representation of entities, attributes, and relationships for a company.

Fact-finding. The formal process of using techniques such as interviews and questionnaires to collect facts about systems, requirements, and preferences.

Fan trap. Occurs when two entities have a 1:* relationship that fan out from a third entity, but the two entities should have a direct relationship between them to provide the necessary information.

Field. Same as *tuple*.

File. A named collection of related records stored on secondary storage.

File-based system. A collection of programs designed to manage (create, insert, delete, update, and retrieve) data in one or more files and to produce applications (usually reports) based on the data in these files.

File organization. A way of arranging the records in a file when the file is stored on disk.

First normal form (1NF). A table in which the intersection of every column and record contains one, and only one, value.

Foreign key. A column, or set of columns, within one table that matches the candidate key of some (possibly the same) table.

4GL (Fourth-Generation Language). A nonprocedural language, such as SQL, that only requires the user to define *what* must be done; the 4GL translates the *what* into details of *how* this should be executed.

Full functional dependency. A condition in which a column is functionally dependent on a composite key but not on any subset of that key.

Functional dependency. Describes the relationship between columns in a table. For example, if A and B are columns of a table, B is functionally dependent on A (denoted A →

B), if each value of A is associated with exactly one value of B. (A and B may each consist of one or more columns.)

Generalization. The process of minimizing the differences between entities by identifying their common features.

Generalization hierarchy. Same as *type hierarchy*.

Global data model. A data model that represents the entire company (or part of the company being modeled).

Implementation. A stage of the database application lifecycle that involves the physical realization of the database and application designs.

Index. A data structure that allows the DBMS to locate particular records in a file more quickly, and thereby speed response to user queries.

Information system. The resources that enable the collection, management, control, and dissemination of data/information throughout a company.

Inheritance. See *attribute inheritance*.

Integrity constraints. Contraints imposed to prevent the database from becoming inconsistent.

IS-A hierarchy. Same as *type hierarchy*.

Local logical data model. A data model that represents a particular user view, or combination of user views.

Logical database design. The process of constructing a model of the data used in a company based on a specific data model, but independent of a particular DBMS and other physical considerations.

Meta-data. Data about data; see *system catalog*.

Mission objective. Identifies a particular task that the database must support.

Mission statement. Defines the major aims of the database application.

Multiplicity. Defines the number of occurrences of one entity that may relate to a single occurrence of an associated entity.

Multi-valued attribute. An attribute that holds multiple values for an entity occurrence.

Nonkey attribute/column. An attribute/column that is not part of a key.

Normal forms. Stages in the normalization process. The first three normal forms are called *first normal form (1NF), second normal form (2NF),* and *third normal form (3NF).*

Normalization. A technique for producing a set of tables with desirable properties that supports the requirements of a user or company.

Null. Represents a value for a column that is currently unknown or is not applicable for this record.

Operational maintenance. A stage of the database application lifecycle that involves monitoring and maintaining the system following installation.

Participation constraint (EER model). Determines whether every occurrence in the superclass must participate as a member of a subclass.

Participation constraint (ER model). Determines whether all or only some entity occurrences participate in a relationship.

Physical database design. The process of producing a description of the implementation of the database on secondary storage; it describes the base tables, file organizations, and indexes used to achieve efficient access to the data, and any associated integrity constraints and security restrictions.

Primary index. An index built on the ordering key field of the file. A file can have at most one primary index or one clustering index. The ordering key is guaranteed to have a unique value in each record.

Primary Key (ER model). the candidate key that is selcted to identify each entity occurrence.

Primary key (relational model). The candidate key that is selected to identify records uniquely within the table.

Privileges. The actions that a user is permitted to carry out on a given base table or view.

Prototyping. A stage of the database application lifecycle that involves building a working model of a database application.

QBE (Query-by-Example). A nonprocedural database language for relational DBMSs. QBE is a graphical 'point-and-click' way of querying the database.

RDBMS. Relational DBMS.

Record. Same as *tuple*.

Recovery control. The process of restoring the database to a correct state in the event of a failure.

Recursive relationship. A relationship where the *same* entity participates more than once in *different* roles. For example, Staff *Supervises* Staff.

Redundant data. Duplicated data that is stored in more than one table.

Referential integrity. If a foreign key exists in a table, either the foreign key value must match a candidate key value of some record in its home table or the foreign key value must be wholly null.

Relation. A relation is a table with columns and rows.

Relational model. A data model that represents data in the form of tables (or relations).

Relational database. A collection of normalized tables.

Relationship. A meaningful association among entities.

Relationship occurrence. A uniquely identifiable association between two entity occurrences.

Requirements collection and analysis. A stage of the database application lifecycle that involves collecting and analyzing information about the company to be supported by the database application, and using this information to identify the requirements for the new database application.

Row. Same as *tuple*.

Second normal form (2NF). A table that is already in 1NF and in which the values in each non-primary-key column can only be worked out from the values in all the column(s) that make up the primary key.

Secondary index. An index that is defined on a non-ordering field of the data file.

Security. Refers to the protection of the database against unauthorized access, either intentional or accidental. RDBMSs generally provide two types of security: *data security* and *system security*.

Server. A software application that provides services to requesting clients. See also *two-tier/three-tier client–server architecture*.

Simple attribute. An attribute composed of a single component.

Single-valued attribute. An attribute that holds a single value for an entity occurrence.

Specialization. The process of maximizing the differences between members of an entity by identifying their distinguishing characteristics.

Specialization hierarchy. Same as *type hierarchy*.

SQL (Structured Query Language). A nonprocedural database language for RDBMSs. In other words, you specify *what* information you require, rather than *how* to get it. SQL has been standardized by the International Standards Organization (ISO), making it both the formal and *de facto* standard language for defining and manipulating RDBMSs.

Strong entity. An entity that is *not* dependent on the existence of another entity for its primary key.

Subclass. An entity that has a distinct role and holds specific attributes and relationships for some occurrences in the (superclass) entity. See also *specialization* and *generalization*.

Superclass. An entity that holds common attributes and relationships for all occurrences in the entity. See also *specialization* and *generalization*.

Superkey (ER model). An attribute or set of attributes, that uniquely identifies each entity occurrence.

Superkey (relational model). A column, or set of columns, that uniquely identifies a record within a table.

System catalog. Holds data about the structure of the database, users, applications, and so on.

System definition. A stage of the database application lifecycle that involves defining the scope and boundary of the database application including its major user views.

System security. Covers access and use of the database at the system level, such as a user-name and password.

Table. Same as *relation*.

Ternary relationship. A relationship between three entities. For example, the relationship *Registers* between Branch, Staff, and Member.

Testing. A stage of the database application lifecycle that involves executing the application programs with the intent of finding errors.

Third normal form (3NF). A table that is already in 1NF and 2NF, and in which the values in all non-primary-key columns can be worked out from *only* the primary key column(s) and no other columns.

3GL (Third-Generation Language). A procedural language such as COBOL, C, C++, that requires the user (usually a programmer) to specify *what* must be done and also *how* it must be done.

Three-tier client-server architecture. Consists of a *client* that handles the user interface, an *application server* that handles the business logic and data processing layer, and a *database server* that runs the DBMS.

Top-down approach (to database design). A design philosophy that begins by defining the main structures of the system and then moves to smaller units within those structures. In database design, you start at the top level by identifying the entities and relationships between the data, then you add more details, such as the information you want to hold about the entities and relationships (called attributes) and any constraints on the entities, relationships, and attributes.

Transaction. An action, or series of actions, carried out by a single user or application program, which accesses or changes the contents of the database.

Transaction Processing Monitor (TPM). A program that controls data transfer between clients and servers in order to provide a consistent environment for Online Transaction Processing (OLTP).

Transitive dependency. A condition where A, B, C are columns of a table, such that if B is functionally dependent on A (A → B) and C is functionally dependent on B (B → C), then C is transitively dependent on A via B (provided that A is not functionally dependent on B or C). If a transitive dependency exists on the primary key, the table is not in 3NF. The transitive dependency must be removed for a table to achieve 3NF.

Tuple. A record of a relation.

Two-tier client–server architecture. Consists of a *client* program that handles the main business and data processing logic and interfaces with the user, and a *server* program that manages and controls access to the database.

Type hierarchy. An entity and its subclasses and their subclasses, and so on.

UML (Unified Modeling Language). The successor to a number of object-oriented analysis and design methods introduced in the 80s and 90s.

Update anomalies. Inconsistencies that may arise when a user attempts to update a table that contains redundant data. There are three types of anomalies: insertion, deletion, and modifcation.

User view. Defines what is required of a database application from the perspective of a particular job (such as Manager or Supervisor) or business application area (such as marketing, personnel, or stock control).

View. A 'virtual table' that does not actually exist in the database but is generated by the DBMS from the underlying base tables whenever it's accessed.

View integration approach (to database design). Requirements for each user view are used to build a separate data model to represent that user view. The resulting data models are merged at a later stage in database design.

Weak entity. An entity that is partially or wholly dependent on the existence of some other entity (or entities) for its primary key.

References

Chen P.P. (1976). The Entity-Relationship model – Toward a unified view of data. *ACM Transactions on Database Systems*, 1(1), 9–36

Codd E.F. (1970). A relational model of data for large shared data banks. *Communications of the ACM*, 13(6), 377–387

Connolly T.M. and Begg C.E. (1999) *Database Systems: A Practical Approach to Design, Implementation, and Management,* 2nd edn. Harlow, England: Addison- Wesley

OASIG (1996). Research report. Available at *http://www.comlab.ox.ac.uk/oucl/users/john.nicholls/oas-sum.html*

Shneiderman D. (1992). *Design the User Interface: Strategies for Effective Human-Computer Interaction,* 2nd edn. Reading, MA: Addison-Wesley

Index

Page numbers in bold indicate where a term is defined in the text.